SKADDEN

SKADDEN

Power, Money, and the Rise of a Legal Empire

L I N C O L N   C A P L A N

F A R R A R   S T R A U S   G I R O U X / *New York*

Library of Congress catalog card number 93-73195

For Susan and Molly, again

Contents

I

History

1

The Snake Pit

Joseph Flom is the senior and only surviving name partner in the law firm of Skadden, Arps, Slate, Meagher & Flom. He is regarded by his partners with ambivalence, curiosity, fear, and awe. Some lawyers who deeply respect him also resent that their firm is spoken of as a one-man show. Others, after years of working closely with him, study him as if he were a distant oracle whose pronouncements yield their true meaning only to minute scrutiny. There are some who perform badly in his presence and steer clear of him, and others, focusing on a primary source of such anxiety, who hold that his talents are incomparable. They are impressed above all by the power of his brain and by his large quota of the vague but bankable resource that lawyers call good judgment. Partners of Flom regard him as the best lawyer of his generation, the finest in the second half of the twentieth century, or the greatest who has ever practiced and, almost seriously, propose that he be bronzed.

A cast of Flom would contrast sharply with heroic statues of lions at the bar. He is short, stooped, and reticent-looking, and has described himself as a hunchback. His feet splay, ducklike, when he walks. He has a squarish face, framed by a big forehead, long ears with large lobes, and a fist of a chin; with minimal shifts of his deep-set blue eyes and wide, thin mouth, his attitude seems to change from a skepticism hinting at cruelty to a patriarch's contentment. Brusque, fidgety, and possessed of self-insulating concentration, he is not well equipped to sort out such turns by furnishing insights about himself.

Flom can be charming and expansive, fervent and delighted. He reminds some people of a benevolent professor and strikes others as almost soft. He is also personally unreflective, frequently irascible, and, by temperament, impatient. When he poses a legal question, colleagues of his feel compelled to answer as if writing a headline. His own views sometimes transcribe like tabloid captions, sassy and unvarnished. But his speech comes out as mumbling and is somewhat nasal, with the bluff ring of Brooklyn. Even when the words are understandable, their meaning can be fuzzy and cryptic.

Among the inexact things that Flom says in the course of business, the following are frequently recycled by colleagues and clients: "It's a small hole, but very deep." "There are a number of ways to slice the baloney, but you don't want to slice it too thin." "You have to ride more than one horse at a time." "If you're carrying too much baggage, you might not get through the door." "The longer there's no news, the better news it is." "We're coming out of the trenches with our bayonets fixed, and we're taking no prisoners." "Their phone is off the hook, and no conversation is going to put it back on." "They've taken their best shot, and it was a balloon with no air in it." "Let's get it broom clean and we'll worry about polishing floors later." "It's just north of trained-monkey work, if you can stay awake." "I'm considering dispensing with the Marquis of Queensberry rules." "There's some real ore to be mined here."

For many years, a series of Flom's colleagues have been looked to as his decoders, fielding questions from other lawyers about what some Flomism really means. To answer, they sometimes refer to other evidence, which he supplies in reams. These are precise, kaleidoscopic doodles, usually made on graph paper with pen or pencil, using the top of a cigar tube for the outline of a circle.

Hanging on a wall of Flom's office are: a platinum version of Twisted

Sister's 1984 "Stay Hungry" album, awarded to one of Flom's sons, as the record's producer, and commemorating the sale of a million copies of the LP; an engraving of John Marshall, America's first illustrious jurist, next to a letter handwritten by Marshall, dated July 16, 1801; and a newspaper advertisement for Merrill Lynch & Company, celebrating Operation Welcome Home, New York City's June 1991 salute to soldiers who fought in the Persian Gulf War, and autographed for Flom as co-chair of the event by General Norman Schwarzkopf ("To Joe, With thanks for a great parade"). A framed sheet of Flom's doodles is also on display.

One Flom cryptographer identifies them as perfect symbols, mazes that he creates and solves as he intuits his way through the problems of his clients and then imagines a solution. Another says the doodles themselves are insignificant. What is, is that, no matter how small the part of a sheet taken up by a drawing, Flom usually does only one per page. Once Flom has explored a line of reasoning, he puts it aside. Flom sometimes jettisons dozens of doodles a day, which, when it's possible to do so unobtrusively, colleagues save and examine. A Skadden partner observed, "One of the problems of getting an answer from an oracle is that you've got to ask the right question."

The contrast between the woolliness of some Flom language and the refinement of his drawings is partially reconciled by his basic rules of practice. He explained them to a protégé: (1) You won't go broke buying options. (2) Never worry about an option until it's about to expire. (3) Don't take a position unless you know what your avenue of retreat is. (4) The goal of a lawyer should be to focus on real problems—to find them and fix them.

Flom believes that decisions should be made when they have to be, and not before, and that it pays to consider all possible contingencies. His figure-filled, often opaque patter serves the simultaneous functions of keeping colleagues engaged while holding them at bay, of coaxing them toward sound judgments while fending off untimely decisions until a problem is ripe for solution.

Then—"crunch time" to him—Flom is capable of making his views plain. "I gotta tell you, it's a blockbuster," he says when he likes an idea. When he doesn't, a favorite Flom expression is directed at the idea's source. "Give him an ambiguous answer," he mutters: "Tell him to go fuck himself."

A partner of Flom's explained why no one gives examples when talking about his genius: "What he does is, he just keeps paring away at something until he gets to the simple core, so everything seems obvious and self-evident instead of flashy and brilliant, as if anyone could have thought of it. But, of course, no one else did."

Flom has been fired by both colleague and client for coming up with new legal arguments after convincing them that he had already framed the best he could. Years ago, according to Skadden lore, he was with an older lawyer on a train from Manhattan to Albany heading for a court date. The position they were expected to advance was memorialized in a brief already submitted to the court. When Flom tried to persuade his colleague to ditch the approach and adopt a fresh one, he found himself by the side of the tracks in Poughkeepsie, temporarily jobless. He disputes the circumstances ("I was never on the train. It was the night before, in his apartment") but not being fired and, within half an hour, rehired. Flom: "He just blew up."

Younger lawyers avow that Flom needs watching—that, for every great idea he offers, there are clunkers, and that he proposes candidates from each category with equal enthusiasm. A lawyer who used to work regularly with him said, "Joe was always an evolving thing. If I wasn't happy with a reaction, I waited for a gestation period. I knew when Joe said 'Fire!' I should hesitate. I counted to ten, and, if he didn't call back by then, I'd shoot."

One expression of Flom's brand of savvy is that, though he is generally a knee-jerk contrarian ("You're being too consistent!" he complains, or "You're being too logical!" or, trapping the unwary listener, "A scalded cat flees cold water!") and though he often hears questions as criticism ("Are you crazy!" is a standard Flom response), he relies on colleagues to help him separate ersatz insight from the real thing. "Milt and the boys are taking my ideas and trashing them" is how he described one such occasion. For lawyers with the confidence to take him on, this is a high pleasure: thinking through a problem with Joe.

A large share of Skadden lawyers do so only irregularly. Speaking about a period some years before, a partner said recently, "You could move into Joe's fear or stay away. Did I say 'fear'? I meant 'sphere.' That's interesting." Pause. "I could never keep up with the man. He's the only one of my partners I think I can't keep up with. After the wounds would heal, I'd try again. I didn't have the capacity to deal with Joe all the time."

Most colleagues call him by his first name, although he rarely returns the recognition. The firm attempted to allay this problem by instituting a game and short-lived Get-to-know-Joe program, in which a series of associates would tag along with him for a month or so. The experiment ended when the first and only associate in the program realized he was being run ragged, trailing after Flom by day and doing his own work at night.

Flom says that he doesn't know how many partners he has, let alone associates ("I function on trends"), and, by a well-informed estimate, he knows the names of relatively few of either. "Bob Zornow is working on a helluva plan," he said about a prized fortyish partner whose first name is David.

On the other hand, when spouses of his colleagues catch their first glimpse of him, they are sometimes underwhelmed. Once a young lawyer was in the firm's offices with his wife. Flom, in a blue suit, a plaid shirt, and white socks, scooted by and, in the lawyer's words, "sort of grunted." The associate announced concisely, "That's Joe Flom," knowing that, in the Skadden camp, the name carried the weight of a legend. His wife refused to believe him.

Flom pays attention to lawyers with whom he works closely, however, and, in dealings with them, he expects reciprocity. In his busiest years, Flom read drafts of legal papers whenever they were delivered to him, in his office or at home, and was known to call colleagues with needling comments at all hours. One remembered: "Some of his midnight interventions were like a finger in the eye, to remind who works for whom."

Another recalled: "Joe used to arrange vacations so that you would have to urgently reach him. My job was to field his calls when he was gone. If nothing had happened, I'd have to make up things. Over beers one night, some others and I decided that, when Joe went on vacation, a part of him was afraid the firm was going to collapse, and a part that it wasn't."

A third said, "Once Joe called me around nine o'clock at night. He wanted the home phone number of the Director of Enforcement of the Securities and Exchange Commission. I put on a full-court press, and, while I was in the middle of it, Joe called five times asking, Did I have it? Why wasn't I on the stick? When I called with it, fifteen minutes later, he said, 'Never mind, I got it somewhere else.' There was no way to satisfy him, but that was a lesson."

The scrutiny that Flom gets from colleagues is magnified by attention from many other quarters, because his law firm is a phenomenon in the world of lawyers, in the United States and abroad. Skadden's name has attained currency as a verb, as in "to Skaddenize." Its financial workings are considered sufficiently distinct so that a noun, "Skaddenomics," has been coined about them as well. Pages of Flom's, or Flomesque, sayings that are used by other lawyers at his firm have been collected and printed out by clients and shared with others, as "Skaddological comments."

The style of Skadden lawyering is judged so characteristic that it is sometimes greeted by other practitioners with a knowing invocation of the firm's first name, like a curse or an oath. Skadden news items (e.g., how much its partners charge per hour) have appeared in gossip columns that usually concentrate on domains other than the law. The firm was paid homage on TV's *L.A. Law* as McFadden Arps, and elsewhere in the annals of popular culture, Skadden lawyers have been showcased in layouts about power people with executives of glitzy enterprises like MTV. When HBO broadcast *Barbarians at the Gate*, about the last corporate blowout of the eighties, the $25 billion leveraged buyout of RJR/Nabisco, the lawyer from Skadden got a cameo at the climax as the guy who clinched the deal.

The firm owes its prominence to a specialty in corporate mergers and acquisitions. The start of the takeover era—for Skadden and the United States—is often given as 1974, when, for the first time in a hostile contest, the most prestigious investment-banking house of the moment, Morgan Stanley & Company, advised a raider (the International Nickel Company of Canada, called INCO) in its attack on a target (ESB, formerly the Electric Storage Battery Company).

Instead of retaining their longtime, established Wall Street legal counsel, the bankers hired Flom. They chose him because he had successfully guided other investment banks and less notable companies in the use of the tender offer, in which a bidder, called the aggressor, offers to buy stock directly from the stockholders of a target company in order to gain control of it.

Flom's firm had seventy or so lawyers and only a limited reputation outside a small circle on Wall Street. But in the previous fifteen years, lawyers at Skadden had proven themselves as specialists in many fights over control of corporations and, just as important, had shown their eagerness to take on business that more established firms did not seek.

The struggles initially took the form of a proxy contest, in which a group of stockholders tried to gain control over a company by electing a majority of its board of directors. The method was less effective than a tender offer: it was slower and more expensive and challengers were often at a serious disadvantage against the incumbent board and managers. They usually lost. Even if they won, they secured less control over the company than if they had bought it outright—which is why the tender offer was imported from England and, with a new twist (American bids were usually hostile), was employed in the United States beginning in the 1950s.

Until then, however, in cycles throughout the twentieth century and especially in the decade and a half after the Second World War, the proxy contest was generally how takeovers of companies were attempted. The common proxy strategy was for the challengers, called insurgents, to paint the managers as a collection of rogues. They sent letters to stockholders filled with accusation, hyperbole, and innuendo, offered unabashedly on the assumption that the other side would balance the record. The "acrimony of proxy contest battles," according to Edward Aranow and Herbert Einhorn in the basic textbook on the subject, made them "repugnant to respectable business managements or financiers."

The main tool of combat was a proxy statement presenting the slate of potential directors for one side. A stockholder was asked to sign it to commit his stock, giving his proxy for others to vote as directed in his place. A stockholder might complicate the vote count in many ways. He or she might sign two conflicting proxies, as the proxy statements were called. He might fail to sign his name on a statement as it was officially registered with the corporation, by leaving out his middle initial. He might own stock jointly with his wife and send in their proxy after signing it himself, without getting her signature as well.

The winner of a proxy contest was determined in the snake pit. (Officially, it was called the counting room.) Lawyers for each side met with inspectors of elections, whose job it was to approve or eliminate questionable proxies. The event was often informal, contentious, and unruly. Adversaries were sometimes in T-shirts, eating watermelon or sharing a bottle of scotch. In rare cases, the results of the snake pit could swing the outcome of a contest and turn on a single ballot.

Lawyers occasionally tried to fix an election by engineering the appointment of inspectors who were beholden to them; inspectors commonly smoked cigars provided by each side. Management's lawyer would contest the proxies of the insurgents ("I challenge this!") and vice versa, and each dispute would yield a story. Sometimes the tale was intricate: A block of stock had been committed on a Sunday by a trust in Rhode

Island, where a blue law still on the books made the signing invalid.

Lawyers who prevailed in the snake pit excelled at winging it. There were lawyers who knew more about the rules of proxy contests, but no one was better in a fight than Joe Flom. He knew by heart the story of virtually every proxy he wanted to challenge (there could be hundreds) and, pacing distractedly, quickly laid out defenses to challenges from the other side. He understood that legal precedent had limited authority in a snake pit, that he was engaged in a free-for-all—lawyering on the run. By his own account, Flom made up arguments as he went along.

A. A. Sommer, a Washington, D.C., lawyer who squared off against Flom in proxy fights and later served on the Securities and Exchange Commission: "I remember, over martinis, Joe would say, 'Always remember that we're engaged in an objective search for truth.' Which I regarded as so much bullshit."

Sometimes Flom's ripostes drew cheers from rivals. ("Joe, you're incredible! This is the best you've ever been!") Sometimes the challenges got almost physical, as when a lawyer tried to throw Flom off by taunting him and, in his version of the story, Flom was so angry at the man's snide remarks that he threatened to rap the lawyer in the mouth.

Flom was fat (a hundred pounds overweight then, one lawyer said, although an ID card of Flom's from then suggests it was closer to fifty), physically unattractive (to a partner, he resembled a frog), and indifferent to social niceties (he would fart in public or jab a cigar close to the face of someone he was talking to, without apology). But, in the judgment of colleagues and of some adversaries, his will to win was unsurpassed and he was often masterful. By the 1960s, Flom sometimes handled half a dozen contests at a time in proxy season, January through May.

Flom's decade and a half of prowess as a fighter in proxy and other contests for control of corporations led to the chance, when he was fifty, to work on the hostile contest that inaugurated the takeover years, when the practices of American and global business and finance, and of lawyers who served them, were radically transformed.

Flom and his colleagues confirmed their abilities repeatedly in that arena, leading to the growth of the group into America's preeminent takeover firm and to Flom's renown as its leader, by the time he was sixty.

In knowledgeable circles, Flom was seen, before he was sixty-five, as one of the most powerful business lawyers during the decades after the Second World War and the brains behind a new kind of law firm— one of the largest and most successful in the world.

At the peak of his firm's prosperity, in 1989, its gross revenues were reported by *The American Lawyer* to be $517.5 million, or roughly $10 million a week. That was first by a wide margin among all law firms in the world. It was almost enough to qualify Skadden for a ranking among the Fortune 500, if law firms had been eligible. Unlike consequential law firms of past eras, which were lunar, reflecting the might and luster of their clients, Skadden developed its own source of energy. It became a big business on its own terms, with epic reach and power.

Once I was talking with Flom in his office and overheard an example of his power in action. He took a phone call about a university fund drive from a man he had called earlier. Flom's side of the conversation went like this:

"Hi. Look, I got a contribution for you from one of my law school classmates. North of ten. Right. A couple of things. He wants to set up a trust so that, in case of a crisis, he can invade the funds. He's not worried about the tax consequences. And he needs a doctor. No emergency, he just needs to see a doctor. My guy is good, but I think his practice is full. Could you ask Ronny Perelman to call, and see if this guy can get in? Good."

(Perelman was a Skadden client and a friend of Flom's. His series of deals in the previous several years culminating with his hostile takeover of Revlon for a time made him the richest person in the country, according to *Forbes*. He recently bought a cigar company in the Dominican Republic for $180 million, in part so he could have its premier cigar roller make "Perelman specials.")

"Now I've got a small favor to ask of you. I'm co-chair of the Bicentennial Commission for the state of New York and in April we're having a celebration down at Federalist Hall for the two hundredth anniversary of Washington's swearing-in as the first President. Right. Fifty thousand dollars. Thank you very much! I'll have my girl send you a letter with the particulars about how you can make your contribution, and about my classmate's gift. Thanks."

Flom hung up, and, in case I hadn't followed what had just happened, he told me, "I got him ten million, he gave me fifty thousand, it's all part of the game."

In 1988, I embarked on a series of conversations about Skadden with Flom, many of his colleagues, some of their clients, and other lawyers, and with a range of observers of lawyers in the United States and abroad. Through a study of one firm, I wanted to explore the transformation since the Second World War of large American law firms.

They had burst in size and salience: Two hundred fifty-eight firms had more than one hundred lawyers that year, representing approximately 5 percent of the lawyers in the United States. Yet they constituted "a vast, mysterious, and almost unmapped interior of American society," in the words of Robert Gordon, a professor at Stanford Law School. Most of this "heartland" on the illusory chart of knowledge was "drawn as blanks, with the occasional mysterious notation, 'Diamond Mines,' or warning, 'Here there be Tygers.'" Skadden was the obvious firm to survey: admirers and critics recognized it as a legal empire favored with riches and filled with lawyers who made a singular roar.

I encountered complications as soon as I began my reporting. Although many spoke with me on the record, many others talked with me only if I agreed not to quote them by name. Those outside Skadden often expressed concern about jeopardizing their relationships with it. Those inside voiced a range of anxieties, the most common being about damaging their standing at the firm. These conditions put me on notice about the delicacy of my task. They also enticed me.

I had first heard of Skadden in the early seventies. I graduated from law school in 1976 and, when I applied to law firms for a job, Skadden offered me one. I decided not to work as a lawyer and maintained no contact with the firm, but I read about it occasionally. In 1983, I spent some time there talking with lawyers about Flom and his role in the rise of corporate takeovers.

When I returned five years later, Skadden was celebrating its fortieth anniversary. The firm held a black-tie gala at the Metropolitan Museum of Art, not far from its midtown office on the East Side of Manhattan. It was attended by sixteen hundred or so people associated with Skadden, who could wander from the medieval collection, where chamber music was performed, to the American wing, which featured jazz, to the Egyptian wing, highlighted by the Temple of Dendur, where a dance band played.

Guests were announced by a herald and a trumpet was sounded as they joined the party. Some lawyers with the firm, including senior partners, enjoyed the pomp so much that they entered, left, and reentered the gathering several times, to keep hearing the trumpet voluntary and their names pronounced. It was an event for which women bought one-of-a-kind dresses, an evening of pride and plenty.

As part of the anniversary festivities, Skadden organized a day of recollection at which lawyers told Horatio Alger tales about the firm's rise. After many storytellers, Joe Flom was the final speaker, in remarks that took three minutes. "I'd like to inject a note of caution," he began.

Flom told a story from 1958, when the firm had ten lawyers and thought it was getting its big break from a corporation that asked it to work on a project with a Wall Street bank: "The major investment-banking firm said, 'Oh, you're not eligible. There are only seven firms of the quality that can do work for this investment bank.' " Flom informed his audience, "Four of those firms no longer exist. The investment-banking firm no longer exists, having been swallowed up by a major client of ours."

The takeover line drew a satisfied, almost vengeful laugh, which seemed to confirm Flom's instinct that the point he was making was timely. He instructed, "We must remember that the history of major institutions is that they are not permanent. The only permanence comes from what you make of it, or what the institution makes of itself. If it becomes a dinosaur, it will disappear."

2

April Fools'

No element of the Skadden name has escaped garbling, ridicule, or doubt. In official correspondence, the firm has been addressed as Skadden, Arbs, Slate, Meher & Flom; Skadden, Arpo, Slate, Meagher & Flour; Skudden, Arps, Slate, Meazer & Florn; Scadden, Harper, Slate, Meargher & Flaun; Skadden, Arps & Flam; Scadden Arts; Scaddens Art; Scadden Knobbs; and Skadden Corps. Skadden has been recast as Skaaden, Skodded, Skaddra, Shadden, and Shoaden; Arps as Ards, Arpa, Arpy, Arips, and Aips; Slate as Sleight, Slater, Slatt, Slats, and Slote; and Meagher (pronounced Mar) as Meager, Meacher, Meaghen, Heagher, and Meier. Mistakes about Flom's name are also rife. The name has come in, among other ways, as Flor, Flow, Flum, Glom, Gloom, and Plum. It has been rendered as Son, as in Skadden, Arps, Slate, Meagher & Son. A British columnist asserted, "I think it must be accepted at the outset that there are not and never have been people called Arps or Flom."

Skadden, Arps & Slate was founded in Manhattan on April Fools' Day in 1948. Marshall Skadden and Leslie Arps had been passed over for partnership at the Wall Street firm of Root, Ballantine, Harlan, Bushby & Palmer, and John Slate joined them from the legal staff of Pan American Airways, to which he had moved after working at the Root firm for four years. Fifteen years old when Slate went there, Pan Am was a daring, romantic venture that was formed to deliver mail between the Panama Canal Zone and South America. It was on its way to becoming the flagship airline of the United States, which it remained for two generations.

The qualifications of other lawyers not asked to be partners at the Root firm put Skadden and Arps in respectable company. But Arps knew that he had to find other work. Skadden recognized that he, too, had topped out and should try something new. Slate felt the same about his job at Pan Am. Skadden told Slate they should start their own firm and, when Arps and another lawyer heard about the idea, they said they were interested.

According to a prospectus of the group's plans, they considered having Skadden and Slate launch the practice, which Arps and the other lawyer would join after working for a year or two in government jobs, to fish for clients. The fourth man dropped out because he didn't have money to risk, and the other three decided it was best for them to open the firm together. In those days, firms put their initials on stationery and the acronym created with Arps's name listed alphabetically was in bad taste (ASS). Skadden won a coin toss with Slate, and his name became the shorthand for the firm's.

It might appear that Skadden and Arps were venturing riskily from a stable, well-anchored base, whose gray-flanneled name suggested its constancy since the nineteenth century. But they were only doing what Elihu Root, Jr., and Grenville Clark had when they left established firms after several years to found their own small group in 1909, and joined forces with Emory Buckner and Silas Howland in 1913 to create the Root firm.

Root was the son and namesake of a former Secretary of War (under Presidents William McKinley and Theodore Roosevelt) and of State (under Roosevelt) who served as a United States senator from New York State. The family name was the new firm's primary asset. "The truth is that the Senator pretty much set us up in business," Grenville Clark later wrote in the firm newsletter, *The Bull*. After the First World War, the firm took off. In 1919 alone, it quadrupled in size to twenty-four lawyers. By the twenties, it had joined the first rank of New York firms.

The "law factories," as they were called by Karl Llewellyn, a legal scholar, serviced the needs of American companies through cycles of depression and prosperity. They adapted legal forms for the fortification of American capitalism, like modern corporations and the cartels called trusts that were designed to monopolize whole industries.

Between 1872 and 1924, the number of American firms with four or more lawyers rose from seventeen to more than a thousand. The highest concentration of "large" firms was in New York City. To the legal observers Marc Galanter and Thomas Palay, the firms were "the great innovation in lawyering in the past century."

The archetype was Cravath, Swaine & Seward, which became Cravath, Swaine & Moore. It began a century before Skadden, in 1848, when the Blatchford firm of Manhattan (1819) merged with the Seward firm of Auburn (1823), about two hundred miles to the northwest, in the heart of New York State, after William Henry Seward was elected to the U.S. Senate. (He had been governor of New York; he was later known for Seward's folly, when he bought Alaska from Russia for the United States as Secretary of State.) By 1906, the firm had three partners and sixteen associates. The senior partner was Paul Cravath.

The Cravath system, as it was called, was straightforward. (Some of the ideas associated with it came from Walter Carter, whose office Cravath had worked in for five years.) As Robert Swaine described in an appreciation of his firm, Cravath "kept moving through his office a current of brilliant, ambitious young lawyers" and the office was "regarded by the law schools and by the profession almost as a graduate school of law." It hired first-rank graduates of leading law schools to do research on behalf of the firm's clients; in exchange for a salary, training, and a decade-long cycle of increasing responsibility as they headed toward partnership, the associates put aside the development of their own practices, which young lawyers had previously pursued, and worked exclusively on firm business; about one out of every twelve associates became a partner; the others left for positions at other firms, at corporations, or in the government.

The Root firm employed the Cravath system, and Grenville Clark and Emory Buckner had exemplary Wall Street careers there. Clark was a moneyed insider (he introduced Franklin D. Roosevelt to Felix Frankfurter when the three entered law practice in New York). Besides being an able bankruptcy and railroad lawyer, he wielded notable private power (he was a member of the small board that governs Harvard University).

From behind the scenes, he directed the successful opposition to the Supreme Court-packing plan proposed in 1937 by Roosevelt, for whom he had voted. He also helped invigorate the American Bar Association, by defining for it a role in defense of civil liberties when war fever during the 1940s convinced many Americans that freedoms at home should be sacrificed for victory abroad. A *New York Times* editorial praised him as "a lawyer in the grand tradition."

Buckner entered the law as a poor outsider (he was the son of an Iowa minister) who learned about the subject as a court stenographer in Oklahoma before it entered the Union, and won the sponsorship of leaders of the bar. They included: Roscoe Pound, a onetime botanist from Nebraska whose influence as a legal thinker was sometimes compared with that of Oliver Wendell Holmes, Jr., and who evolved from a prairie reformer to a conservative dean of Harvard Law School; Learned Hand, perhaps America's finest judge in the middle of this century; and Henry Stimson, an esteemed private lawyer who was the first person to serve in the Cabinets of four American Presidents, culminating with his tenure as Secretary of War during the Second World War.

Buckner's public achievement came as a U.S. attorney. Despite his personal opposition to Prohibition, he shut down speakeasies throughout New York City. He came within a vote of persuading a jury to convict Harry Daugherty, the Attorney General of the United States, of taking bribes from men who had violated the Prohibition laws. (Daugherty was forced to resign.) To his followers, Buckner's special capacity was for choosing and cultivating unusual legal talent. John M. Harlan, Jr., the admired conservative Justice of the Supreme Court, was his best-known protégé. Buckner's main vehicle was the Root Clark firm. He led it until illness forced him to give up practice in 1933.

In *A History of American Law*, Lawrence Friedman observed that the bar attracted "seizers of opportunities." An archetype was John J. McCloy, whose mother supported the family as a hairdresser and who rose to become a name partner in Milbank, Tweed, Hadley & McCloy and chairman of the American establishment, as chairman of the Council on Foreign Relations, of the Chase Manhattan Bank, and of both the Ford and Rockefeller foundations. Insiders like Grenville Clark had to reach less far to seize theirs, but outsiders like Emory Buckner could also grasp opportunities on Wall Street, within limits.

With one exception, every man who became a partner at Root Clark while Buckner was in charge attended either Harvard or Oxford. This apparent snobbery was grounded in a sense of merit. In 1925, the firm passed a milestone when it took into the partnership Leo Gottlieb, who had been first in his class at Harvard Law School. It became one of the first white, Anglo-Saxon, Protestant firms on Wall Street to admit a Jew.

The firm of Sullivan & Cromwell had made a Jew a partner in 1894 (and, in 1869, the Cravath firm had taken into its partnership a descendant of West Indian Jews), but Root Clark was still a generation ahead of most of its peers. Until after the Second World War, Jews and Catholics were generally excluded from partnership at such places. (The Cravath firm named its first Catholic partner in 1940, and its first partner who was a practicing Jew in 1959.) Women and African Americans were all but entirely refused admission for another generation.

Such exclusivity felt part of a natural order to the firms, as did other practices that later ended. Until 1968, for example, when Cravath unilaterally increased its starting salaries by more than 40 percent, the associates were paid a "going rate" established at an annual luncheon of the managing partners from the leading twenty or so New York firms. The "big employers' trust" had been started in 1927, when Emory Buckner, as the leader of his firm, decided that recent law school graduates were foolishly choosing which firm to join on the basis of small differences in salary.

The Root firm innovated on its own as well. It treated clients as the firm's instead of an individual lawyer's, and, according to Martin Mayer, Buckner's biographer, it was the first reputable New York firm to share its profits with associates through annual bonuses. By the time Skadden and Arps left, with the blessings of their former employers—Elihu Root, Jr., helped them secure office space in a tight Wall Street market and the firm sent two dozen roses to honor the Skadden opening—the Root firm was among the most prestigious on Wall Street.

Yet it had changed since Skadden and Arps had joined the decade before. In 1940, when Buckner was no longer its leader and Elihu Root, Jr., and Grenville Clark had turned their attention to outside interests, three partners, including John Harlan, asserted that they were responsible for more business than others at their level of seniority and demanded a higher share of the firm's profits.

They got it, but, in doing so, altered the all-for-one Root Clark concept that Buckner had championed. The change also solidified the authority of Harlan and company. Leo Gottlieb wrote in his memoirs that it was the main factor in convincing him and others, who included the leading Jews of Root Clark, that they should start a new firm that they could control. One of his new partners, Henry Friendly, called Gottlieb the leader of the "secessionists."

In 1946, they founded Cleary, Gottlieb, Friendly & Cox, and Root, Clark, Buckner & Ballantine became Root, Ballantine, Harlan, Bushby & Palmer. Not long after, Thomas Dewey, the former prosecutor, presidential candidate, and governor of New York State, joined the Root firm. Its name was changed to Dewey, Ballantine, Bushby, Palmer & Wood. Elihu Root, Jr., became of counsel to Cleary Gottlieb, with which Clark had already affiliated. ("Of counsel" was an honorific title meaning he had senior status but didn't own a share of the firm.) Root brought with him the portraits of the founders of Root Clark and, by his lights, the firm's legacy—although Dewey Ballantine is usually identified as the successor to the Root firm and the one that had no place for Skadden, Arps, and Slate.

When they left the Root firm and Pan Am, the three were varied in experience and somewhat tarnished. (Looking back at that time, Arps's wife described them as "marvelous rejects.") They hadn't been offered partnerships in an established law firm at the center of Wall Street practice. They lacked their profession's seal of approval.

Skadden was a compact, orderly, and formal man from Toledo, Ohio, who had graduated from the University of Michigan at nineteen and worked in Ohio with his uncle (Lothar T. Konopak) and his father (Marshall H. Skadden) as a certified public accountant for seven years before going to Harvard Law School. He finished with honors in 1936, and was forty-one when the new firm opened. He had pleasant features, a sunny outlook, and the earnestness of a go-getter. Meticulous in his grooming, he dressed in the upstanding image of a Root Clark partner (three-piece suit, gold watch fob, handkerchief in his breast pocket).

Arps, also forty-one, was born in Germany and grew up in Columbus, Ohio, the site of Ohio State University. His father was dean of the education school there (its Arps Hall is named for him) and Arps attended Ohio State for three years of college. Then he followed family tradition and transferred to Stanford University, where he earned his bachelor's degree and a Phi Beta Kappa key. He was tall and slope-shouldered, with a genial face and an open, excitable manner.

After graduating with honors from Harvard Law School in 1931, he spent many years as an aide to John Harlan, both at Root Clark and in the U.S. Army Air Forces during the Second World War, when Harlan led the first operations analysis section of the Eighth Air Force, in Europe. The group was composed of world-class mathematicians and physicists, in addition to Arps and others. Their studies of the Air Force's bombing missions helped increase the effectiveness of its tactics: in 1942, less than 15 percent of the force's bombs hit their targets; two years later, the figure had quadrupled to 60 percent.

Harlan and Arps became friends. (Arps called him Chief, and went horseback riding with Mrs. Harlan.) They remained so through Harlan's service on the Supreme Court. But the friendship had an element of strain. Arps complained to an interviewer that, before the war and during it, Harlan didn't guide Arps to promotions that he felt were his due and had expected Harlan to help him secure.

In 1941, Harlan took him to lunch to say that a contemporary of Arps's was getting the partnership that Arps had hoped for in the Root firm. A few years later, in the service, Harlan again didn't protect Arps's interests. "He sat on his ass," Arps complained. Another officer received a promotion that Arps wanted. He scolded Harlan, Arps later reported: "You have done the same thing to me here that you did to me back in New York."

Harlan claimed not to know what Arps was talking about, although the intensity of Arps's rebuke shouldn't have surprised him. ("Arps called up in a state of agitation," he recorded on an earlier day in his wartime diary.) Harlan preferred to avoid confrontations and had likely been only one of many votes bringing about each of Arps's disappointments. Still, as Arps recalled, Harlan promised, "I will do everything I can to make you a partner."

Not long after, when Harlan was about to leave the Army and return to the United States, he asked Arps, "What are you going to do after the war?" He didn't refer to his promise of sponsorship. With that, Arps realized he had no future at Root Ballantine. In January of 1946, after being discharged from the service as a lieutenant colonel, he went to Ohio to join a cousin in a small Toledo law firm. He missed practicing in Manhattan, and decided to return to New York. On the theory that he should return there with a job lined up, if only as a stepping stone, he asked Harlan for a temporary position at Root.

Harlan hesitated, but said yes, and Arps arrived in October of 1946, at a salary of five hundred dollars more than he had made before the war. When he learned that other Root associates returning from wartime service were receiving raises of five hundred dollars multiplied by the number of years they had been away, he knew that he had gotten Harlan's message. For a while, Arps admitted, he was "very bitter." He carried traces of the feeling for four decades. But he never again mentioned his disappointment to Harlan.

Slate was born in Windgap, Pennsylvania. His father was a civil engineer who built bridges and, when a job took him and his wife to South America, they left John (a baby) with her parents. John's grandparents taught him Welsh before he spoke English. When his parents returned, he couldn't talk with them. The family later moved to Pittsburgh and then Brooklyn, where Slate graduated from high school.

He went to Columbia College, where his friends congregated at the *Jester*, the school's humor magazine, and tended to be artsy and intellectual. They included Robert Lax, an editor, a screenwriter, and a poet; Thomas Merton, later famous as a Trappist monk; Ad Reinhardt, a lauded modern painter; and Herman Wouk, the best-selling novelist. Slate graduated as salutatorian (second in his class). He planned to take a job teaching philosophy at Northwestern University, near Chicago, but his father died unexpectedly and left Slate with financial responsibility for his mother and an aunt. Slate turned down a partial scholarship at Harvard Law School for a full one at Columbia, where he made the law review. He finished in 1938.

When Skadden Arps was started, Slate was thirty-four—mischievous, moody, and conspicuously informal. He alternated between a pair of brown crepe-soled shoes and blue Top-Sider boat shoes, and wore only black knit ties. He had a large head and favored stagy hats: a gray fedora in winter; in summer, a straw panama. They complemented his brush mustache, wide-set eyes, and dry, sometimes antic manner.

Skadden, Arps & Slate opened for business, without a formal partnership agreement (the partners made a draft of an agreement and then discarded it), on the top floor of the Lehman Building near Wall Street, not far from the southern tip of Manhattan. They picked April, because they believed that the law business was at its peak in the spring. They had $12,000 of working capital, pieced together from personal savings (Arps's and Slate's) and the sale of U.S. war bonds and Pan Am stock (Slate's). Skadden was exempted from chipping in, but was expected to bring in most of the firm's early business.

Both Skadden and Slate were married and had children, and money was tight. To keep costs down, the Skaddens sold their house on Long

Island and rented another. They took a loan from a relative to pay for expenses during the firm's first year. The Slates, in a Greenwich Village apartment (they soon moved to a house on Long Island), lived on funds borrowed from his in-laws.

"Dear Daddy," began the letter of request to Slate's in-laws written jointly by him and his wife, Mary Ellen: "John and I were just sitting around tonight and decided, so saying, 'Things are getting a little dull. I guess it's about time to put the bite on the old man for some of that folding stuff.' John is going to finish this letter with a totally preposterous scheme about starting a law firm. Don't you believe a word of it. Actually we're going to take the money to Tia Juana and put it all on the spin of a wheel."

The partners gave themselves a trial period of two years. If the firm went under, they bantered edgily, they could move with their families to a farm in Illinois. Arps had inherited it from his mother and expanded it to five hundred acres. With a decorator's discount (Mary Ellen Slate qualified, as a contributor to *House & Garden*), the lawyers bought three partner's desks, two armchairs for visitors, and Winslow Homer prints for the walls. Skadden's and Slate's wives made drapes for the conference room/library from green burlap. At a party to celebrate the firm's opening, the women served potato chips and beer, chilled in a wastebasket loaded with ice.

Skadden, Arps & Slate received its first fee, of $532.50, in May of 1948. It was from Root Ballantine, and the check was signed by John Harlan. Soon after Skadden opened, Harlan circulated a memo to his partners recommending that any who had a case too small for their firm should send it to the former Root associates. He set an example by letting Arps take a case they had worked on together. The client was an American accused of trading with the enemy during the Second World War— conspiring to conceal the German ownership of an American soap company, to avoid paying half a million dollars of taxes. The matter was typical of early Skadden business: another firm had declined it.

It was also typical for Arps. He was designated the firm's courtroom lawyer, but he initially brought in money as a sleuth. His plum engagement was as an aide to the New York State Crime Commission's inquiry into corruption on the waterfront, for which Harlan was general counsel. Arps won a commendation for putting together (against unnerving odds) the picture of the gangsters' world that the commission unveiled at public hearings. The commission reported, "Many longshoremen, recalling the long series of unsolved murders on the docks, were deterred by fear from testifying." At the scene of an accident later, New York City's police commissioner said to a lawyer who identified himself as a Skadden associate, "Isn't Les Arps the Thin Man there?"

Marshall Skadden did general business law (he was the firm's "corporate lawyer") and had two main clients. First were Thomas Fizdale and his wife, Patricia Stevens Fizdale. They ran a series of beauty salons, talent agencies, and charm schools that used her maiden name. They licensed the use of the name to others. The agencies referred actors and models to "advertising agencies, business establishments, motion and slide picture companies, radio and television studios and other enterprises desirous of their services," according to a 1952 contract; the charm schools offered training in "modeling, motion picture, radio and television acting, make-up, figure control, hair styling, voice, diction, fashion and kindred subjects. . . ."

The other was Allan A. Ryan, Jr., the grandson of Thomas Fortune Ryan. Thomas was a self-made tycoon who, at various times, controlled the American Tobacco Company, the Equitable Life Assurance Society, the Royal Typewriter Company, and New York City's transit systems. At the Democratic National Convention in 1912, he was singled out by Williams Jennings Bryan, the populist who led the party, as a symbol of its foe, the "privilege-hunting and favor-seeking class."

The grandfather was not well liked on Wall Street either: his financial speculation was sometimes considered shady. When he was sixty-six, he was widowed and remarried twelve days after the death of his first wife. His son, Allan, called that "one of the most disrespectful, disgraceful, and indecent things I've ever heard of." Ryan retaliated by cutting Allan out of his will (Ryan left him two shirt studs) and dividing his estate— $135 million when he died in 1928—into many pieces.

His grandson, Allan A. Ryan, Jr., at age twenty-five, received over $3 million, worth ten times that today. He bought a seat on the New York Stock Exchange, served as chairman of the board of the Royal Typewriter Company, and, at the Ankony Farm, in Rhinebeck, New York, bred prize-winning Aberdeen Angus cattle. Marshall Skadden handled Allan Jr.'s personal business, like the legal work for the farm. He also represented the inventor of the collating machine (Louis Mestre), the founder of a chain of movie theaters (Walter Reade), and the originator of the *Ma Perkins* program, one of TV's first soap operas (Orin Tovrov).

John Slate's field was aviation law. While he brought in Idlewild (renamed Kennedy) Airport as his first client, the bulk of his work was for the general counsel of Pan Am, Henry Friendly (a co-founder of Cleary Gottlieb, he divided his time between the offices of the airline and the firm). Friendly was later a revered, and intimidating, judge on the United States Court of Appeals for the Second Circuit, in Manhattan, and one of the dominant figures in American law during the middle years of this century.

To lawyers at Skadden, Friendly described himself as the firm's godfather—in its early years, fees from Pan American sometimes represented over half its annual income. Joe Flom, looking back, said that "but for Henry Friendly's help in sending us business, we would not have survived." The Pan Am business led to other airline work (e.g., for Aeronaves de México) and it led to other clients (a former President of Mexico).

At the end of 1948, Charles Lyon joined the firm. When the others had asked him to join them, he was deputy chief of the team of lawyers who prosecuted Nazi war criminals at Nuremberg, so he had not been a founding partner. But he had taken two months' leave from his Nuremberg work to help them get started, and was treated as an equal by the founders. His name was added to the firm's.

Lyon was thirty-two and a tax specialist, with an owlish look and a wry manner. The group knew about him because his wife and Slate's wife were friends. The two couples played cards together. Lyon stayed at the firm for two years, until it became clear that, despite his ability and the firm's profits (on revenues of $37,660 their first year, the partners netted $6,510, which they plowed back into the firm), Skadden, Arps, Slate & Lyon lacked enough business to require a tax counsel.

Not long after, Lyon went to work in Washington, D.C., on a congressional investigation of corruption among collectors of federal taxes and, as it turned out, at the highest level of the Internal Revenue Service. Looking into the related activities of two senators and officials at the Justice and Treasury departments, Lyon made a name for himself by sequestering some telling documents that the IRS was planning to seize in order to hide wrongdoing. He did it like an undercover agent, spiriting them away in an old station wagon at night.

The inquiry led to the resignations and, in some cases, convictions of a spray of senior officials, including the Assistant Attorney General in charge of the Tax Division at the Justice Department. To fill the vacancy,

Lyon (then thirty-five) was appointed to the slot by President Harry Truman. He served for half a year, until Eisenhower named his replacement. Later, Lyon became a professor at New York University Law School and he occasionally did projects for the firm. In 1986, Skadden Arps helped to endow a chair in his name at the law school.

3

Accident

Joseph Harold Flom was the first Skadden associate. He was born in Baltimore, Maryland, in 1923, and his family moved to New York City when he was three. He grew up in Brooklyn—"Borough Park and Flatbush and that place at the end of Coney Island where Trump built his place." The family moved often: a landlord would offer three months' free rent for an apartment, and, when the rent came due and the Floms couldn't pay, they would move to the next place.

His father, Isadore, was a Russian immigrant. Until the Depression, he worked full-time as a union organizer. (Flom: "My father was a guy who had a great deal of charisma.") Flom's mother, Fanny, was also Russian (her family name was Fishman) and did appliqué at home. ("That was a helluva job with little scissors," Flom recalled.) When times were hardest and the union hadn't paid Isadore for months, the Floms survived on money from friends and food from the government. Their situation got so bleak that the parents considered suicide. They decided against it, Flom said, because of him and his sister, Florence, who was two years younger. Eventually, Isadore found a job with the Works Progress Administration of the federal government. Later, in a small sewing shop, he made shoulder pads for ladies' dresses.

Isadore was a nonobservant Jew, to his son a "sort of free soul in the group." Fanny kept a kosher household and, as Flom put it, she was "convinced that I was going to be the shining light. My sister was convinced that this reflected the chauvinism that was characteristic of Jewish families—the Prince." Fanny wanted Joe and Florence to go to a yeshiva. The Floms couldn't afford it, but Joe was among a few students in his junior high school picked to take the qualifying exam for a selective public school, Townsend Harris High School, then part of City College of New York. ("In grade school, fortunately, at that time, they weren't on the anti-elitism kick that we are today.") He was the only one who got in.

Each morning his mother gave him a dime for subway fare and another for breakfast (a dime bought a carton of orange juice, three doughnuts, and a cup of coffee at Nedick's). He rode to school in Manhattan, about fifty minutes from his stop in Brooklyn. He did his homework on the subway and, typically, his grades were middling: good in some courses (English, history, and math) and poor in others (Latin and Spanish). After the rigor of Townsend Harris, Flom said, "everything was duck soup."

During his junior year in high school, Flom pushed a hand truck in the Manhattan Garment District to earn pocket money. The following year, Roger Baldwin, the founder of the American Civil Liberties Union, to whom Flom got an introduction, helped him land a job as an office boy at Cook, Nathan & Lehman, one of New York's recognized Jewish firms. A partner there was Nathan Greene, a reserved, handsome man in his late thirties, who had gone to City College and Harvard Law School. (He had co-authored with Felix Frankfurter a legal classic, *The Labor Injunction*, which provided the basis for a landmark New Deal law that protected unions and their members.) Greene became a role model for Flom.

Flom graduated from Townsend Harris in 1941, and worked at Cook Nathan for a second year while attending City College at night. In 1942, after the United States entered the Second World War, he signed up with the Army. He took courses wherever he was posted: at Rutgers

University, in New Jersey; at the University of New Mexico; at Texas A&M University. When he wanted to, he said, he was an ace: the Eighth Army gave a history exam for all comers and, according to Flom, he received the highest score. After he was discharged, in 1946, he followed Nathan Greene's lead and applied to Harvard Law School. He wanted to go for "the usual reasons: the immigrant's way into life was politics, and law was the way into politics." Without a college degree, he was accepted.

Flom entered with a veterans' class that was marked by experience and practicality. He was known for his irreverence. "He saw through the power structure," said Charles Haar, a classmate who became a professor at Harvard Law School and a consultant to Skadden Arps. He expressed it by not taking notes in the classes he went to (Flom: "I would correct other people's notes") and by never going to other classes that he was enrolled in ("They didn't appeal to me"). He did very well. (About a teacher known for his severity, Flom said, "There was one professor, named Eddie Morgan, who I guess gave me the highest grade he'd ever given anyone.") His academic success earned him a place as an editor of the *Harvard Law Review*: it published an A paper he wrote about the lawfulness of limits on picketing under the U.S. Constitution. Eventually, he stood fifteenth or sixteenth in a class of 325.

But toward the end of his last year he had not found a job. In some cases because he was Jewish and in others because he wasn't "an obvious fit," Flom explained, he received no offers from the New York firms for which he hoped to work. His first choice was a thirty-lawyer firm now called Paul, Weiss, Rifkind, Wharton & Garrison, which was then known for its specialties in tax, theatrical, and other legal areas. The firm hired two or three associates a year.

To Flom, the rejections confirmed that he was an outsider. In reality, the story was more complicated. Until 1946, Paul Weiss was Cohen, Cole, Weiss & Wharton; with Jews helping to run it, Flom's religion wasn't an issue there. Many Jews had been successful in the law during the previous generation, and some Wall Street firms had ended their exclusion of Jews. They increasingly had the option of practicing as insiders if they were seen as fitting in.

Flom didn't exercise his option. Because of their "size and rigidity," he didn't feel comfortable with the non-Jewish firms that invited him for a second set of interviews and for which he felt he might be asked to work. They were Cahill, Gordon, Zachry & Reindel, a twenty-nine-year-old firm with fifty-five lawyers, started by Irish Catholics who couldn't get jobs at Wasp firms; and Cravath, Swaine & Moore, the epitome of the establishment, with seventy-five lawyers. Flom: "I'll never get over the firm, although I won't say which one it is, that talked with me about its baseball teams—A teams, B teams. Baseball! What the hell did that have to do with me?"

In June, three months before his class was set to graduate on an accelerated schedule, after two and a quarter years, Harvard Law School's placement office told him about a new firm in New York being started by two Harvard grads and a Columbia grad, and recommended that he interview with them. It was Skadden, Arps & Slate. The firm had written to Harvard, Columbia, and Yale, in the hope that "among the really top-notch men" at those law schools, "there might be some who would prefer a small new law firm to the much larger ones."

The partners took Flom to lunch at Delmonico's, a Wall Street fixture since the Gilded Age. As Flom recalled, they spent most of the time talking about the risks of joining their venture. "A flyer," they called it. The more they warned, the more he liked them. None was Jewish (Skadden and Arps were Protestants, as was Lyon, and Slate was a Protestant turned atheist), but he felt comfortable with all three. He accepted their offer of a job, to begin in October of 1948, two weeks after he graduated, for the going rate at Wall Street firms, $3,600 a year. Charles Lyon said Flom was "the smartest thing I ever saw." Flom was twenty-four.

According to firm lore, the partners couldn't pay Flom when he started work, so they held a pinochle game every Friday afternoon and gave the pot to Flom. Or they could pay him, but not themselves, so that Flom became the highest-paid lawyer at Skadden the day he arrived. In fact, during the firm's first year, the partners paid Flom and took no draw themselves. The second year, the partners paid Flom and Marshall Skadden took a draw to cover his family's expenses. The third year, when Flom made $4,500, the partners had a net profit of $28,946.

Flom's arrival at Skadden wasn't auspicious. In high school, he had been a member of an organization called Friends of Democracy, an anti-fascist, anti-totalitarian group founded by the Reverend L. M. Birkhead, a Unitarian minister from Kansas. He was known as the preacher whom Sinclair Lewis consulted while writing *Elmer Gantry*, his satirical novel about religious scams, and for his series of Little Blue Books (e.g., "Religious Bunk over the Radio"). Flom: "Birkhead was basically a guy who believed in pamphlets—the wisdom of the written word." Ira Wender, a onetime Friend who became a lawyer and a financier, said, "Joe used to street-speak for Friends of Democracy," about Birkhead's message of tolerance.

Flom disclosed his membership in the group when he applied for admission to the New York State bar in 1948. In that early year of the Cold War, the tie raised suspicions that Flom was a Communist. A discrepancy between his birth certificate (it said he was born December 20) and what he claimed (December 21) added to the concern. (Flom: "Aha! A big inconsistency!") After Flom passed the bar exam, the admissions committee required him to sign an affidavit saying that the birth certificate gave the correct date. ("I thought: What the hell, I guess I can sign it. I was there.") He also had to submit a reference (he got one from Wender) vouching for the patriotism of his part in Friends of Democracy. He was sworn in.

Flom on his early days at Skadden: "They had nothing to do early on, right? Slate was off working on Pan American and Arps was working for the Crime Commission. Skadden said, 'We have to have an important partners' meeting.' It was stuff like 'Is this secretary going to get a five-dollar raise?' And then Skadden said, 'We've got to talk about Joe's extracurricular activities.' Slate said, 'Have you thought of suggesting masturbation?' Everybody broke up, and that was the last partners' meeting for about six months."

Flom began as a jack-of-all-trades. He helped file a lawsuit about infringement of a copyright on a chimpanzee doll, and looked into the idea of importing lobster to the United States from the Virgin Islands for a client. He did some estate planning and libel work, and, on one vacation, took a job on a cattle-breeding farm so he would know firsthand the details he wrote about for Allan Ryan, Jr.

He also helped Arps defend William Ward Pigman, a former chemist for the federal Bureau of Standards, which tested secret weapons. Along with Alger Hiss, Pigman was accused by Whittaker Chambers of supplying government documents to him when he was an agent of the Communist Party. Pigman denied the charge and was investigated by the same grand jury as Hiss. Hiss was indicted for perjury and convicted in a case that still mints controversy. Pigman wasn't indicted. Soon after, in a landmark case called *U.S. v. Dennis*, Flom helped write a brief for the American Civil Liberties Union. It sought unsuccessfully to convince a federal appeals court to overturn the convictions of members of the

National Board of the Communist Party for advocating the forceful overthrow of the U.S. government.

With John Ray, a former vice president and general counsel of the American Telephone & Telegraph Company, who became of counsel to Skadden Arps in 1951, Flom handled a case about a British company that made nylon. It was argued in the House of Lords, and resolved in favor of the firm's client. Flom liked quoting the Lords' legal frippery ("with due regard for the comity of nations . . .") and memorized part of an opinion they issued. To Skadden, Ray had stature. His affiliation elevated the firm. In 1952, he was elected to Congress, as a Republican from Staten Island, and he left for Washington, D.C.

Representing the Crown Prince of Yemen gave the firm another sort of distinction. The prince was in New York as an envoy to the United Nations, and got himself in trouble by printing and selling stamps with a likeness of his country's ruler. That was a blasphemy against Allah. On behalf of the Kingdom of Yemen, men in caftans carrying swords retained Skadden Arps to have the stamps destroyed. When Arps and Flom completed the job, the kingdom paid their fee. It expressed gratitude for the firm's services with coffee beans: two hundred pounds for Arps, seventy for Flom. They were delivered in sacks to the lobby of the Lehman Building. Flom was summoned to fetch the gift.

The coffee-bean story suited the tone of the firm: "anti-pomposity, pro-kook," a partner called it. Others called it sophomoric. It was set by Slate (the joker) and Arps (the foil), or by lore they generated, since other lawyers were sometimes involved where Arps was credited. Slate dropping pennies behind Arps as they walked, so Arps would think he had a hole in his pocket. Slate and Arps sharing a hotel suite in Washington, D.C., the night before a hearing at which Arps was going to argue, and Slate (after Arps fell asleep) finding an all-night cobbler to add a lift to one of his shoes, so Arps felt wobbly when he got dressed the next morning. Slate going to a Manhattan night spot where a jazz band played and, when the band finished, around 2 a.m., inviting the musicians to Arps's apartment for a drink. With Slate as conductor, the band rousing Arps with some Dixieland. Each was "a Slate thing to do."

Arps had a strong sense of protocol: when he got serious about a girlfriend (who became his wife), he wrote the other women he was dating, saying he was no longer eligible; for male associates whose shoes were scuffed, he insisted on buying a shine. The Dixieland escapade particularly unnerved him. In one version, Arps had been out partying and was awoken from a drunken sleep, certain he was dead. Arps's and Slate's drinking was not only nocturnal. They regularly took long, boozy lunches. Arps rationed himself to a martini and a half before lunch, but apparently observed no limit during the meal. Sometimes he and Slate didn't make it back to work.

In 1954, Lehman Brothers asked Skadden, Arps, and Slate if they would free up space for the investment bank by moving to new quarters. In the fall, the law firm moved to the Fred F. French Building, a landmark at 551 Fifth Avenue, near Forty-fifth Street, then known as the location of a men's clothing store called Browning King. It was a genteel, art deco structure, with low ceilings, narrow offices, and varnished wooden plaques with gold-leaf lettering announcing its tenants. Skadden was among the first firms on, or near, Wall Street to move midtown.

The move coincided with Flom's election to a partnership, which may have been expedited by Marshall Skadden's recent stroke. Not long after, Flom began to attract some notice in the press. When Pamela Woolworth, a distant relative of the founder of the famous five-and-dime retail chain, and a partner bought a controlling interest in a cattle ranch that was the largest American company in Paraguay, *The New York Times* identified Flom as her counsel.

In the spring of 1957, Flom traveled to Boston to interview potential associates at Harvard Law School. ("Proselytizing," he called it.) The next morning, he started out by cab from Harvard Square to the airport. A car driven by an off-duty policeman who had fallen asleep at the wheel crashed into the cab head-on. The collision killed the cabdriver and knocked Flom out cold. Sometime after, Flom heard a voice say, "He's dead, too." Noting that his right foot was resting on his left shoulder, and that he had never seen a picture of a scene like this that he would be able to remember from his grave, Flom concluded that he wasn't dead. He decided, correctly, that his problem was a broken right hip.

Flom was taken by ambulance to the Massachusetts General Hospital in Boston. His hip required a dicey operation and three steel pins to fix. Flom called his office to ask lawyers to cover for him. Although he downplayed the accident, an associate flew up to Boston to see him. The lawyer called Les Arps to encourage him to come as soon as possible, advising that Flom might die before he got there. (Flom: "I must have looked pretty gruesome, with tubes up my nose and my foot strapped, my face black and blue.") Arps rushed along. He found out who was the best nurse on Flom's ward, and maneuvered the man (the word "stole" is also used to describe the act) from another patient to care for Flom.

For a month, Flom's right leg was encased in plaster and elevated by a pulley. He couldn't get out of bed. He also had a dozen other injuries, including a broken nose, cracked ribs, and a bruised spleen. He spent two months in the hospital. Flom read a lot while recovering (a favorite book was *The Wreck of the Mary Deare: A Story of the Sea* by Hammond Innes). By his lights, he enjoyed himself: "Churchill said that everybody oughta go through being in the hospital for an extended period of time, where all of your wants are taken care of and you have nothing to do but read books and expand your mind—it really gets your thinking process freed of a lot of preconceptions."

He received $15,000 in settlement for the accident, worth four times that today. ("If we had been hit by somebody with money, I would have been able to retire," Flom said. "Christ, I really got hit!") With weekly disability insurance on top of his salary from the law firm, he felt in "great shape." It was the first time he had "two nickels to rub together." Flom rented an apartment on the Upper East Side of Manhattan. (He had been living with roommates downtown.) To decorate the place, he hired Claire Kramer. (Her maiden name was Cohen.) She impressed Flom in part because she had done work for the senior partners of Cahill Gordon.

She was tall, dark-haired, and beautiful, with unblinking green eyes, a dusky voice, and a ten-year-old daughter from a first marriage that had ended in divorce. She found Flom "arbitrary and capricious," and exasperating to work for. (Joe: "I guess she said I was the worst pain in the ass she ever had as a client." Claire: "I discovered just before the job was finished that Joe was color-blind, and that was a big part of the problem.") He appealed to her, however, and she to him: she especially liked that men confided in him; he liked that she said what was on her mind. Because he lacked obvious glamour, friends of Flom's said, hers was especially alluring. Within a year, they decided to get married.

Flom told Arps about their plans, and Arps (then still a bachelor) said he had a diamond ring for Flom's fiancée: he had bestowed it on a girl he planned to marry; when things hadn't worked out, she had given it back. In a version of the story from Claire Flom, Joe gave her the ring

(Claire: "modest, very pretty") and told her its history over dinner. When a friend of hers complimented the ring soon after, she replied, "Les Arps gave it to me"—a Skadden thing to say. According to Arps's future wife, Flom asked Claire to stop by the firm and Arps got the ring out of the firm vault. Flom slipped it on Claire's finger, and then he and Arps went back to work.

4

Showing the Bastards

Flom was busy because of William H. Timbers. Timbers became a Skadden partner in 1956, after resigning as general counsel to the Securities and Exchange Commission in Washington, D.C. He had served in the government for two years. His stint ended in a flurry, when he was sentenced to sixty days in jail for refusing to release confidential FBI files sought in a lawsuit. He spent half a day behind bars, until a judge who could free him was located at a baseball game.

Timbers knew about Skadden through Les Arps, who played cards with a friend of Timbers's. When he left the SEC, he narrowed his choices to Skadden and a small young firm in Washington, D.C. (Its junior partner was Lloyd Cutler, later a counselor to President Jimmy Carter.) In part because Timbers was from Connecticut and wanted to return North to live, he picked New York. Timbers was not prepossessing: he was a man of medium height with tiny ears, a receding hairline above a roundish face, and a dumpling's frame; he wore thin bow ties and glasses with thick dark frames. Even when he smiled, he pursed his lips in reserve.

But Timbers was unreservedly proud of his accomplishments. He hung dozens of diplomas and awards on his office walls. Behind his desk, he displayed an American flag, on a brass staff topped by a brass eagle, which the SEC had given him. Timbers's vanity irked Slate, who laid down newspaper under the staff, as if to catch droppings from the bird. Slate intrigued Timbers, however, and the feeling was sometimes mutual. The two occasionally took a break for dinner together when they had work to do at night. One evening, Slate excused himself early from dinner at a restaurant. When Timbers returned to his office, he found Slate armed with a BB gun, shooting his certificates one by one.

Until Timbers arrived, the firm had done no big-time corporate legal work. (Its advice to Pan Am dealt with airline regulations and was secondary to the counsel given by Cleary Gottlieb about other business matters.) His main client was an insurance company that owned a subsidiary represented by Abe Fortas, the future Supreme Court Justice, who was then a partner in the decade-old Washington, D.C., law firm of Arnold, Fortas & Porter. Fortas was notoriously brilliant and arrogant.

According to Timbers, "Fortas hated Flom," who was a regular member of Timbers's insurance team, because he challenged Fortas—"he was so bright and dominant." Flom: "Abe Fortas liked to be front and center on everything. I'm not exactly a shrinking violet. And, actually, he was older than I was, so he wanted to be given total homage, and I just didn't buy it."

Timbers brought in two pieces of business that, over time, transformed the fortunes of Joe Flom and the firm. In 1958, the law firm of Davis, Polk, Wardwell, Sunderland & Kiendl (now Davis, Polk & Wardwell) represented the investment bank of Harriman, Ripley & Company, and asked Timbers to serve as counsel to the Dixon Chemicals Company, another Davis Polk client that was trying to raise funds through Harriman for a new venture. Timbers had worked for the law firm as an associate; his son was the godson of John W. Davis, a onetime presidential candidate, a famous lawyer's lawyer, and the firm's reigning partner. The Davis firm was one of Wall Street's leaders, with regular business for Morgan Stanley & Company as its cornerstone. Timbers asked Flom to handle the deal and appeared to give Flom his first chance to work for a Wall Street bank.

But Joseph Ripley, the bank's chief executive, didn't like the idea of using Skadden: it was not one of the law firms regularly picked for such work. When Dixon Chemicals said it would go to a different bank rather than insult Skadden, Flom related, he advised that Dixon needed the financing more than it did his firm and that it should hire another. Within a year, the deal fell apart and the chemical company discharged its counsel. Dixon again raised the idea of engaging Skadden. With Flom in the room, Joseph Ripley called a senior partner at Davis Polk for a reference.

"Oh, yeah, they're a good firm," Flom reported the partner saying about Skadden. "We use them." The deal was consummated and, a year later, Flom was directly hired to represent Harriman Ripley in another matter. When that deal closed, Flom said, he brought in a fee of $750,000, Skadden's largest yet. It was almost as much as the firm's total revenue since it had been founded, eleven years before.

Marshall Skadden had died in December of 1958, after a second stroke. The last of the Skadden name partners, William R. Meagher, arrived at the turn of the year. Meagher was the first Skadden partner hired laterally from another firm. A compact Irish American, with a pronounced nose, swept-back hair, and striking good looks, he was a graduate of Fordham College and of Fordham Law School (he had been in the top ten of his class) and a former Fordham Law lecturer. Out and around, he wore a homburg and doffed it to the ladies.

Like Arps, he had served as an investigator of corruption, in New York State's Kings and Queens counties. He joined Davis Polk at the age of thirty-nine, and worked closely with Theodore Kiendl, a name partner, on a long-running U.S. Supreme Court dispute about apportioning water from the Colorado River. At forty-nine, he began to assist John W. Davis in *Brown* v. *Board of Education*, the case of the century, unsuccessfully defending the position that the U.S. Constitution permitted public education for blacks and whites that was separate but equal.

Meagher was passed over for partnership at Davis Polk—in his opinion, because of his unclassy background, symbolized by his law degree from Fordham. It was thought of as a school for recent immigrants or their children, who were intent on climbing the social ladder and hadn't made it to the Ivy League rung. At fifty-four, long past the age most lawyers were made partners in established firms, he moved to Skadden as a senior partner.

He knew about Skadden through Bill Timbers, with whom he had overlapped at Davis Polk. That firm favored him with good referrals (to soothe its guilt about not making him a partner, according to a Skadden theory), and he generated enough business to be a substantial contributor to Skadden's profits until the late sixties. His biggest client was the Stereotypers Union, which represented workers who made molten plates for printing newspapers. The Skadden reception area was commonly filled with men in ink-stained coveralls waiting to see him.

Meagher was a raconteur. He liked to tell a story about one of his early jobs of legal research. A ship had been seized and a senior lawyer called Meagher into his office. "We've got to get a writ of pluckaddendum," he told Meagher excitedly. "We've got to get one fast!" Meagher had little idea what the lawyer was talking about, so he went to the library and spent the night searching for a clue about the writ. In the morning, empty-handed, he went back to the lawyer. What was a writ of pluckaddendum? The senior lawyer said, "You don't know? It's where somebody took something and you go and pluck it back!"

Meagher also had a righteous streak, which led to some minor reforms at Skadden. ("He was a very formal guy," Joe Flom said, "as formal as an Irishman can get.") Associates had treated the firm's petty-cash box as a source of pocket money. He put an end to that. Lawyers had hired stenographers for overtime work, and then kept them waiting while the lawyers went out for well-lubricated dinners. Meagher stopped the spendthrift practice.

When the firm held a meeting about the request by some associates for the chance to take on legal projects for public causes, known as pro bono work, Meagher said, "I think you're right. But you people have to keep this in perspective. You think you invented pro bono. *I* represented one of the main parties in *Brown* v. *Board of Education*!" He didn't say which one.

John Slate reacted to Meagher's dour side according to form. Marshall Skadden had been cremated, and Slate kept his ashes in a box on his desk. One day he carried the box into Meagher's office. "You know what this is?" Slate asked. "It's Skadden."

In 1959, William Timbers got Flom involved in Flom's first proxy contest. His clients were the managers of the United Industrial Corporation, who were being challenged by a group of stockholders. United Industrial was a onetime manufacturer of automobile bodies that was turned into a financial holding company. In the previous four years, it had gone from owning three-fourths of a company that made missiles to owning approximately one-quarter. The sold-off stock had been purchased by the managers of United Industrial and their families, and the missile company's profits had soared.

The insurgents contended that the missile company was now worth more than United Industrial and that the public corporation was being run like a private club for the benefit of its members. The company's president, Rensselaer Clark, with Flom as his guide, countered that it was worth over $13 million, more than half of it liquid, and that these assets represented a prize the insurgents sought to capture. In mail attacking the leader of the insurgents (one letter about him was titled "How Bernie Fein Operates"), Clark portrayed the challenge as a devious plot masterminded by a disgruntled former director of the corporation. Against the usual odds, the insurgents won four seats on the company's board, although they didn't gain full control.

In September of 1960, Bill Timbers left the law firm to become a federal trial judge in Connecticut. (His sponsor was Prescott Bush, the Republican senator and father of George Bush. Timbers was elevated to the U.S. Court of Appeals for the Second Circuit in 1971, and became a senior judge in 1981.) The firm changed its name to Skadden, Arps, Slate, Meagher & Flom. The name was settled, but the firm was not.

On Timbers's departure, Robert Ensher was named a partner to replace him. He was a talented associate of Armenian stock with a shock of dark hair and a lopsided smile. The number of partners remained at five, but with Ensher's elevation, the ranks of associates fell to four. The firm had barely doubled its initial size. Skadden still had few corporate clients and those were relatively small. No corporate clients were listed on the New York Stock Exchange, only one was listed on the American Stock Exchange, and only one had stock that was traded over the counter.

Aside from occasional lucrative assignments like Flom's for Harriman, Ripley & Company, the firm was still sustained by airline business. Its main client (the last on which it was heavily reliant) was a helicopter company, New York Airways. The company went bankrupt after two of its helicopters crashed, one on top of the Pan Am Building.

To fortify the ranks, Peter Mullen was brought into the firm as a senior associate and its tenth lawyer. He had been passed over for partnership at Dewey Ballantine, as was the other candidate left in his class. In the lore of that firm, he was the last associate ruled out solely because he was Catholic. Mullen was tall and self-confident, and had an unreadable demeanor that made him appear serene. At thirty-two, he had been recommended as (Joe Flom's words) "a terrific piece of talent."

Claire Flom met him at a buffet dinner that the Floms gave for the Irish Historical Society. (Robert F. Wagner, New York's Irish American mayor, also came.) Claire: "Everybody was fed and I was moving around the room, and I got into a conversation with Peter Mullen. I thought to myself: Oh, boy, he's solid and impressive. If I were in trouble, that's the guy I'd want to represent me. He was already in conversation about coming into the firm." A friend of the Flomses' reported her saying to Joe, "You hire that guy." (Claire said she had no such influence.) The same friend said, "Mullen was bloodless, and offered an anchor against the firm's absolute chaos. It was a circus over there on Fifth Avenue."

The Skadden that brought in Mullen, he allowed, was "a dinky little firm." No partner was satisfied with that status. Of the firm's five partners, three were castoffs with something to prove (Arps, Slate, and Meagher) and two (Flom and Ensher) were young lawyers who, no matter where they had gone to school (Harvard Law) or how well they had done (very), felt like outsiders. A lawyer who was an associate then said, "They all wanted to prove they weren't shlubs."

The firm composite would have been a high-strung, gung-ho lawyer with a sizable chip on his shoulder. In the status-conscious world of lawyers, Skadden's were unusually attentive to markers of success. The first-rank Wall Street firms didn't know it (they would have considered the challenge premature), but Skadden eyed them as its competition. "The biggies," firm lawyers called them.

The twenty largest ranged from Cleary Gottlieb, with forty-six lawyers, to Shearman & Sterling (then Shearman & Sterling & Wright), with a hundred twenty-five, and a franchise as the primary counsel for the bank now called Citicorp. They included the alma maters of half the lawyers in the firm, who set out to extend the traditions of places they had left and then to best them. At firm meetings where Arps and Slate explained how things had been done at the Root firm, Flom countered with examples from his days at Cook Nathan. It didn't faze him that the experience he drew on was a messenger's.

As it was represented by the large firms that led the New York City bar, the legal profession in the early sixties was measured, self-protective, and clubby. Louis Auchincloss, the chronicler of Wall Street manners and morals who began his legal career as an associate at Sullivan & Cromwell, one of the law firms in the Wall Street establishment, described a fictional archetype as being "marked by gentility and disorderly grandness." To him, the ideal firm was "a group of gentlemen loosely associated by a common enthusiasm for the practice of law."

Nancy Lisagor and Frank Lipsius, in a history of Sullivan & Cromwell, recount that the gentlemanly aura at Auchincloss's onetime firm veiled some coarse episodes, like the firm's collaboration with the Hitler government during the 1930s, which was led by its managing partner, future Secretary of State John Foster Dulles. Similar stories are told about other established firms. Still, the bar acted as if it controlled its own destiny —although, to some observers, the law appeared to be a "dwindling profession," because the number of American lawyers was not keeping pace with the growth in the population.

Arps coined the term "upper-margin work" to describe what his firm aspired to do, to break into the bar's inner circle. The Skadden goal was to get the kind of work that first-rank firms did and, in the range of acceptable results produced by them, to perform at the upper margin. To Flom, who sometimes recalls his past thoughts in the present tense and knows how to use a straw man for effect, the firm's impetus was elemental: "We've got to show the bastards that you don't have to be born into it."

To reach the upper margin, the firm defined as its method doing more for a client than other firms were willing to do. Skadden lawyers had to be faster and more responsive. At the Root firm that Arps and Slate remembered, a lawyer was considered to be doing something wrong if he was at his desk past early evening. (If so, the firm was atypical among established firms, where, the journalist Spencer Klaw reported in 1958, "hard work and long hours are such an honorable tradition that young associates boast of watching the sun come up over Wall Street.")

At Skadden, Flom lectured, lawyers didn't have the luxury of working banker's hours. Other firms had long-standing relationships with clients ("Corporations owned their counsel and their counsel owned the corporations," Flom said), but Skadden was building from scratch and (Flom) "whatever came in the door was the greatest thing in the world." The work of Skadden lawyers was an act of salesmanship. They had to shun the mentality of ten-to-six.

Flom's aim was for the firm to distinguish itself substantively, too. To him, the Skadden franchise was to help a client solve its problem rather than simply to counsel whether a solution it proposed was legal. He considered this standard a breakthrough, as did others at his firm.

In fact, it was the same as one handed down by Elihu Root, the father of the lawyer who helped found Root Clark: "The client never wants to be told he can't do what he wants to do; he wants to be told how to do it, and it is the lawyer's business to tell him how." Yet, even if other firms prided themselves on doing that, Skadden lawyers felt that Flom gave them an advantage.

In 1960, Skadden was asked to take part in its second proxy contest as a result of an unrelated piece of problem solving that demonstrated the firm's chutzpah. A woman had a stroke, and her niece and her brother (not the niece's father) disagreed about where she should be treated. The brother, a Skadden client, thought she should go to a hospital. The niece thought she should stay at the home the two women shared.

Skadden advised that the brother had the right to move his sister to the hospital and that he ought to do it soon—say, after the niece went to work one day the following week. The brother took the advice and the woman recovered nicely. In Skadden lore, which tends to exaggerate for impact, the case is called the dead-body story.

The brother had worked for Thomas Fortune Ryan. The Skadden firm was the executor of the brother's will. His son was Arthur Long, who worked for one of the leading firms of proxy solicitors, D. F. King & Company. Long advised corporations on the most important part of proxy contests, how to win votes of stockholders. He was impressed enough to recommend Skadden as counsel for management in a proxy contest over control of the Alleghany Corporation in 1960. It was among the last of the big proxy contests of the postwar era, and a showcase for Joe Flom's talents.

The contest involved the New York Central Railroad (the nation's second-biggest system), Investors Diversified Services (the largest mutual fund in the world), a pair of wealthy Texas brothers (John D. and Clint W. Murchison, Jr.), and Allan Kirby, a once-passive investor who had belatedly assumed the chairmanship of the Alleghany holding company.

In 1954, Kirby had supported a proxy contest staged by his longtime ally, Robert Young. Alleghany gained control of the New York Central in the apotheosis of that form of corporate warfare after the Second World War. For a couple of years, the railroad flourished. So did the holding company. In 1957, the New York Central began to flounder, along with many of America's railroads. The next year, four days after the Central board voted not to pay a dividend to stockholders for the first time under Young's leadership, he killed himself.

The Murchisons mounted a proxy campaign that focused on Allan Kirby, casting him as a "back-seat" investor (as president, he had let Young run Alleghany for nineteen years) who had not developed a skilled team of executives or made good investments for Alleghany. "How Can Kirby Take Credit When Young Ran the Show?" asked a proxy solicitation from the insurgents.

"But what qualifications do the Murchison sons have for taking over your Company?" management retorted. Kirby portrayed the Murchisons as puppets of their father (he got them started in business), whose only goal was to regain control of IDS. They had sold it to Alleghany, bought it back, and sold it again to Alleghany. Kirby argued that, in the previous two decades, he had helped take the corporation's common stock from a value of minus $89 million to plus $92 million.

Skadden's job was to count the proxies for Kirby and the Committee for Continued Responsible Management of the Alleghany Corporation, rather than guide it through the whole contest, but Flom eagerly signed on. "Not very heady or sophisticated stuff, but that put us at least one ahead of everyone else in New York City," Flom said, overlooking at least one. A lawyer with more experience was George Demas, who represented the insurgents in the bid for control of Alleghany. Demas's clients won.

Despite the loss once again for Skadden's client, Flom's counsel won respect. In 1962, he was asked to represent the management of the General Fireproofing Company, of Youngstown, Ohio, in another contest. There, the insurgents were led by Alfons Landa, a director of the company, whose five previous fights for control of companies made him a seasoned corporate raider. Landa and others contended that General Fireproofing's profits were down, that its costs were up, and that its growth had been neglected. They also charged that nepotism in the company was a scandal.

The management argued that Landa had previously run another flourishing company into the red and should be stopped by any legal means, including by staggering the terms of corporate board members to keep him from gaining control through the board. Management prevailed. Skadden won its first victory in a proxy fight. Belatedly, proxy work became the firm's way to show the bastards—its "bell ringer," in another phrase of Flom's.

A contest later that year gave Flom the chance to sound off again. He was asked to represent the management of the American Hardware Corporation in a fight against challengers led by another experienced raider, Victor Muscat, and his counsel, George Demas. Muscat headed three holding companies, which had interests in a bank, an insurance company, and companies making automobile parts and machine tools. The holding companies were financed by an unusual amount of debt. One of the companies, BSF Company, of which Muscat had recently gained control, owned one-third of American Hardware. Instead of asking for the list of American Hardware's stockholders, which he almost surely would have been given, Muscat made his challenge by accusing that the company was mismanaged. The charge rattled Flom's client. " 'What the hell are you doing? Go home! I'm finished!' " Flom recalled the client saying.

The accusation played into Flom's hand. The contest became a court test about the issue of mismanagement, and a state judge in Connecticut ruled decisively for American Hardware. "The judge wrote a lengthy opinion about how this was one of the best-managed companies in the United States," Flom recounted, reading heavily between lines that reached a less grand conclusion. (The judge stated that the firm's "conservative management and financial stability" produced "annual profits and regularly paid cash dividends.")

More accurately, Flom said, "They took on a higher burden of proof than they had to, and they blew it." Flom then helped to strip Muscat of his stock (". . . and how the hell do you keep him from getting fifty percent? You start looking into his sources of financing") and to bring about a merger between American Hardware and another company, in which his clients retained control. American Hardware became the Emhart Company, which remained a Skadden client for twenty-five years, until it was taken over by the Black & Decker Corporation for $2.8 billion.

To Flom, who went on to major proxy contests involving companies like Elgin Watch, Studebaker, and Metro-Goldwyn-Mayer, the American Hardware fight was the "high-water mark" of his proxy experience: he had kept "a guy with a third of the stock from getting a seat on the board." He also marked it as his "big break." During the American Hardware case, *Barron's*, the financial weekly, noted Flom's arrival as a counselor to corporations in struggles for control. It reported that the company had "enlisted the services of Joe Flom, a lawyer who successfully stood off the Alfons Landa forces last year at General Fireproofing."

5

Takeoff

Skadden began to take off, and Flom celebrated by spending. He bought a racehorse with Arthur Long, the proxy fighter (Long: "A cheap little nag, but we won three races in four starts at Belmont and Aqueduct"). On his own, he bought expensive cars. Claire disliked the habit, and checked it. "You can't give back a car you've used, but I did sell them," she related. "He would buy a Cadillac convertible, and I would sell it." In the meantime, the first thing each morning at his office, Flom would open the mail to see if any checks had arrived from clients. At the end of the week, he would bug lawyers to hand in the sheets on which they recorded time they put in for clients, so the firm could send out bills.

It was not uncommon late on a Friday afternoon for Flom to read a document that an associate had just finished drafting, and gripe, "This has to give me an erection, and I'm not getting one." The associate handed in a second draft at 7:30 that evening and, as Flom marked it up with a red pen, heard him mutter, "This is shit" or "This sucks."

By the third draft, which the associate brought in as Flom ordered, at 6:45 on Saturday morning, the document was rounding into shape. Each lawyer conceded points. They wrote the fourth draft together. When it was done, they went out to celebrate over a piece of cheesecake. The associate chalked up the abusive moments to Flom's quest for perfection.

Louis Goodman, a partner who worked for Flom as an associate, said, "That wasn't just to motivate you. He was frustrated and wanted to get the solution right." Another lawyer who trained under Flom: "I actually don't like Joe. He can be extremely difficult to work with. But he is a Rosetta stone of practice. Once you see him practice law, you think differently about it."

For much of the year, Flom spoke at bar meetings to publicize the firm—often at seminars put on by the Practising Law Institute, in Manhattan. Other Skadden lawyers did routine corporate work, like drafting the minutes of annual board meetings for a small group of regular corporate clients. The companies were still relatively modest, but the proxy business turned a busy firm into a growing one. Flom attracted business because (his words) "Wall Street has big ears." By 1965, the firm had more work than it could handle. Shifting the focus from quality (upper-margin work) to quantity, Les Arps adopted the motto "If you don't grow, you die!"

At New York City's established firms, it was an almost ironclad rule that partners had to be developed through the ranks. Skadden's spurt of business made the normal cycle of hiring and training associates out of law school a luxury it could not afford, so it hired some lawyers from other firms, as it had taken Meagher into the partnership. The firm attracted associates who felt they had made the wrong choice by going to bigger firms with slower practices ("I was bored to tears," James Freund, a partner who arrived in 1966, when he was thirty-one, said about his previous experience) and liked what they heard about Skadden.

Sometimes they expressed doubts about the move. Jim Freund is a vigorous, articulate man, whose taste for writing has made him the unofficial historian of Skadden. One of his first assignments was to figure out how to use semen from a prize bull as collateral for a loan. Like Flom eighteen years earlier, he felt the need to inspect a cattle-breeding farm before addressing the question. Stepping around the barnyard in Florsheim loafers, Freund recounted in a memoir, he didn't feel much like a Wall Street lawyer. But the lure for associates was the chance for a jump in responsibility at a firm that wanted them (Freund: it "put a big make on me") and appeared to be "small and peppy and on the move."

Compared with most of the places that associates left, Skadden felt like a sweatshop. But young lawyers said they found exhilaration in its pace. One who left a more established firm recruited a friend from there: "This is it! This is where the action is!" An associate met a partner going down the elevator one evening and coined a Skadden cliché: "Thank God it's Friday. Only two more workdays this week!"

Skadden lawyers felt they were part of a legal counterculture: as they saw the world, established firms billed their clients once a year, and assumed business would come to them; Skadden lawyers felt they could take nothing for granted. When Skadden teamed with the Cravath firm on a case, the intense style of the small firm led a senior partner at Cravath to compare it, not altogether approvingly, to the Israeli Army. Cravath was known for its work ethic, so Skadden lawyers heard the remark as high praise. A Skadden partner said about those days, "We thrilled ourselves . . ."

From the firm's point of view, its hallmarks were pragmatism and openness. Skadden had a mix of Democrats and Republicans, and of Catholics, Jews, and Protestants. At work and otherwise, they banded together to advance their interests, as when Flom, through Arps, got John Harlan (in addition to Allan A. Ryan, Jr., and J. Pierpont Morgan III) to serve as a reference for his application to buy a co-op in a building that had never had a Jewish tenant. (Flom: "I figured that would break the logjam." It did.)

In addition to its castoffs, the firm consisted of late bloomers and, if not misfits, then not quite smooth fits. It prided itself on shaping them into a crack outfit, like a bomber crew in the Second World War. Performance counted. Birthright was irrelevant. Skadden made a virtue of taking in lawyers who were less highly valued by other Wall Street firms.

Sometimes they came from first-tier schools: Blaine Fogg is a Harvard Law School grad (he is known as Fin, a nickname he picked up at Exeter and carried with him to Williams College). He had been called into the office of a partner at the old-line New York firm where he worked during the summer between his second and third years at law school. Without being given a reason, he was told he wasn't cut out to be a lawyer. (Fogg: "I was devastated, and figured they didn't know what the hell they were talking about.") After he graduated, he spent a year and a day at a second firm, and then transferred to Skadden.

They were also from Fordham Law School. William Meagher created a channel to his alma mater in 1959 by asking the Fordham dean to recommend a student for a summer job. The dean sent over John Feerick. He was first in his Fordham class after the first year and typical of the school: from the Bronx, the son of a first-generation Irish immigrant and New York City bus driver, he was also the first member of his family to go to college, at Fordham. Feerick became a Skadden associate and partner.

Most of the lawyers were men, but the firm faced the gender issue in 1959. In New York then, some corporate law firms favored men as secretaries as well as lawyers. At least one Wall Street firm, Milbank, Tweed, Hadley & McCloy, forbade spouses of its lawyers from practicing with another firm, on the ground that the firm had to avoid the appearance of engaging in conflicts of interest. For many years, only women were affected, for the firm had only male lawyers. The rule was changed in 1960, after the firm hired a woman whose lawyer husband refused to give up his solo practice in Brooklyn.

Elizabeth Head applied to Skadden during a stint as a teacher of legal writing at Columbia Law School. (She later became the university's general counsel, after working as a partner in a large New York firm.) She had good qualifications, including a law degree from the University of Chicago. The five Skadden partners were rounded up to meet her. With her still in the room, the huddle focused on whether they should hire a female lawyer.

At thirty-five, Flom was the youngest partner by a decade. Head recalled him saying, "What the hell does it matter as long as she can do the work?" (Flom: "To me, it was: What's the bullshit? I can see why she would remember it.") No one had a rejoinder, so she got the job. She quit after almost two years, when she got pregnant. It didn't occur to her, or anyone else, that she could be given a maternity leave. For the next dozen years at the Skadden she had worked for, it was O.K. for a senior partner to write on the interview sheet of a female law student who was applying to be an associate: "A terrific broad," as one noted about Peggy Kerr. In 1981, she became the firm's first female partner.

As John Slate's airline work became less crucial to the firm, he went public as a humorist. Math had been one of his hobbies since college. He turned the line of a song—"If you loved me half as much as I love you"—into an equation. He once picked a fight with his wife, who didn't know much math, about whether a certain proof was elegant. Slate also liked working with his hands. Helping one of his daughters make a primitive computer for a science project put an idea into his head about how to combine his hobbies.

For several years, on weekends and at night, he disappeared into his basement and pieced together a large analog computer. While the work was in progress, in 1964, Slate showed off what he was learning in *Fortune*. He wrote an article called "The Warning Impulse Timing and Computing Haversack (TWITCH)" (haversack = backpack), in which, twelve years before the computer industry proved him farsighted, he predicted the advent of a portable computer.

During the next two years, between December of 1964 and September of 1966, Slate contributed five pieces to *The Atlantic Monthly*. He showed a flair for puns, twists of logic, and all-around verbal high jinks. He wrote a piece about how to build an ocean liner; "A Note on Man-Animal, Animal-Man, and Animal-Animal Perception"; a cautionary spoof about what he called the home surgery movement ("Lay Lobotomy—Go Slow"); a primer about how to survive a hospital stay; and a send-up of capital punishment.

Thomas Merton read the hospital piece and got back in touch with Slate by letter. After their days at Columbia College, the two had heard about each other through mutual friends for almost thirty years, but hadn't communicated directly. Merton asked Slate to handle the legal side of his literary estate and Slate traveled to Gethsemani Abbey, in Kentucky, where Merton lived, so they could talk about the details.

During the reunion, Slate charmed Merton's Trappist brothers by speaking Welsh and reciting passages of Mary Baker Eddy's teachings about Christian Science. Merton deduced that Slate was "living rather wildly, burning everything out." Not long after, in September of 1967, Slate died of a heart attack, on his fifty-fourth birthday.

A few months before, Robert Ensher had died as well, from a stroke. He had recently turned forty and was the firm's rising courtroom star. The two deaths cast a shadow over the place. On its twentieth anniversary soon after, the number of partners stood back at seven. Skadden and Slate were gone, and Arps toiled mainly on criminal and corporate investigations. (The United States Trotting Association was his big client.) As a result of Ensher's death, the firm's growth in litigation lagged. Associates worried out loud whether the firm would hold together. For the next ten years, one lawyer kept Ensher's obituary in a desk drawer as a reminder of fate's turns.

Skadden's therapy for its depression was hard work. It was increasingly engaged in struggles for control of corporations. In 1964, Joe Flom had helped a New York investment partnership called the Arcady Corporation take over a small San Diego-based investment company called Electronics International Capital, after Arcady's bid had stalled. It was Skadden's first tender offer.

The next year, the firm helped the U.S. Smelting, Refining & Mining Company gain control of the Mueller Brass Company and, the year after that, guided the Gulf & Western Corporation when it took over Paramount Pictures. But, as in its counsel of the Holly Sugar Corporation against a bid from the Houston Oil Field Material Company, most of Skadden's early takeover work was on defense.

In 1967, for example, the firm represented the Norwich Pharmaceutical Company when it received an unwanted offer from Revlon. Norwich manufactured Pepto-Bismol, among other products. Revlon wanted to acquire the company for a division that made antacids, like Tums. Flom was hired by Norwich. The firm defended the company, arguing that a merger would violate antitrust law by creating a monopoly in the market for noneffervescent stomach pills.

The theory was only partially Flom's. Skadden had a new associate, Stephen Axinn. He had grown up in Queens expecting to follow his father's footsteps into the family lumber business, and had considered the law a woman's profession: the only lawyer he knew as a boy was his mother, who had gone to New York University Law School. Axinn's father died when he was fifteen. A few years later, at his mother's suggestion, he went to law school, at Columbia University.

Axinn put in stints at a large firm in Manhattan and as an assistant to a solo practitioner who did antitrust work. He concluded that he didn't want to specialize in the field. On summer duty in the Army Reserve, he noticed another soldier who used his spare time to work on a legal brief. To Axinn, he "looked liked he was going places." It was John Feerick.

He got Axinn to apply to Skadden as an all-purpose trial lawyer, or litigator, on the understanding that Skadden was a small firm and wasn't likely to have room for Axinn as a partner: Feerick was also a litigator and a year ahead of Axinn, and expected to fill the upcoming slot. (For such candor and other virtues, Feerick was called St. John.) Axinn was offered a job, and he took it.

Skadden was tight for space when Axinn arrived, so his office was the small firm library. One day, Flom came in and said, "Do you know where the antitrust laws are?" Axinn said yes. Flom said, "There's a law about mergers, right?" Axinn replied, "Yes, there is. A merger that is anti-competitive won't be allowed." Flom said, "What the hell does that mean?" Axinn became Flom's antitrust lawyer. The duo comprised the team that successfully defended Norwich against Revlon.

In 1968, Congress passed an amendment to the Securities Exchange Act of 1934, one of the important securities laws of the Depression era, which had been enacted to prevent abuses in stock trading. Called the Williams Act, the new law was intended to close a gap in the old, by ending the possibility of surprise takeovers.

Until then, an aggressor could quietly accumulate a block of a target firm's stock and, through advertisements in newspapers read by the financial community, offer to buy enough of the target's outstanding stock directly from the stockholders to gain a controlling interest. The mechanism was called a tender offer because the aggressor asked stockholders of the target to tender their shares for purchase. If the aggressor received enough shares, it could buy them at the price it had announced in its offer. If not, the aggressor could return the shares to their owners.

Under the Williams Act anyone buying 10 percent or more of a company's stock in the open market was required to disclose that fact (the threshold was later lowered to 5 percent) and say whether he intended to try a takeover. The act also set some rules for takeovers. Framers of the new law tried to make it impartial to the stockholders of aggressors and targets—to establish a "level playing field." But one of its main sponsors referred to takeovers as financial rape. The act was intended as a moderate restraint on the hostile deals that were done increasingly during the 1960s and had been basically unregulated. Between 1956 and 1966, by one study, there were 286 cash tender offers for companies. Almost half were made in the last two years of the span.

Some respected corporate lawyers opposed the new law, saying that takeovers helped to keep managers accountable to stockholders and were good for the economy. Their concern that the law would limit the use of a valuable policing mechanism seemed realistic for two years—the number of tender offers fell precipitously in 1969 and again in 1970. But the new law had a paradoxical effect: It made takeovers legitimate. In 1971, the number of takeovers began to climb again.

Still, Skadden proceeded on its tender-offer work without much competition from established firms. Taking their cues from longtime business clients, the older firms considered takeovers unsavory. The view that was "common then among many lawyers at major firms," according to Stephen Volk, then an associate and later the senior partner at Shearman & Sterling, "was that gentlemen didn't do takeovers."

In *New York Law Forum*, in 1969, Edmund Kelly wrote: "Many executives, even some of the more acquisition minded, have protested that they would never use the surprise take-over bid approach, for a variety of reasons." Louis Auchincloss told me recently, "The concealment, the creeping up on somebody, the tactics: The whole concept of the takeover is very smelly."

Experts from Wall Street and from the Ivy League like Samuel L. Hayes, then a professor at Columbia Business School, told Congress during hearings about the Williams Act that, by the mid-sixties, takeovers had proven a "respectable" means of merger and acquisition, and were "an accepted tool in the expansion efforts of many corporations." But Professor Hayes chose his language advisedly. In the *Financial Analysts Journal*, he and a co-author framed their support for hostile tender offers as an answer to a question then at large about sudden raids, "Are Cash Take-over Bids Unethical?"

And there were practical concerns. Established firms represented corporations and financiers whose prestige was reduced to sundries—blue chips, white shoes—and that were involved in other enterprises. According to Stephen Volk, "Some of the major firms didn't go after the takeover work because they felt they were doing important corporate work already, they were busy, and they didn't have excess resources." To them, Skadden's commitment to takeover work was a dubious flyer: The firm tacked off on its own while the Wall Street establishment held their unassailable position at the front of the pack.

For some firms, covering Skadden by competing with it for takeover business meant risking the loss of far more important business—like an investment-banking client, by guiding a corporation in the takeover of another that was represented by the bank. (Flom: "If you were in the business of working with an investment-banking firm and you were gonna go after one of their core clients, they would be pissed.") Some firms thought that, if they helped a company do a takeover, other clients might bolt out of fear that the firm would help the raider go after them. Some lawyers were convinced that the business was not profitable: A takeover fight kept lawyers busy while it was going on, but a slack period often followed when a firm might not be able to fill the lawyers' time. The field was wide open, in part, Flom said, because there was "no repeat business."

Skadden had none of these problems. According to Jim Freund, the firm "moved into that void." It considered takeovers an exciting area of the law, and had few longtime relationships with corporations and none with investment banks that it might jeopardize by taking part in a deal. Its specialty in the defense of corporations had the opposite effect: It made Skadden popular among executives. They passed along the firm's name to others who found themselves in a takeover fight. The business was profitable for the firm because it "had the deal flow." It didn't have to worry about the downside of devoting lawyers to a takeover. When one was completed, another came along for them to do. Flom aimed "to keep their plates full." He did.

By Flom's estimate, half of Skadden's work in the early seventies was for other law firms. Sometimes the firm's role depended on a narrow expertise. An investment company owned 13 percent of a mining firm, which owned about 1 percent of the investment company. The mining firm wanted to know if it was all right, under a federal law that was intended to deter some kinds of cross-ownership, for the firm to double its stake in the investment company. The mining firm consulted an established firm, which bumped the case to Skadden.

Sometimes the firm's expertise was hard to pin down. When Flom showed up without advance warning at the board meeting of an investment company, to represent a director in a ticklish negotiation, the client (Peter Sharp, who owned the Carlyle Hotel on Manhattan's Upper East Side, among other properties) pegged him in an introduction: "This is Joe Flom, special counsel for special purposes."

Often the firm's role as a specialist depended on its enthusiasm for fights that others lacked. In Flom's view, other lawyers were bewildered or frightened by takeovers: "These guys said, 'Someone's shooting at my client. What am I gonna do?'" There was no apparent cost to bringing in Skadden, because the firms that sought Skadden's counsel regularly got credit for it. Skadden was like an original equipment manufacturer that supplied reliable products to established companies that sold them under their own brand names.

The Skadden archives hold many legal papers drafted by its lawyers but signed by another firm. (One 1968 filing, on behalf of the defendant in a case called *Electronic Specialty Company* v. *International Controls Corporation*, lists a well-known New York firm as counsel and a well-known Washington, D.C., firm as of counsel, or secondary adviser. Skadden—the ghostwriter—appears nowhere.)

Sometimes the firm's opportunities came not simply because of its enthusiasm but because it was willing to do what others wouldn't. In 1967, Norman Donald was an associate at Davis Polk. A corporation that was a firm client, for which Donald regularly worked, wanted to make a hostile tender offer for another company. According to Donald, the presiding partner of Davis Polk, F. A. O. Schwarz, Jr., said, "Absolutely not." The firm would not guide a contested offer. Skadden would. "I'm a maverick," Joe Flom explained. "I didn't have the baggage." Soon after the matter went to the upstart firm, Donald moved there, too. In 1968, he became a partner.

As Skadden grew from twenty lawyers in 1968 to twenty-nine in 1970, it dispersed from the thirty-first to the twenty-fifth to the twenty-first floor of the Fred F. French Building. Increasingly, it felt both constricted and spread out. At the end of 1970, Skadden changed its address and its image. From Fifth Avenue and the settled neighborhood of Grand Central Station, it moved to a new forty-seven-story building at 919 Third Avenue, between Fifty-fifth and Fifty-sixth streets. It was the northernmost office tower on the East Side and, for a Wall Street firm, an outpost.

The skyscraper was constructed of black steel and glass. The decor was classically modern: off-white walls; furniture, carpets, and trim in earth tones; recessed lighting; no marble or draperies; and plenty of polished blond wood. Outside the elevator doors on the thirty-fourth and thirty-fifth floors, where Skadden rented space, the firm was identified by a logo of rounded white letters on off-white walls—when the comparison was exalting, Skadden lawyers said it was like IBM's. To the northwest a few blocks away, Central Park appeared as a swatch of green, immediately to the east the Queensboro Bridge spanned the East River, and to the south in the middle distance rose the Chrysler Building, the Empire State Building, and other icons of Manhattan.

The sleekness and controlled aura of the new offices belied the reality of Skadden. After Bob Ensher's death, the associates at the firm had paid a backhanded tribute to him by originating the Beast of Burden

(BOB) Award. For a few years, the award went irregularly to an associate who, in the reckoning of his peers, had endured the most punishment during the previous month. It was named after Ensher on the theory that the stress that killed him might get the winner, too. Sometimes it was awarded solely on the basis of who had billed the most hours. One month, the top-billing associate lost out to another, Peter Atkins. He had put in killer hours and his young daughter had asked him on the phone, "Are you *ever* coming home again?" (She grew up and became a lawyer.)

The award reflected an attitude of can-do macho and an aggressive nonchalance. Associates who liked to work out didn't join health clubs. They kept barbells and weights in a corner of their office and lifted when they got the chance. Once when Jim Freund (by then a partner) went to see Fin Fogg (still an associate), who was on the phone, Fogg mouthed, "I'll come see you soon." The partner kept talking, so the associate threw an ashtray at him.

By firm lore, Freund helped another associate win the Beast of Burden Award by calling him "a fucking idiot" in front of others. Twenty years later, both Freund and the onetime associate said they didn't remember the incident, but Freund explained that he had always tried to offer lawyers who worked for him appropriate measures of praise and blame. A former partner of Freund's, speculating why Freund might have been tagged in the story, said, "When he was younger, he used to really shit on lawyers. He's mellowed now." In 1991, the mellowed Freund wrote and starred in an educational video for lawyers called "Ten Tough Times: Advice to Associates on Handling Some Hairy Situations."

Associates bonded in other ways besides giving each other awards: On Friday afternoons, a group of associates regularly went to the Long River, a Chinese restaurant near the firm, chosen because it served free hors d'oeuvres. Yet within a year or so of the firm's move, Skadden became explosively busy. Camaraderie among young lawyers sometimes wasn't enough to overcome their discontent.

Thomas Schwarz, a Skadden partner who arrived as an associate in 1969, told a reporter about the early days on Third Avenue: "For a time, we were like a town where gold was discovered. I mean, everybody's building houses, and the sewer system doesn't work."

William Frank is also a Skadden partner. In 1970, he was on vacation in Peru, riding a horse in the Andes Mountains. A farmer galloped up and said, "Señor Frank? Señor Frank? Call your office!" Associates felt overworked and underappreciated. For a number of months in 1971, young lawyers quit faster than Skadden could replace them. The partners held a morale dinner, at which they made speeches about how much they valued the associates. In exchange for aid in building an institution, they pledged to bring in more lawyers. The firm hired a legal recruiter to reverse the decline.

The headhunter found Morris Kramer. He was a 1966 graduate of Harvard Law School and a sixth-year associate at the firm of Cahill Gordon, who had been told that he wasn't likely to make partner. Kramer wanted a fresh start. He had sent his résumé directly to Skadden and been turned down, but the firm hired him on the recruiter's recommendation.

To Kramer, most of the firm's clients appeared to be individuals and medium-sized companies, and included few first-rank corporations or financial institutions. Skadden now fit the profile of a small, up-and-coming midtown firm, and kept track of how fast it was rising. It circulated a memo showing that in 1973 it had only half as many partners as the firm ranked last in size among New York City's twenty-four largest firms, but that from 1963 to 1973 the total number of Skadden lawyers had increased 357 percent (from fourteen to sixty-four)—four times as fast as the fastest-growing of the largest firms.

In May of 1974, Skadden began publishing an in-house newsletter which suggested the straight-ahead feel of the firm. Vol. 1, No. 1 announced an annual spring party given by Les Arps and his wife at their country house in Connecticut, the installation of a TWX machine (a forebear of the fax), an expansion of the firm library, and the publication of an article by John Feerick about the impeachment of an English Prime Minister.

Feerick's hobby was studying how the Constitution deals with the transfer of presidential power—as an adviser to the Judiciary Committees in both houses of Congress, he helped write the Twenty-fifth Amendment, providing for succession by the Vice President if the President can't perform his job, and this was the era of Watergate, when Richard Nixon's misdeeds made the question of succession paramount. It was a point of pride for Tom Schwarz that, as a student editor of the *Fordham Law Review*, he had rejected an article by Feerick, who was Skadden's hiring partner.

The main firm victory reported by the newsletter was humble, a decision in New York State's Surrogate Court about the technicalities of a will. *The Word*, as it was called, reprinted without comment an item from *Variety* about a lawsuit between the movie studio 20th Century-Fox, which Skadden represented, and David Merrick, the producer. The entertainment weekly reported that Skadden's name partner "Arthur Flom" was "directly involved."

In a comprehensive internal listing of contested takeovers done in the United States, Skadden began with a bid by the Curtiss-Wright Company for Airco, in November of 1973, when it represented Curtiss-Wright. But the world changed for Flom and for Skadden in July of 1974, when he was asked to advise Morgan Stanley & Company in the takeover by INCO of ESB. In twenty-fifth place chronologically on the master list, the deal marked a watershed.

INCO was the world's leading nickel producer, and ranked 122nd among the three hundred largest industrial companies outside the United States. ESB was the world's leading independent battery maker. As a company in the energy field, with a good reputation and strong potential for growth in earnings, it met INCO's requirements for an acquisition whose performance might help it ride out downturns in the nickel industry.

INCO offered to pay $153 million cash for outstanding shares, ESB's stockholders received another offer from the United Aircraft Corporation (renamed United Technologies), and, drawing on a deep reserve of cash ("We had the ass to swing it," Charles Baird, the chief executive of INCO, told a reporter), INCO took over the company for $224 million.

INCO approached ESB's president, announcing the attack the day before he was scheduled to leave for a safari in Kenya. The takeover was completed in a few weeks—"a slam-bam-thank-you-ma'am kind of deal," Morris Kramer called it. Flom issued the orders at Skadden; Alfred Law, a former *Wall Street Journal* reporter and a graduate of New York University's night law program, interpreted them; and Kramer and another associate drafted the legal papers. The legal rules governing the deal could have been written on a single sheet of paper. The fee for filing INCO's offer with the Securities and Exchange Commission was one hundred dollars.

Not long after, deals seemed to pour into Skadden. According to one longtime mergers-and-acquisitions, or M&A, lawyer at another firm, Flom had been anointed by Morgan Stanley and Lazard Frères & Company, the most conspicuous investment banks in the M&A field during the rest of the seventies. (Flom: "Let's just say that, in short order, we became known as the firm of choice.") They told their blue-chip clients that it was acceptable to go after other companies through a takeover. Rather than recommending Skadden as special counsel to another firm, they steered them directly to Flom as counsel. Skadden had achieved brand recognition.

By September, Skadden associates competed to set new records for days worked without sleep and for other badges of commitment, like having their vacations interrupted, according to *The Word*. So did partners. Fin Fogg was in Kenya, ballooning over the Masai Mara Reserve, when he got word to check in. The reserve had no telephones, so he communicated with New York via shortwave radio through Nairobi, one hundred miles away.

In the mid-seventies at Skadden, lawyers like to recount, there was sometimes little distinction between night and day. One evening, an associate told his wife that he'd be home late and she shouldn't wait up for him. She awoke several times during the night, missing him, and finally called the office at 4 a.m., to see if he was still there. A receptionist explained that he was in a meeting and would have to return the call. Another lawyer, who reported for work not long after, said, "My first day of work at Skadden, I told my wife I might be a little late. During the next three years, I had dinner with her on a weekday three times." To help Skadden lawyers answer the question "Does the job require much travel?" the newsletter asked "a typical associate" to compile a list of places visited on firm business. After three years, the list included thirty-one cities spread across the country.

On weekends, half the firm was usually in. Those who didn't plan to work might be summoned. The newsletter reported that Peter Mullen, by then the firm's managing partner, "turned in a winning performance singing and dancing in the chorus of 'Mame' at the Lake Waramaug Country Club in Connecticut" and "was the only member of the cast with an understudy standing by—just in case he got a call from the office."

Skadden lawyers said they embraced takeover work because of the intricacies of the deals, but the niceties of transactions were enhanced by their size, which seemed to be measured a new way each deal: "Great Western United Corporation, a Denver-based conglomerate, issued a 280-page proxy statement asking security holders to approve a recapitalization plan involving the sale of its major asset (the largest U.S. refiner of sugar from sugar beets), and a possible spin-off of its Shakey's pizza parlor subsidiary."

Size was burnished by the aura of corporate power and stealth, as when Skadden represented the investment bank that was advising the Standard Oil Company (Indiana) in an uncompleted bid for the Occidental Petroleum Corporation. The firm gave the deal the code name Thor, the Greek god of thunder, because Occidental's chairman was Armand Hammer.

Firm life was not entirely consumed by deals: One associate found time to give free counsel to the Lab Theatre Company and Rosebud Coffeehouse in Manhattan; another produced a study for the American Bar Association called "Public Financing of Elections: A Constitutional Division of the Wealth"; and Jim Freund published a textbook, *Anatomy of a Merger.* Joe Flom surfaced for a taste of celebrity, in December of 1974, when the Lawyers Division of State of Israel Bonds honored him at a dinner chaired by Manhattan's district attorney, Robert M. Morgenthau.

But deals were paramount: Sapphire (a tender offer by a German company); Meteor (an offer by one maker of electrical equipment for another); and Stallion (the takeover by Colt Industries, a conglomerate whose best-known division made guns, of a manufacturer of packing and sealing products called Garlock). During the Stallion fight, Garlock used the phrase "Saturday Night Special" in a newspaper advertisement to describe Colt's unwelcome tender offer. The phrase stuck as an epithet for hostile takeovers.

Not long after, *New York* magazine published a profile by Steven Brill of Joe Flom and Martin Lipton, from the Manhattan firm of Wachtell, Lipton, Rosen & Katz, who had represented Garlock. They had faced each other in proxy fights, without drawing wide attention. Their first contest—the maiden proxy fight for both Lipton and Flom—was the United Industrial fight in 1959.

Lipton was seven years younger, and viewed Flom as a master whose reputation in the takeover business he hoped to match. In 1976, the two linked efforts in a two-volume primer about deals, *Takeovers and Take-outs: Tender Offers and Going Private,* which bore their names along with a third lawyer's. According to Jeff Madrick, a business reporter, Lipton's business plan was to oppose Flom whenever he could. The challenge served Flom's interests: He could recommend Lipton as an adversary or, if Flom couldn't take a case, as an alternative. Instead of eroding Flom's standing, Lipton enhanced it.

In keeping with the Garlock deal's motif, Brill paired the two as the guns to hire if a company planned to bid for another or needed a defender.

Other lawyers had competence and experience to match, and were bitter that Brill hadn't given them as much notice, but the two were set apart. At a Skadden Christmas party, held at the Roseland dance hall and featuring "Wanted" posters of the partners, some firm lawyers put on a skit that reveled in the rivalry between Flom and Lipton. Nineteen seventy-five ended for Skadden with a "drafting" party on New Year's Eve, on behalf of T. Boone Pickens and his Mesa Petroleum Company, which was poised to launch a hostile takeover of the Aztec Oil and Gas Company.

Business

6

Opportunism

Robert Pirie, a onetime Skadden partner who left the firm to head the American branch of the Rothschild investment bank, said that, as early as the 1950s, Joe Flom described a vision of a Skadden that would surpass the leaders of Wall Street, built on a foundation of counseling in contests for control of corporations.

Charles Haar, a professor at Harvard Law School who is a longtime friend of Flom's, recalled that, during the summer of the INCO takeover of ESB, in 1974, Flom predicted the coming of large national law firms, a decade before they emerged as a feature of the legal profession, and of large international firms, a decade and a half before they emerged. Flom declared that his firm would be among them—although Skadden wasn't yet counted among the leading firms in New York City.

When he left Skadden in 1978 to become a federal judge in Manhattan, Robert Sweet wrote a letter to his partners that paid tribute to Flom's vision: "I salute you all, especially Joe, and leave to you the task of frantically putting the blocks in place to accomplish his grand design."

Claire Flom agreed only about the spirit of Joe's augury: "I remember the first time it came up. We were on the road from the home of a charming gentleman who had invited us for the weekend in Maryland. We were on the road from his house to Friendship Airport—this is 1957, probably. He said, 'Do you want to marry *me*?' I said yes, I had given it some thought. Immediately, he said, 'Maybe we oughta move to the suburbs. It would be good for Nancy.' My daughter.

"Then I said to him, immediately, 'If we want to have children, that's a lousy idea, because then they'll never see their father.' And I distinctly remember that I asked him, 'Why do you work so endlessly, seamlessly? You're always working.' He said, 'Well, I gotta build up the firm to where we have twenty lawyers.' I said, 'That's ridiculous, because when you have twenty, then you'll say the same thing about forty' "—which wouldn't have placed Skadden among New York's twenty largest firms. She paused, and said, "I don't think he responded."

Barry Garfinkel is a senior partner who met Flom on a double date in 1955. (This was before Flom had met Claire, and he was out with a Yale Law School classmate of Garfinkel's, the granddaughter of Louis Brandeis, the legendary Justice of the Supreme Court.) Garfinkel asked to be released from a commitment he had made to Davis Polk, so he could join the young firm. He concurred with Claire: "I remember in the sixties, on a Saturday, sitting with Joe at the Trattoria, in the Pan Am Building, on Forty-fifth Street. The firm then had twenty or twenty-two lawyers, and Joe said, 'If we do more work in the proxy area, we may have to have as many as thirty lawyers. How do you feel about that?' There was no big vision. That is bullshit. We were entrepreneurial. We had no grand scheme. We improvised."

Flom: "It would be wrong to say that anybody predicted, 'This is all where it's going to go.' Nobody is that smart on any subject, to see that far ahead. There are too many variables. You have to do enough home-work so that you can take advantage of opportunities when they occur, and then try to create opportunities. Do you ever play pinball machines? If you don't push, you lose. If you push too hard, they tilt."

In the Skadden lexicon, aggressiveness exercised to capitalize on opportunity was called opportunism. It was an affirmative response to luck. Unlike in the dictionary, where the word is defined negatively as taking advantage of circumstances without regard to principles or consequences, at Skadden it was considered a laudable trait that was more important than vision.

Flom: "Look, you can't ignore serendipity. If I hadn't come to this firm, I wouldn't have had the opportunity to get into the proxy thing in the first place. Bill Timbers wouldn't have been there to give me my first proxy case, and who knows what would have happened. I have a very strong feeling that, sure, you have to be able to take advantage of opportunities, but you have to be where the opportunities are—and a lot of that is either luck or serendipity or whatever you want to call it." And: "Did we sit down and plot our opportunity in mergers and acquisitions? No. We got in by accident, and then took advantage of the opportunities presented."

In the 1970s, Skadden was positioned as well as any American law firm to take advantage of a dramatic evolution in the world of business, which created fifteen years of steadily escalating mergers and acquisitions, largely unaffected by the state of the general economy. Alfred Chandler, an emeritus professor at Harvard Business School and the leading historian of American business, judged that these changes created a new era for capitalism.

One factor spurring change was the desire of corporate executives to maintain the growth of their companies in the face of increasing competition within the United States and from abroad. In the 1960s, for the first time in American history, companies expanded into markets where they had no experience or obvious advantages. The flattening out of corporate returns led many managers to support the theory that they could obtain higher returns by investing in new markets than if they expanded in the markets they knew best. Between 1965 and 1969, the number of mergers and acquisitions in the United States tripled, to over six thousand. Most of them represented efforts by small and medium-sized companies to diversify.

Another element was the change in the composition of investors in corporations, and the desire of new investors to maximize the returns on the stock that they owned. Before the Second World War, the majority of the ownership shares in American industry were held for long-term growth. Wealthy individuals, insurance companies, and trust departments of banks were the primary investors. After the war, an increasing percentage of shares were held by mutual funds and pension funds that were managed for short-term gains.

"For the first time," Alfred Chandler wrote, "individuals, groups, or companies could obtain control of well-established companies in industries with which the buyers had no previous connection, simply by purchasing the companies' shares on the stock exchange."

Many corporations encountered basic problems in managing their newly acquired portfolios of businesses that were unrelated to their main enterprise, which led later to a run of sell-offs, known as divestitures. The ratio of these deals to mergers and acquisitions rose from less than one in eleven in 1965, to one in two between 1974 and 1977.

By 1981, the economists F. M. Scherer and David Ravenscraft estimated, at least one-third of all the businesses that had been acquired as part of the diversification movement in the 1960s and 1970s had been sold off. A divestiture by one corporation was often the acquisition by another. The heavy concentration of deals created an opportunity for an entirely new business. Chandler described it as "the buying and selling of corporations."

The new business flourished in the fourth, and longest, wave of mergers and acquisitions by American corporations since the turn of the twentieth century. It followed the era of consolidation leading to famous industrial monopolies, like U.S. Steel and Standard Oil, from 1897 to 1904; the era of mergers creating corporate oligopolies, in which small groups of companies controlled different markets, from 1925 to 1930; and the go-go years of conglomerate mergers, from 1967 to 1969, that led up to it.

Contrary to a popular assumption, the takeover era of 1975 to 1990 (some say it began in 1980) did not set a record for the number of corporate deals. That occurred at the height, and end, of the conglomerate era, in 1969. Even in its busiest year, which was 1986, the takeover era had little more than half as many deals as the go-go years. What distinguished the major transactions of the takeover era was their size, scope, and method of financing.

Before the eighties, a transaction of $100 million or more was uncommon. A billion-dollar deal occurred only once. In the takeover era, hundred-million-dollar deals occurred hundreds of times a year. By the late eighties, transactions worth one billion dollars or more were commonplace. They took place dozens of times annually. From 1975 to the peak of the takeover era, in 1988, the amount exchanged annually in mergers and acquisitions increased more than twenty times, to almost one quarter of a trillion dollars. All of the one hundred largest deals in history were done then, almost three-quarters of them in the five years between 1985 and 1989.

The size of the deals is explained, in part, by the stock market. In 1974, the Dow Jones Industrial Average fell to 577.6, its lowest level in a decade. In the view of investment bankers and corporate executives, the level made cheap deals readily available on Wall Street. The Dow wandered upward in the next few years, slipped back to the 700 range in 1978, and, in 1979, stayed below 900. In 1982, however, it began the climb that helped define the 1980s, reaching a high of 2,791.41 in 1987, before crashing 600 points in October of that year—to a level that was still almost three times as high as it had been a decade earlier. The rise in the stock market served as a shorthand for the increase in the value of corporations involved in deals. As it went up, so did the value of mergers and acquisitions.

The size of the deals in dollars is also explained by their scope in business terms. In the 1980s, the curtailment of antitrust enforcement and the deregulation of American finance enabled the takeover wave to rise with almost no impediment. Beginning in the mid-eighties, large firms and relatively small ones that sought to take over large ones were able to make big acquisitions for the most part as a result of a potent coincidence—the increase to $100,000 of the amount of savings deposits insured by the federal government and the availability of new means of financing, the best-known being below-market-grade, high-yield instruments, or junk bonds.

Financial institutions, especially savings and loan associations, became a plentiful source of money for junk bonds. Accounts were opened or increased to take advantage of the increase in the size of deposits insured by the federal government, and the bonds became a source of high interest rates for the banks. Michael Milken, of the investment bank of Drexel Burnham Lambert, linked the banks and the bonds as no one else had.

Of course, banks would have had no bonds to purchase if there were no companies issuing them, but recognizing and creating the market for junk bonds was part of Milken's complex legacy as a financier—along with his 1990 admission of wrongdoing and his plea of guilt to six felony violations of securities and tax laws; his payment of a $600 million fine; and the substantial, if murky, evidence that, out of greed and an intent to succeed on a monumental scale, he masterminded broad corruption of the junk-bond market.

Beyond the dimensions of size and scope, the domain of mergers and acquisitions was expanded by geography. In 1975, foreign firms made only two purchases of American companies for $100 million or more. At its peak, in 1988, although they represented only about one-fifth of the value of all deals done in the United States, there were scores of purchases that size. A dozen were worth a billion dollars or more. The total cost of the foreign purchases was $55.5 billion. The foreign purchasers were concentrated by country of origin. Throughout the period generally, three-fourths of the transactions were done by companies based in Japan, the United Kingdom, France, the Netherlands, and Canada.

Purchases by American firms of controlling or minority interests in foreign companies also rose notably. In 1975, there were no purchases by American companies of foreign firms worth $100 million or more. From then to 1989, the annual value of American acquisitions abroad increased by fifty times, to over $22 billion. The sum still represented only one-tenth of the total value of deals announced that year throughout the world. Most of the purchases were based in the United Kingdom, followed by Canada, and France, and then, after a large drop in dollars, Australia, Sweden, the Netherlands, Japan, Hungary, and New Zealand.

The size, scope, and increasingly global reach of mergers and acquisitions made many industries throughout the world an arena for them. As different industries became unsettled, their rapid ascent in the value ranking of industries (measured by dollars paid for companies) reflected the tumult. During the first half of the eighties, deals involving oil companies topped the lists: experts said it was cheaper to find petroleum reserves on Wall Street than to find them in the ground, because crude-oil prices were down and exploration was so expensive. Railroad holding companies and financial services companies sometimes joined oil companies at the head of the industry ranks, as did other kinds of firms.

Between 1985 and 1989 in the United States, the highest ranking passed from control by oil and gas to banking and finance to retail to conglomerates, and, finally, to drugs, medical supplies, and medical equipment. Throughout that period, the entertainment, broadcasting, food-processing, paper, chemicals, paints and coatings, transportation, fabricated metal products, communications, and insurance industries joined the others as sectors in which the value of deals also remained high. Brand names replaced oil as Wall Street's hottest commodity, and companies that sold to consumers (with products like foods, drugs, tires, records, magazines, and cosmetics) decided that it was cheaper to buy whole companies with well-known brands than to develop new products and brand names from scratch.

Abroad, industries at the top of the list that attracted American companies as buyers included oil and gas, retail, autos and trucks, paper, and food processing. Many other sectors were involved. In the late eighties especially, the weakness of the dollar in comparison to other currencies made American firms attractive to foreign ones. After the 1987 stock-market crash, foreign companies took little time to restart the action; contrary to most predictions, American deals quickly boomed once more, along with the foreign.

This activity among corporations is sometimes described as an ener-getic reordering of different markets, as firms sought to seize, regain, or protect some competitive advantage. It can also be seen as a giant casino-like game, in which banks, law firms, and others exchanged massive amounts of paper on behalf of corporate chieftains often moved more by ego than good economic sense, and equally often instigated by investment bankers with a vested interest in seeing that deals got done. The bankers raised the odds by proposing companies for deals ("putting them in play") against the wishes of executives.

In the mid- to late eighties, divestitures became simply the last phase of an acquisition in a category known as bust-ups. Some who bought companies sold off parts of the newly acquired firms to realize profits based on the difference between their value before and after the breakup. Others had to sell parts to help pay off debt taken on to accomplish the deals. Sometimes buyers, who called themselves entrepreneurs and func-tioned as brokers, were in both categories at once. They used junk bonds and bridge loans from banks to finance billion-dollar purchases, and sold off parts of busted-up companies for a middleman's profit.

The investment banks were not prepared for the growth in mergers, acquisitions, and divestitures that carried them to great prosperity and led to a restructuring of the financial world as comprehensive as the restructuring it helped shape in other lines of business. From the late nineteenth century, when investment bankers prospered by financing the construction, reorganization, and consolidation of the American rail-roads, they mainly raised large sums of money to pay for the activities of corporations, governments, and other institutions, through under-writings—guaranteeing clients a certain amount of capital and then reselling the placement to investors for a profit. In the sixties, a few investment banks created new departments to handle mergers and ac-quisitions, but mostly as a favor to clients. Joe Flom: "You did M&A services as a freebie."

The M&A department of Morgan Stanley & Company was started in 1972. Beginning with the INCO deal in 1974 and for the next several years, according to Robert Greenhill, for many years the firm's best-known dealmaker and later its president, Flom was as much the teacher of the bankers he worked with as their colleague. He played the same role in the development of the M&A department of First Boston and elsewhere in the deal world. Flom was in a strong position to do business with bankers because of Skadden's readiness for changes in the world of law that were as momentous as what was going on in business.

In Skadden's first two decades, the established law firms with which it hoped to compete often succeeded as a result of continuing relationships with longtime clients. In many instances, it was possible to identify which firm handled the legal business of a big corporation by learning the affiliation of the most notable lawyer on its board of directors. Skadden couldn't compete on those terms ("Small firms just didn't crash the party," Jim Freund said), because they started without a similar set of clients. Instead, they developed a specialty in proxy and takeover work, and the capacity (through the overwork of their lawyers) to handle intensive jobs.

By the mid-seventies, many corporations decided to save money by expanding their legal staffs and doing on their own much of the work that they had previously farmed out to law firms. Instead of relying on one firm for specialized counsel, corporations shopped for lawyers who seemed best suited to a project and firms increasingly competed for one-time jobs. In the aggregate, this was known as transactional work. It called for the kind of specialization and service that Skadden had developed as a method of survival.

Flom: "People say, 'What was your concept of the firm?' At one point, I decided that, the way the practice of law was changing, it was too expensive for law firms to do the routine legal work that we occasionally were doing. Indeed, when we didn't have a lot of business, I had a client—a Canadian company—that was paying us about a hundred thousand dollars a year, which was a lot of money for us, for doing minutes of corporate board meetings. I called him and said, 'You know, you guys are making a mistake. You ought to have a U.S. general counsel, because you can save money. You can't justify paying us to do that.' They were shook up, so they whistled me up to Canada, and I went through it again, and we actually gave them one of our associates, who went up there. Our bills went down to twenty thousand dollars a year."

The coincidence of the surge in corporate takeovers, in which Skadden had specialized before any other law firm, and of the unbundling of relationships between major corporations and large law firms, which Flom claimed to promote before most observers of the legal profession recognized the trend and to which Skadden had already scrambled to create an alternative in any case, was serendipity of the highest order.

To Skadden and to some observers of the firm, however, this coincidence illustrated the full impact of the firm's opportunism. Having developed particular expertise about takeovers and having employed it with notable success, according to Jim Freund, the firm "had a lot to do with" the breakup of exclusive ties between companies and law firms: Skadden's success as a specialist fed the demand for its counsel from companies; and law firms that once hired Skadden on behalf of longtime clients jumped in to compete as specialists themselves, accelerating the erosion of long-standing relationships. In 1976, *New York* magazine quoted "one top lawyer" as saying, "Joe's done the most magnificent thing anyone's ever done in the law business. He's broken the link between the old investment-banking firms and blue-chip companies and their Wall Street lawyers."

7

The Market

Jim Freund: "The thing I'll never understand is why, when the takeover wave happened in earnest, the major securities law firms didn't get involved. I could understand that they might not want to represent a raider, because there was something almost antisocial about that in the early days. But why they wouldn't want to represent their good client in extremis, when the client needed good lawyering and, let's face it, the fees were unbelievable, because it was such intensive work and nobody worried too much about dimes and nickels when the company was at stake, I'll never understand. One has to feel that, if they had wanted to, they would have blown us away."

The answer may be that Skadden's status as an upstart, its partners' need to prove themselves, and the dynamic nature of its specialty led the firm to operate by rules that many other firms did not. Some large law firms were like American industrial companies and other enterprises that failed to respond to new conditions in the mid-seventies. As the industrial companies stayed with outmoded manufacturing techniques, plant and equipment, management styles, and uses of labor, the law firms continued to practice as they had for a generation. They were as ill-prepared for, or generally opposed to, redeploying lawyers to new areas of opportunity, like takeovers, as industrial companies were to retooling. Their success kept them from preparing for the future.

The senior partner of an established New York firm said, "I did my first hostile takeover in 1964. But it wasn't my specialty. I did other corporate work, too. When I started to move my firm into M&A work, everyone was happy to do it, but people had their own work and they weren't going to give up resources to me. My battle was getting up and running and developing a practice. I started specializing in the late seventies. Skadden had a five-year head start, easily, and by then had a whole firm specializing in takeovers."

John Coffee, a professor of law at Columbia Law School who once practiced corporate law, said, "When I was at Cravath, Swaine & Moore, in the mid-seventies, Skadden had twenty-five partners. People at Cravath said that takeovers were a one-time blip, that they would be destroyed by defense tactics or by state anti-takeover laws. They said that Skadden was riding a short-term wave, and that it would be caught in a terrible crunch when it crashed and disappeared. One effect was that Skadden became more sensitive to the forces of the market than any other law firm. Their game plan was to be conscious of where the market was and to diversify so that, if the market actually did collapse, they wouldn't be caught."

Out of necessity, Skadden was attentive to several markets. The first was the one for clients, which included other law firms, financial institutions, and corporations. Peter Mullen: "We were not reluctant to say, 'Hey, we'll go after that client.'" If another lawyer brought the firm business, Skadden didn't horn in on his territory. That was enlightened self-interest. "But in the normal situation," Mullen said, "where the lawyer told the client not to come to us and the client came anyway, we have had no hesitancy about trying to make the client our own."

Skadden also competed in the market for services, with its specialty in proxy contests and takeovers and with other areas of expertise, and in the market for lawyers—at law schools, at other law firms, and elsewhere. Its attitude equipped the firm to deal with and, in some ways, to contribute to a transformation of the American legal profession, which went far beyond the shift in relations between large law firms and their clients. The era of change began as Skadden was taking off.

The 1960s touched the profession as deeply as they did other institutions of American society. Until then, the legal kingdom had considered itself autonomous, shaping the law yet largely immune from its disciplinary force. The rules of lawyering, or legal ethics, were briefly stated in a series of pronouncements called canons. Geoffrey Hazard, a professor at Yale Law School, wrote that the canons "gave voice to an ethical tradition" and assumed that "right-thinking lawyers knew the proper thing to do and that most lawyers were right-thinking."

When leaders of the bar sought to tighten the discipline of the profession, however, they turned to the courts to shore up their authority and, in the process, gave up some autonomy. Or, since courts had originally delegated the power of self-discipline to lawyers as court officers, leaders of the bar returned some of the power to the courts. In the meantime, some lawyers went to court to challenge the bar's leadership and authority. In 1964, the Supreme Court eroded a long-followed rule against solicitation of new business by lawyers in certain cases. With this ruling, the legal profession was opened to the forces of the market, in addition to those of the law.

In 1970, the profession adopted a new code of conduct which ended the era of the bar as a cohesive, self-governing fraternity, and acknowledged the arrival of one in which lawyers would be ruled like everyone else, by law. The new code was written by conservative lawyers. It included canons and commentaries as grand and hortatory as the old formulations that some liked to think still bound the profession together.

In retrospect, they seem to have been written by lawyers who didn't realize how profoundly their livelihood was changing. A set of disciplinary rules in the new code distinguished it from the old. In Geoffrey Hazard's words, they "legalized" the practice of law. They "functioned as a statute defining the legal contours of a vocation whose practitioners were connected primarily by having been licensed to practice law," instead of as a code of conduct for professionals committed to a calling.

Some lawyers challenged key elements of the rules in court, and the Supreme Court ordered further changes. In 1975, the Court struck down minimum-fee schedules, which bar associations had adopted to prevent lawyers from competing with one another on price and thus, theoretically, undermining the quality of work done by the profession, as "a classic illustration of price fixing." In 1977, in the best-known decision affecting the legal world, the Court ruled that the bar could not prohibit advertising by lawyers because doing so violated the guarantee of free speech in the First Amendment. In a footnote, the Court called the claim that the practice of law was noncommercial and, therefore, should be allowed to keep out some business practices, "sanctimonious humbug."

The bar had initially looked to the courts as partners that would reinforce the standards that the profession established for itself. It was willing to give up some control in exchange for a stiffening of its authority. Instead, the forces of the law and of the market gathered strength, and the bar lost control over key rules governing the practice of law. The rules affected the bar's self-image as well as its conduct. In the next decade, the loss of control was compounded by a rise in the number of lawsuits against lawyers and by an increase in sanctions imposed by judges on lawyers.

In the meantime, predictions of the bar's decline in membership proved spectacularly wrong. The demand for the services of lawyers increased dramatically (from $8.2 billion in 1960 to $47.5 billion in 1985, in 1985 dollars). So did the supply. The number of American lawyers leaped as it had only once before, a century or so earlier: between 1870 and 1890, it went from 41,000 to 90,000; between 1965 and 1990, from 296,000 to 800,000. The number of American lawyers increased more than four times as fast as the population of the United States; the ratio of lawyers' representation in the population jumped from one in 600 to one in 350.

The evolution in the nature, size, and geographic range of economic transactions among corporations and between corporations and other large social institutions, and the growth in the amount and complexity of law made by legislatures, administrative agencies, and courts, contributed heavily to the increase in demand for lawyers, especially at large law firms.

The growth in the size of typical corporate transactions meant that legal teams had to be bigger in order to handle the work, so that firms either had to grow as well or, if they wished to remain relatively small, had to concentrate on one segment of practice. The growth in the amount and complexity of law and in the nature of legal transactions meant that generalists had to become specialists, that specialists had to narrow their focus still further, and that firms had to retain more specialists to solve a widening range of problems.

An example was anti-takeover laws. When they were adopted by states in the seventies, they didn't have the effect that some observers predicted. Rather than preventing takeovers, they created obstacles that lawyers simply helped their clients get around. But the laws governed how takeovers could be conducted and made knowledge about them essential to any corporation involved in a takeover, creating a new legal specialty.

John Pound, who teaches at Harvard University's Kennedy School of Government, and a Skadden partner, Louis Goodman, were once asked to testify before a Massachusetts commission established to consider whether takeovers were good or bad for the state's economy, and if bad, how to regulate them. Pound: "Goodman was the consummate lawyer: patient, friendly, low-key, and very confident. He basically said, 'Enact anything you want. I'll find a way to get around what you do.'"

To Stephen Gillers, a professor at New York University Law School, "a profession that once had great control over its operation and direction, a profession whose members could fairly well predict and determine the course of their professional lives," had given up a large measure of authority to other institutions and to the sweeping dictates of the market. Out of discomfiting anxiety, in Gillers's opinion, many lawyers sought to "reaffirm professionalism and decry commercialization" as a way of complaining about, and in some cases denying, the significant changes at work.

Skadden did the opposite, treating the apparent polarities of professionalism and commercialism as one and the same. From 1975 to 1978, its motivation was similar to what it had been for a generation: The firm hustled to prove itself against established ones and recorded its progress.

"Some interesting observations," Barry Garfinkel wrote in a 1978 memo to his partners about a survey that ranked Skadden thirtieth in size among all American firms and showed that it had grown by 75 percent since 1975: "1. At present we rank 15th in size of the New York firms alone. 2. If the new '78 associates are added in, we are approximately 25th in size—nationwide. 3. Of the 50 firms surveyed, we have had the largest percentage increase in attorneys during the '75–'78 period (excepting the Kutak firm in Omaha which is a recent combination of firms)."

Now Skadden's sights were set higher. Their goal was to be the best commercial firm in the country, and to be recognized as such. To get there, the firm reached for every advantage it could find in the legal market. The primary one was its reputation as a counselor in takeovers.

Joe Flom was again responsible. The senior partner of a longtime firm explained that, while Flom's abilities as a lawyer were impressive, "he was light-years ahead of everyone else in terms of his marketing sense."

Flom was an operator. He regarded even mundane acts, like binding the legal papers from a deal in leather volumes, as opportunities for self-promotion. (Peggy Kerr: "Flom told me, 'We used to bind everything. We thought it was good advertising.'") Sometimes his enthusiasm carried him into hyperbole. (Flom: "Some of my partners and I edited a book which was the definitive piece on its subject for a while." Another Skadden partner: "Joe's turned out no writing." On the book in question, he was "more an auditor" than an editor: "What is writing? It's a form of reflection. He hasn't done that.") But in dealings with the press, Flom's zeal paid off. He displayed his comprehension of the new market forces and his ability to market himself and the firm.

In the mid-sixties, Alf Law reported for *The Wall Street Journal*. He had gone there, with a degree from Princeton University, after five years as a reporter for the Associated Press. His beat was retailing: jewelry, shoes, toys, etc. One assignment that landed on his desk was to cover a proxy contest that Flom was involved in for control of the Elgin Watch Company. Law was drawn to Flom because, in his opinion, Flom was one of the two lawyers he had met who knew how to deal with the press. (The other was Milton Gould, a well-known New York lawyer and an adept self-promoter.) Flom liked Law because he was "the only guy who got the story straight in proxy fights."

In Law's view, many lawyers were afraid of the press. They had good reason. The bar rule that prohibited lawyers from advertising their services ("It is unprofessional to solicit professional employment by circulars, advertisements, through touters or by personal communications or interviews not warranted by personal relations") had explicitly been interpreted to prohibit a firm from cooperating "in the publication by a magazine of a laudatory history of the firm." Not long before, a respected New York firm had been censured by the state bar for violating the rule when it let *Life* tell its story and illustrate the feature with photographs of its partners.

The rule also defined as "reprehensible" and offensive to the "traditions" of the legal profession "indirect advertisements," like "furnishing or inspiring newspaper comments." To many lawyers, that meant they couldn't be quoted by the papers. To the punctilious, it meant that they shouldn't speak with reporters about their work.

Most of the lawyers who did speak with Law were, in his words, "extremely inept." They tried "to bluster or they patronized." Flom was "a breath of fresh air." He understood that Law had deadlines to meet. ("He knew enough to say, 'Be at your phone tomorrow afternoon,' or 'Where can I reach you tomorrow?' ") If he couldn't answer a question, he said so straightforwardly. He was never indiscreet about what he said for attribution. ("He said, 'There are some things I can only tell you off the record.' ") He gave Law "input."

He also knew what questions he could ask a reporter. Law said, "Flom saw opportunities in dealing with the press." Flom and Law developed "a sort of friendship," and when Law finished law school at night (he hadn't told Flom he was attending), he asked Flom for a job. Flom satisfied himself that Law really wanted to work at Skadden, and hired him in 1967.

Law became the first of a series of lawyers known as Joe's boys (or guys—never a gal), who occupied an office near Flom and functioned as an executive assistant. He did everything from making hotel reservations, because Flom didn't trust a secretary to get them right, to attending a meeting of the board of directors at General Motors and explaining why Flom couldn't be there. He also interpreted Flom's Delphic comments (Flom: he "was supposed to be able to read my mind"), and, as a former reporter, he schmoozed the press.

Flom first learned about the utility of the press as a counselor in proxy contests during the 1960s. By the seventies, takeover fights were often waged in the newspapers. Some of Flom's most important colleagues outside the firm were public relations people, like Gershon Kekst, who heads his own successful firm and calls Flom *boychik*, and Richard Cheney, who became vice-chairman of Hill & Knowlton, one of the largest in the field, and who is credited with supplying to Garlock Industries the phrase "Saturday Night Special," as a description of a hostile takeover.

Flom grasped that the public spin given a point of contention in a takeover fight could heavily influence how the whole conflict came out. He had scant use for the self-effacing style that Wall Street lawyers had perfected since the turn of the century. Flom understood a basic lesson of American advancement: the payoff of publicity. The reward was especially high in legal maneuvers over deals. Typically, their outcomes were ambiguous, making perception the reality in the crowning of a victor.

In New York City for many years, the main printed source of information about lawyers and legal decisions was the *New York Law Journal*. The paper was published by the Finkelstein family, who were friends of Flom's. (Andrew Stein, the longtime president of the New York City Council, is in the family.) Flom became a member of its editorial board and, from 1978 to 1990, served as chairman of the editorial board of its sister publication, *The National Law Journal*.

From the papers' point of view, it was as if the head of the New York Stock Exchange had become the editorial chairman of *The Wall Street Journal*. (*The National Law Journal* no longer has an editorial board stocked with lawyers.) To Flom, there was no downside to filling those posts. They helped him master the chameleon's art of changing from a source into a subject and back again. Flom, on what he learned: "Today, if you don't talk to the press, for background and things like that, they'll kill you, because they'll put the other guy's story in."

Recently, Gershon Kekst observed, "We have all been, in one way or another, shaped by Joe." Richard Cheney said, "The press tries to tell the story. But they're limited by time constraints, space, and the understanding of their readers. We try to help out by giving reporters information. Without falsifying the facts, sometimes it's of the heads-we-win, tails-they-lose variety."

To Flom, the ability to spin opinion about a deal was just one of the unusual mix of skills required of a takeover lawyer. He was confident he had them all. "When I was at CCNY," he said, "I took an aptitude test. The results said I should be a lawyer first, an investment banker second, and, third, a used-car salesman. I got something that combines all three."

Steven Brill's 1976 *New York* profile of Flom and Lipton was the most fruitful payoff from an opportunity for Flom in dealing with the press. It heralded Flom's dominance among takeover lawyers (Brill, in that profile: "Flom today enjoys unprecedented pre-eminence in the field"). It established a new domain for his reputation to flourish in, the market of public opinion. For a deal-oriented lawyer, keen on selling his name to ensure a steady flow of work and build a firm, it was an essential forum to master. A year later, the Supreme Court ruled that the legal profession could no longer prohibit advertising by lawyers. The following year, Brill helped found *The American Lawyer*.

The monthly became the first in a chain of publications about lawyers that thrived because of advertising from lawyers, palpable interest among

lawyers expressed through the purchase by law firms of expensive sub-
scriptions, and cooperation from lawyers that ranged from wary through
calculated to eager. It presented itself as performing a public service, by
exposing the previously hidden workings of law firms and other legal
institutions—the business of the law.

In its world, the magazine became a shaper of a sharp-edged picture
of reality that established a new order of status. Eventually printed on
thick, glossy stock as an oversized tabloid, the monthly ran big photographs and large headlines that made their subjects appear larger than
life. Despite its limited circulation (at its highest, 21,000 copies), it heavily
influenced how other media presented the legal profession.

The American Lawyer went through various incarnations (muckraking,
celebrating, predicting the future), but for many years it remained constant in treating the legal world primarily as self-contained. Paying less
attention to forces outside the law that heavily shaped it than to its
internal dynamics, the monthly presented lawyers—heroes and vil-
lains—as many liked to think of themselves: central, powerful, masters
of their universe.

For many private practitioners, professional life could be reduced to
a series of benchmarks: law boards; quality of law school; law school
grades; job prospects; and career advancement. Instantly, *The American
Lawyer* zeroed in on a blunt, tantalizing measure of ultimate success:
how much money lawyers made. The symbol was a dollar sign, as in
"M$A." The magazine's first issue featured an article about the financial
achievements of Skadden, under the headline "Flom Firm Takes Over
as Top Money Maker in '78."

In the case of the Supreme Court ruling, luck followed opportunism
for Skadden twice over. Steve Brill: "The reason I wrote about them in
the first issue of *The American Lawyer* is that I had written about them
for *New York* magazine and I knew about them. I believe in going with
what you know, and it was a good story." To Brill, fate deserved a lot
of credit for his singling out Flom.

But Flom had provided a model for how lawyers at his firm should
speak with the press, a decade and a half before many others considered
it proper, let alone necessary, or had developed the knack. For his cover
story, Brill found Skadden lawyers "very frightened and quite uncoop-
erative," although "less anxious than most other firms, or more resigned
to the reality" of being written about. They preferred to think of themselves as canny.

In 1978, the firm newsletter instructed, "Lawyers are increasingly being sought by news reporters for their views on various issues, for help in understanding complex legal developments, and as sources for news. As a firm we welcome this increased interest and we will maintain our policy of being responsive within responsible bounds. However, it is important to review our policies in this area and point out some of the potential pitfalls." Personal comments of Skadden lawyers could embarrass the firm. Reporters might "stampede a source" into a hasty and ill-considered observation. Journalists were "never really 'off-duty.' " Some of their best material was collected "at cocktail parties, sport events, beaches and other informal gatherings."

The newsletter advised, "With our particularly interesting and visible practice, it is always a temptation to share our enthusiasm with others. The only way to maintain discretion here, as with chance comments in hallways, restaurants and elevators, is to develop the discretion discipline." But Skadden lawyers were firmly instructed to cooperate with the press. "Never say 'No comment,' or 'We really have nothing to say now.' Say 'Someone will call back,' and see to it that that happens." Skadden fielded inquiries, and the firm's name stood out in the market created by the burgeoning legal press.

A common view of Skadden's willingness to deal with the press is that the firm understood the new forces in the legal market and was eager to compete in it. In fact, Skadden sought to stand above the competition, by seizing advantage over other law firms. Alf Law told *The American Lawyer*, "A client came to [Flom] with one of the first takeovers. Joe and I sat with him, and when the meeting was over, the guy asked Joe if there would be a retainer. Joe was kind of taken aback; he hadn't thought of that. He kind of coughed and said, 'Yes.' The guy asked how much? Joe coughed again, and said, 'Thirty-five hundred dollars.' The guy was about to leave when he turned and asked Joe if the thirty-five hundred dollars would be good only for this takeover matter, and Joe hesitated again and said, 'Yes, just for this matter.' "

In the late sixties, Skadden began taking retainers from corporate clients in exchange for being on call to represent them in the event of a possible takeover. The roster grew with Flom's reputation. Retainers appealed to clients because they promised that Flom would be available to give counsel. Or, in a practice known as "sterilizing Joe," according to John Shad, who worked with Flom when he was head of Merrill Lynch & Company and later as chairman of the SEC, they promised that he would not end up on the other side. If a company got involved in a takeover, it could apply the retainer to the firm's charges for its services. If the company didn't use up the retainer, it would have to sign up again the next year.

By the mid-seventies, retainers provided an important source of income for Skadden. By 1978, according to the legal press, the number of corporations retaining the firm climbed to approximately two hundred, with the amount they brought in rising to $40,000 apiece and, in moments of crisis, to $50,000. (By 1984, the fee rose to $150,000 and as many as three hundred companies were in the program.) To Louis Lowenstein, a professor at Columbia Law School, who observed Skadden's rise as a partner in another Manhattan law firm, Flom and his partners had "stepped into Nirvana."

In 1978, the firm's guaranteed annual income from retainers was at least $13 million, out of a reported $30 million total. *The American Lawyer* estimated that half the guaranteed amount was pure profit, since the firm expended little effort for the clients paying those retainers. The estimate was probably low, since only a "minor portion," or fewer than half, of the retainer clients engaged the firm in billable work. "You see a notice about a new, retainer client," *The American Lawyer* quoted a Skadden lawyer as saying, "and then you never hear about them again."

Jim Freund: "It was terrific money. A guy was paying you in case something happened." The firm treated the money as a windfall. Peter Mullen said, "For a period of years, the retainers were often not used up, although sometimes they were and, if anything happened with a company, they would be used up very quickly." Also: "In the late seventies and early eighties, the unused portion of the retainers was of some significance to our profit-and-loss statement." Bill Frank, a Skadden partner: "Skadden was often hired for protection or because we were known as the most aggressive sons of bitches. That benefited us and helped account for growth."

Some lawyers outside and inside Skadden criticized the retainer policy, on the grounds that it was improper to accept money for providing insurance rather than doing legal work. (About the retainer program, a partner then: "It was a form of holdup.") But Flom was undeterred. Others went further and accused Skadden of using its retainer system as a form of blackmail—paying off Joe.

Flom: "I've never gone to a guy and said, 'Come hire us or we'll go with someone else.' Not in a million years. If the guy indicates that he

wants to pay us so we won't be on the other side, that's not acceptable."
Yet Flom was confident that a client got his money's worth if he did
nothing at all, because opponents didn't like having him on the other
side. He said as much. A client in a tight spot might ask, "What do I
do now?" Flom would say, "Tell 'em you've hired me."

Flom modified his position when proof came to light in a lawsuit that
a Skadden retainer was less an insurance policy, a form of limited
protection, or even a retainer, than an option to hire Flom if he chose
to make himself available when called.

In 1973, as it had done for several years, Skadden included a clause
in a retainer agreement which read: "Should your corporation or any
person affiliated with it seek to acquire or invest in any company which
is a client of our office we will be free to represent that client and the
same shall not result in a reduction of the retainer." Called a waiver, it
allowed the firm to take money from a client, in exchange for the promise
of counsel, and to keep the money if it decided not to do any work. The
firm asked all of its retainer clients to accept the clause, and most did.

"You had to start getting these waivers from as many people as you
could," Flom explained recently, because almost any corporate client,
old or new, was both a potential aggressor and a potential target, and
might make a persuasive case that Skadden should represent it. The
waiver gave Skadden the option of representing whichever company it
wanted.

In 1978, Flom decided to represent a new client in a takeover rather
than a retainer client for which Skadden was also counsel in an inactive
court case. The retainer client sued to disqualify him on grounds that
he had a conflict of interest. A federal trial judge denied the motion of
the client. Before it appealed, the company and its adversary reached a
compromise. An element of their agreement was that no one in the suit
could discuss any part of it, including Flom's possible disqualification,
with anyone not involved.

Skadden rewrote its waiver, to make clear that the clause allowed the
firm to represent a new client as well as an existing one instead of a
retainer client. In response to criticism from Monroe Freedman, a professor at Hofstra Law School and an expert in legal ethics, that the
waiver was "unprofessional," and to observations from many lawyers
that the arrangement it set out was "greedy," the firm announced that,
in most cases, it would return the year's retainer when Flom invoked a
waiver clause. Afterward, Lester Brickman, a professor at Benjamin N.

Cardozo School of Law, and Lawrence Cunningham, a former Cardozo student, called nonrefundable retainers "impermissible" under all forms of law. In the *Fordham Law Review*, they wrote that even Skadden's new waiver was "arguably unethical." It limited the firm's losses as a result of conflicts of interest by assuring fees from at least one client.

The lawsuit provoked some other changes. To defuse criticism, apparently, "reliable sources close to" Flom told *The American Lawyer* that he was considering "giving up" the retainers. He didn't, but he seemed to realize that he had to justify his firm's retainers on grounds other than the indispensability of his counsel. This instinct was fortified when Flom and his retainer were cited in another lawsuit as evidence that the board members of a company in Chicago that retained him had no intention of seriously entertaining an offer from another corporation, because, according to a lawyer involved, "hiring Flom was a sign that they'd never consider selling to anyone in a takeover bid." The lawyer also said, "If they'd ever been forced to go to a trial on that, Flom could have kissed off his retainers."

Skadden began to say that its retainer program was a way of protecting itself—against the problem of conflicts of interest. The legal profession's rules required that a firm giving counsel to a client refrain from representing the client's adversary in another matter. In Flom's words, "If you didn't have some way of assuring a guy was serious about hiring you, everybody would talk to you about some tiny problem and you'd be conflicted out of everything."

The rules took no account of the financial consequences of a conflict, so advising a corporation with a small share of a market and a modest legal question might prevent a firm from representing a "serious player" who sought counsel later on about a similar problem. If a serious player wanted to ensure that Skadden would be available, it had to retain the firm. From Skadden's point of view, some corporations engaged in "sabotage": they retained the firm and consulted it about a minor problem, to keep it on the sidelines in a major takeover fight. Retainers softened such blows.

Flom and others also agreed that the firm should make a point of telling clients that it wasn't interested in simply banking its retainers. According to Flom and others, Skadden had informed its retainer clients from the beginning that they could draw against the sum for any sort of legal work that the firm did. Beginning in the late seventies, it actively solicited clients to try out other lawyers besides its dealmakers.

To Flom, with his new perspective, it was "bad business to put the retainers on ice." They represented a potential loss of opportunity for the firm. If a retainer prevented the firm from representing another corporation, the firm might bring in less revenue than it would have as counsel in the second matter. Lost opportunity meant lost money.

Alf Law was put in charge of asking retainer clients how else the firm could be of service. Sometime later, he insisted to *The American Lawyer* that Flom had recognized the opportunity for increased exposure from the retainer program almost as soon as it was suggested to him. "The next morning, Joe said to me that he'd made two mistakes. One, he should have charged five thousand dollars. Two, he should have encouraged the guy to use the five thousand for anything the firm did. His point was that this was the way to get clients to see what else the firm could do."

The firm applied the concept to dealings with most of its clients and not just those in its retainer program. Jim Freund: "If we were brought in by an investment bank or a company's general counsel, we could show our stuff." In the wake of the retainer suit, Flom was determined that his firm would have more stuff to show. Morris Kramer: "Flom articulated that there were other areas of business that we could do, that were intensive, cutting edge, high profile, high margin, not M&A. The firm found people who had quality and interesting prospects, and we thought: What the hell? We're doing so well, we'll take a flyer. If it works, it will soften the downside when M&A dries up."

According to a Skadden partner then, the retainer suit brought home to Flom that the firm's prospects would be increasingly hampered by conflicts of interest if it continued to focus so heavily on the takeover work he generated. A common question among Skadden lawyers about the firm's dependence on Flom was "What happens if Joe gets hit by a bus?" His answer was to diversify the practice—before it happened again.

The firm's retainers provided the capital to fund the expansion into new areas of practice. They also gave companies on retainer an incentive to try the added services. Because Skadden was often hired to help a client out of a one-time jam, the firm was usually new to the client and needed to win its confidence quickly. If a client paid Skadden a big retainer up front, Morris Kramer instructed, it was more likely to do as it was counseled.

Skadden also retained the option of dropping clients. Flom explained,

"They would call up to renew their retainer and we'd say, 'Look, you don't need a retainer. Come see me when you need me.'" The firm sounded like it was thinking of the client's interests. To corporations that worried about not having Joe Flom as counsel in a takeover or about having him appear on the other side, the message had to come across as "Use us or lose us."

The retainers defined Skadden's remarkable achievement in the few years from the start of the takeover wave: garnering a large measure of power. The firm was the most chased-after counsel in the area of law that was then more important than any other to many of the largest American corporations. Skadden's power was manifest in related ways, as when the firm expanded its practice in corporate finance in the early eighties and investment bankers who wanted it to work with them in M&A gave the firm some finance business "as a kind of sweetener" (Matthew Mallow, head of corporate finance at Skadden). But the power of the firm could be gauged neatly by the large number of corporations that wouldn't risk losing its counsel in deals.

Paul Starr, a professor of sociology at Princeton University and a student of the professions, explained that clients depend primarily on the "knowledge and competence" of professionals, including lawyers, but that sometimes clients' needs are "entirely subjective." The success of Skadden's retainer program proved that the difference didn't matter.

8

Building the Church

Among the many Skadden partners in different fields of corporate law, the only one on a recent firm roster who was identified as a generalist was Peter Mullen. He was also the only lawyer who didn't actively practice law. In 1982, when he was fifty-four, he officially became the firm's full-time leader as its executive partner. He had already functioned as its managing partner since 1967, an extraordinarily long tenure for anyone in that role at a major firm in New York City.

Mullen has thinning silver hair, tired eyes, and erect, almost military, posture. He has an appreciator's smile, a gravelly voice that rolls with confidence, and, for the most part, an unthreatening gaze. His temper flares at grievances, but his manner is generally buoyant and patrician. At certain moments, especially when he wears a three-piece suit, he has the forbidding look of a onetime spy, which he was not, or of a lawyer from the generation before his. Stories about him are scarce, because he avoids vivid gestures and smooths rough edges, including his own.

Mullen was born in Manhattan in 1928. He grew up on Eighty-sixth Street in Yorkville, between York and East End avenues. His mother, a librarian in the Yorkville branch of New York City's public library, was a third-generation American with German forebears. His father, a third-generation American of Irish stock, was a lawyer and, for twenty years, a state Criminal Court judge who considered himself part of a war against organized crime. Frank Costello and other figures in that world, down to Three Fingers Brown, a local hood, were tried before him. According to his son, "He sentenced some of the most colorful criminals of the mid-twentieth century to jail."

The family was Catholic, and Mullen went to a private Jesuit high school, Loyola, at Eighty-third Street and Park Avenue. He attended Georgetown University, in Washington, D.C., where he edited the school paper and led the college honor society. From there, he moved on to Columbia Law School, where he also did well. He spent nine years at the firm of Dewey Ballantine, and when he didn't make partner, he decided to look around.

"In those days, the big firms were very Waspy. They had token 'others.' Dewey Ballantine was typical. I was told that I didn't quite fit the mold," Mullen recalled. Many years later, Mullen's mentor there, a name partner, William Palmer, wrote him a letter in which he listed all the reasons that did *not* explain why Mullen had not been voted in. Conspicuously, being a Catholic was absent. A Dewey partner told Mullen that Skadden was looking for a lawyer with experience like his. He made the move in 1961, with the understanding that he would be admitted as a partner soon, if things worked out. He became a partner in 1962.

Alf Law observed, "Mullen infuriates you by sounding out, moving cautiously, deferring decision." Mullen's explanation for this style of management is that his power depended on persuasion: any expression by him of imperiousness would have been greeted by unrest among his partners, who would have quit rather than take orders. For years, he was described as acting like the president of a large university, with a range of departments and campuses, whose job was to lead an organization vertically that was defiantly horizontal.

To Joe Flom, however, speaking about Mullen at the height of his reign, he "operates beautifully by consensus. He looks like he's following, but he's leading." When he was named executive partner ("or whatever the hell he called himself," Flom said. "They didn't want a chief executive officer"), Mullen became well positioned to lead by leading, when he chose. The last time the full Skadden partnership voted on an expenditure of money was in 1982, when a majority opposed the construction of a restaurant-sized kitchen at the firm's Manhattan office. At Mullen's direction, the kitchen got built anyway. By his reckoning, he was the only Skadden lawyer with the time and mandate to consult fully with his colleagues. Since he was the only lawyer who knew each partner beyond pleasantries, he was also the only one to learn firsthand about the range of ambitions that he was expected to fulfill.

Mullen has sometimes acted like the shepherd of a diverse flock. Jonathan Bowie, a gay Skadden partner who arrived from the law firm of Sullivan & Cromwell in 1985: "Not long after I joined the firm, an acquaintance at Sullivan who was gay but very closeted was passed over for partnership and he committed suicide. Not a single Sullivan partner went to the funeral, or acknowledged the event. At Skadden, which had nothing to do with this, Peter Mullen came to talk with me. He sat in my office, and wanted to make sure that I was O.K., and that we did what we could to make sure the same thing didn't happen at Skadden. Personally, Mullen is very uncomfortable with the gay issue. He is a good Catholic. But he is fully committed to a belief in openness and to learning about different points of view. While his discomfort with the issue makes me uncomfortable talking with him about it, we do talk about it. He has been both a friend and a supporter."

Skadden partners like to say that Flom is the firm's spiritual leader and Mullen the apostle who built his church, or some variant. (Joseph Halliday, head of the banking practice: "Joe was Jesus, and Peter was the rock on which he built his church.") In Mullen's diplomatic view, however, from the day he arrived at Skadden, "Joe was the key." With power flowing from his status as the firm's giant star, Flom's word about matters that interested him was usually supreme. A partner at Skadden during the 1970s once went to see Mullen about something important and realized he was talking to Flom: "If you wanted something taken care of—to get more money for a lawyer or to secure him a partner-ship—you went to Joe."

According to Les Arps, Mullen and Barry Garfinkel "did Flom's dirty work"—from firing a secretary to giving a partner unwelcome news about compensation to getting rid of a client. Sometimes, other partners said, Flom and Mullen used Garfinkel as a go-between when they didn't want to deal with each other directly. (A onetime partner: "If Flom wanted to do something that seemed wrong, and Mullen had only a limited number of times to go to Flom and say, 'I really think you're on the wrong track here,' he could send Garfinkel.")

Beginning in the late sixties, Mullen functioned as the firm's managing partner. He oversaw hiring, decided how much to pay associates, and signed checks for the firm. He once told a reporter that he filled that role because of "my ability to work not just with Joe but around Joe, to control his ideas." A former partner of the two suggested that the remark was evidence of Mullen's ambivalence about Flom and a tendency he developed over the years to put Flom down in public. An enduring Skadden mystery, the lawyer said, was the relationship between Flom and Mullen.

But, as his colleagues saw Mullen during the rise of Skadden, he knew his role: Flom wanted to attract and do deals, the firm's lifeblood, and he needed someone to run the firm; Mullen was willing and able. He was a builder of consensus as well as its barometer. He created a working social order to discipline Flom's potent, if sometimes raw, energy.

He also recognized the limits of his authority. He checked in regularly with Flom. Alf Law, on how often Mullen and Flom spoke during the sixties and seventies: "Twenty times a day." Law explained: "Joe is not a steadily consistent person. He could be institution-minded, and the next day he could have an ego attack."

In 1972, the firm formed an administrative committee to guide the firm and spare the full partnership (then nineteen) from meetings about all but essential issues, like who should become a partner. Mullen became its chairman and Flom a member, but Flom rarely attended meetings. Ambiguities that had prevailed for several years about firm leadership continued, with authority ostensibly spread among the partners, Mullen the firm's overall manager, and Flom guiding critical decisions, like how to divide the firm's profits.

To most Skadden lawyers in the 1970s, managing the firm seemed far less consequential than practicing law. The significance of management became more apparent in 1978. Skadden had a hundred fifty lawyers by then, and Flom took part in twenty-one of the twenty-two major hostile takeover contests in the United States that year. He was kept out of the twenty-second because he had recently represented both companies involved.

A lawyer who was at Skadden then said, "Flom's day was divided into chunks of going from one meeting with high-powered people to another. It was the perfect example of the pyramid structure of a law

firm. Each of his meetings could keep fifteen people busy for days."
Hustling between conference rooms, Flom would actually tell his secretary, "Hold my calls!" Pause. "Unless it's new business!" According
to *The American Lawyer*, his firm's dominance in its specialty, and its
retainers, made Skadden partners the best-paid at any corporate law
firm in the country.

The next year, in a move known as the Palace Revolution, a quartet
of takeover lawyers whom Flom had trained as the next line of command
asked for a role in running the firm. Roger Aaron, Peter Atkins, Fin
Fogg, and Morris Kramer called themselves the Young Turks.

Aaron and Atkins had arrived for a summer at the firm the same
day in 1967. Both were tall and dark-haired, and wore nerdy, black-
rimmed glasses. Aaron was from Yale Law School and Atkins from
Harvard, but they were called the Bobbsey Twins. They joined the firm
as associates in 1968, and, sharing an office, earned reputations for being
able, disciplined lawyers for whom a sense of humor was a tool of the
trade, like mastering a calculator. They represented a new chapter in
the Skadden story. Instead of succeeding at the firm on the rebound,
each said recently, they could have gone to any law firm in New York.
They chose Skadden for its verve and promise.

A friend of Atkins's told me that he is a thoughtful, warm perfectionist,
who showed up unexpectedly at the funeral of her brother, plays the
guitar well, and is a great dancer. An investment banker observed, "He's
like the law professor who still follows the facts and the law," and "he
has a mind that won't pontificate." A biographical sketch of Atkins
available from Skadden said about his part in deals, "He is *directly
involved* in all phases of these transactions, including initial planning,
structuring, negotiation, implementation and advice." (Emphasis added.)
Another banker said, "Atkins is totally dedicated to his role in the firm.
He is without doubt the best corporate lawyer there."

I found him taciturn and guarded, and his explanations of his work
truly nebulous, as if the crisp picture he was capable of describing were
caught in a fog of circumspection. "I've been practicing law for twenty-
plus years, and there have been lots of changes," he said. "But I personally
never really felt in the area of the fiduciary duty of directors, which is
at the heart of guiding directors of corporations, which is what I do,
that the law has changed that much."

Or when I asked him for examples of Skadden's leading deals: "I
don't think there is anyone here, Joe included, who could pick out the

ten or twenty most significant transactions we've done, by any standards. Some are significant because they have some particular construct, legal or otherwise, that was fashioned so that the transaction, in a time frame, under pressure, with risks, actually worked." Atkins personified the deal lawyer as existentialist: severely absorbed in the present, and either uninterested in or incapable of making the meaning of his past vibrant.

About Roger Aaron, a onetime Skadden associate who worked regularly for him said, "I know him. I like him. He was always nice to me. He worked like a madman. Seven a.m. to eleven p.m., on a regular basis." Others at the firm and outside it praised Aaron's intellect and commitment, and told me that he ranked with Atkins as one of the outstanding corporate lawyers in the firm. A lawyer at Skadden said about the duo, "It is a pleasure to have them as partners, and impossible to work with them." A recent biographical sketch of Aaron began concisely: "For many years, Roger S. Aaron has represented clients in some of Skadden, Arps' most significant merger and acquisition, leveraged buyout and other corporate transactions."

Perhaps because of Aaron's devotion to his work, I tried unsuccessfully to meet with him, off and on, for five years. In one stretch, I decided that intensity might be a strategy he would respond to, so I called, faxed, or wrote Aaron a dozen requests for an interview in a two-week period. I was at Skadden's New York office regularly then and caught glimpses of him in corridors, so I knew Aaron was around. His secretary answered promptly every time, and we developed an understanding, but Aaron never called me.

In 1993, as I was winding up my work, I made a final request, and Aaron gave me twenty minutes. A lean, fit, angular man, with straight graying hair falling over his collar, he recited brief anthems like "We tend to look forward, and think about our clients' needs," and came across like a man practicing sound bites for a business feature. I had been told that some Skadden partners were opposed to the idea of letting me write about the firm, and Aaron acted like one of them.

As he stood to signal our time was up, he asked me about my background. I told him, and he became animated. He said that his son had recently graduated from college and was out in Hollywood, trying to make it as a writer, or maybe a producer, in movies and TV. "The other night, he called and said, 'You know, sitting in front of a computer screen all day isn't that much fun.' His mother and I looked at each other, like"—Aaron's eyebrows shot up and he lifted his chin suddenly,

in a compelling pantomime of surprise—" 'Well, what did you *think*
you'd do as a writer?' "

Fogg was the senior member of the group, having moved to the firm
in 1966. With a mercurial face highlighted by narrow eyes and a crooked
nose, he smokes big cigars and sometimes masks his acuteness behind a
jovial smile. He is likable, if unpredictable—a Wasp *mensch* with survival
skills. For a man with charm and polish, he sometimes seems to be
coarse on purpose. The first time I spoke with him, in 1990, he told me
about an important early client. The story ended with a dialogue:
" 'Fin Fogg,' he said. 'What kind of a name is that? You don't sound
like a Jew to me.' I said, 'I'm not. I'm a Wasp. But if it's any consolation,
I married into your camp.' He said, 'Funny, I married a *shiksa*. Jewish
women don't fuck enough.' I said, 'Oh, I thought that Jewish men
couldn't get it up.' We got along great."

Morris Kramer moved to the firm in 1972, and became the man of
incarnations. He arrived dressing in conservative business suits, and soon
adopted the mod style (bright-colored shirts, jackets with wide lapels,
bell-bottom pants, and long hair). Another partner said that he was as
monochromatic as Aaron and Atkins, "but in chartreuse."

When Kramer was asked to name the stars at Skadden in the mid-
seventies, besides Flom, he told a reporter, "I'd say I'm one of them.
And I'd bet you that every other partner would say he's one of them.
That's the kind of people we are." Another partner told me about
Kramer, "My position on Morris is that you couldn't find a guy who is
more normal." He was a quiet Jewish guy who learned to project a
shimmer of eccentricity. "It's his product," Kramer's partner said. "It's
his trademark. Long hair? You might not remember his name, but
whatever it takes, you try to distinguish yourself from the pack."

Fogg was named a partner in 1972. Aaron, Atkins, and Kramer
became partners in 1975. In 1979, Fogg turned thirty-nine, Kramer thirty-
eight, Aaron thirty-seven, and Atkins thirty-six. With a nod to the
Beatles, they were called the Fab Four.

The Palace Revolution that they launched is variously recalled. Fogg:
"Aaron, Atkins, Kramer, and I had breakfast at Kramer's house, on
Seventy-first Street. The firm had an administrative committee, and we
thought we should be on it. We had this breakfast to plot, and we asked
and they said, 'Sure.' "

Steve Axinn, who was then on the committee: "They wanted a voice
in the important things, like who made partner and how much each

partner made. Lots of firms whose hulks you see in the harbor went down on this rock. This issue kills firms. Flom and Mullen, the shot callers then, said, 'We are going to share money and power with these kids.' "

In 1979 as well, Mullen took a prosaic-seeming step toward the firm's goal of diversification. Skadden hired the accounting firm of Arthur Young to analyze the firm's information systems (accounting, financial, and word processing) and advise how to manage the firm effectively in the 1980s.

Mullen: "We always paid more attention to planning than other firms. We had to because whatever we did last year wouldn't necessarily work this year, our firm was growing so rapidly. Growth alone required different systems for managing it. We liked the idea of growing, so we wanted to cope with growth in a way that allowed us to continue to grow."

Earle Yaffa, a graduate of Tufts University and MIT's Sloan School of Management, in Boston, where he grew up, was the brand-new partner in charge of Arthur Young's law-firm consulting practice. His experience was in advising entertainment companies, financial firms, and a variety of other businesses. He was an incisive, high-strung man, with a taste for systems. At forty, he had just been given responsibility for Young's law-firm practice, and decided to take a couple of assignments from law firms to learn about the work he was overseeing. The second call came from Skadden.

Yaffa concluded that the firm needed to overhaul its information systems and organize them by practice areas. By monitoring how many lawyers worked in each area, how busy they were, how their work translated into billings, and how the billings contributed to the firm's profits, Skadden could learn the growth rate of each practice. It could study practice areas as units of business to be left to their own devices, nurtured, or recast.

Once the firm had the systems in place, however, it needed someone to interpret the data they produced. Mullen felt that a person with enough experience to do the job well would be unlikely to fit easily into Skadden's "egalitarian environment." The firm wasn't satisfied by any candidate that Arthur Young proposed. Over time, the job was redefined so Yaffa seemed right for it.

The prevailing view in the consulting world was that law firms were boring businesses. Yaffa initially turned Skadden down. But he saw that the legal profession was changing and that Skadden seemed different from many firms: it was thinking about how to prepare itself for the future; it was committed to being "a major factor" in the profession; and it was willing to let a nonlawyer help achieve that goal. In 1980, when the firm had approximately two hundred fifty lawyers, Yaffa became the firm's managing director.

His first move was to alter the systems that he had designed while at Arthur Young and fashion ones that deposited all of Skadden's data in a central computer. There, the data could be sorted by almost any category: practice area; type of legal service; client; or deal. Skadden regularly used the information to learn how much time it was spending for a client and what the firm's monthly billings were going to be, and how busy the firm's lawyers were, individually and by practice area. Each transaction was processed into the computer. The computer could answer almost any financial question of significance to the firm.

Yaffa's arrival gave Peter Mullen a respite from some management chores and allowed him to concentrate again on his legal practice. As chairman of the administrative committee, he was meant to spend one-fourth of his time on firm management. The rest he was supposed to devote to clients, as head of the firm's corporate department. They included companies like FlightSafety, whose corporate secretary Mullen had become in 1961 (it grew to have a value in the stock market of over one billion dollars), and Athlone, a company that Mullen had helped create in the mid-sixties, when its chief executive bought a shell corporation with a tax loss on its books and began to use the loss to shelter the income of other companies he purchased.

Within a year, however, it became clear that Skadden's growth was outstripping the new structure in which Yaffa played an integral part. The partners were pleased by Yaffa's performance, but he didn't have the stature to lead the firm. In 1981, Irving Shapiro joined Skadden after retiring as chairman of the board of E. I. Du Pont de Nemours Chemicals, one of the country's largest and most respected corporations. (Shapiro's son Stuart was a Skadden partner and the firm had an anti-nepotism rule; it made an exception to allow the parent of a partner to join.) He was intent on transferring to the firm some of the knowledge he had gained as a captain of industry. "I'll be a full-time partner. I won't goof off or anything," he told a reporter when he came aboard.

Shapiro advised, "You guys are getting to be a big business, and you've got to run yourselves like one." Shapiro, Flom, Mullen, and Yaffa formed a committee to determine what new leadership position to establish, so the firm could act on his advice. They approved a Flom idea of having a partner serve as the first full-time chief executive of a large American law firm. Mullen was the obvious choice, and, in the fall of 1981, Flom asked him to take the job.

Flom recalled: "Mullen told me, 'I'll do it on one condition: You're not going to second-guess me.' I said, 'Peter, you've got my word. I'll only second-guess you to your face.'" Flom promptly did, when Mullen wanted Fin Fogg to succeed him as head of the firm's corporate practice (he was forty-one and the senior member of the Fab Four) and Flom insisted that Peter Atkins get the job (although he was three years younger). Flom was named chairman of the partnership.

In 1982, Skadden was a New York law firm with three small satellite offices and a bold, but limited, reputation. ("Excels only in the takeover area," a *Fortune* survey of America's twenty-five biggest law firms said about Skadden, which was number eleven. "Even partners work like coolies.") On the firm's silver anniversary, in 1973, it had opened a Boston branch "for the guy"—to make a place for Bob Pirie.

Pirie was then a Boston lawyer; Flom had gotten to know him working on proxy contests. On the surface, his story was one of inheritance: of money from the Chicago family that built the department-store chain of Carson Pirie Scott & Company; and of a sense of destiny. Pirie was also an iconoclast who loved a fight. A lawyer who worked with him said, "He bulls his way through everything in a larger-than-life way, and he knows he's doing it. He affects a kind of entitlement, with a confidence and a flair that enable him to pull it off."

Pirie wanted to live in Boston, so Skadden petitioned the Massachusetts Bar Association to overturn a rule that kept an out-of-state firm from establishing a local office under its own name. The Massachusetts rule was changed, and Pirie set up shop. He then spent most of his time in New York, where he kept his main office and lived at a private club. For the first decade of the Boston branch, it was treated like an extension of the firm's Manhattan headquarters, with relatively little business of its own.

Skadden opened a Washington, D.C., office in 1976. It paused over the decision, compiling a list of all the major New York firms that didn't have branches there (Cravath, Davis Polk, Shearman & Sterling, etc.). The firm was also put off by a proposed rule of the D.C. bar that would require a firm to withdraw from a case if it hired a lawyer who had played a big part in the matter while working in the government.

But Steve Axinn, the head of the firm's antitrust department, wanted another partner to help on a new, large case and hired one out of the Justice Department. He was John Fricano. A memoir by Jim Freund: "John finally accepted, and the day he arrived at the firm in New York, Steve presented him with a white cowboy hat, a sheriff's badge, and two six-guns—which John proudly wore around the office—to prove that John hadn't lost his power and was still on the 'right side.'"

A statement of policies for the D.C. office said that "we all shun the concept of a political outpost for lobbying and related activities," and that the branch shouldn't grow by acquiring another firm in a city "where most of us lack knowledge as to the right buttons to push, the people who have the clout, the areas of specialization that can prove most productive . . ." The firm should be "(without the pejorative connotation) opportunistic; we have tended to avoid fixed conceptions which artificially limit our alternatives. If a good man comes along, we are likely to reach for him, even though he might not fit a particular need or fall into a specified category."

In 1979, Skadden opened an office in Wilmington, Delaware, with six lawyers from a local firm that had handled business for Skadden in the state. Over half the Fortune 500 are incorporated in Delaware, where the companies deal with legal issues about their governance, so Skadden viewed the new outpost as an opportunity for the firm to do on its own what it had previously farmed out. Legal newspapers described Skadden's move as a raid on the local bar: To them, the branch was the idea of the New York firm. Skadden said that the decision to jump firms was the Delaware sextet's; it simply provided a place to land.

Under Mullen's and Yaffa's direction, and with Flom's eagerness to expand in mind, Skadden took stock of itself and articulated fresh goals. "From the firm's inception," a group of partners stated in a 1982 memorandum, "our intent has been to build a quality law firm that would stand the test of time. While a high degree of profitability has come to be expected, short-term profits were always a less important consideration than ensuring a stable, viable, and high quality law firm." Skadden's objective was to "enhance the reputation of the firm and insure its continued viability and its ability to earn substantial income for its partners . . ."

To the partners, the firm had four basic means. The first was to maintain "our dominant position" in mergers and acquisitions and to strengthen the firm's related corporate, litigation, and antitrust groups, in which three-fourths of Skadden's lawyers then practiced. "[W]e should never lose sight of the importance of this area to our overall practice—both on its own and as a feeder for other business."

The second was to "expand the scope of legal services offered to existing clients and attract new clients to the firm in the areas in which our skills are well known." The third was to "expand the products (services) offered to the business community by using our existing skills in new and different areas." In its litigation department, the firm had defended companies sued for damages alleged to have been caused by products they made. In its corporate department, it had counseled financial companies about underwriting offerings of stocks, bonds, and other instruments. These and other specialties provided "significant opportunities to obtain work in areas where we have little business or reputation but do have the capability to perform the work." Such efforts might, "on occasion, require the addition of a key specialist," but they entailed "little downside risk."

The fourth method represented significant change for Skadden. It was to develop "new specialties" or move into "new geographic areas." The specialties were meant to be "self-sufficient and independent" of the firm's existing practice. They were described as boutiques into which expansion could be important for the firm in the long term, for one of several reasons: The specialty would help maintain the firm's "reputation"; it was "highly profitable"; it would attract clients that would bring "significant profits" in existing practice areas; it would keep the firm from losing "desirable business to competitors," even though it was "only marginally desirable in itself"; or it was likely to be "a most important practice area in the future," and the firm should enter it early.

In 1980, drawing on the treasury it was amassing from its retainers and from its takeover business, the firm had begun to be avowedly "expansionist," seeking new specialties (it called the initiative "practice development"), by bringing in bankruptcy experts from another firm. In 1981, it brought in experts to start real estate, energy, and environmental practices. When the energy practice didn't pan out, because the change in administrations from the Democrats to the Republicans killed the deals that the new lawyers had said they would handle, Skadden demonstrated its strength by carrying those lawyers for a year or so while they realigned their sights and found other work.

The expansion took advantage of a new trend that was a sign of competition among law firms, called lateral mobility—the movement of partners from one firm to another, although they were welcome to stay at their original base. It also took shrewd advantage of the legal press. The attention the press paid to how much money lawyers were making, and to how much Skadden lawyers made in particular, heightened the firm's attraction to prospective lateral entries. Profiles of successful partners in other firms helped Skadden identify candidates (Mullen's words) "for acquisition."

Skadden had also debated opening other offices, especially in Chicago and Los Angeles: they ranked second and third to the New York area, respectively, in the number of large companies and of Skadden clients located in each. In 1982, the idea of a Chicago office was rejected. The legal market there appeared to be well served by firms already established in the city and the bar seemed unusually insular, so Skadden concluded that it would be difficult for the firm to make a place for itself.

The combination of a national recession and of opposition from a corps of partners, particularly Flom, led the firm to table the Los Angeles idea as well. A memo had argued that an L.A. office would be "very desirable" for the firm ("What it all comes down to is that Los Angeles appears to be booming [like us]"). The memo had also surveyed the "Major Negatives." "The biggest apparent problem" was that L.A. is "a long way from New York." Flom latched on to the point. He said that none of the firm's current offices was more than a jet shuttle ride from another and that it would be hard to manage an office three time zones away.

But Skadden soon made progress on all fronts. Its most obvious expansion was geographically. In 1983, because "expansion into the Los Angeles area" was "the most important step in fulfilling" the firm's objectives for overall growth, it lured a partner from the Los Angeles office of a New York firm to found and build up a Skadden branch in L.A. In 1980 and 1981, the firm had calculated, it had taken part in over 40 percent of the mergers and takeovers involving publicly owned companies when one or both of the companies were headquartered in the East or the Midwest, and in less than 18 percent of the deals where one or both companies were headquartered west of the Mississippi. To Skadden, four of every ten deals seemed its fair share of the market. It wanted to climb to that level out West.

In 1984, it opened a Chicago office. A group of partners from one of Chicago's leading firms, Mayer, Brown & Platt, approached Flom through a friend of his, who was the father-in-law of one of the lawyers, and asked if Skadden was interested in a branch there. The Mayer

Brown group was disaffected with its old firm, according to *The Wall Street Journal*. The leader of the group was Wayne Whalen, a longtime Democratic activist, whose father had founded Whistling Wings, a duck farm producing more mallards than any other in the world. He had pressed Mayer Brown to rely less on the Continental Illinois National Bank & Trust Company, one of its major clients, and to change its compensation system so that it rewarded rainmakers more fully. In a struggle for control of the firm, his appointment to its policy and planning committee had been defeated in a vote for ratification by the partnership. Skadden considered the chance to start with a respected cadre too good to pass up. Without doing any detailed financial projections, as it had for the L.A. office, it became the first New York firm to open in Chicago.

In 1984, the firm began new practice groups in the areas of products liability and finance and, in 1987, when it learned that an expert in finance who was based at a firm in San Francisco was available for a move, it opened a branch there, too—less because it fit a strategic plan than (again) "for the guy." The firm also went international, opening a branch office in Tokyo.

By 1987, over 40 percent of the firm's one hundred fifty-five partners practiced corporate law (sixty-seven) and litigation remained the second-largest group (with thirty-three). But tax (twelve) replaced antitrust (nine) in third place, real estate, a relatively new area, moved into fifth place (eight), and the firm's twenty-six other partners practiced in ten separate fields. In the spring, the firm had approximately seven hundred lawyers: more than four hundred were in New York; a hundred or so were in Washington, D.C.; eighty were in Los Angeles; sixty were in Chicago; twenty-five were in Wilmington; twenty were in Boston; and five were in San Francisco.

In the meantime, the firm's profits were larger than anyone's rosiest projections. The firm's leverage at the bargaining table redounded to its own benefit, allowing it to command a form of payment from its clients that made the extraordinary flow from the firm's retainer program seem trivial.

In theory, how a law firm makes money is simple: clients hire the firm, its lawyers spend time on matters, and they bill for their time; at the end of the year, after the firm has paid its expenses (including associates' salaries), the firm's partners split the profits. Most lawyers in the United States operate this way, although savvy clients have long realized that an hour is a piece of string to some lawyers and that it is impossible to know precisely how they measure it. An idea called value billing is gaining favor, in which clients hire lawyers for a fixed sum per job as an incentive for getting the job done efficiently as well as competently. By the late seventies, intense demand allowed Skadden to raise its hourly billing rates to as high a level as any firm's in New York City.

Skadden partners improved on this arrangement by milking the labors of associates. The ratio between partners and associates there (approximately one to four) was higher than at any other large American firm. In one survey, the only legal institutions with higher partner-to-associate ratios were storefront chains offering cut-rate legal services to a very different market. The ratio of partners to associates is called leverage. With this extreme leverage, partners spread their work among as many other lawyers as possible. They freed themselves of the limits on income at many firms, whose profits were determined by the billings of partners themselves and a smaller number of associates. The fact that clients paid the firm's high bills confirmed the value of its services, Skadden lawyers told each other. They were proud of being expensive.

On the other hand, in the firm's view, in transactions in which a corporation's existence was at stake, clients were far more concerned about getting their lawyer's attention than they were about his fees. Bet-your-company deals turned legal work from a commodity of service, whose price played a big part in whether it was in demand, to an uncommon métier. Price became an afterthought or, even, a come-on. Skadden believed that lawyers who brought unusual expertise to a deal could ask for a premium above an already high hourly rate for their services.

According to Jerome Kohlberg, a founding partner of Kohlberg, Kravis, Roberts & Company, the best-known leveraged-buyout firm of the 1980s, he suggested the idea. It happened in the mid-seventies, after a deal in which Joe Flom helped a corporate client get a good price when it was bought out. Kohlberg recalled: "He was going to send them a bill on the hours he had worked, and I said he should bill them for the wonderful job he did. He billed them either five or six times what the hours added up to, and they paid it willingly." In the early eighties, million-dollar premiums began to roll into Skadden's coffers. The firm took the final step for workers intent on beating the clock, by charging fees that were liberated from time.

In 1988, Mullen complained: "Something that has gotten a little out of whack in recent years is billable hours and what are your billing rates, as if we were rendering services like an electrician or a carpenter." There were a dozen key factors in determining Skadden's bill on a matter: how tough the deal was, whether the firm had to drop other work or forgo new work to do it, whether the firm had expertise that made its contribution unusually valuable, and what the results were, among others. Above all, results mattered.

To Mullen, billing strictly by the hour was "simplistic." Sometimes Skadden did it, in practice areas like bankruptcy, where bills had to be approved by a judge. Often, the firm went through its factor analysis, and when it concluded that enough factors showed a job had been demanding and successfully completed, it charged more than its time multiplied by standard fees would have warranted.

Internally, the firm described the difference as a "premium," as other law firms did. But Mullen called the word imprecise, because it assumed there was a standard to serve as a baseline for the premium. In Skadden's view, there was no standard. The firm charged what it did in each case because it thought the number was appropriate. Each case was unique. To give itself leeway in billing, the firm gave clients that engaged it an open-ended letter. One general counsel for a corporation described it as "bullshit." The lawyer: "It said, 'We charge on the basis of time and "success."' It was a who-the-hell-knows-what-it-means kind of letter."

A big factor in the firm's billing, apparently, was its sense of what the market would bear. In the eighties, it seemed to prefer erring on the high side, on the theory that a client could always ask for a bill to be reduced. This sometimes happened. The general counsel of a corporation that had used Skadden in a large, successful deal in the mid-eighties was told confidentially by his boss that he could pay up to $5 million for legal work. That would have been a good, unexceptional fee for the firm. When a Skadden partner went through a factor analysis with the general counsel and ended by asking for a fee under that amount, the counsel quickly agreed. The partner responded, "Shit," apparently realizing he could have charged more.

Skadden's best-known specialty, M&A, was demanding in terms of manpower, intensity, and expertise. As important, unless a conflict of interest kept the firm out of a deal, it had an excellent chance of being asked to take part in the largest ones. Many deals involved at least four law firms on each side (for the acquiring or defending company, members of its board of directors, the company's investment banker, and its main supplier of financing). Only a dozen or so law firms were regularly involved in such transactions. As a result, during the takeover era, Skadden often charged clients four times hourly billings, following ancient laws of supply and demand.

In 1988, the practice was news to the London *Sunday Times*, because it was so foreign to England. The paper carried an item about a report from the British Department of Trade and Industry regarding a takeover in which Skadden had planned to charge £312,000 (roughly $555,000) for its services if a deal it was involved in didn't go through and four times as much if it did, as happened.

Time charges themselves would have been large, given Skadden's high legal rates and the round-the-clock work of many takeovers. At the height of the era, it was common for a firm takeover lawyer to bill two hundred fifty hours a month, or 40 percent more than a lawyer working at an already demanding pace.

Bernard Black, a former Skadden associate, who became a professor at Columbia Law School, gave students there a handout showing that the monthly average of the hours he billed between 1983 and 1986 was two hundred thirty, with long stretches when the average was around two hundred seventy, and one month when he billed three hundred twenty-five. He reported that he had been "far from the hardest-working associate at Skadden."

Since half the firm was sometimes caught up in takeovers in the mid- and late eighties, according to Mullen, Skadden's typical billings at hourly rates would have been roughly 20 percent higher than those of a normally hardworking firm of comparable size and rates. When those billings were quadrupled, Skadden enjoyed a bonanza. The party went on all year round. Takeovers were not a seasonal business.

Like the firm's retainers, its premiums were criticized on ethical grounds. The payments were, in effect, contingency fees that gave the firm an interest in the outcome of a deal. In some legal cases dealing with criminal charges and divorces, the fees are considered unethical, because they promote conflicts between the interests of lawyers and clients. In business deals, accountants are barred from charging contingency fees, for the same reason: An accountant might be torn between a client's interest in not having a deal go through and the accountant's interest in getting a fee after a deal is consummated.

Skadden didn't invent the concept of contingency fees in M&A. Its rival Wachtell Lipton was viewed as the leader among takeover firms in charging its clients "performance fees"; it drew attention for charging a client $20 million for two weeks' work. But Skadden justified the practice on grounds of fairness. The idea was that the firm contributed as much to deals as investment bankers did and was usually paid far less. Skadden shrugged off the point that the bankers were usually paid only when a deal went through, whereas Skadden, at a minimum, could count on a fee that covered its time.

The power of the firm in the takeover market regularly assured that it got paid what it asked for. Premiums replaced retainers as the source of the firm's deep treasury, and Skadden sometimes savored a "double whammy." It received a fee for counseling the financial company that underwrote a deal in addition to a premium for advising the corporation that did the deal.

For many years, the American bar had tried to assure the independence of lawyers by prohibiting them from accepting investments from non-lawyers. The rule was seen as a primary restriction on the size of law firms, since it limited their ability to raise capital like other businesses. For Skadden, premiums made the problem disappear.

9

Olympus

By the spring of 1990, Skadden had offices in New York, Boston, Wilmington (Delaware), Washington, D.C., Chicago, San Francisco, and Los Angeles, as well as Toronto, London, Brussels, Hong Kong, Tokyo, and Sydney, and it operated informally in Beijing. It had plans to open offices in Paris and Frankfurt and to operate informally in Prague and Budapest. The firm had 226 partners. While comings and goings there made it difficult to arrive at a fixed count, it employed a thousand or so attorneys and approximately twenty-five hundred others, including secretaries, librarians, legal assistants, law clerks, security guards, physical trainers, and other staff members, dealing with accounting, data processing, employee benefits, and other functions of a large service business. The firm had planned to honor its one thousandth lawyer, but no one could figure out who it was.

Almost half of Skadden's lawyers worked explicitly on corporate legal matters. They were specialists in mergers and acquisitions, corporate finance, banking, and other areas. About one-fifth were litigators, and the rest, in order of distribution, concentrated on tax, antitrust, energy, real estate, products liability, environmental, employee benefits and executive compensation, labor, trusts and estates, communications, and commodities law. Skadden described itself as a full-service law firm. This was true unequivocally for clients that were corporations, in particular very large ones like members of the Fortune 500, of which Skadden said it represented approximately one-third.

A significant share of the firm's business came from areas unrelated to corporate deals. In the firm's litigation practice, for example, Skadden represented Guess? in a dispute with Jordache Enterprises about its knocking off designs for Guess? jeans; in the products-liability practice, the firm defended the Ford Motor Company against allegations that some of its vehicles were defective because they lacked air bags; in the environmental practice, it defended the South Florida Water Management District, in a suit by the state's attorney general claiming that the district had polluted the Everglades and the Loxahatchee National Wildlife Refuge. In 1989, the environmental practice alone, employing only twenty-two of Skadden's lawyers, accounted for 46,399 hours of legal work—an average of approximately 2,100 hours per lawyer.

But the dominant area of practice, drawing on corporate and other specialists (from the tax, antitrust, labor, and employee benefits and executive compensation groups, for example), was corporate transactions: advising clients about making, repairing, recovering from, and bailing out of deals. In 1989, over 40 percent of the tax group's billings was for work on mergers and acquisitions, and over 70 percent of the group's billings was for work on corporate transactions of some kind.

From the seventies through the eighties, Skadden worked on more big mergers and acquisitions than any other law firm, and especially on more major takeovers than any competitor. Either directly or peripherally, Skadden had taken part in what, to dealmakers, were the deals of the year for a solid decade:

1980: Kraft merges with Dart ($2.5 billion)
1981: Du Pont buys Conoco ($7.5 billion)
1982: U.S. Steel takes over Marathon Oil ($6.2 billion)
1983: Allied buys Bendix ($1.8 billion)
1984: Chevron buys Gulf Oil ($13.3 billion)

1985: Pantry Pride takes over Revlon ($1.8 billion)
1986: General Electric buys RCA ($6.3 billion)
1987: Unilever buys Chesebrough-Pond's ($3.1 billion)
1988: Campeau takes over Federated Department Stores ($6.6 billion)
1989: RJR Holdings buys Nabisco ($25.3 billion)

In 1989, Skadden was involved in four of the five largest mergers and acquisitions, six of the ten largest, nine of the fifteen largest, and so on, to twenty-nine of the hundred largest—more of the key transactions than any other firm. By its count, the firm took part in two hundred and five financially significant deals. That year the *Institutional Investor* published a feature about competing views in takeover law which listed the landmark rulings made by the Delaware Supreme Court. Of the six decisions since Skadden was founded, the firm had represented a party in five.

In the RJR/Nabisco buyout, Skadden was credited with getting the deal done and was accorded Solomon-like status. Skadden was counsel to a special committee of RJR's directors, serving as auctioneer in the deal. According to *The Wall Street Journal*, Skadden received a payment of $10 million soon after the auction was completed. A Skadden partner said it received a total of $25 million.

To Skadden, its M&A practice was a part standing for the whole. The firm résumé asserted that clients turned to Skadden for help with their "most challenging and complex cases."

In 1989, for example, Skadden represented Eastdil Realty and Nomura International, which owned half of Eastdil, when it lent $600 million to a New York developer for the purchase and renovation of a skyscraper on Sixth Avenue in Manhattan. The loan was divided into tranches of $300 million each. In exchange for placing the senior portion of the loan with Japanese insurance companies, banks, and other institutions, the lender received an interest rate of 11 percent. To lower its costs, from U.S. taxes, among other things, the lender set up an offshore corporation in the Cayman Islands.

The junior portion of the loan was known as a securitized participating mortgage (a mortgage in which the lender participates by having a share in the value of the property). The lender spread the risk of the loan by dividing it into units, turning the units into bonds, and selling them through a public offering on the Luxembourg Stock Exchange to Japanese investors. The deal involved the tax laws of four countries, the corporate securities laws of four countries, and negotiations in New York, Luxembourg, and Tokyo. Twenty Skadden lawyers—in the firm's New York, Washington, D.C., London, and Tokyo offices—took part. They completed the financing in sixty days.

Eastdil Realty ranked as Skadden's twentieth highest-billing client in 1989. Among the top twenty, eleven specialized in finance of some kind. These included Skadden's three biggest clients (Drexel Burnham Lambert, Merrill Lynch, and Morgan Stanley), five of the following seven (Prudential-Bache, Smith Barney, Dai-Ichi Kangyo Bank, Temple Holdings, and American Express) and three of the following ten (First Boston, Shearson Lehman, and Eastdil). No client represented more than 2 percent of the firm's revenues. The turnover among the firm's top twenty clients since 1986 had averaged 50 percent, increasing each year, with A. H. Robins Co. at the head of the list in 1986 and 1987, replaced by American Stores in 1988 and American Express in 1989. Skadden worked for many clients on a wide range of matters.

The high rankings of financial institutions among the firm's clients highlighted the firm's frequent role as an adviser in intricate deals involving large sums of money and financial arrangements that had yet to make it into textbooks. Peter Mullen said, "We like to think of our client as Wall Street." It was the most lucrative type of counsel that a corporate law firm could engage in. As the universe of finance broadened and deepened explosively in the 1980s—by the end of the decade, Skadden had done deals financed by over sixty types of securities, in contrast to the traditional two of stocks and bonds—the firm's fortunes did, too.

From 1984, when *The American Lawyer* began compiling financial data about law firms and Skadden's revenues were reportedly $129 million, until 1989, when they were said to have climbed to over $500 million, the firm's reported revenues had annually towered over those of all other firms—by an average margin of 40 percent over those of the second-ranked firms. Skadden was the richest law firm in the world.

On the record, Skadden neither confirmed nor denied the figures. But according to a lawyer familiar with how *The American Lawyer* gathered data, Steve Brill got financial information directly from Joe Flom the first year the magazine did its survey, and, each year after, an editor learned from Mullen or Earle Yaffa about changes in the firm's financial performance.

From 1984 through 1989, the *American Lawyer* survey reported, the firm's revenues quadrupled. They increased by an average of almost one-third a year. Only lawyers at a few, much smaller, corporate firms averaged higher annual partnership shares. During this run, the average annual compensation of Skadden partners more than doubled, reaching $1.2 million—more than three times as much as partners at the two American firms that had more lawyers.

Throughout this period, the Skadden partnership paid directly for the firm's growth. Instead of borrowing money to open new offices and otherwise expand, in the late seventies the firm began systematically to accumulate a large account for expenditures out of partners' earnings. Partnership laws required the firm to pay out all its earnings each year, so there was no tax-effective way to build the fund. Skadden partners paid taxes on 100 percent of their income, but left 7.5 percent a year in the account.

In 1983, the firm established a second reserve (the Rainy Day Fund), intended to carry the firm through hard times, if they ever came. The goal was to save enough money to cover all the firm's expenses for six months without fresh income. In some years, partners received only 83 percent of the income they were taxed on. Skadden stopped adding to the fund after five years, because the firm had collected more than its target.

In financial terms, the Skadden approach was bedrock conservative. But for a service business known not to be capital-intensive, it was radical. It left Skadden with a mountain of cash—100 percent more capital than it needed, by the firm's estimation, and the means to grow in any direction it wanted.

When *The Wall Street Journal* compiled a list of sixty-six global "Companies for the Future," as part of its 1989 centenary celebration, Skadden was the only law firm included. In promotional materials, Skadden referred to itself as "one of the largest, most visible and most innovative firms in the world" and "the preeminent firm in mergers and acquisitions." Internally, in planning documents, Skadden referred to itself as "the preeminent law firm" in the country. Lawyers there readily described the firm as unique.

So did other observers of the legal profession, like Brill in *The American Lawyer*. He featured Joe Flom in the magazine's tenth anniversary issue (as he had in the fifth), in a profile that called Flom "an Old World generalist," "the consummate lawyer-businessman," "a visionary entrepreneur," and "the embodiment of the lawyer as public-spirited citizen." The article was so flattering that Skadden public relations aides and partners warned about its lack of balance as they gave away reprints.

In 1990, Skadden had recently hired over a hundred lawyers a year straight out of law school, making its incoming class bigger than that of all but a few firms in most of the world's largest cities. Between 1980 and 1985 the number of lawyers in the firm had jumped from 205 to 526, and between 1985 and 1990 it had doubled again, to more than 1,000. In 1987, Skadden hired even more associates from other firms than it did from law schools. The total of new recruits alone crossed the 200 mark in that year; new lawyers comprised almost one-fourth of the whole firm. In lawyers' vernacular, they alone qualified as a mega-firm.

The Skadden associates in 1990 were graduates of eighty-eight law schools. About half came from seven schools: 10 percent from Columbia, 9 percent from New York University, 8 percent from Harvard, 7 percent from Fordham, 6 percent from Georgetown, 5 percent from the University of Chicago, and 4 percent from the University of Michigan. The other half came from eighty-one different schools, with single representatives of thirty-three schools.

Geographically, they ranged from the University of California at Davis Law School and Western New England College of Law; to University College, Dublin; to the University of Paris; to Tel Aviv University; to East China Normal University Institute of Law; and to the University of Sydney Law School.

Of the firm's partners, thirty-four were from Harvard Law School, twenty-three from Columbia, eleven from Yale, and nine from the University of Michigan—all first-tier schools. But Fordham (with twenty-two), New York University (eighteen), and Georgetown University (twelve), which were less widely recognized as prime sources of big-time corporate lawyers, joined those four law schools among the seven whose graduates made up 60 percent of the Skadden partnership. Comprising the other 40 percent were graduates of forty-one different law schools, including single representatives of twenty-three schools covering a broad spectrum (among them, Benjamin N. Cardozo Law School in Manhattan, the University of Detroit Law School, and Vermont Law School).

Among the firm's associates, by 1990, a hundred seventy held advanced degrees in subjects other than the law, in addition to their J.D.s. The degrees were in accounting, anthropology, biological oceanography, business administration, chemical engineering, chemistry, civil engineering, clinical psychology, communications, counseling, divinity, East Asian studies, economics, education, English literature, finance, fine arts, forestry, history, human services, international business, international politics, Islamic art, library sciences, linguistics, mathematics, molecular biology, music, nuclear engineering, organic chemistry, philosophy, politics, psychology, public administration, public health, public policy, social work, theology, and urban planning.

Among the firm's lawyers, over four hundred claimed fluency in at least one language in addition to English. These included Arabic, Chinese (Cantonese, Mandarin, and other dialects), Czech, Fijian, French, German, Greek, Hebrew, Hindi, Hungarian, Italian, Japanese, Korean, Latin, Persian, Polish, Portuguese, Russian, Serbo-Croatian, Spanish, Tagalog, Thai, and Yiddish. Thirty-five were fluent in French, twenty-one in one or more of the Chinese dialects, seventeen in Spanish, and seven in Japanese. Others had working knowledge of Afrikaans, Dutch, Malay/Indonesian, Romanian, and Urdu, as well as American Sign Language.

In 1990, about half of Skadden's attorneys were based in Manhattan. The flagship office filled twenty of the forty-seven floors of the firm's building, and had more lawyers than any other firm in New York City. At other Manhattan firms, Skadden was sometimes singled out as the premier user of a service known as Dial-a-car. Its calls for transportation around Manhattan went out twenty-four hours a day, because the firm never shut down. If you phoned the firm at four on a Sunday morning, an operator would answer as if you were calling during business hours, because, for Skadden, you were. At the entrance to the library in the New York office stood an American eagle (a century-old copper cast covered by gold leaf, from a firehouse in Glens Falls, New York). Like some casinos in Las Vegas, Skadden's library had no doors to seal off its entry because it was never closed.

A primary element of Skadden's strategy for success in legal practice was time. What legal work the firm couldn't do more efficiently than others, it still attempted to complete sooner by wasting less time on other parts of office life. To make the lot of Skadden lawyers surpassingly productive, the firm treated almost every detail of its operations as a target for refinement.

The firm's interoffice directory, updated and reprinted monthly, included an international time chart to ease communication between the branches (for example, "From: NY, BOS., TOR., WASH. & WILM., To: London + 5 hours, Paris + 6 hours, Hong Kong + 13 hours, Tokyo + 14 hours, Sydney + 16 hours"). It also held numbers for reaching most people employed by the firm, no matter where in the world, by telephone, fax, cable, telex, or TWX.

In the library, the firm stocked fresh pads and sharpened pencils in lawyer's carrels, but they were not meant for copying passages from law books. Post-it notepads were handy, so lawyers could mark the pages they wanted photocopied and conserve their time for lawyer's work. Messengers were available around the clock to do the photocopying. If a lawyer wanted a fresh version of something he was drafting, word processors were always on call.

It was possible for Skadden lawyers in New York to spend whole weeks without straying far from their desks. When they arrived in the morning, slips for ordering food hung on their office doors, as in hotels, and the firm kitchen, run by the restaurant chain Trusthouse Forte, provided meals (breakfast, lunch, snacks) that could be delivered to a lawyer's office from early morning until midafternoon. As a Skadden dining room at lunchtime, the firm took over Michael's Pub, a restaurant in the lobby of its building, which was open to the public in the evening as a jazz spot.

For lawyers who wanted to exercise, the firm maintained its own fitness and training center, run by twelve professional trainers and equipped with Stair-Masters, Tunturi exercise bikes, and other high-tech machines. (The firm had similar centers in Washington, D.C., Chicago, and Los Angeles.) Lawyers who left their gym bags at home sometimes sent a Dial-a-car to get them. The fitness center recommended that lawyers keep a pair of exercise shoes there. If male lawyers were willing to exercise without shoes, they didn't have to bother with Dial-a-car, because the fitness center supplied fresh T-shirts, shorts, jocks, and socks. (Skadden women chose to supply their own gear.)

For lawyers who needed a change of business clothes, messengers regularly picked up suits and dresses at cleaners that didn't deliver. An independent contractor who could be reached through a paging system at the firm and who worked full-time at Skadden shined shoes at the office, by appointment. The firm rented apartments in buildings nearby, so lawyers in town from other Skadden offices had alternatives to a hotel. Skadden represented the American idea of the Japanization of the law firm. It took care of lawyers twenty-four hours a day, to free up their time for work. For partners who didn't have time to oversee their investments, the firm set up a program that bought into eight to fifteen deals a year, in real estate, oil and gas, and so on. It was called Project Capital.

Contrary to lore at some law schools, Skadden didn't have a floor in its Manhattan offices set aside as a dormitory. While firm lawyers sometimes told recruits that the firm supplied rollaway beds or futons to lawyers pulling all-nighters, Skadden officials said that was a joke. Pulling an all-nighter was a common Skadden phrase and habit, but Skadden employees who needed a nap had to find quiet spots around the firm —often under tables in conference rooms not being used. It was difficult to find tranquillity, because the firm's paging system was audible throughout the firm, not only in the offices of lawyers but in hallways, in the library, and elsewhere. It regularly summoned associates and partners to phone in.

To all employees, Skadden offered the free counsel of psychiatrists, social workers, and other professionals at an agency that specialized in dealing with personal problems. They were not meant primarily to counsel the employees; the idea was for the agency to step in on behalf of a Skadden lawyer or staffer and help quiet a crisis that would otherwise distract him or her from work (the employee's brother had a drug problem, or her mother was diagnosed as suffering from Alzheimer's disease).

In most instances, Skadden employees used the service confidentially; for billing purposes, the firm knew how many were using it, not who. In other cases, if as a result of a crisis an employee's performance slipped or he missed a lot of work, the firm asked him to call the agency. The agency was told to expect him to call and to report back if he did. Skadden offered this counsel through each of its American offices.

The firm also offered three kinds of help with child care: a referral service, for employees who needed a short-term substitute for a regular caretaker; an emergency dropoff center, which Skadden set up with six other law firms at a YWCA nearby, for employees who had no alternative for a day or two; and emergency assistance, or care at home, for up to several days, which the firm set up with six other companies.

Other firm benefits included: a family leave policy; life, medical, and disability insurance; a retirement policy; a tax-deferred savings plan; a matching gifts program for donations to law schools; reimbursement of fees for bar examinations, bar-review courses, bar-association memberships, and continuing legal education programs; and a start-up bonus for associates ($5,000 in 1990), which many used to buy a corporate wardrobe. In 1990, salaries ranged from $85,000 for first-year associates to $178,000 for seventh-year associates, including bonuses, according to the *New York Law Journal*.

The firm gave four weeks of paid vacation annually, although some Skadden associates were not well acquainted with the concept of vacation. They had to be ordered to take time off when, after a binge of work, their productivity fell. The firm also supplied a personal computer to each lawyer who wanted one, for drafting and research. Lexis is one of the leading computerized legal-research services. Skadden was an early subscriber and the first firm to which Lexis supplied terminals free of charge, because it counted on getting paid well through hourly charges. In its use of Lexis, Skadden ranked first among American law firms.

In New York, Skadden employed approximately fifteen hundred support staff members, and posted an average of fifty new jobs a week. It sometimes appeared to be an experiment in social engineering, geared to rewarding self-improvement with upward mobility. For employees with no previous experience in an office, like some of its messengers coming out of high school, from a fast-food job, or off the streets, Skadden ran a seminar to introduce them to the work force. The curriculum taught what was expected on the job, like showing up neatly dressed and on time, and gave tips on how to succeed. When entry-level workers proved themselves, they could transfer to other posts in the firm.

The most difficult members of the staff to hire were qualified secretaries. (The Skadden office in New York employed about four hundred.) The firm recruited at community colleges throughout the New York area and offered internships to introduce potential secretaries to the firm and vice versa. Skadden's training sessions for secretaries covered the firm's specialties, so they could understand its business. Secretaries who didn't like working directly with Skadden lawyers, because they yelled or swore or were grating (as a supervisor told me), sometimes transferred to the word-processing pool, which employed approximately two hundred people. From word processing, they could become operators of telecommunications and other equipment. The support staff's model of upward mobility was Anthony Arbisi, who came to the firm as a temporary secretary in 1958 (he had recently learned to use a stenotype machine so he could become a court reporter, and was waiting for an opening), worked for eight years as Joe Flom's secretary, and eventually became Skadden's director of administration.

The New York office maintained four shifts of legal assistants for Skadden lawyers: day; evening; late night; and cleanup, in the early morning. (Skadden employed more legal assistants than any other law firm, and in 1989 the assistants throughout the firm accounted for billings of $30 million.) At night, calls to the dispatch desk for legal assistants were generally urgent, like calls to 911.

Sometimes they were for food. Relying on comments about takeout restaurants compiled in a Skadden notebook, "Chez Nous," lawyers ordered out and sent an assistant in a Dial-a-car to pick up the meal. Calls were usually for help in proofreading a document or shepherding it through word processing, photocopying, binding, mailing, and delivery. Midnight calls for help were common. When the shift's complement of assistants was spoken for (normally around thirty-five were on duty), the dispatcher contacted an assistant (each carried a beeper) and asked if he or she could move to another job.

A typical job for a night para, as night assistants called themselves, modifying the old term paralegal, was to help get a document delivered to a corporate board meeting the next morning. Skadden regularly used Federal Express as most people did the U.S. mail, when there was no rush; it used specialized couriers as others did Federal Express, when there *was* a rush, such as when the document was done at midnight, ready for pickup at 4 a.m., and due by nine in Washington, D.C.; and it had legal assistants travel by commercial airliner, and sometimes by private charter, as others used specialized couriers, when the need was critical, such as when the document was done at 7 a.m. and due in Washington by nine. Assistants who had been caught up short by the delay of a plane learned to cover themselves. They sent a document by two means simultaneously and, on at least one occasion when papers were indispensable, by plane, helicopter, train, and car all at once.

The night paras referred to demanding shifts as Jamaican Independence Days, after what they had heard were especially rough ones for police officers in New York City. On those, lawyers would stub out cigars on documents that were being prepared for delivery. Or they would drive underlings so hard to meet a deadline that someone (man or woman) would end up sobbing in the crepuscular hours before morning.

For some night paras, the flexibility and financial stability they found at Skadden was the day job that let them pursue other interests. One supervisor, who received a salary and benefits for three ten-hour shifts a week, was a writer and the executive secretary of the Bibliographical Society of America. Her pool of one hundred sixty or so assistants and proofreaders included actors, directors, playwrights, authors, painters, and musicians. Would-be paras sometimes heard about the firm on the performers' grapevine. To apply for work, they sent their résumés and photos of their faces, called head shots, as if they were auditioning for a show.

The youngest was twenty-one, the oldest fortyish, and the average age twenty-eight. One was a lawyer who hadn't liked the pressure of practicing. As a result of a book he co-authored about the Oscars, he annually took off a few days during the week of the Academy Awards to be on call for the media, like *The Oprah Winfrey Show*. Others were writers of children's books, food books, novels, screenplays, and episodes of *Sesame Street*.

An author of detective stories got ideas from Skadden security guards, who were ex-New York City policemen. Assistants on the active roster had starred on Broadway, off-Broadway, and in regional theater as far away as California. They had appeared in Hollywood movies and on TV soaps. They had danced with the Martha Graham Company and shown sculpture in New York galleries. One regularly played the saxophone in jazz spots around Manhattan.

For the daytime legal assistants, who were usually recent college graduates more intent on progressing in a career than in the arts, the starting salary in 1990 was $22,000 a year. With overtime, assistants often doubled their income (assistants sometimes put in a hundred hours per week). Paying them good money had previously backfired for the firm, because assistants would join Skadden for six to nine months, work as much as possible, and quit to goof off before going to law school or somewhere else. To address the problem of losing assistants just when they had learned the job, Skadden devised a legal internship in 1987. It provided incentives for assistants to stay at the firm and for the ones who left for law school to consider working there later as lawyers.

The program guaranteed an assistant one thousand dollars toward his law school tuition if he stayed at the firm for a year; half the tuition for his second year of law school if he applied to work at the firm as a summer associate after the first year of law school, met the firm's standards, and took the job; and two-thirds of the tuition for the third year of law school if he was asked to work at the firm after graduation and accepted the offer. The guarantees were better for an assistant who stayed for twenty-two months. If he returned as a summer associate and then as a permanent one, he could expect to make at least $40,000 a year as an assistant and the firm to pay all but two-ninths of his full law school tuition.

For assistants contemplating law school, Skadden also sponsored a course to prepare them for the law school aptitude test and reimbursed them for courses they took on the outside. Some first-year assistants reasoned that it wasn't in their long-term economic interest to stay for a second year because, for income and tuition worth perhaps $60,000, they would postpone for a year the chance to make $85,000 as a starting associate at the firm. They called this kind of analysis Skadden thinking. As of 1990, a dozen Skadden associates had come through the interns program.

The firm's large size increased the likelihood of its diversity, but diversity gave a texture to Skadden's scale that was matched by its aura of enterprise and opportunity. Skadden partners had left the firm to run investment banks, to serve as state and federal judges, to direct the Internal Revenue Service, and to retire early, but through 1990, lawyers there said regularly, no partner had left to practice law with another firm. At the highest reaches of the legal profession, Skadden was the firm against which others were most often measured—with envy or curiosity, on one hand, and disdain, on the other. Its Olympian features seemed to be etched out of a deep layer of inevitability.

Culture

10

The Bar's Race to the Bottom

Joe Flom said recently that he valued most the integrity, as well as the imagination and technical competence, of Skadden lawyers. At the funeral of Les Arps, in 1987, Jim Freund told the many who were assembled that if even a hint of scandal about Skadden had surfaced in the years when it was challenging established Wall Street firms, it never would have recovered. Some lawyers who are familiar with the history of Skadden would treat these statements as self-serving palaver. The firm's rise was in fact accompanied by periodic questions about its practices.

Sometimes, after dealing with Skadden on a matter, lawyers singled out the firm by name for obloquy. According to the senior partner of one Wall Street firm, Skadden was thought to operate by a code different from that of the more established firms: "I remember getting a call from a crusty investment banker. They called up and said, 'Our client is going after someone else. We want you to represent us. We know you'd rather represent the company, but we're bringing Flom in for that. We feel we need a sewer rat—someone who will fight dirty and win at any cost.' "

Sometimes questions were directed at Skadden because of the firm's association with takeovers, that unpopular method of merger. In 1974, for example, William L. Cary, an authority on corporate law and a professor at Columbia Law School, chastised the entire bar for its part in corporate takeovers, in a speech at the New York City bar association. Although he didn't name the firm specifically, it was impossible to exclude Skadden from his sights. He observed that takeover lawyers seemed "to countenance any means to justify the ends" and that "the standards of brokers" appeared to be "higher" than those of lawyers. He asked sadly, "Are we never shocked?"

Louis Auchincloss explained to me, "Originally in the bar, you brought a lawsuit to right a wrong or to collect a sum of money owed to you. That changed with takeovers. One of the techniques used was to bring harassing suits. On the surface, the purpose was to right some wrong, but the real purpose of the suits was obviously harassment. It's like laying down a barrage of artillery. The purpose is to force a target to the point of conciliation or surrender."

To Auchincloss, in the 1960s the overall standards of Wall Street legal practice began a dramatic slide that was directly traceable to takeovers. The decline was the fault of Skadden, the pioneer in takeovers, he charged, as well as of the old-line firms that belatedly competed with it. He commented to the *American Bar Association Journal* in 1990: "That all the finest firms [now bring takeover suits] is the single most corrosive factor in the ethics of the bar."

Skadden is hardly surprised by this kind of criticism, general or specific. When I told Joe Flom that he had been called a sewer rat, he replied, "I can live with that." But Skadden and its critics fit into a large, complex story, which explains why both can lay claim to being in the right.

Since the 1970s, the organized American bar has experienced a crisis of confidence about the purpose and character of its members. The sense of crisis has been reinforced by habitual criticism from the press and the public that often amounts to automatic lawyer bashing.

The most prominent statement of the bar's alarm appeared in a 1986 report called ". . . In the Spirit of Public Service: A Blueprint for the Rekindling of Lawyer Professionalism," prepared by a commission of the American Bar Association. In its exploration of the question "Has our profession abandoned principle for profit, professionalism for commercialism?" the commission made plain that, in its view, the character of American lawyering had never been more strained.

Lawyers and nonlawyers alike tend to believe that the profession's problems reverberate far outside the legal world, and it is indisputable that the reach of American law is extensive. Because of its unique foundation in law, the United States has long depended on lawyers to an extraordinary degree. It seems to be the ABA's conviction that the Republic's well-being is closely linked to that of the legal world.

In practical terms, the United States has more lawyers than any other country (it has somewhere between one-quarter and one-third of the world's total, by a respected tally), and as a share of the population, more lawyers by far. Lawrence Friedman wrote in *A History of American Law* that, since the nineteenth century, lawyers in the United States have been "exceedingly nimble at finding new kinds of work and new functions." Lawyers fill roles in this country's business, finance, and government that they do abroad to a far less significant degree.

Lawyers have often been cast as American heroes. The country's pantheon includes lawyers (Thomas Jefferson, Abraham Lincoln, Franklin Roosevelt), and the profession's luminaries include lawyers whose significance transcends their legal role (Daniel Webster, Clarence Darrow, Thurgood Marshall). Stories about lawyers' triumphs are part of national lore, illustrating American qualities of power and moral purpose.

Yet, while lawyers are undeniably integral to the country's life, the reputation of the bar has never been as fine as some lawyers like to believe. Even at high points it was shadowed by ambivalence. Scorn has sometimes eclipsed respect for lawyers from the country's earliest days, and the country has had periods of great prosperity and strength when lawyers have been held in low esteem.

There were thirty-three lawyers among the fifty-five members of the convention that wrote America's Constitution and, with religious ministers, they are generally given credit for midwifing the birth of the nation. But, according to the historian Perry Miller, legal practice was unorganized then (there were no American law books and no reports of legal precedents), and hostility to lawyers and to the very idea of law was deep-rooted in the former colonies, as it had been in England.

In a significant feat, lawyers largely overcame these obstacles and achieved social sway within two generations of the first major European settlements. As Robert Ferguson, a professor of English at Columbia

University, documented in *Law and Letters in American Culture*, lawyers drew on their legal training to help animate and order the nation "in a seemingly endless stream of words instructing and strengthening the American people in the meaning of republicanism."

By Ferguson's account, lawyers drew broadly on the range of Western knowledge to lead people in the task of self-governance and did much to create the country's distinct civilization. The best of them led model lives of conscience and engagement, as lawyer-statesmen. Robert Gordon, of Stanford Law School, defined the model as "the independent citizen, the uncorrupted just man of learning combined with practical wisdom." Recently he commented that the model "has been since so completely eclipsed that it now seems almost a joke."

In the nineteenth century, the bar's dominance was greeted by widespread distrust, which Alexis de Tocqueville—known for describing the leadership of lawyers during the 1830s as an aristocratic calling—was in his own time criticized for overlooking. The kind of justice provided by an increasingly technical legal system was suspected to be a betrayal of morality. The vision of the bar as a dignified vocation was also befogged by an abundance of stories describing legal chicanery.

"The American lawyer was never primarily a learned doctor of laws," Lawrence Friedman judged, "he was a man of action and cunning." In the mid-nineteenth century, formal constraints on lawyers were minimal. There were no grievance committees with which to file complaints against lawyers because there was no organized bar. "[A] lawyer could do pretty nearly anything he wanted," wrote the historian George W. Alger. "Most of them did."

The first major American bar group, the Association of the Bar of the City of New York, was formed in 1870 expressly to reform the practices of lawyers and to refurbish their honor in the wake of damaging scandals caused by corruption in New York City and by an epic struggle to control the nation's railroads—the first corporate takeovers. For a generation, Tammany Hall and its Irish Democrats had controlled city hall and local judges ("a community worse governed by lower and baser blackguard scum than any other city in Western Christendom," wrote a contemporary lawyer and diarist named George Templeton Strong).

After the Civil War, well-known lawyers joined with famous speculators like Jim Fisk and Jay Gould to bribe legislators, improperly influence judges, and otherwise abuse the legal process in order to gain advantage in the consolidation of the nation's railroads. These outrages threatened the legitimacy of the law itself. They propelled the leadership of the bar to self-healing reform.

The effort culminated in 1908 with the passage by the American Bar Association of the first national code of conduct for American lawyers. (The ABA was then thirty years old and had been founded mainly to organize summer outings for members at Saratoga Springs, New York. Its thirty-seven hundred members comprised about 3 percent of the lawyers in the United States.)

The code was grandiloquent and often unenforceably vague, yet it expressed the essential challenge that lawyers set for themselves as officiants of a kind of secular religion. "Above all," declared a typical canon, or pronouncement, "a lawyer will find his highest honor in a deserved reputation for fidelity to private trust and to public duty, as an honest man and as a patriotic and loyal citizen." To Stephen Gillers, a professor at New York University Law School and an expert in legal ethics, the most important question about the legal profession since the code was composed and issued has been "the proper point of reconciliation" between the lawyer's duty to his client and his obligation to serve the public, addressed by this canon.

It is now generally agreed by observers of the legal profession that the main influences on lawyers when they make this reconciliation are what they learn from lawyers they practice with, in the same office or in similar circumstances, and the expectations they glean from the legal culture, expressed most obviously in talk among lawyers, in the legal press, and in directives from the bar about the duties of the profession.

But the 1908 code paid scant attention to how lawyers should deal with each other within firms and in daily practice. The duties that the code stressed were loyalty, confidentiality, and candor. The first and second a lawyer owed to his clients. The third he owed to courts, which lawyers served as officers. The code's thirty-two canons concentrated primarily on relations between lawyers in the courtroom.

The code was based, however, on one written in Alabama in 1887, which, in turn, was derived from a series of lectures given by a Mississippi judge, George Sharswood, in 1854. Sharswood emphasized the benefits of legal fraternity, and admonished that a lawyer should "never unnecessarily have a personal difficulty with a professional brother," should "never give nor provoke insult," and should "shun most carefully the reputation of a sharp practitioner." The canons assumed that lawyers knew what was proper, and that they would act accordingly. From the outset, observed Charles Wolfram, a professor at Cornell Law School, they were seriously dated and widely ignored.

On the other hand, the code's very existence suggested that the organized bar had acquired the traits of a profession, both laudable and less so. Lawyers made their own rules, required new members to have training that they prescribed, and practiced free of direction from the government. Through an unspoken social contract—lawyers were granted the privilege of self-regulation in exchange for worthy service to clients and the public—they had a special role in American life.

Like other professional organizations that coalesced in the late nineteenth century, the American Bar Association and state bar groups were dedicated in part to defining and to maintaining the social standing of their members. Besides the evident advantages to members, there was another practical motive: The groups equipped lawyers to bestow social acceptance on clients, too, to their mutual benefit.

There is now no serious dispute that, in the period before the First World War, rules about membership in some bars and about the group's operations were designed to play on fear of foreigners and to prevent newcomers from practicing law or, if they gained entry to the profession, to limit their practice to clients from their own kind. As Jerold Auerbach documented in his study *Unequal Justice*, many of those who suffered directly from the exclusion were Catholics and Jews.

The closed quality of the American bar did not immunize it against public disapproval. During the middle years of this century, as the sociologist Rayman Solomon wrote, the bar was regularly criticized. Prohibition-era lawyers were blamed for the spread of bootlegging and related crimes. Depression-era lawyers were accused of abandoning all but the wealthy. The bar's opposition to proposals for independent regulatory agencies during the New Deal led to charges that it was partisan and aligned with big corporations. The low point for the reputation of lawyers may have come in the late forties and early fifties, with the American Bar Association's sustained leadership in the national witch hunt for Communists, extending far outside the legal world.

The blame leveled at lawyers during those decades substantiated a famous piece of criticism made in 1934 by Harlan Fiske Stone, whose experience as a former dean of Columbia Law School, a onetime lawyer at Sullivan & Cromwell, and a sitting Supreme Court Justice gave his words special weight. He observed that, by focusing on "petty details of form and manners," the bar missed the larger issue on which a code of ethics should focus: how the profession's "activities affect the welfare of society as a whole."

Lawyers have long been on the defensive against the charge that the practice of law has been debased by commerce, and that business lawyers in particular have tended to their clients' interests at the expense of the public's. The accusation was first made extensively at the end of the nineteenth century and has been voiced regularly almost ever since. Lawyers soon adopted this criticism as the focal point of their own self-examination.

In 1905, for example, Louis Brandeis gave a talk to the Harvard Ethics Society which became a classic article called "The Opportunity in the Law." In it, he wrote: "Lawyers are now to a greater extent than formerly business men, a part of the great organized system of industrial and financial enterprise. They are less than formerly the students of a particular kind of learning, the practitioners of a particular art. And they do not seem to be so much of a distinct professional class."

Brandeis's analysis revived and sharpened a theme that had already been developing in the nineteenth century. He charged: "Instead of holding a position of independence, between the wealthy and the people, prepared to curb the excesses of either, lawyers have, to a large extent, allowed themselves to become adjuncts of great corporations and have neglected the obligation to use their powers for the protection of the people." As a devout progressive, Brandeis believed that the "public interest" could be identified and that, through the ethical practice of law, as well as through efforts to improve the mechanisms of the legal system and of government, lawyers had a duty to pursue the public interest as independent professionals.

Brandeis was seriously chastised for his point of view. In 1916, his nomination to the Supreme Court was opposed by seven past presidents of the American Bar Association, among others. One reason given for the opposition was that, although an extraordinarily successful corporate lawyer in Boston, he did not "act according to the canons" of the bar. An opponent complained to the U.S. Senate: "The trouble with Mr. Brandeis is that . . . he always acts the part of a judge toward his clients, instead of being his client's lawyer, which is against the practices of the Bar." Nonetheless, he was confirmed as a Justice.

Other members of the American establishment concurred with Brandeis's reproachful views about the bar:

"Lawyers have been sucked into the maelstrom of the new business system of the country," President Woodrow Wilson declared a few years later. "They do not concern themselves with the universal aspects of society."

Judge Learned Hand, of Manhattan, commented in 1925: ". . . in my own city the best minds of the profession are scarcely lawyers at all. They may be something much better, or much worse; but they are not that."

In 1932, Justice Harlan Fiske Stone observed: "Steadily the best skill and capacity of the profession has been drawn into the exacting and highly specialized service of business and finance. At its best the changed system has brought to the command of the business world loyalty and a superb proficiency and technical skill. At its worst it has made the learned profession of an earlier day the obsequious servant of business, and tainted it with the morals and manners of the market place in its most anti-social manifestations."

Geoffrey Hazard, a professor at Yale Law School, recently suggested that the long-standing discomfort about the ties between lawyers and business spring from anxiety about the bar's primary role—in his words, "to aid the development and protection of business property within a political system committed to both popular government and constitutional restraints on government." The aristocratic position of lawyers recognized by Tocqueville derives from more than class, learning, or power. To Hazard, its roots lie in a "distinct, constitutionally based role in the governance of the community at large."

For a century, the bar's primary role (by Hazard's definition) has been filled most strikingly by lawyers gathered in the largest law firms. These firms became a special target of rebuke as legal practice transformed itself in the past generation. In 1989, in a book called *Rascals: The Selling of the Legal Profession*, Peter Brown, who was once a partner in a large Wall Street firm, stated the case against such firms in particularly harsh terms.

To Brown, the bar has become blemished by "crime, perfidy, greed, and sloth" and "many lawyers" treat the practice "as a trade solely for profit rather than as a profession for service to the public interest." Many of "the greedy ones" are "found practicing in the large law firms," which promote "selfishness" among their partners, the "oppression and abuse" of their associates, and a general decline of "manners and morals."

Brown didn't pinpoint all of what he sees as the sources of these problems, but a major one, by his lights, was "severe, economic pressures"—on "self-serving and gross" firms led by "new barbarians," as well as on smaller, less savage firms. To him, the impact of all this has been more dramatic than what Brandeis and others described in the first decades of this century: The bar is "spinning out of control" and the consequences for the bar and American civilization are dire. Brown suggested that the impact of the bar's current downward spiral could be like that of the decline of lawyers during the fall of the Roman Empire. He quoted Gibbon: "The ordinary promotion of lawyers was pregnant with mischief and disgrace."

The prominence of very large (or mega-) firms has itself caused changes in the practice of law, and has led lawyers to contemplate and confront a range of related issues, including: what it's like to work in those firms; how well they train young lawyers; the quality of the work they do; and the value of that work to clients and to society. The theme often tying such topics together is the challenge posed by intense economic competition to broad principles of professional responsibility.

The belief is widespread that competition among large firms has increased tensions between the goals of worldly success and of social purpose among lawyers, between the goals of completing a project on a tight schedule and of doing first-rate work, and between the goals of doing work because a client hires a firm to do it and of seeking assignments that are meaningful and productive. The overarching tension lies between the dictates of the market and the duties of the profession— described in terms of how lawyers do their work, and what they do in the community besides providing legal services for a fee.

The large-firm critique goes like this: In these firms, more purely than in any other institution where legal work is the main occupation, the overriding goal is to make money. As competition has intensified among them, firms have put increasing pressure on partners and associates to bill long hours and to reduce the time they spend on matters that might be a distraction from the most profitable work. The growth in the size of law firms has made them increasingly like corporations, and has further reduced their sense of intimacy and common purpose.

As a result, large firms are more stressful to work at than they were a generation ago. The pressures of competition have reduced the amount of time available for experienced lawyers to train junior ones, and to help inculcate values of professional responsibility. Through force of circumstance, lawyers are less often counselors than hired guns, less often fiduciaries than mouthpieces. The pressures have also made individuals at large firms more likely to commit improprieties—the evidence being scandals, which were previously rare, at many Wall Street firms and common reports of intimidation, distortion, lying, and other forms of unacceptable behavior in their lawyers' work.

Lawyers have attempted to counterbalance such problems by giving time to public projects, in the form of pro bono work, but they have less time to offer now than a generation ago. It is generally estimated that well over half of all American lawyers devote no sustained time to pro bono work. Lawyers who do must measure what the projects cost their firms and themselves in the cold hard numbers of forsaken billings and income. More broadly, the growth of large firms has in the past generation increased their demand for recent law school graduates and decreased the supply of lawyers available for public-interest jobs.

The high and rapidly increasing level of salaries offered by large firms compared to the level of salaries available in public-interest jobs since the early 1970s has aggravated this imbalance, as has the steady climb in the cost of legal education. Some who might work in public-interest jobs instead go to large private firms to help pay off their large debts to colleges and law schools. The number of public-interest jobs for which lawyers were paid declined sharply between the seventies and eighties, although the trend appears to have reversed in the early nineties.

The premise of this analysis is that economic pressures on lawyers at large firms have undermined their professional ethics and that the year 1970, which saw dramatic growth in America's largest firms, marked the beginning of the current ungenteel era. Anthony Kronman, a professor at Yale Law School, asserts that the times are distinguished by the disappearance of the lawyer-statesman, who represented the Brandeisian ideal, and warns that the American bar "now stands in danger of losing its soul."

Lawyers have actually spent a century falling short of the ideal of a noble profession, at least as it is popularly understood. The size of the gap between the profession as an occupation (requiring special training, knowledge, and intellectual skill for the representation of clients) and the profession as a calling (with the promise of public service) has varied over time, but it has never been narrow enough for lawyers in the established bar to claim the purity of commitment of some professionals, like old-fashioned family doctors or ministers. For commercial lawyers at least, the practical standard that has long governed major firms boils down to this: The profession they are in is a business distinguished by a sense of civic duty, not a vocation that happens to yield a profit.

While recent economic pressures may also have further undermined lawyers' ethics, the view is not entirely right. The world of legal ethics embarked on a sea change before 1970, and the tide of change has since developed its own momentum. The first of the series of Supreme Court decisions that reshaped the practice of law, in 1964, and the American Bar Association's adoption of a new code of conduct, in 1970, had already helped open up legal practice to the forces of law and the market as never before. Shifts in the rules of ethics for lawyers also invited changes in the economic pressures attendant upon the practice of law.

In 1977, the ABA appointed a commission to study and rewrite its ethics code. It began what the legal scholar Theodore Schneyer called "the most sustained and democratic debate about professional ethics in the history of the American bar." The commission was headed by Robert Kutak, a practicing lawyer from Omaha, Nebraska, who was a visionary to allies, a radical to adversaries, and a reformer to all.

An early version of the commission's proposals was drafted boldly to include rules that would apply to subjects of wide interest to the public and to lawyers: a requirement that every lawyer give forty hours a year of free legal service, as a general contribution to the American system of justice; a requirement that lawyers disclose any perjury or misrepresentation of facts by their clients, as a contribution to finding the truth in court proceedings; and a requirement, called the whistle blower's proposal, that lawyers disclose any information that could keep a client from seriously injuring someone else.

These and other recommendations proved highly controversial. The Association of the Trial Lawyers of America, for example, a group whose members generally represent plaintiffs in civil suits for damages, drafted a counterproposal that, in effect, required lawyers to allow clients to lie in court. It asserted that lawyers had always to maintain the confidences of clients, without exception and without fail.

In 1983, after considering the proposals made by the Kutak Commission and subsequent criticism, the ABA adopted a second modern code, called the Model Rules of Professional Conduct. These model rules were written to finesse the controversy stirred by the early draft and to quiet the concerns of the many bar associations, representing different states and specialties, that had opposed it. The pro bono, disclosure, and whistle blower's recommendations did not appear in the final rules. The rules' statutory nature—and in fact their very identification as rules instead of a code—confirmed the bar's passage from an organization defined by tradition, whose character as a profession was said to derive from its own virtue, to one shaped by expediency.

Charles Wolfram observed that in both the 1970 code and the 1983 revisions "little is required of lawyers that is not already required by other law," and that "many provisions" of both codes are obviously "imprecise." In partial excuse he noted: "Drafting is inherently a process of finding the lowest common denominator." But to him, the bar's efforts reached bottom in 1983: "It seems apparent, after three-quarters of a century, that the A.B.A. no longer has the capacity to generate a single set of standards of lawyer conduct that lawyers will generally accept."

Each state was entitled to adopt its own version of these suggested rules. Thirty-five states adopted the model rules in some form, making them the major source of standards for most American lawyers. But even where accepted in full, the model rules were only one of many codes establishing standards for lawyers. In addition, there were special codes for arbitrators, criminal lawyers, divorce lawyers, government lawyers, judges, mediators, trial lawyers, and so on, developed by their own professional subgroups. The proliferation of codes underscored the variety of preoccupations concerning lawyers with different practices and the wide range of views about legal ethics among lawyers—"ethical pluralism," Theodore Schneyer called it.

Lawyers heard a cacophony of opinions about how they should practice. With ambiguities in the model rules and competing standards proposed by other codes, practitioners looked increasingly to the courts and to other institutions to resolve the contradictions. The bar's new susceptibility to law, apart from its own code, was confirmed by a rise in the number of lawsuits filed by clients against lawyers and by an increase in sanctions imposed by judges and other authorities against lawyers.

To those outside the legal world, the bar's attention to the process of self-regulation, through the fresh articulation of its rules of practice, commitments to better enforcement, and other means suggested welcome attention to an earnest need. To a large degree, the perception was correct. But well-informed observers of the bar contend that the apparent improvements in the process were wrapped around a hollow core.

The American system of justice relies on a basic and perhaps obvious tenet, that a lawyer should not be held responsible for the actions of his client—"a principle of non-accountability," in the words of the legal scholar Murray Schwartz. In addition to the unfairness of holding a lawyer vicariously liable for the actions of his client (especially before he became a client), the theory is that a lawyer couldn't be a fully reliable advocate if he was held morally accountable; the lawyer's personal beliefs might constrict his advocacy and prevent a client from receiving his due under the law.

When nonlawyers ask how a criminal lawyer can defend a drug dealer or a vicious killer, the accepted answer is that when representing a generally repugnant defendant, a lawyer upholds the ideal that everyone is innocent until proven guilty in a court of law, under the U.S. Constitution. Justice most regularly emerges from legal encounters in which the parties on opposing sides are both vigorously represented. This is the premise of our adversary system.

The lawyer can serve these ideals because he is not punished for his client's past acts. American legal ethics permit a lawyer to refuse to take on a prospective client on certain moral and other limited grounds. But once a lawyer takes a case, he becomes bound by a duty of zealous advocacy. Even for a client he detests, a lawyer is obligated to give his all.

To some lawyers, there is no compromising the devotion owed to a client. Lawyers serve the public interest best, they maintain, by representing clients with total commitment. The classic statement of this view was made by Lord Henry Brougham in 1820: "An advocate, in the discharge of his duty, knows but one person in all the world, and that person is his client."

Few lawyers think much about this logic day-to-day, but when they contemplate it, many routinely apply it to the full spectrum of lawyering jobs. For them, the standard of zealous advocacy reaches civil litigation as well as criminal work, and, in some instances, counseling in business deals as fully as in civil litigation.

If lawyers set variable limits on the extent to which they were willing to represent their clients' interests, the measure of what advocacy a client should expect would be too vulnerable to a lawyer's personal judgment and unhinged from any objective standard. And many clients see their civil matters (a divorce; a libel suit; a sizable business affair) as plainly suitable for the most energetic and aggressive advocacy.

Robert Gordon summarized the tenets of the model like this: "Lawyers should not commit crimes or help clients to plan crimes. They should obey only such ethical instructions as are clearly expressed in rules and ignore vague standards. Finally, they should not tell outright lies to judges or fabricate evidence. Otherwise they may, and if it will serve their clients' interests must, exploit any gap, ambiguity, technicality, or loophole, any not-obviously-and-totally-implausible interpretation of the law or facts."

The broad application of the duty of zealous advocacy has been seriously questioned. David Luban of the University of Maryland, Deborah Rhode of Stanford Law School, and others contend that it has received too much weight as a standard by which to judge lawyers' conduct. They argue that the principle of partisanship that animates it is in fact appropriate only for the fraction of legal work that they see as truly adversarial, and maintain that much else involves counseling that should be conciliatory.

Even in adversarial cases destined for court, they continue, unrestrainedly zealous advocacy is only sometimes justified as a standard. Created to encourage vigorous representation of the criminal defendant, the goal was to counterbalance the power and disproportionate resources of the government as prosecutor. It was meant to give substance to the presumption of innocence.

But in civil cases, the standard can be effective only if both sides have equal resources and are served by lawyers with similar abilities. In many instances, that prerequisite is notably absent. Empowered by the standard of zealous advocacy to use disproportionate means, one side can bury the other. And even when two sides are well matched, there is no reason to believe that a fairer result emerges from a system in which opposing advocates are compelled to argue as unfairly as possible.

In addition, as David Wilkins of Harvard Law School has observed, the legal realists' view that legal rules are inexact and subject to the prejudices and power of those who apply them has come to dominate the field of legal ethics, as it has other areas in the law. In the traditional model of legal ethics, the lawyer's duty to represent a client zealously was tempered by his responsibility to do so "within the bounds of the law." It was assumed that those bounds could be adequately identified.

In the era of legal realism, however, much of the law is seen as vague and changeable, and the traditional model of legal ethics seems increasingly unsatisfactory. The duty of zealous advocacy has seemed to overwhelm lawyers' sense of responsibility to operate within legal bounds, in part because the bounds don't amount to much when the law is so variable. Even lawyers known for their care and caution feel obliged to test the limits of propriety in the name of a duty, or ethic, imposed by rules of professional responsibility. Robert Gordon: "The difficulty with such an ethic, as its critics have pointed out, is that it is a recipe for total sabotage of the legal framework. . . . The lawyer under such an ethical regime is by vocation someone who helps clients find ways around the law."

Some legal scholars have proposed a redefinition of the concept of advocacy so that, besides serving a client, a lawyer strives to fulfill obligations to society as well. Their model is Brandeis. They invoke Brandeis's "opportunity in the law" to do good for the public, and implore lawyers to use moral discretion while representing clients. The goal for a lawyer should be to fuse his duty to his client and his obligation to the public, and for the lawyer to accommodate a client's plans to the purposes of the law governing it.

In the example of a lawyer who furthers the immoral or illegal ends of a client, say, by helping him to launder money from a drug deal or to obtain permits to ship weapons to a repressive foreign government, a standard of moral discretion seems easy to apply. (Some of this kind of behavior is unethical under the old and new codes.) The lawyer has become, in effect, an accomplice of his client. If the client deserves moral blame, so does the lawyer. In these examples, the reasons for granting a morally guilty accomplice professional immunity don't hold as they would for an ex post facto advocate in court.

But calls for moral discretion rely heavily on lawyers making judgments about the nature of the public interest and of moral good that would only sometimes be as clear-cut as these. They would turn lawyers into judge- or philosopher-advocates. Compared with the longtime standard, which has lawyers serving society by playing a role in a seasoned process, the touchstones of the proposals seem too highly subjective to constitute an enforceable standard—especially in an era marked by deep, multifaceted disagreement about the common weal and "goodness." Even their proponents must regretfully acknowledge how far from the mainstream such ideas remain and present them as a mix of reason and exhortation that might lead the next generation of lawyers to practice more nobly.

In the meantime, lawyers work according to a conception of professionalism in which they define themselves primarily through their relationships to clients, not to society. "Lawyers lull the public into a view of the lawyer's role as less client-centered and as more public interest-oriented than it really is," Stephen Gillers observed. But "the client is the center of the lawyer's universe." When clients head out into the fray of the market, as those of large law firms usually do, they jostle, brawl, and scrap to stay upright, bringing their lawyers into the tumult.

When clients play a part in influencing the habits of lawyers, some observers of the legal world contend, it is rarely for the better. Professional rules have long required lawyers to defer heavily to the wishes of their clients, who are often more concerned about their case or deal than about minding their own morals or their lawyers' tactics. As scholars like Wilkins have observed, when corporations began to do much of their own routine legal work and to hire outside counsel only for unusual, often one-time transactions, they increased their control over their outside lawyers and decreased the opportunity for lawyers to know enough about a company and its business so that they could serve as true counselors.

Many lawyers feel obliged to exploit every advantage they find as advocates, including the wealth of their clients and the resources that it buys. Although the law rarely holds them responsible for their clients' actions, lawyers often come to identify strongly with clients' causes and, in large firms especially, regularly justify round-the-clock efforts as urgent client needs. This lawyering with the intensity of emergency-room medicine is done in the name of client service and professional duty.

The dilution of client loyalty may have liberated lawyers from some elements of client control. An intricate but revealing example is how some lawyers handle conflicts of interest. At large law firms, and at Skadden in particular, there has been a wholesale review of the notion of conflicts in recent years. In a common view, the basic rule—that a law firm can't represent a client if its interests are in conflict with those of another client—was formulated when a small-firm lawyer represented a family or a small company in many matters and knew much of what there was to know about his client's activities. It would have been unseemly in those circumstances for the lawyer to oppose the family or company in any matter, even if he hadn't handled anything related to it for his usual client.

Today, the argument goes, when a large corporation hires many different law firms to represent it in a range of matters, the basic rule of conflicts and some of its offshoots are vestigial. A large corporation has many interests and, as long as there is no substantive relationship between two matters, in one of which a law firm represents the company and in the other is asked to oppose it, there is no conflict. "You can understand how a guy in Peoria thinks that his lawyer is his lawyer," observed Jonathan Lerner, Skadden's main expert in legal ethics. "But for today's multinational lawyer, with multinational companies as clients, it's a different matter." Questions about conflicts are now the most common for experts in legal ethics; the group at Skadden called the ethics committee deals primarily with questions about conflicts.

But the sharpest criticism of the current large-firm approach to the subject, including at Skadden, is that it uses alleged or potential conflicts as an excuse not to take some matter because another will be more lucrative for a firm. When Skadden lost a prominent partner recently, Peter Mullen stated that the issue of economic conflicts was relevant: "He [the lawyer involved] believes that his ability to develop a practice has been hampered by the extent to which there were conflict problems or perceived conflicts, when the firm might be conflicted out of more attractive legal work"—that is, more lucrative—"if it took on a potential client who came to him." The firm had no compunction about not accepting work in order to hold itself open for business that would yield a higher return. Unbeholden to one main client, Skadden accepts and rejects potential clients in part the way banks set priorities among customers, as do other law firms.

Once engagements are begun, however, the desire and need to impress corporate clients, the instinct to guard against malpractice suits, and the urge to triumph lead many lawyers to practice by sharply aggressive standards of partisanship. They rarely run a real risk of sanction, and rarely can be charged with egregious violations of the bar's rules of conduct. Like a well-designed experiment, the prevailing imbalance of forces in legal ethics—of a duty exerting a strong impetus for action against a weakened standard of restraint—regularly leads to predictable results. One overruns the other.

The vast majority of lawyers' daily actions, outside the courtroom, are not expressly regulated by any authority. Guided generally by their professional rules, lawyers set the terms of encounters with each other as they act on behalf of clients in counseling and planning, in private dealmaking, and even in some routine aspects of litigation. Law in this sense, as it governs the activities of private parties, is made by lawyers working with, and against, other lawyers. Private encounters between lawyers, Gillers noted archly, are "consensual acts, like bribery."

If the vague, unelaborated idea of "professionalism" as self-restraint is discounted, as it has been over the past generation especially, there is little incentive for lawyers to practice by gentlemanly standards when out in the fray with their clients. ("In the American legal system," concedes a partner at a well-known firm that believes it offers a good combination of intensity, detachment, and professionalism, "being a complete asshole for your client has a high payoff.") To the contrary, while the legal culture establishes a range of tolerances for questionable deeds and there are many lawyers who are unwaveringly principled, the current ethos among many lawyers in the bar has led to a race to the bottom.

Legal ethics becomes a paradoxical element of competition among lawyers: Those who practice closest to the line without crossing seem to gain an advantage. Goaded by the market, conscientious lawyers ask whether they do their clients a disservice if they don't exploit every opening. Some legal scholars warn that any lawyers who don't reach the limit are in breach of their professional obligations.

For Skadden, the upshot of the gradual evolution of generally acceptable legal ethics has been this: The firm's critics fault it for not practicing by gentlemanly standards, and its leaders tout their firm's integrity, since it admonishes Skadden lawyers to operate within the codified rules of practice. Integrity, like opportunism, has come to have a special meaning at Skadden. The firm, like many, is now playing by pliant rules, in a system where there is no ready sanction against looking out for one's own interest first and where there is far more agreement about the mandate for serving the interest of a client than that of the public.

11

Hardball

Litigation has long been suspected of bringing out the worst in clients and their lawyers. The 1908 canons contained strong warnings against going to court to resolve disputes. Canon 8: "Whenever the controversy will admit of fair adjustment, the client should be advised to avoid or to end the litigation." Canon 28: "It is disreputable . . . to breed litigation by seeking out those with claims for personal injuries or those having any other grounds of action in order to secure them as clients. . . ." Canon 30: "The lawyer must decline to conduct a civil cause or to make a defense when convinced that it is intended merely to harass or to injure the opposite party or to work oppression or wrong. . . ."

Until the 1950s, some of the most respected American law firms showed their support for this standard by distancing themselves as far as possible from litigation. They did not have litigation departments. Sometimes they had a trial partner who took matters to court for other partners, but they often farmed out cases destined for the courthouse, or falling for other reasons in the gray areas of acceptability, to firms like Skadden, euphemistically called "specialists."

The 1970 code of conduct for lawyers retreated from the position of the 1908 canons. It was more neutral about litigation, and only prohibited lawsuits whose purpose was "to harass or maliciously injure another." In the next decade, litigation became a dominant fact of legal life. Heading to the courthouse became a norm rather than an exception. What lawyers like Louis Auchincloss considered harassment became a common form of advocacy.

In takeovers, lawsuits became a way for companies or their management to show backbone and to maintain the support of investors, to extend time for negotiation or to develop options, and to accomplish other ends. Ronald Gilson, a professor at Stanford Law School, wrote: "The tactical history of the tender offer movement resembles an unrestrained arms race," because of the escalation in aggressiveness of techniques used to try a takeover of a company or to block one. Litigation was integral to innovations dreamed up by both offense and defense.

The bar's 1983 model rules of professional conduct removed all vestiges of official disapproval of litigation. Lawsuits simply had to be lawfully accomplished. The main standard that they had to meet was that they not be "frivolous." Yet, while the pace of development in the law and the ingenuity of lawyers often allowed them to finesse even that standard, litigation regularly fell short of it.

An official interpretation of the rule stated, "Realizing financial or other benefit from otherwise improper delay in litigation is not a legitimate interest of the client." But delays in litigation were frequently used to drag out a deal precisely so that a client could realize a financial gain. Especially in takeovers, that was often the aim. According to Gilson, the rule against the practice has not been enforced.

The weakening that occurred in the ethos of litigation was duplicated in many other areas of legal practice. As takeovers contributed to litigation's increasingly adversarial quality, they also intensified the kinds of business tactics that lawyers counseled corporations to use, for effecting or thwarting various transactions.

In 1981, a federal court handed down a decision involving Joe Flom and a Skadden client that became a textbook example of the newly acceptable standards in the arena of deals and suits. It was called *Panter v. Marshall Field & Company*.

For the U.S. Court of Appeals for the Seventh Circuit, in Chicago, Judge Wilbur Pell wrote: "On several occasions in the late 1960's and continuing to the mid-1970's, [Marshall] Field's management was approached by would-be merger or takeover suitors. In 1969 Field's sought the help of Joseph H. Flom, an attorney with expertise in such matters, in determining how best to respond to the overtures of interested parties. Flom advised the board that the interest of shareholders was the paramount concern, and that management should listen to such proposals, evaluate whether the proposal was serious, and whether the proposal raised questions of antitrust violations. He also advised Field's directors and management to invest the company's reserves and use its borrowing power to acquire other stores, if such acquisitions were in accord with the sound business judgment of the board, and in the best interest of the company and its shareholders. He counseled that such acquisitions were a legal way of coping with unfriendly takeover attempts."

Flom had recommended that Field apply a "pyramid theory," which would have the company buy other stores and become too large to be acquired or acquire so much overlap with another retailing chain that the proposed new company would have antitrust problems. Judge Pell, for the majority, endorsed the tactic. A dissenting opinion by Judge Richard Cudahy pointed out that after Field hired Flom the store "made a major acquisition and/or raised antitrust problems to fight off virtually every serious merger or takeover attempt."

In 1969, for example, when Associated Dry Goods, with stores mostly in Ohio and Pennsylvania, expressed interest in acquiring Field, Field bought stores in Cleveland and Erie. In the next decade, those stores never turned a profit. In 1976, when the Dayton Hudson Corporation tried to take over Field, Field started the process of acquiring stores in Oregon and Washington that competed in the same markets as the bidder's stores, claiming that the purchases were part of a long-range plan. When the Dayton Hudson bid for Field ended, so did the company's interest in the Pacific Northwest. Their enthusiasm was revived only after one of Flom's colleagues suggested that Field acquire stores there, to "bolster our potential competition theory" against a merger with Carter Hawley Hale Stores, whose 1977 bid for Field led to the Panter suit.

In 1977, Field's stock traded at $22 per share. CHH offered $36. The Field board rejected the offer as inadequate, and two months later CHH announced plans to offer $42. Field's stock rose to $34. The board rejected the second offer, too, on the grounds that to combine the chains of stores would violate antitrust laws. After CHH dropped its offer, Field's stock fell to $19.

This series of events prompted a suit to be filed by a group of shareholders who believed that the Field board had deprived them of the chance to sell their stock at a large premium over its value in the stock market. Applying the business-judgment rule, which says that courts won't second-guess directors of corporations when they have made decisions for their company in good faith, no matter how imprudent the judgments later appear, the U.S. Court of Appeals ruled for Marshall Field.

In dissent, Judge Cudahy wrote: "I emphatically disagree that the business-judgment rule should clothe directors, battling blindly to fend off a threat to their control, with an almost irrebuttable presumption of sound business judgment, prevailing over everything but the elusive hobgoblins of fraud, bad faith, or abuse of discretion."

In its description of the key role played by Flom in charting the Field strategy, the court's majority captured the important part played by lawyers generally in advising corporate officers what actions they could risk. As long as the executives (guided by their lawyers) avoided Judge Cudahy's three hobgoblins, the business-judgment rule gave them wide latitude to be intensely combative. It gave lawyers—Flom and his law firm most explicitly—the same range to concoct tactics.

Skadden was involved in many examples of the intense combativeness that dominated in takeover fights. In 1975, Flom devised the "Jewish-dentist defense," used by a dental supply company called Sterndent to fend off a bid by a firm called Magus. The Kuwait Investment Company, a 10 percent owner of Magus, had led an attempted boycott of certain underwriters of Euromarket bonds, because they were Jewish. Magus's bid for Sterndent was defeated after Sterndent argued that its business would decline steeply if it was taken over by Magus, because many Sterndent customers were Jews who would boycott the Kuwaitis in retaliation. Only two years after the shock of large oil-price increases by Arab-controlled OPEC, Magus was made even more vulnerable to this defense by the press's identification of the Kuwaitis as Arabs.

In 1978, the Occidental Petroleum Corporation made a bid valued at almost one billion dollars for the Mead Corporation, in the paper and other forest-products businesses. This case also became a Skadden classic. Occidental's chief executive and primary stockholder, Armand Hammer, traveled to Dayton, Ohio, where the headquarters of Mead was located, to formally deliver the offer to James McSwiney, the chairman of Mead.

Hammer's autobiography recounts: "Mr. McSwiney looked at me coldly across his desk and said, 'Let it be plainly understood, Doctor Hammer, that this company is not for sale. I have nothing more to say. You will be hearing from our attorney, Mr. Joe Flom.'"

The Mead defense that Flom quarterbacked had two prongs: the first, a claim that the merger would create antitrust problems; the second, an attack on how Hammer ran his company. Occidental was a glamorous corporation whose operations were veiled in mystery. According to *The New York Times*, it was the only corporation in the Fortune 500 believed to have been investigated by the Securities and Exchange Commission as many as four times in the previous decade.

Mead relied on investigators to piece together the SEC material and to uncover other possible and proven wrongs by Occidental. The investigators reported environmental problems caused at Love Canal, near Niagara Falls, by a company that Occidental had later bought; Hammer's improper control over the corporation's board of directors, exercised by undated letters of resignation that members had signed and given the chief executive so he could fire them anytime; and an allegation that Hammer had improperly paid $100,000 to a Soviet official who aided him in collecting art.

By the *Times* account, when Mead's investigators turned to look into Hammer's art business (he controlled the Knoedler Gallery in New York), Occidental halted its takeover effort, citing "the ferocity of the Mead management opposition." According to Hammer, Occidental "took care of" the allegations that Flom assembled, but no "acquisition was worth this battery of problems." Hammer on Flom, in his autobiography: "It is a great comfort to have Joe on your side and a sore distress to have him against you."

Flom and his colleagues treated Occidental's official explanation of its withdrawal as high praise. T-shirts for the Mead team were made up with "FEROCITY CREW" printed on them. Not long after, Hammer hired Flom to represent his company in other matters (he had previously used Flom once), and the two became fast friends.

A third Skadden classic was minted three years later. In 1981, as James B. Stewart, Jr., reported in *The American Lawyer*, a lawyer and investor named Samuel Heyman bought about 5 percent of the stock in the GAF Corporation, which made photographic supplies and other products.

GAF's longtime chairman, Jesse Werner, had announced he would retire. GAF was known as an ill-managed company whose performance had long fallen below analysts' expectations. It was then Skadden's highest-billing client. The firm was representing it in a large antitrust suit against Kodak. When Werner announced that he wouldn't step down, Heyman formulated a plan to protect the value of shareholders' stock by selling off certain parts of GAF and keeping others. The plan was well received by Wall Street investors, but Werner dismissed it. In 1983, Heyman devised a challenge to Werner using a proxy contest.

Joe Flom represented Werner. Among other reasons, Flom took the case to prove a point: Jerry Finkelstein and a group of investors had hired Skadden to help them attack Chock Full o'Nuts in a proxy contest. They did not succeed in gaining control of the company, and the *National Law Journal*, which Finkelstein owned, ran a piece about proxy contests and law firms. It included some items that were critical of Skadden (e.g.: "In representing management that eventually lost control in . . . two contests, Skadden Arps billed its clients twice as much as the firms on the prevailing side"). When the GAF fight came along, Flom immersed himself in it more fully than he had in a proxy contest in many years. Augustus Oliver, who worked with Flom during the fight: "Everyone else headed for the hills, but I was the most senior nonpartner with proxy experience, and I was drafted."

By *The American Lawyer*'s account, Flom and his client used their power in the loosely defined takeover club, consisting of investment bankers, lawyers, and others, to prevent Heyman from hiring experienced counsel in the field. When Heyman tried to retain specialists, like a proxy-solicitation firm called the Carter Organization, they wouldn't take his business. In litigation later, Heyman obtained documents showing that GAF had paid the Carter Organization not to represent Heyman. Heyman had hired Salomon Brothers to advise him on banking issues in the contest, but after GAF gave some bond business to the bank and asked it not to represent Heyman, Salomon withdrew. GAF also raised questions about Heyman's character by calling attention to a legal dispute he was having with his sister. (A Skadden lawyer, looking back: "We did not cover ourselves in glory with that one.")

Given Werner's poor reputation as a manager and GAF's poor business performance on the one hand, and the praise drawn by Heyman's plan for salvaging the value of the company on the other, Flom could not justify Werner's tactics by claiming that they served shareholders' interests. But, according to *The American Lawyer*, they served his client's interests: "By playing both tough and dirty," Flom demonstrated that he was "without peer as a tactician in a battle for corporate control." Sam Heyman, who eventually ousted Werner, called the moves "scorched-earth tactics at their very worst." To Skadden's pride, Flom was the acknowledged grandfather of the notion of scorching a corporate opponent to defend against a takeover.

Flom was also retained in 1981 to be part of the team of lawyers that defended Conoco, the ninth-largest American oil company, against a bid for its Canadian subsidiary by Dome Petroleum Company. That bid was joined by a bid from the Mobil Oil Company, and eventually led to Conoco's complete takeover by the country's largest chemical company, Du Pont, for $7.5 billion.

"We had a three-ring circus going," Flom told the *Institutional Investor* about the best-known example of the Skadden takeover-defense style. In one ring, Conoco was chased by the Seagram Company, the large Canadian corporation, which negotiated with the oil company on friendly terms and then made a surprise hostile offer for some of its shares. In a second, Conoco dealt with Du Pont as an alternative buyer—as a white knight. In a third, there were Conoco and Mobil.

In the press and in a lawsuit, Conoco claimed that a takeover by Mobil would violate antitrust laws. *The American Lawyer* reported: " 'It was thought,' recalls one lawyer involved, 'that Skadden Arps should not do the suit because Skadden Arps and Flom are always bringing frivolous takeover defense suits, and we wanted this one to look legitimate. But we classed it up a bit by making sure Bill Mulligan was involved and his name on the papers.' " (Mulligan was a Skadden partner and a former member of the U.S. Court of Appeals for the Second Circuit.) While not frivolous, the lawsuit was based on rhetoric more than law, since a merger between Conoco and Mobil would have created antitrust problems in only a few markets. Nonetheless, the suit served its purpose.

To ward off Seagram or delay Seagram's bid long enough to allow another company to make a counteroffer, Flom came up with three key tactics, according to Philip Heymann and Lance Liebman in *The Social Responsibilities of Lawyers*. (Their book features the Conoco deal as an example raising questions about practices of corporate lawyers.)

First, Conoco should find states with laws that forbade wholesale liquor sellers like Seagram from owning retailers of alcohol, like Conoco, which sold beer at some gas stations. Second, it should publicize the theory that a merger with Seagram would threaten Conoco's foreign, especially Arab, oil supplies—as David Luban of the University of Maryland put it, the tactic was to rouse anti-Semitism and manipulate prejudice to further the company's end. (Muslims in the Arab oil states disapproved of liquor, and Seagram's chairman, Edgar Bronfman, was an ardent Zionist and president of the World Jewish Congress.) Third, it should stir up congressional disapproval of the deal, by arguing the inequity in taking over vital American natural resources while Canada hindered American companies from entering its markets.

Not long after, Congress held hearings about Canadian ownership of American resources, and *The Wall Street Journal* reported that the governments of Dubai, in the United Arab Emirates, and of Norway threatened to stop supplying oil to Conoco if Seagram took an interest in it.

The Conoco team eventually staved off Seagram's bid and assured the success of Du Pont's through court victories in Florida and North Carolina. As Heymann and Liebman wrote, a lawyer persuaded a Florida state judge "in an ex parte discussion in chambers"—with no Seagram lawyer present—"that the $7 billion merger should be put on hold because Conoco sold six-packs at Florida gas stations."

When Edward Weinfeld, a distinguished judge in Manhattan who was in charge of federal court matters related to the Conoco deal, learned of the Florida decision, he said that "he would not tolerate further secret actions on behalf of clients," Heymann and Liebman reported. Flom's Conoco team didn't heed him. The Florida judge lifted his order, but the oil company's lawyers immediately obtained a similar one in North Carolina. By the time Seagram undid it, Du Pont had prevailed with the stockholders.

About its unilateral dealings with state judges, a lawyer on Skadden's Conoco team commented: "Whether you are required or not to notify opposing counsel about such discussions is only a matter of state law. Sure, it was an elbow in the eye and probably does not meet everybody's expectation of what a good guy is. But these two companies were in a life-and-death struggle. From our standpoint, we did nothing inappropriate."

The kind of lawyering permitted by current norms and regularly done by big-firm practitioners is called hardball. In the ongoing debate about the character of the legal profession, it is a central topic. It has been addressed in an informal national campaign for civility and self-restraint—through creeds that bar associations ask members to subscribe to, in extraordinary opinions by judges exhorting lawyers to reform unseemly habits, and in other arenas.

At a recent annual meeting of the Litigation Section of the American Bar Association, one session was tellingly called "The Great Civility Debate: A Cop-out for Incompetence?" A panel of judges and lawyers could not agree on a definition of "hardball," but one panel member, Robert Sayler, a partner in the old-line Washington, D.C., firm of Covington & Burling, described it as "meanspiritedness," "son-of-a-bitchedness," and "different from being stern, firm, and seizing the strategic advantage." He renamed the behavior "Ramboism," a term broad enough to encompass a range of purposes, which has since been adopted by Supreme Court Justice Sandra Day O'Connor and other bar leaders who have spoken out against this trend.

To focus the discussion, the members of the panel and their audience were asked to comment on a series of hypothetical cases designed to highlight choices between tough (but acceptable) lawyering and Ramboism. One panel member was Susan Getzendanner, a former federal trial judge, who joined Skadden as a partner in 1987. Getzendanner is a popular speaker at bar gatherings because, by her own description, she can be counted on as a provocateur. In Chicago that day, she sounded like she was coming down on the side of Ramboism.

One case involved a trial lawyer calling a witness who hadn't been identified to the other side. Since the lawyer came into the case at the last minute and hadn't had any prior dealings with his opponents, there was no evidence that he had intended to mislead them and, therefore, had done something wrong. Getzendanner said, "I used to kid around about sending the woman in the mink coat to sit behind your opponents at the trial. These things are done. I don't see anything wrong with them."

When the moderator pressed her to acknowledge the disputable nature of her view, Getzendanner explained later, she responded with an attitude that was intended to jerk him off his high horse: "Don't forget. I'm at Skadden Arps now. We *pride* ourselves on being assholes. It's part of the firm culture." (Later, she allowed, the A-word she should have used to drive home the point was "animals.")

Some other members of the panel supported Getzendanner's commitment to playing hardball, but she seemed to want to correct any impression that Skadden's culture (caricatured or not) always merged with her personal views. She recounted: "When I joined Skadden Arps, we had a firm-wide conference. And I got up and said to the litigators, 'You know, you oughta practice law in such a way that, in ten years from now, every one of your opponents would say that you're eligible to be a federal judge. That's how you should practice, you should be reliable, people should depend on your word.' Yack, yack, yack. Then the guy from Los Angeles got up and said, 'If I catch any of you being nice to an opponent . . .' In that instance, it did come from above, and that is the predominant view, and I think it's the predominant view at most firms right now."

In a speech to new lawyers at Skadden not long ago, a senior partner listed aggressiveness as a cardinal virtue at the firm. He gave tips about how lawyers there could disguise their pushy style, if that seemed called for, like when a client announced that he didn't want to take orders from a "New York" lawyer. ("Never wear a vest when you go outside New York City," he said to a roomful of men and women, and "Talk about your humble antecedents.") But surface shifts in style ("This is a firm with a lot of pluralism when it comes to that," another partner said) wouldn't alter the underlying approach.

There was no conflict between the firm's sense of integrity and its aggressiveness, in the judgment of Skadden lawyers. The rules of conduct were designed to restrain lawyers, like a leash. But the firm style was to test their limits. It expected a lot of give. Here's a move that a Skadden lawyer highlighted when telling me about his experience at the firm: settling a case for a client that was one of many defendants in a hundred-million-dollar lawsuit on the insistence of insurance carriers, contrary to an agreement the lawyer had made with the other defendants in the case that none of them would settle on their own.

"We made some enemies," said Shepard Goldfein, a well-respected, middle-aged Skadden partner. He explained the move on the grounds that the agreement had been invalid, that he had informed the other defendants that Skadden would hold its client's interests paramount, and that another party to the agreement had breached it first by settling on its own. A court upheld the Skadden view.

Another Skadden partner in the star category gave an example of what he saw as effective advocacy, and others called hardball, when I spoke with him. Thomas Dougherty became a partner in the Boston office in 1984. Bob Pirie worked regularly with Dougherty before Pirie left the firm. Pirie recalled: "He's warm and friendly, with that angelic Irish face, and he'll cut your balls off."

Dougherty became a favorite of Pirie's as a litigator in takeover contests. One was the Life Investors case, active in 1981. An insurance holding company in the Midwest, it did business through twenty-four corporations, from New York to California. A Dutch company owned 40 percent of Life Investors and sought a majority share. Pirie was asked to defend the owners of the remaining 60 percent of Life Investors.

The Dutch company could acquire more shares only if it got approval for the purchase in all of the states where the insurance company operated. Pirie's strategy was to use litigation to keep that from happening. He divided up the United States into the federal circuits and assigned teams to each area. Dougherty drew Michigan and Ohio, in the Sixth Circuit. Pirie wanted to keep a court order enjoining the sale of stock to the bidder in effect in at least one state at all times.

From a Thursday until the next Tuesday, for example, an injunction might be outstanding, pending an appeal, but by the time it dissolved he needed a victory in another state. Pirie would say, "Get me Tuesday! I want Tuesday!" The team marked its activities with colored flags on a map of the country. From Labor Day to Thanksgiving, at least one state was flying red at all times.

The Dutch company had made a tender offer for 11 percent of Life Investors stock, so the owners of the 49 percent that would remain were unlikely to be able to sell for as much as the tender price. Dougherty recalled that the company had been advised that it could win in a month. Pirie wanted the Dutch to buy all 60 percent of the outstanding Life Investors stock for the same price, and his argument had a strong claim to fairness. He believed that the best way to bring that about was to play hardball, by stymieing the deal indefinitely through litigation while negotiating with the Dutch. The strategy worked. It earned Skadden a million-dollar premium.

Skadden's aggressiveness sometimes hasn't worked. Jonathan Lerner is a third Skadden star (he became a partner in 1981) who, before heading the Skadden ethics committee, established himself at the firm by helping to uncover misuse of corporate funds by a businessman and Brooklyn congressman, Frederick Richmond. (It was in a takeover fight against a company of which Richmond was the chief stockholder.) The work led to Richmond's conviction for tax evasion and for illegal payment to a government employee. He was fined $20,000, sentenced to three years in prison, and forced to resign from office. "We arranged for the jailing of at least one congressman," a senior partner told new Skadden lawyers in a welcoming speech, entering Lerner's feat in Skadden lore.

In 1990, Lerner made headlines by seeking to block publication in the

United States of a book called *By Way of Deception: A Devastating Insider's Portrait of the Mossad*, on the grounds that the book's release would imperil the lives of Israeli intelligence agents. The book was written by Victor Ostrovsky, a former agent of the Mossad (the Israeli intelligence agency), and by Claire Hoy, a Canadian journalist. Skadden was retained to represent the government of Israel by a leading Israeli law firm, S. Horowitz & Company, with which Skadden had worked on other matters.

Distribution of the book in Canada had already been halted by a judge's temporary restraining order. Lerner led with a well-publicized and extraordinary midnight session at the Manhattan apartment of a state judge, at which a temporary suppression order was obtained. He took a hard line with the U.S. publisher. "I wrote a snotty letter," Lerner said about his first communication with the publisher, St. Martin's Press. "It gave them the basic information about the temporary restraining order in Canada, and told them to cease and desist or die, basically." Intense litigation, and media coverage, followed. Lerner inadvertently helped turn a book that he intended to suppress, and that was expected to have only modest sales, into a number one national best-seller.

There are two main views about his effort. Lerner's is that he had no choice. He explained: "If you're worried about Abu Nidal and other terrorist enemies of Israel getting a copy, then your concern is that no copy get out and you don't worry about the difference between ten and one hundred thousand copies. If they hadn't pressed the case, they would have felt that they had blood on their hands if any Israeli agent was killed."

Despite his reputation among some for "running an anti-First Amendment practice" (his words), Lerner maintained: "I actually believe in the First Amendment" (the section of the Bill of Rights that guarantees freedom of the press). He explained: "I just think we need to honor other values like national security." When Ostrovsky joined the Mossad, he signed a contract never to reveal any secrets of the agency, and his book contained identifying information about some operatives that Israel said could endanger their lives. To Lerner, who relied on a settled U.S. Supreme Court precedent, the Snepp case, to support his argument, this was basic: "You had a rogue agent violating his contract. If they hadn't taken action, what's to keep the next agent from doing the same thing?"

The other view is that Lerner's approach was a prime example of overkill, of turning a large but containable embarrassment into a public relations disaster for his firm's client by playing hardball. In addition to the material that was thought to endanger Israeli agents, the book disclosed other facts that were problems for Israel: among them, that the Mossad had advance knowledge of plans for the 1983 suicide truck-bomb attack on U.S. Marine Corps barracks in Beirut (it killed two hundred forty-one American servicemen) but withheld the information so American relations with Arab states would be damaged.

When William Safire, in *The New York Times*, expressed the opinion that the Israeli lawsuit was a debacle, Lerner answered with an indignant letter: "Fortunately, the Israeli government feels a stronger moral imperative, and a higher regard for human life, than Mr. Safire evinces. To be sure, once the book was written, preventing disclosure of its contents was no simple feat; but neither was the raid on Entebbe nor the destruction, at least temporarily, of Iraq's nuclear capability, for which the world should be grateful."

Lerner overlooked Israel's apparent disregard for the life of the American marines, which weakened his claim, and his analogies were strained. He and four colleagues had showed up at the judge's apartment at 11 p.m., seeking to stop publication. They had no written complaint, no legal brief, and no other admissible supporting material. (Lerner, later: "I apologized for the less than usually elegant Skadden presentation.") They relied on oral representations to secure a temporary restraining order against the distribution of a book that he knew was already out of the publisher's control. Eighteen thousand copies of it had already been shipped to bookstores across the country and galleys had been sent to four selected book reviewers. This ragged post hoc effort did not compare easily to the raid on Entebbe.

When Skadden filed a formal complaint the next day, it was marred by typographical, grammatical, and other errors, which made it look like the work of a harried solo practitioner, not of an awesome firm. By then, St. Martin's Press, which said it had satisfied itself that the book endangered no lives before agreeing to bring it out, was delighted by the publicity that the lawsuit was generating, especially a front-page story in the *Times* by Roger Cohen. Lerner, who keeps in his office a Plexiglas block holding a miniature of the *Times*'s front page with the Cohen article: "He wrote an hysterical and unbalanced piece, palming it off as news."

Soon after, St. Martin's received a court decision allowing the book to be distributed to an audience that had now been dramatically enlarged by the lawsuit. The court reasoned that the book's previous distribution to reviewers and bookstores made superfluous an effort to balance the values of free expression and those of national security, and that distribution should continue. Still, in typical Skadden fashion, Lerner made no concession. He insisted that Israel and its counsel were right to attempt to suppress it, on legal and moral grounds. His letter to the *Times* closed: "In this case, it was better to have tried and failed than never to have tried at all."

Below Skadden, Arps & Slate was founded in Manhattan on April Fools' Day in 1948. In those days, firms put their initials on stationery and the acronym created with Arps's name listed alphabetically was in bad taste. Skadden won a coin toss with Slate, and his name became the shorthand for the firm's (*Skadden, Arps, Slate, Meagher & Flom*)

JOHN H. SLATE
MARSHALL K. SKADDEN
LESLIE H. ARPS

announce the formation of a partnership

for the general practice of law under

the firm name of

SKADDEN, ARPS & SLATE

with offices at

One William Street

New York 4

April, 1948   Digby 4-1074

Top Marshall Skadden worked as a certified public accountant for seven years between college and law school. He had a sunny outlook and the earnestness of a go-getter, and dressed like an old-line Wall Street lawyer. The founder who contributed least to Skadden, because of his early death, gave the firm its name (*Skadden, Arps, Slate, Meagher & Flom*)

Middle In the early years of the firm, Leslie Arps's plum engagement was as an aide to the New York State Crime Commission's inquiry into corruption on the waterfront of New York harbor. New York City's police commissioner said to a lawyer who identified himself as a Skadden associate, "Isn't Les Arps the Thin Man there?" (*Skadden, Arps, Slate, Meagher & Flom*)

Bottom For several years while he was at the firm, John Slate pieced together a large analog computer as a hobby. Slate wrote a humor article for *Fortune* magazine called "The Warning Impulse Timing and Computing Haversack (TWITCH)," predicting the advent of a portable computer years before one was invented (*Skadden, Arps, Slate, Meagher & Flom*)

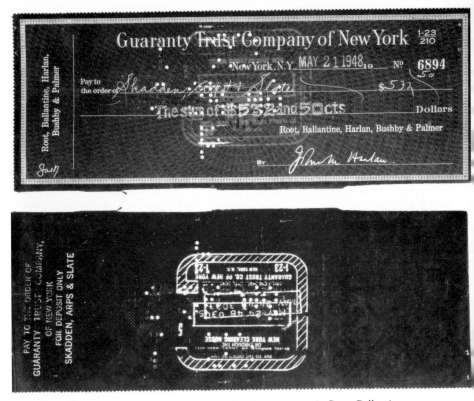

Soon after Skadden opened, John M. Harlan, Jr., a partner in Root, Ballantine, Harlan, Bushby & Palmer (and future Justice of the United States Supreme Court), circulated a memo to his partners recommending that any who had a case too small for their firm should send it to the spin-off from the Root firm. A matter that another firm had declined was typical of early Skadden business (*Skadden, Arps, Slate, Meagher & Flom*)

Opposite Joe Flom's election to partnership may have been expedited by Marshall Skadden's having had a stroke. Not long after, when Pamela Woolworth, a relative of the founder of the famous five-and-dime chain, and a partner bought a controlling interest in a cattle ranch in Paraguay, *The New York Times* identified Flom as her counsel (*Skadden, Arps, Slate, Meagher & Flom*)

Charles Lyon was deputy chief of the team of lawyers who prosecuted Nazi war criminals at Nuremberg before joining Skadden. Treated as an equal by the founders, he stayed until it became clear that Skadden, Arps, Slate & Lyon lacked enough business to require a lawyer in his field, which was tax (*Skadden, Arps, Slate, Meagher & Flom*)

William Meagher was passed over for partnership at a well-known New York firm—in his opinion, because of his unclassy background. At fifty-four, he moved to Skadden as a senior partner—the first Skadden partner hired laterally from another firm (*Skadden, Arps, Slate, Meagher & Flom*)

SKADDEN, ARPS & SLATE
551 FIFTH AVENUE
NEW YORK 17

JOSEPH H. FLOM

HAS BECOME A MEMBER OF OUR FIRM.

MARSHALL K. SKADDEN
LESLIE H. ARPS
JOHN H. SLATE

NOVEMBER 1, 1954

"I gotta tell you, it's a blockbuster,"
Flom says when he likes an idea. When
he doesn't, a favorite Flom expression is
directed at the idea's source. "Give him
an ambiguous answer," he mutters: "Tell
him to go fuck himself" (*Skadden, Arps,
Slate, Meagher & Flom*)

William Timbers became a partner after resigning as general counsel to the Securities and Exchange Commission. Behind his desk at Skadden he displayed an American flag, on a brass staff topped by a brass eagle, which the SEC had given him. Slate laid down newspaper under the staff, as if to catch droppings from the bird (*Skadden, Arps, Slate, Meagher & Flom*)

Following Robert Ensher's early death, the associates at the firm paid a backhanded tribute to him by originating the Beast of Burden (BOB) Award. The award was named after Ensher on the theory that the stress that killed him might get the winner, too (*Skadden, Arps, Slate, Meagher & Flom*)

Opposite A framed sheet of Flom's doodles is on display in his office. One Flom cryptographer identifies them as perfect symbols, mazes that he creates and solves as he intuits his way through the problems of his clients and then imagines a solution (*Skadden, Arps, Slate, Meagher & Flom*)

John Feerick's hobby was studying how the Constitution deals with the transfer of presidential power—as an adviser to both houses of Congress, he helped write the Twenty-fifth Amendment, providing for succession by the Vice President if the President can't perform his job. His Skadden nickname was St. John (*Skadden, Arps, Slate, Meagher & Flom*)

When Robert Sweet left Skadden to become a federal judge, he wrote a letter to his partners that paid tribute to Joe Flom's vision of a Skadden that would surpass the leaders of Wall Street, built on a foundation of counseling in contests for control of corporations (*Skadden, Arps, Slate, Meagher & Flom*)

Robert Pirie was an iconoclast who loved a fight. A lawyer who worked with him said, "He bulls his way through everything in a larger-than-life way, and he knows he's doing it. He affects a kind of entitlement, with a confidence and a flair that enable him to pull it off" (*Skadden, Arps, Slate, Meagher & Flom*)

For years, Peter Mullen was described as acting like the president of a large university, with a range of departments and campuses, whose job it was to lead an organization vertically that was defiantly horizontal. A colleague observed, "Mullen infuriates you by sounding out, moving cautiously, deferring decision" (*Ida Wyman*)

The Skadden eagle is a symbol of the firm's epic American success and of its style. In the Skadden lexicon, aggressiveness exercised to capitalize on opportunity is called opportunism. It is an affirmative response to luck. In contrast to its dictionary definition, at Skadden it is considered a laudable trait (*Skadden, Arps, Slate, Meagher & Flom*)

Roger Aaron, one of the "Fab Four," said: "Every lawyer who wants to succeed at Skadden has to learn sales and marketing as well as production." I was told that some Skadden partners were opposed to the idea of letting me write about the firm; when I spoke with Aaron, he acted like one of them (*Skadden, Arps, Slate, Meagher & Flom*)

Above Blaine "Fin" Fogg smokes big cigars and sometimes masks his acuteness behind a jovial smile. He is likable, if unpredictable—a Wasp *mensch* with survival skills. For a man with charm and polish, he sometimes seems to be coarse on purpose (*Skadden, Arps, Slate, Meagher & Flom*)

Lawyers who know Peter Atkins say that he is taciturn and guarded. A friend of his told me that he is a thoughtful, warm perfectionist, who showed up unexpectedly at the funeral of her brother, plays the guitar well, and is a great dancer (*Harvey Wang*)

Morris Kramer was asked to name the stars at Skadden, besides Flom, and told a reporter, "I'd say I'm one of them. And I'd bet you that every other partner would say he's one of them. That's the kind of people we are." Another partner said about Kramer, "My position on Morris is that you couldn't find a guy who is more normal" (*Harvey Wang*)

At the end of 1970, Skadden changed its address and its image. From Fifth Avenue and the neighborhood of Grand Central Terminal, the firm moved to 919 Third Avenue, a forty-seven-story building between Fifty-fifth and Fifty-sixth streets. It was the northernmost office tower on the East Side and, for a Wall Street firm, an outpost (*Robert Klein*)

The American Lawyer zeroed in on a blunt, tantalizing measure of success: how much money lawyers made. The symbol was a dollar sign, as in "M$A." The magazine's first issue featured an article about the financial achievements of Skadden (*The American Lawyer*)

Skadden, photographed for *Fortune* magazine in the spring of 1982, was then a New York law firm with three small satellite offices and a bold, but limited, reputation. "From the firm's inception," a group of partners stated in a memorandum that year, "our intent has been to build a quality law firm that would stand the test of time" (*Neil Slavin*)

In 1990 Skadden announced a new management structure, the Office of the Executive Partner. It gave Peter Mullen, the first executive partner, the chance to use six colleagues—Aaron, Atkins, and others—"like a stereophonic booster: he could put his message through these other speakers and blast it throughout the firm"

Earle Yaffa (*Skadden, Arps, Slate, Meagher & Flom*)

Michael Diamond (*Skadden, Arps, Slate, Meagher & Flom*)

William Frank (*Skadden, Arps, Slate, Meagher & Flom*)

Benjamin Needell (*Skadden, Arps, Slate, Meagher & Flom*)

James Freund's taste for writing made him the unofficial historian of Skadden. One of his first assignments as an associate was to figure out how to use semen from a prize bull as collateral for a loan. He felt the need to inspect a cattle-breeding farm before addressing the question (*Skadden, Arps, Slate, Meagher & Flom*)

Peter Mullen and Robert Sheehan began to compile a list of lawyers who should be considered for election to partnership the following year—to decide who should go on "the morning line." The phrase was drawn from the horse-racing-style pool sometimes formed by firm lawyers who assign odds to the chances of candidates

Robert Sheehan (*Skadden, Arps, Slate, Meagher & Flom*)

J. Michael Schell (*Skadden, Arps, Slate, Meagher & Flom*)

Kent Coit (*Skadden, Arps, Slate, Meagher & Flom*)

Brian Hoffmann (*Carol Clayton Photography*)

In the 1970s, Douglas Kraus was the first and only associate in the Get-to-know-Joe program. Twenty years later, he grew frustrated with Skadden and called for democracy at the firm, so all partners would feel that the system was "responsive to them." Some Skadden leaders believed that, in his attack on current management, Kraus was accusing them of corruption (*Skadden, Arps, Slate, Meagher & Flom*)

Sheila Birnbaum built the products liability group into one of the fastest-growing at the firm. Birnbaum located her advocacy on the moral high ground. "I like representing the underdog," she said about her clients. A law professor pointed out that they tended to be rich, powerful corporations, and commented, "Lawyers posture all the time" (*Harvey Wang*)

il Général

Kurzbeschreibung

Skadden, A

vec à peu près mille juristes, Skadden, Arps est un d
juridiques les plus importants dans le monde. En 1
.ctions le seul cabinet d'avocats cité dans "The Wall St
ne faisant partie des 60 "Entreprises du Futur." The
ver, un des mensuels juridiques les plus renommés a
, considère comme le chef de file des cabinets améri
eile.
Skadden, Arps est basé à New York, avec sept bureaux
ston, Chicago, Los Angeles, San Francisco, Washington
f à l'étranger (Bruxelles, Budapest, Francfort, Hong Kor
Iney, Tokyo et Toronto). En plus nous avons des bureau
Prague, à Moscou et à Pékin. Cette stratégie globale nou
pondre avec efficacité aux besoins de notre clientèle inte
Skadden, Arps fournit une gamme complète de servi
onde financier, industriel et commercial. Skadden, Arp
banques, compagnies d'assurance et

Mit über 1000 Rechtsanwälten zählt Skadd
und renommiertesten Anwaltskanzleien d
einzige Anwaltssozietät, die im Wall Str
Jubiläumsausgabe zum 100-jährigen Bestehen im
"Companies for the Future" aufgeführt wurde. T
der bedeutendsten juristischen Fachpublikationen
uns sogar als "die Herausragende (preeminent)" F
weiteren Büros in Boston, Chicago, Los Angeles, S
D.C. und Wilmington. Im Ausland unterhalten wi
Frankfurt, Hongkong, London, Paris, Sydney, T
Unsere Präsenz in den Kapita
York und Tokio sowie die 24-stünd
(auch an Wochenenden) der meist
e, die Interessen unserer M
nehmen. Dies hat für vie
Vorteile geführt. Sein
Arps dem Grundsatz v
mit höchstqualifizierte
ente Beachtung dieser N
atendsten und global at
meinhin wird Skadd
asitions angesehen. Do
n Rechtsgebieten tät
m:

rsen- und Versi
treten amerikan
er/geber, Invest
länder und Ve
ktionen, insbes
rung neuer Pr
onalen Kapit

Skadden, Arps, Slate, Meagher & Flom
スキャデン・アープス・スレート・マー＆フロム

Fusiones y Adquisiciones

Skadden, Arps ha sido nombrada continuamente
firmas de abogados que participan en operac
adquisición. Durante siete de los últimos nue
ubicado primera entre las firmas de abogados en la
American Lawyer's "Corporate Scorecard," como la
de las cien fusiones y adquisiciones más importantes
abogados de fusiones y adquisiciones trabajaron en de
grandes operaciones.
Los abogados de fusiones y adquisiciones de Ska
operaciones ne... que incluyen tanto fusiones, co
cadas, como operaciones de
disputas de poderes de accionis
el control social. Además, he
restructuraciones de empresas
s adquirentes, compañías a ser a
ión y a instituciones financieras
Nuestros clientes abarcan tanto
anjeras.
Arps en operaciones de fusión y a
incluye participar en la formulació
estructuración y táctica. Frecuente
lo referente a las decisiones de me
a los mismos, lo que comprende pu
e reglamentos y comunicación con
mantienen a los clientes al día sobr
ciales aplicables a las fusiones y adc
áreas que van desde leyes impositiva

Arps son representativas de las grandes
Skadden, Arps ha participado en los añ

To potential foreign clients Skadden
now announces itself in their native
tongues as one of the most important
law firms in the world and describes
the legal services it offers (*Skadden,
Arps, Slate, Meagher & Flom*)

When Isaac Shapiro joined Skadden,
he was known less for his legal
expertise, which was substantial, than
for his cosmopolitan background. He
was born of Russian parents and grew
up in Japan. He is fluent in Russian,
Japanese, English, and French and was
the first member of his family to
emigrate to the United States (*Skadden,
Arps, Slate, Meagher & Flom*)

In a conference room of Skadden's New York office hangs an oil painting of Joe Flom: himself, yet not. This is the way the lawyers who make Skadden's future will see Flom when he's gone (*Skadden, Arps, Slate, Meagher & Flom*)

12

The Skadden Culture

Since the early 1980s, in a variety of forums, Joe Flom has tried to put his firm and the legal profession into perspective. In a debate at the Federal Bar Council against Peter Brown, the author and critic of large law firms, and as a speaker at the banquet celebrating the one hundredth anniversary of the *Harvard Law Review*, for example, Flom has challenged the theory of decline in the profession subscribed to by lawyers he calls "these creeps who keep talking about their gentlemanly practice."

He poses a series of rhetorical questions: "When law firms were run with the fathers handing them down to the sons, what was so great about that? What was so great about the fact that certain people could get into these clubs and others couldn't? Or that women or blacks couldn't work at these firms? Or that there were Jewish, gentile, and other separate firms? What was so great about the fact that you had to go to one of the four or five major law schools in order to get into one of the major firms? What was so great then that it was more important what your family background was, in terms of whether you got into one of those firms, than what your academic background was? You say something was lost when those practices disappeared. Every change involves some loss. The question is whether things are better off or worse off."

To Flom, the answer is clearly: Better off. In some moments, he is almost diplomatic, and observes that the "gentlemanly profession" was "gentlemanly for some, but not for most." In others, he "gets so pissed" at the "whole gestalt of the guys who don't want to move with the temper of the times." In his view, they are nostalgic for an era when a handsome Victorian façade hid a dingy profession. Flom argues that valuable changes were ushered in by market forces a generation before those that reshaped the profession in the 1970s came into play.

During the Second World War, the number of students enrolling in law school dropped to sixty-four hundred, less than one-sixth the number reached just before the Depression. After the war, the support of the GI Bill of Rights, the strength of the economy, and other forces multiplied enrollment by a factor of eight, to fifty-one thousand. Although women and blacks remained largely excluded from the ranks of law students (Harvard Law School admitted women for the first time in 1950, the year blacks successfully challenged segregation of southern law schools in the Supreme Court), the prospective lawyers represented a greater cross section of Americans than ever before.

Following the war, as Flom recalled, "there was a shortage of top lawyers—enough of a shortage that the big firms had to stop limiting their hiring to the top four or five law schools. But as the demand for legal talent increased and the pool changed, you had an opening up and firms brought people in primarily because of talent." In the 1950s, "the profession changed dramatically. The large corporate law firms became less of a club and more of a meritocracy."

In Flom's view, bolstered by others at his firm (like Peter Mullen), the new openness in hiring at corporate law firms worked directly to the advantage of the clients, because, they assert, the new lawyers' work was generally better than that done by those who arrived and succeeded at firms primarily as a result of their social connections—as Mullen put it: who only lost a client if they "screwed up."

A generation or so later, another shift—away from permanent relationships between clients and lawyers and toward competition for business among law firms—also strengthened clients' hands. Firms began to vie for business, giving clients bargaining power on cost and other facets of the legal product. When a client required specialized counsel, it could now avoid paying for the education of a neophyte at a firm that was its longtime counsel—or (Mullen again) it could elude a lawyer from that firm who "faked" both knowledge and competence. It could choose among lawyers already familiar with the legal questions it was asking. Consumers of legal services and smart lawyers, both, were the winners.

Take the story of Skadden.

Flom's and his colleagues' assertions about how the legal profession has changed for the better meld easily with their proud references to the firm's parochial detail. By the mid-1980s, other firm leaders were, with Flom, subtlely restyling the official tale of Skadden's birth and growth, shifting their emphases and attempting to achieve a neater fit between the past and their conception of the firm's essence in the present. Now conceiving of the firm as an institution, they pondered how best to define and perpetuate the firm's "culture," which had been so successful. To Skadden, its culture was a positive force—the best answer it could offer to doubtful inquiries about the state of the legal profession and about the firm's character.

The impetus for the effort was Skadden's dramatic growth. If the firm did not act to control its character, outside factors would. By 1990, most of the firm's partners were relatively new: more than half had been elected since 1985 and almost three-fourths since 1981. Their average age was forty. When I asked a cross section of Skadden lawyers about the firm's "good old days," without saying when I had in mind, most talked about the period just out of reach of their own experience, a few years before they arrived—for a partner elected in 1988, who joined the firm after graduating from law school in 1980, the late seventies were the *belle époque*.

Many believed that the firm's professional identity had crystallized with the INCO–ESB deal in 1974—as Matthew Mallow put it: "The stuff before was so much history." The days of Skadden, Arps & Slate, according to a former partner, were "the Age of the Sumerians." In a 1985 memo called "Culture of the Firm"—a Skadden manifesto—Jim Freund presented this view of the gap between past and present as dogma. He asserted that as late as 1970 "few people were aware of Skadden Arps; our roster of clients was small and not particularly distinguished."

Les Arps objected to Freund's memo. "As near as I can tell," he wrote in a memo of his own to Mullen, "it would appear that from 1948 to 1970 the firm was in fact a nonentity." Arps's view was that Skadden had attracted fine lawyers from its start; this would not have been possible if the firm was as "undistinguished" as Freund had described.

Mullen sided with Arps in judging that Skadden had succeeded, and its character had formed, well before 1970. To Mullen, the source of Skadden's success and distinctiveness, whenever it occurred, was its "shared values," which resided in the unabridged story of the firm. Since most of the firm's partners, let alone associates, hadn't been around to watch the genesis of those values, he and other firm leaders now had to pass on what they knew.

Although they did not have a large legacy of well-established tradition, the Skadden elders did have some advantages in their quest to define and spread the culture. In the 1980s, many law firms grew by merger and acquisition. Skadden had never merged with another law firm, and was not unsettled by the culture clash that could have resulted from such a merger.

As of 1990, three-fourths of its partners had been promoted from within the firm, and one-fourth had come in laterally from other law firms, from the government, or from business. Of the partners who had also been associates at the firm, one-third had worked only at Skadden; two-thirds had moved to the firm from another as young lawyers. Partners at other firms deduced that immigration from other firms and other sources of legal talent made Skadden a less integrated firm than those that brought in few outsiders. The Skadden view was that laterals kept the firm nimble and fresh.

A variety of organized efforts were undertaken to promote what the elders saw as the Skadden culture. None was more important than the firm's initiation of newcomers at an annual retreat called Arrowwood, after the conference center in Westchester County, not far from Manhattan, where it was held beginning in 1985. Mullen described the retreat as an "indoctrination." At Arrowwood, the firm tried to stress one primary concept: the importance of "merit" at Skadden.

"Merit" had two key meanings. One was the high quality of the firm's product. "If there is any one feature that has produced the success of Skadden Arps, we all firmly believe that it is the quality of the work we do," Mullen announced to all at an Arrowwood gathering in 1988, as memorialized on a firm videotape. "Merit" meant first that Skadden's work must be top-notch.

The second meaning of "merit" was excellence in individual performance on the job. Jim Freund said, "What you did before doesn't count. What you do here does. People who do the job get rewarded. Isn't that the way it should be?" Freund didn't mean that what lawyers did before they got to Skadden was irrelevant. The firm lauded the young people it hired as being among "the best and the brightest" of their generation. They wouldn't have been hired if they hadn't met that standard, they were told. To Flom, merit meant hiring and promoting lawyers "on the basis of talent." Merit was the firm's "number one test."

The idea was that Skadden had succeeded, in part, because it embraced the concept of pure merit sooner and more fully than most law firms of consequence in New York City. The long list of law schools from which Skadden lawyers came represented its commitment to merit. If Skadden had followed the pattern of established firms, it would have hired only from select schools rather than taking people who led their classes at less prestigious places or others who appeared strong but had some unorthodoxy on their résumé.

Never mind that Skadden did so originally out of default, because relatively few graduates of Harvard, Yale, and Columbia, for example, had been interested in joining it in the early years. Augustus Oliver, who graduated from Yale College with a mediocre average, and from the Washington College of Law, at American University, *summa cum laude*, was hired in 1975. He recalled that when he took the job "Skadden was an 'outside' firm, unlike Cravath and some others. It took top students from second-tier schools, many of whom had done other things before."

(Oliver was elected to partnership at Skadden in 1983, and left the next year to join an investment group, where, according to *Fortune* magazine, he proved his "merit": he and his two partners once earned $50 million in a few months' time during the eighties by buying a block of stock in a company to put it in play and reaping the rewards when the price of its stock climbed during the contest that followed.)

Never mind that the firm's rapid expansion in the 1980s required the firm to cast an increasingly wide net, which inevitably would catch more than "the best and the brightest." An investment banker who hired Skadden observed: "The ideal law firm would have only associates who a client would say have a good chance of making partner. But Skadden, like other large firms in the eighties, couldn't afford that standard. They will tell you that that was the standard, but I think they're wrong."

Flom's accomplishments made him the firm's paragon, of course. It was generally believed that neither Skadden, nor Arps, nor Slate had much to do with the law firm's growth into a giant. To most Skadden lawyers, the founding partners existed only as syllables in the letterhead, with the name most frequently spoken that of the group's most paradoxical member, Marshall Skadden. He was the firm's originator, but, because he died in 1958, he contributed least directly to the firm's success.

But the firm wasn't content to trace its meritocratic origins to Flom. Mullen and others asserted that the firm's success was rooted in the character of each of its founders. They sometimes attributed key elements of Flom's development as a corporate lawyer to Skadden, with whom he had worked for five years. "Care" and "thoroughness" were Flom traits that he was said to have learned from Skadden.

Senior lawyers also shaped the firm's sense of merit so that it was tied, in part, to John Slate and Les Arps. "Skadden Arps was always a meritocracy," Jim Freund said at a retreat. "There was nothing stuffy or artificial about it." Old stories about Slate's practical jokes were important for new Skadden lawyers to hear, Mullen said, because they made clear the founder's "anti-pomposity fixation," which shaped the firm. "One thing John could not stand was people who put on airs." Slate's lack of pretension ostensibly allowed the firm to focus on merit over status. Les Arps was the firm's ethical standard-bearer, and his sense of right and wrong was said to make the firm toe the line of rectitude.

The best expression of the Skadden culture, of course, lay in individual lawyers practicing at the firm. Hired as a managing clerk, not as a lawyer, Edward Yodowitz arrived at Skadden in 1969 from the University of Baltimore School of Law, a third-tier school, where he was an average student. He was put in charge of tracking deadlines for firm lawyers, filing papers in court, and handling other chores. He volunteered to help out associates at night, and, after several months, John Feerick asked him to put in overtime doing research on an article about the U.S. Constitution's provisions for impeaching judges.

When Yodowitz ventured that he would like to try his hand as an associate, some lawyers greeted the request skeptically. ("This isn't 'Cinderella,' " one groused.) But Feerick put the proposal to his partners and they backed it. Having taken the new job, Yodowitz wondered if his prospects as an associate at Skadden would be limited. (He recalled: "I had questions about whether people would still see me as a managing clerk.") But he prospered as a litigator and, with the endorsement of Flom as well as Feerick, he eventually became a partner.

According to Skadden lore, Robert Zimet flunked out of Cornell University after one year and had to go to night school in order to get into Queens College. By Zimet's account, he transferred to Queens after his switch from pre-med to pre-law at Cornell cost him a New York State scholarship and he couldn't afford to stay at the Ivy League school. He attended the Washington College of Law, at American University, from which graduates rarely went to large prestigious firms. (He was in the class ahead of Gus Oliver.) Zimet won a place there as an editor of the law review, and, he said, he wrote to every large firm in Washington, D.C., and New York City, looking for a job. From four offers, he accepted Skadden's, in 1974. He became a leading Skadden litigator.

Irene Sullivan, who became the head of hiring for the firm in 1990, went to Mount Holyoke College on a full scholarship. After graduating, she worked for eight years at Time Inc., rising to the job of circulation manager for *Money* magazine. She also attended Fordham Law School at night. She recalled: "In 1975, when I interviewed at some other major New York City firms, there was clearly a negative inference drawn about, or a barrier created by, my having gone to school at night. Large firms preferred people who went right out of college into a day program. My career path was different and not as easily accepted. I was amazed. I'd gone to a good undergraduate school, and done well. I had a job at *Time* magazine and proved myself at that. I'd gone to law school and done well. They would say, 'How do we know you really want to be a lawyer?'

"I was working as an executive, and making more money than I would as an associate. Why would I have switched to law if I hadn't wanted to? Skadden's hiring became a sort of self-fulfilling prophecy: There were a lot of very good people out there who didn't have the typical career pattern, who found themselves well accepted here, and found themselves here."

How did Mullen account for the large number of Skadden lawyers whose life stories include chapters that seem like deviations from the making of a corporate lawyer? He replied, "People change." But reliance on "merit" also provided a plausible explanation.

A corollary of Skadden's reliance on merit as the firm's essential hiring standard was its tolerance of the range of individuals who met that standard. They included ex-construction workers, an ex-contract bridge player, an ex-dockworker, an ex-labor relations specialist, ex-rabbis, an ex-roadie for rock-and-roll bands, ex-salesmen, ex-scholars, an ex-surfer, ex-teachers, an ex-translator, and many others who were on their second careers.

They also numbered preppies, children of corporate chieftains and American plutocrats, and real intellectuals, some of whom felt the need to hide their shine beneath a layer of adopted grit or to remind colleagues that they hadn't forgotten their families' plain roots. One partner tweaked and honored this Skadden shtick when he said about Tom Dougherty, a former Marshall scholar and graduate of Harvard Law School: "His father died young. He grew up in South Boston and Quincy"—areas that could be tough proving grounds. "That's his slightly overstated but still valid motivation."

Gay partners marched in New York City's Gay Pride Parade, gay associates kept photographs of their lovers on their desks, and gay lawyers brought their significant others to firm functions. Jonathan Bowie, who in 1989 became the first gay Skadden partner to bring his companion to a retreat of the partners and their spouses: "I believe that some gay associates have found the atmosphere unreceptive, in particular in M&A and litigation, because those are such macho worlds. To an associate who is insecure about his future or maybe where he went to school, that style can be very intimidating." And: "There's no law firm, and hardly any corporate entity, that's better on the gay issue than Skadden, but there's no institution that's perfect."

Bowie, on how he got to Skadden: "I spent seven or eight years at Sullivan & Cromwell, a very white-shoe firm. I had finally figured out I was gay when I was twenty-nine, and a third- or fourth-year associate. I was not wholly out of the closet, but I had a boyfriend who joined Sullivan & Cromwell, and people knew about me. I was passed over for partnership in the normal rotation in 1985, and since Sullivan & Cromwell had an up-or-out policy, I had to find someplace to go to. No one had ever gone from there to Skadden. The two firms were very unfriendly. I had this image of the great barbarians up the street. Anyway, I had some interviews at Skadden and liked the place, they offered me a job and I took it. About a year later, I was told about how I was hired. A group of lawyers, including Peter Mullen, were going over my file. They said that my recommendations from clients were fabulous, I was personable, I got along well with different kinds of people. Why hadn't Sullivan made me a partner? Someone said, 'It might be because he's gay.' Mullen apparently said, 'Oh, *that's* it. Let's make him an offer.' "

By 1990, the firm had two African American partners and four Latino partners. Like other large law firms, Skadden admitted that the number of nonwhite lawyers and partners there was still too low, but it strived to be a hospitable environment for this kind of diversity, too. Some observed that many Skadden lawyers were in "mixed religion" marriages, and they had been so when those were rarer, twenty-five years ago.

By 1990, the firm had thirty-three women partners (13 percent of its total partners) and three hundred twenty women lawyers (32 percent of its total lawyers). For associates who preferred to be at home with their children for more than weekends, the firm allowed part-time work (defined as at least three days a week). The impetus for the program was an imbalance between supply and demand. The firm needed more lawyers it judged capable than it believed it could hire full-time, and it believed that a fair share of the part-timers who helped ease the shortage in the near term would return to work full-time in the long term. In 1990, forty-two associates chose the part-time option, most of them mothers with young children. They did nothing to advance their chances for partnership.

For partners, the Skadden approach to nondiscrimination was strict: No healthy partner was allowed to work part-time, which meant no woman partner had that option. No young woman partner with children could cut back at work to spend more time at home. *The New York Times Magazine* published an article about women at Skadden that featured Peggy Kerr, the first woman partner at Skadden, who was raising two adopted children as a single mother. At the firm, it generated resentment of Kerr for calling attention to herself as a trailblazer, and for drawing the spotlight to some exigencies of the Skadden culture. The firm came across like a military service that had accepted women into combat roles and, to make the system work, felt it could recognize no distinctions among officers as a result of gender differences.

Three perspectives from women at Skadden: One partner described the place as "nurturing." Another partner engaged me in a dialogue that made me wonder for the first time as a reporter if I'd just been sexually harassed. ("So what's your project about?" "The best way to describe it might be as a piece of anthropology." "Oh, you're much too cute to be an anthropologist!") A special counsel to whom I was directed to talk about the issue of women at Skadden broke a couple of dates because of the press of business and became unavailable.

In a place that sometimes seemed a men's club (men, not women, asked me if anyone had told me about the male deal lawyers who traded stories about "shtupping" female associates), the rule of the firm that demanded equal commitment by men and women partners might have been a requirement for obliterating a glass-ceiling attitude even if the ceiling itself had been removed.

The partners, male and female, were alumni of dozens of law firms —competitors of Skadden and noncompetitors, some that went out of business and some that still flourished. Among the most senior were men who had sought the firm as a haven. Mark Kaplan arrived in 1979, after losing a power struggle as the president and chief executive officer of Engelhard Minerals & Chemicals. (Joe Flom counseled with him about his departure from Engelhard, and offered him a job. Kaplan: "Joe said, 'Sign the fucking resignation, and come work for us.' ") It pleased Kaplan that the firm tried not to distinguish between those who had been there ten years and those like him who just arrived. "At Skadden," he said, "we're adoptees, immigrants, ancestors rather than descendants."

Kenneth Bialkin, the senior partner and co-chairman of the executive committee at the established firm of Willkie, Farr & Gallagher, ran into serious difficulties there in 1987, almost a quarter of a century after he joined the firm out of Harvard Law School. (Lawyers at the firm claimed that, without informing his partners, he had offered counsel to a company in a way that raised a serious conflict with the interests of a major firm client; he said there was a misunderstanding about his role, since he had provided advice as a company director, not as its lawyer, and that his real sin lay in causing jealousy among his partners through his public activities on behalf of the American Bar Association and major Jewish organizations.)

When Willkie asked Bialkin to resign his partnership, Kaplan took him for a drink to help him decide where to go. Bialkin ended up at Skadden—and brought with him the desk that he had inherited from a Willkie senior partner. Bialkin chose Skadden, in part, because "so many other partners were laterals: I would be one of a series of partners coming from the outside, and I would feel less like an outsider."

Having departed from another home, some immigrant lawyers embraced the firm and felt embraced back. Some found spouses there (Skadden witnessed marriages between lawyers and lawyers, lawyers and paralegals, lawyers and secretaries, paralegals and paralegals) and best friends (they cruised together on their sailboats, they showed up at the bar mitzvahs, first communions, and the weddings of each other's kids).

When lawyers went off on a retreat, the firm primed the frolic by supplying them with water pistols and guns that shot rubber bands. The firm recorded the blood type of everyone who worked there, so it could organize donations quickly, if needed. When lawyers and others fell ill, they felt understood and taken care of: The firm let them know they would be put back to work when they were ready, until then getting others to cover their assignments. Jonathan Bowie, in 1993: "I found out I was HIV-positive four years ago and the firm has been very supportive, in terms of flexibility, and financially. At first, I continued to work full-time. Now I work very little."

In scrapbooks filled with memorabilia and photographs from 1948 on and running through fourteen volumes, the firm kept records of Christmas parties, country outings, and other events. For the most part, in the pictures lawyers and their spouses are smiling and a little stiff, like any group that's gone along with requests for snapshots from a well-intentioned relative. (Over the years, they seem to shed a cocoon of humdrum dress—baggy, frumpish, or, if fashion-forward, loud—for a more elegant look. Senior men exchange boxy suits with natural shoulders for fitted Italian threads with shoulder pads.)

Besides the fortieth-anniversary gala, held at the Metropolitan Museum of Art, the pictures show: the firm's thirtieth-anniversary party at Lincoln Center; a skating party at Rockefeller Center, with a demonstration by some Olympic hopefuls; and a spring fling on the aircraft carrier *Intrepid*, highlighted by the Kit McClure Big Band, whose musicians are all women. Videotapes of firm events show Skadden guys (women have rarely been featured) making fun of their leaders, being flip and sarcastic, getting sentimental. The events seem to be both celebrations and chances to blow off steam as a group—bonding experiences that tie the firm's members together and set Skadden apart.

At the annual Skadden indoctrination at Arrowwood for several years, one of the major sessions was called "How the Outside World Views Us." Senior partners of the firm made a general accounting of praise and blame that the firm received from clients, other lawyers, the legal press, and various observers. Their conclusions were that the outside world generally viewed it with respect and envy: Clients were flocking to Skadden and other law firms were emulating it.

The self-consciousness of the Arrowwood session's topic resonated with the urgent need to prove itself that had motivated Skadden from its earliest days. Mullen: "We tend to keep looking over our shoulders, because we haven't been around for three generations." In another reflection of some insecurity, the firm had a strong habit of immodesty. "My impression from clients is that they think we're excellent lawyers, the best, top-drawer, terrific," Roger Aaron, of the Fab Four, said in 1988. "More and more, we are the standard." Associates maintained that Mullen believed the hyperbole he sometimes used in after-dinner remarks, when, as they remembered, he called the firm "the greatest accumulation of talent in the history of the earth," or something close.

The firm called its lawyers "Green Berets." "We swagger," Alf Law told new lawyers at a gathering. "This is fun!" He also maintained that no one "appreciated" Skadden's value better than its competition. (If so, the appreciation was sometimes shown in odd ways. Law reported that, for a time, Sullivan & Cromwell, which in the 1980s competed effectively with Skadden in the M&A world, had told its clients, "If you use Skadden Arps, we'll resign," and that Skadden "got a lot of good clients that way.") Law also instructed his colleagues: "Our competitors are very good at 'sharpshooting' "—the Skadden term for calculated, unfair criticism. "We have to deal with that."

Sometimes Mullen remained neutral about the criticism that he believed other lawyers made of the firm. "Not everyone in the profession is an admirer of ours. Some of the changes that have been caused by us or in response to us haven't pleased everyone."

He could also be pointed in defense: "The establishment couldn't imagine how a firm could either catch up with them or pass them unless they were doing something weird. People don't like to admit to the fact that they were sleeping at the switch. That they were not doing everything they could to keep up. It's like a pitcher in baseball who cleans up. The first thing they do is check to see if he's throwing a spitball."

No one who spoke with me about Skadden praised it as broadly as lawyers there did themselves, or slammed it as hard as Skadden lawyers predicted. In talks with clients and competitors, I heard plenty of praise. "Skadden has a strong group of partners and not just one guy, and that is to their credit," an investment banker in New York who had used the firm said. "To have even fifteen world-class lawyers in the business is an accomplishment." At the same time, he declared, "I could have gotten the same service I got from Skadden from half a dozen firms." Another said, "There are four or five firms in this city which are in a different league from everyone else." To him, Skadden was one. I asked a law professor who had worked at Skadden whether it was a great firm. "I'm not sure any law firm can be called great," he said. "Skadden is first-class."

I also heard bile: about Skadden's arrogance; about the firm's hyper-aggressiveness in going after business; about its attempts to intimidate, which in the case of federal-trial judge Robert R. Merhige, Jr., who felt he was a victim, led him to reprimand a Skadden partner in court for holding "a club over my head"; about lawyers there too relentlessly pursuing client ends through petty maneuvering and hardball, which made the practice of law against them flagrantly unpleasant; about the gap between Skadden's rich notoriety and its dodgy reputation among some lawyers, or between the high expectations of clients before they engaged the firm and its pedestrian performance; and about inconsistent quality, which, one lawyer said, sometimes fell to "execrable" standards. "No lawyer wants to question the quality of another lawyer," this partner in a competing firm said. "Skadden gives very good service in M&A and good work in other areas, but spottily."

One solo practitioner: "I had a case in state Supreme Court, and a young lawyer from Skadden kept repeating the same request for a motion, over and over. Every time, the judge said, 'No, I'm not going to allow it.' Outside the courtroom, I said something snotty to the lawyer, off the record, and, generally speaking, the things that lawyers say off the record are kept among themselves. When we went back into court, the lawyer repeated it to the judge. When we got done and I was talking to the lawyer, I said, 'I suppose when I get back to my office, you'll be back in court pressing that motion.' It was sarcastic and not serious, but he got touchy and thought I was accusing him of unethical behavior. When we were having difficulty finding a time for another hearing, the lawyer suggested that the judge hear the case at lunchtime. She [the judge] looked surprised and I said, 'But, Judge, this is Skadden Arps.'"

A senior partner at an established firm in New York: "I was at a meeting on a deal, in which my firm was representing the underwriters and lawyers for Skadden were representing the issuer, and a problem came up. It was a question on which the SEC had taken a position.

"The Skadden lawyers said, 'Don't worry about that. We'll deal with that. We knock down walls.' It was: 'Don't worry about this legal question, Mr. Client, by the time you're ready to go to market, we will have knocked down that wall.' The wall was not knocked down, and those of us accustomed to working in a more traditional way had to listen to that bravado."

Skadden also had to endure plenty of direct criticism for its role in some well-publicized cases. In 1984, to take a prime and perhaps unique example, Skadden earned heavy criticism for its part in the Texaco-Getty-Pennzoil case, one of the wildest takeover contests of the eighties, in which Texaco eventually acquired the Getty Oil Company for $10.1 billion.

The takeover also led to a $10.5 billion judgment for Pennzoil against Texaco (the largest jury verdict in history, awarded on the grounds that Texaco had illegally interfered with a prior contract for the sale of Getty to Pennzoil); a fee of $420 million for Pennzoil's lawyer, Joseph Jamail; and, eventually, a settlement of $3 billion to Pennzoil from Texaco, which was granted protection by a bankruptcy court while it straightened out its affairs.

Skadden had been brought into the deal by Texaco, when it looked like Texaco was about to purchase Getty. Skadden counseled that the deal it was supposed to help close was legal, as many lawyers thought, and didn't respond to a lawsuit by Pennzoil against Texaco in a Delaware court. Because of that "procedural catastrophe," according to Benjamin Stein in *Barron's* (a lawyer involved in the case called it the "ten-million-dollar boo-boo"), Pennzoil had been able to sue in "populist, big-money-juries Texas."

"They were in the takeover business, where lawsuits were like rockets," explained the writer Steve Coll. Lawsuits "took off in a fast and fiery explosion and then faded quickly from view."

Coll wrote: "The attorneys at Skadden Arps tried to explain to John McKinley and Texaco's other top executives that their failure to answer in Delaware was an innocent error, that they followed reasonable assumptions and analysis, but the firm's embarrassment was compounded by the fact that all of the other Delaware defendants had avoided Pennzoil's trap by routinely filing their answers."

In *Barron's*, Stein contended that the deal's only lasting losers were the Texaco shareholders. Besides paying $3 billion, they were forced to indemnify the company's executives, investment bankers, and lawyers (including Skadden) for their part in the mess.

Matthew Rosen is a fortyish Skadden tax partner. One evening, as I spoke with him about Skadden, he asked me what lawyers at other firms were telling me about it. Before I could answer, he continued that he was "tired of sniping from other firms." Skadden's reputation among clients was in "a high ascendancy," but lawyers at "other major firms love to knock Skadden." A lot of that is "jealousy," he said, as in " 'I'm every bit as smart as those clowns at Skadden. How come I'm not making as much as I'm led to believe they earn?' "

Joshua Schwartz traced the route he took to Skadden, as a mid-level associate: "All the other firms I spoke with said, 'Where else are you interviewing?' When I said, 'Skadden,' other firms would always com- ment. It was ostensibly neutral, but there was always an undercurrent of a sense of superiority; it was as if they were attempting to justify why they weren't as successful financially. The idea was that Skadden does certain things that they wouldn't do. That was the inference I drew. You'd say, 'Skadden Arps'; they'd smirk and nod their head, as if to say, 'If I weren't so polite, I'd tell you some stories.' People have a chip on their shoulder about Skadden."

And the firm had a chip on its shoulder about others.

A significant reason was the firm's psychology. Its sense of its "merit" was highly relative—the firm was always measuring itself against others and guarding against slights. This attitude seemed to function like a prod implanted in the firm's collective brain. Without the vigilance that "merit" prompted, "others" (competitors, critics-at-large, whoever) would see to it that Skadden's hard-won advantages were whittled down in the public record and that its achievements were diminished in history. This competitive vigilance—anxiety, even—was a less acknowledged part of the Skadden culture.

A senior partner at Skadden described it positively like this: "It was a heady and straightforward goal, to be the best, and one worth pursuing. 'You've gotta be so focused and dedicated—whatever it takes.' " Peter Atkins said, "My fervent hope is that we never lose the sense that every day we have to fight for our existence, because that's the only way an institution stays healthy."

Yet Skadden was agitated by the law-firm equivalent of the law school's *in terrorem* method, a form of unforgiving inquisition used by generations of professors to sharpen the minds of lawyers-in-the-making and push them to succeed through anxiety, if not outright fear.

This disequilibrium was a permanent state because the goal that Skad- den sought was unattainable. In a line of work as subjective, personal, and changeable as lawyering, no firm could honestly claim to be the unequivocal best. Some Skadden lawyers recognized the fact, noting that theirs had been the firm of choice for a particular national corporation that needed counsel in Delaware and Los Angeles, but had been overtly spurned by the same company in New York; and that it had been the firm of choice for a second major corporation requiring counsel in New York, but which avoided Skadden in the other cities.

In the outside world, the firm tried to muscle its way around this conundrum with the extremely direct approach that firm lawyers used to market themselves. Henry Wasserstein, a senior partner who headed a firm committee set up to guide Skadden lawyers about the development of their careers, explained the first piece of advice he gave new partners, right after they were elected: "What I told people is 'You have an opportunity to have some control over your own destiny, over a period of time. My job is to tell you what it means to be a partner here. Until now, it has been your job to get out the work. As a partner, it is servicing clients, managing costs, and developing business . . . by having lunch with clients, meeting "the right people," and so on.'" He said, "I asked people to keep a record of client relations. 'Did you take a client to lunch? Discuss business? Ask for business?' I tried to raise the consciousness of every young partner."

Jim Freund wrote in the 1985 firm manifesto: "We realize that there are many ways to get across the message that we feel we're pre-eminent. So, many of our partners and associates write books and articles, chair or participate in professional forums, and reach out to clients through written material and oral presentations." A standard close for a Skadden lawyer on the phone was "If there's anything I can do for you, give me a call." The essence of the Skadden sales system, a partner explained, was this: "If you don't ask for business, you might not get it." Every lawyer who wanted to succeed at the firm had to learn sales and marketing as well as production, in the words of Roger Aaron.

Skadden lawyers marketed the firm's practice areas intensely. As Freund said, they gave seminars and held receptions and other events for groups of current and potential clients. They sent mailings to clients. They used the firm's referral list (of lawyers to whom it had sent business and vice versa) as a basis for identifying lawyers to contact in the search for new business.

In 1990 alone, to take one year, the firm devoted significant time and money to sophisticated marketing efforts. About the firm's marketing of its counsel to financial services companies, an internal memo related: "Initially, the effort had been focused on Japanese insurance companies prepared to enter the U.S. market or to substantially expand their position or range of products." About the firm's efforts in tax, the memo stated: "The current focus has been on two areas—(1) German Nomura/Tishman deal—how to capitalize on our role and get additional transactions, and (2) Korea—how to establish working relationships with leading Korean investment bankers and multinational companies (NY seminar, Salomon contacts, Asian Wall Street Journal seminar, Korea trip, letter and phone contacts, etc.)." About futures and options: "We have been working on a program to use existing working relationships with foreign commodity exchanges to reach their member firms through joint seminars and workshops. The initial target (MATIF, Paris) has agreed in principle and discussion of the seminar content is underway."

The firm's client seminars for 1990 began on January 3, with one in New York called "Doing Business in the USSR," and ran through another on December 11, called "Utility M&A in the Nineties: Issues and Opportunities." Skadden hosted seventeen other seminars, including "Proxy Fights and Shareholder Activism in the 1990's," "Energy Price Risk Management in Today's Turbulent World," and "Current Critical Issues in Power Plant Project Finance."

The Deputy Foreign Minister of the Socialist Republic of Vietnam discussed investment opportunities in his country at a reception and a luncheon organized by Skadden. The assistant governor of Hainan Island, off the southern coast of China, briefed Skadden guests at a seminar called "World Bank Programs in China: Economic Reform and Opportunities in Hainan Island." In Prague, under the auspices of the Ministry of Industry of the Czech government, the firm put on a seminar called "Privatization Approaches and Techniques." In Stockholm, it presented a seminar on "International Mergers and Acquisitions and Financings: The Current Climate."

The firm made promotional mailings to clients on eighty days in 1990. Its packages consisted of memos, handbooks, letters, outlines, and articles. On January 18, it mailed out a handbook for an event called the "Tenth Annual Bankruptcy Litigation Institute." On February 5, it mailed an outline titled "New Trends in Class Action Litigation." On March 30, the firm mailed eight articles written by its lawyers and reprinted from, among other publications, the *New York Law Journal* ("A Progress Report on Merger Enforcement"), from *Boardroom Reports* ("How to Solve Telephone Service Contract Problems in Advance"), and from the *Southwestern Law Journal* ("Corporate Successor Liability Under

CERCLA: Who's Next?"). There was a letter about doing business in Israel (April 11), a memo about a court decision on insider trading (June 11), and writings about many other technical topics—all in only the first half of the year.

The Skadden marketing memo reported four hundred sixty referrals of new clients in 1990: 18 percent from client calls made directly to partners; 17 percent from friends of partners; 13 percent from lawyers at other law firms; 13 percent from banks or investment banks; 12 percent from new clients "affiliated with" current clients; 11 percent from new clients referred by old clients; 8 percent based on the reputation of Skadden attorneys and the firm; and 7 percent from a variety of other referrals—not to partners, but to special counsels, associates, or personnel who weren't lawyers.

The firm's culture reflected the test of the markets in which it competed. Henry Baer, a onetime partner who became of counsel to Skadden, said, "It's no longer enough to be the best lawyer you can be. Now you have to market yourself, too. A young woman in my department won a major motion in court, and I suggested she get news of it in the firm's newsletter and in the *New York Law Journal*. I told her, 'Take what you are and tell the world about it.' "

Every other week, the firm newsletter carried reports of victories. On one level, the newsletter was a tabloid for the firm, providing common ground to a law firm operating in many time zones. On another, it was a showcase for self-promotion. The firm wasn't the place for shrinking violets. While back-office lawyers whose skills projected could succeed there, the standouts stole bows without waiting for a cue.

One afternoon, I was sitting in a reception area near Joe Flom's office, waiting to see him. He walked in, signaled for me to follow, and headed toward his office. On the way, he was intercepted by an established partner who hadn't realized that I was with Flom. He was a lawyer I'd talked with at some length. In the privacy of his office, his manner suggested supreme self-confidence.

To Flom, however, his behavior was different. "That meeting with"—he mentioned a client I'll call Hall—"went very well. I was sorry you couldn't be there. At the end of it, Hall asked me where I learned to negotiate like that. I said, 'From a master,' " and he bowed slightly from the waist, with his head nodding deferentially to Flom.

Attention to the psychology of power went hand in hand with self-promotion. One evening at the firm, a partner caught up with a onetime associate as he was leaving the office. That day, a paralegal whom both men were working with had been a few minutes late in delivering a piece of research. The paralegal had another assignment due the next day. The partner said, "Tell the paralegal I want that work on my desk by nine o'clock tomorrow morning." The associate said, "I won't do that. It's not that important, you won't be in then, and she was only five minutes late this morning." Referring to the fear he expected to induce with a tight and unnecessary deadline, the partner said, "Don't you understand? *It* works."

To some lawyers at Skadden, the fear induced by "it"—by assertions of pure cower power—was untamed and produced undesirable results. A senior associate, who had worked elsewhere before going to the firm and said that Skadden was "a good place to be" and "a very egalitarian place," described the firm as being without a culture: "The way you can tell that there is no culture here is that people try to get away with things that people at firms with established cultures wouldn't. I think there's more dishonesty about hours—with people inflating them. People here will try to take credit for things they shouldn't. The walls don't tell you to do that here. It's not everybody. But people with a natural propensity to do that will at Skadden—in terms of time and credit—because they don't see anything in the eyes of other people saying no."

Some would argue that this observation was more about fear (or stress or responsibility) than the absence of a culture. The history of Skadden included black-humored tributes to unavoidable pressure and the efforts of lawyers to relieve it, like the Beast of Burden Award, circa 1970, and, fifteen years later, the dubbing of the Screamers, a group of young M&A partners known for expressing their wants and needs loudly, and for always screaming down at associates, legal assistants, and secretaries, rather than up at senior partners.

The incentive was to own a piece, or a bigger piece, of Skadden—of its imposing position of financial strength among law firms. The firm regularly boasted about its revenues, for many years higher than any other firm's, and a client list among the most impressive in the world. Other lawyers prospered merely on the strength of business turned away by Skadden, one partner claimed; respected firms in New York were proud to be on the Skadden referral list. Skadden was at the center of the deal world. It functioned as a gatekeeper, a talent scout, a dispenser of favors. Mark Kaplan summed up: "This is a big, powerful firm, and, if you want to be in certain kinds of areas, it pays to have this firm as a friend."

Skadden preferred to have its power described as Kaplan did—in general, suggestive terms rather than concrete detail. In 1982, Joseph Nocera wrote an article for *Texas Monthly* magazine about a deal done by T. Boone Pickens, counseled by Flom, for which Nocera was allowed to accompany Pickens into private settings as the deal was negotiated, and reported on those interactions. When I mentioned the article to Flom and said I'd like to see him in similar action, he vowed: "No one'll ever do a piece like that again, if I can help it!"

Flom had been the chief counselor in the Pickens deal, and became a central character in Nocera's writing. The most durable insight Nocera's reporting provided about Flom was how little he revealed even to his client: "Just then a phone call came in for Joe Flom. It was Marty Lipton. *At last!* Lipton would no doubt be relaying word from First Boston [the investment bank on Lipton's side of the deal]. Flom trundled off into one of the bedrooms to take the call. His negotiations with Lipton were almost always conducted in deepest secrecy; not even Pickens got to listen in on their talks."

The firm prided itself on pulling off feats of advocacy that others wouldn't try. The writers David Vise and Steve Coll reported that in 1983 Flom managed to get himself and the chief executive of Aetna Life & Casualty Company invited by John Shad, the chairman of the Securities and Exchange Commission, into a closed meeting of the commission, where no outsiders had been allowed for more than a decade. Flom was permitted to argue there that a controversial accounting practice of Aetna's, which had increased its reported profits by $203 million, was widely accepted. (In part out of pique at Shad's breach of protocol, a majority of the SEC commissioners voted to charge the company with a violation of its rules.)

But the firm preferred not to be scrutinized in action. A Skadden partner told me a story that was intended to be about the egalitarian nature of the firm: "I have a very unpolitical associate, whose father had a stroke. The best place for treatment was the New York University Medical Center, but there was a waiting list. The kid got a list of the hospital's board and saw Joe's name on it. Instead of talking with me, or asking me to talk with Joe, he called Joe. And Joe helped him out." Then the partner said, "Be careful how you use that, because it sounds like the kid asked Joe to use his influence to get special treatment"— which he had. If not the product of knowledge, skill, and hard work, Skadden wanted its achievements, large and small, to appear to come from art and mystery, a form of magic, emphasizing the force of the firm.

With the preference for secrecy came a strong desire for control over as many parts of the Skadden universe as possible. Once I called a Skadden client, the designer Ralph Lauren, on the prior recommendation of Skadden partner Mark Kaplan. (Kaplan: "He's a superb businessman. He is there ahead of us. As we get bigger at Skadden, we can learn from him. When his new store opened on Seventy-second Street, he said, 'Think of this as my house, and when people come in, think of them as guests in our houses.' I want him to talk with our lawyers about that.")

Soon after, Mullen phoned me to say that Kaplan had rung him in a tizzy to complain that my calls to clients could "damage" Skadden's relationships with them. I had to be stopped. (I had been required to speak with three intermediaries before I reached Lauren. When I finally did, Lauren said things like: "I think that a fine lawyer is defined, first of all, by his personality. First, he's got to be a fine man. I wouldn't work with him if he weren't a fine man. I need someone with the same kind of morality and sensibility, who's on the same wavelength. He's someone who advises on things that come up in your life. Mark I work with for many reasons.")

Skadden's relationships with its clients were more likely to churn on their own. One morning, in the office of a partner, I noticed he had removed a picture that had been prominent. The missing photograph was of the tycoon Robert Maxwell, which made him look as crude and overbearing as his reputation. Wearing a baseball cap labeled "Skadden," he appeared the loyal client touting the name of a favorite law firm. Skadden had guided Maxwell through important deals.

"I put it [the photo] away when he took his swim," the partner explained, referring to Maxwell's mysterious death over the side of his yacht as his financial empire was unraveling amid inquiries into his apparent fraud and other criminal activity.

"Did you feel tarnished by Maxwell's fall?" I asked the lawyer, who had handled some business for Maxwell.

"Nah, I always knew he was a hard charger. I just didn't know he was a crook."

The Skadden desire for control reflected the soul of the firm. In ways that lawyers measured professional and social prestige, by 1990 Skadden enjoyed a coating of glitter: On its roster were two past presidents of the Women's Bar Association of the State of New York, three past commodores of the Larchmont Yacht Club, and, as the firm regularly noted in its newsletter, scores of former law clerks to state and federal judges, including two former Supreme Court clerks. It also had two former federal judges as partners.

Skadden had no former U.S. Attorney General or Secretary of State whose past service might lend the firm the gloss of high public service (as former Secretary of State Cyrus Vance's did for the New York firm of Simpson, Thacher & Bartlett, for example), but scores of Skadden lawyers had filled lesser governmental posts. And, for most of the previous decade, the Chief Judge of the U.S. Court of Appeals for the Second Circuit (long one of the most influential courts in America, after the Supreme Court, and the most important in the development of federal law about corporations) had asked Skadden lawyers to organize its annual conference for leaders of the bench, bar, and academy, an honor that combined a limited public service with power politics.

Yet, while Skadden lawyers were unabashed about the firm's and their own professional accomplishments and public recognition, a core of them seemed to share some concern about gloating too freely over the firm's achievements. Isaac Shapiro, a senior partner, mused: "I remember being disturbed at the time that the tenth-anniversary issue of *The American Lawyer* came out with a very favorable article about Joe Flom and the firm, and when *The Wall Street Journal* came out with that ranking of Skadden as one of the leading companies in the world. I rode down on the elevator with one of my partners and he was in ecstasy over this attention. I thought: This is dangerous."

Bob Pirie also singled out the firm's hubris as a weakness. He said, "Skadden got too big, too fast—they got too dependent on a big revenue stream from M&A. Those guys were making too much money. If you make that much you say, 'Gosh, aren't I clever. I make a million dollars a year.' I used to tell them, 'What you should say is: "Aren't I lucky that I happened to work for Joe Flom."' "

At a retreat focusing on the firm's culture, Peter Mullen dealt with the issue head-on. He presented the Skadden ambition for quality as an imperative, arguing that as Skadden grew ever larger, the performance of each firm lawyer became that much more important. The consequence of a grievous mistake by any individual was, perhaps paradoxically, jeopardy to a colossus. Fear of disaster was magnified by the conviction that others would take pleasure from the fall.

As a matter of fact, the threat described in Mullen's scenario was exaggerated: Twice in the 1980s and once in the 1990s, employees at Skadden (never a partner) were indicted or convicted for insider trading, having used information they learned at the firm to make, or help others make, illegal profits in the stock market, ranging from $99,000 to $3 million. (Similar breaches had happened at other firms.) Skadden stressed its cooperation with the authorities in bringing the suspects to justice. When the SEC used one particular violation as an occasion to review the other improprieties that had occurred, Mullen recounted, Skadden pointed out that the low number of violations connected with its operations was remarkable for a firm that had done so many deals and far below what the odds would have predicted. The colossus did not fall.

Still, Mullen's imperative emphasized Skadden's nature. A partner commented: "The same qualities that made this firm a big success create a lot of internal turmoil. That's just the way we are." Behind its smooth veneer and displays of bravado, the firm was motivated by a sense of insecurity that helped keep it intense, watchful, and highly ambitious.

13

Green

The Skadden culture was being defined to bind the firm, which was sprawling and sometimes a vessel of contradictions. The firm prided itself on its informality and, touting its reliance on teamwork, claimed to be free from rigid structure and bureaucratic procedures. Yet, like many, the firm had a clear hierarchy: On the firm's internal roster, Skadden's partners were listed (within departments) according to the dates of their arrival. Many partners knew their precise seniority ranking and presented a low number as a form of status, like a low-numbered license plate handed down through generations of a family.

Associates knew their relative status as well: For several years, the firm left no doubt about it by using the term "indenture" to describe a Skadden system of apprenticeship. Many cases had a strict hierarchy of a senior and a junior partner and a senior, a mid-level, and a junior associate, with fungibility inherent in the structure. Associates learned that if they proved unreliable, they would be replaced. An associate named Samuel Scruggs told me about being temporarily reassigned on short notice to help out in another Skadden office, on a different continent. I asked who decided whether he would go. "There must be an element of personal choice for me," he said, "though a rather subtle one."

Associates knew at what level of seniority they would get a desk that could be locked, an office of their own, and a speakerphone, and gauged the importance of an incoming call from someone in the firm by the number that appeared on their phone's digital screen. It was well known that partners had numbers ending in zero and the most powerful of them had numbers ending in double zero.

"Twenty-five hundred. That's Garfinkel. Shit," a lawyer said when a call came in from Barry Garfinkel, who ranked fifth on the firm roster, as I talked with him one day. The phone display left room for surprises, though. Guessing that an associate might not pick up his call late one Friday afternoon, a partner rang from the library instead of his office, and greeted him: "Gotcha!"

The firm boasted a jackets-off, first-names-always, open-door "collegial" policy among all Skadden lawyers and others. The general counsel of one major investment bank that worked with the firm commented dryly, "That's a very good sales pitch." But, like other words in the firm vocabulary, "collegial" had a Skadden meaning. Getting along collegially didn't necessarily mean harboring affection for each other. When I asked a longtime partner about the front-office claim that Skadden was especially good at integrating new partners from other firms, he said, "I wish the fuck I'd never heard of . . ." and named a partner who had arrived laterally. In one Skadden circle, another partner was called the "shithouse rat." He got his nickname when an associate repeated to a second partner something that the rat-to-be had proclaimed. "Why are you listening to him?" the second partner asked about the first. "He's crazier than a shithouse rat!"

As for how the firm makes its decisions, Matt Rosen explained: "My view is that we operate on a variant of democratic pluralism. It isn't a democratic process as such, nor is it a benevolent dictatorship. The concept of the place is that if there are problems and areas of disagreement and dissent, they will surface. A person can decide how much he or she cares. Management doesn't actively solicit agreement in many cases. On the things that really matter, like the growth and direction of the firm, the number of people involved is really small. If there's really a problem, it will make itself known. It would be more democratic to go solicit views in these instances, but it's democratic enough to deal with issues as they arise. Because of all this, people have to decide what's really important to them—when it's worth speaking out and when it makes sense to be restrained. There's tons of subtext."

Like about the meaning of the Skadden phrase "One Firm": In firm memos, the first letters of the phrase are often capitalized to emphasize that Skadden conceives of itself as a unified place, with all clients treated as the firm's rather than an individual partner's, in the practice first developed by the Root firm, where Skadden, Arps, and Slate started out. Jim Freund wrote: "This is a firm in which specialists from many areas of practice work closely together to accomplish our clients' goals."

Size and specialization were prime impediments to Oneness. I overheard the following scrap of talk between junior Skadden associates in an elevator at the New York office:

"If things pick up any more for me, I'll be dead. Did you hear we [a client] got sued?"

"What?"

"Clayton Act violations. Did Cohen talk to you?"

"Which one, Harlan?"

"No, David."

"I don't even know who he is."

"He's a litigator."

"I've been out for an hour and a half."

"He'll find you."

In the mid- and late eighties, in particular, when it was striving to become One, the firm tried to minimize practices that would underscore its compass and stress its internal divisions. Mullen and other leaders received computerized data about the economics of the firm's different offices, broken down by costs, billings, profits, and other categories, such as yield rates (the percentage of client bills actually paid), but the information was closely held so Skadden lawyers would not be distracted by their own parochial interests from the goal of seeking overall prosperity. Throughout its American offices then, Skadden paid all associates at rates established to compete with those offered by other major New York firms. (When the firm opened foreign offices, associates abroad received cost-of-living adjustments.) The firm also compensated partners without regard to where they lived, so partners in Wilmington, Delaware, with the lowest cost of living of Skadden's locations, enjoyed a windfall.

According to a mid-level partner, a One Firm protocol guided dealings throughout the Skadden network. She said to me one evening, "Today, I had to call a partner in Los Angeles, whom I'd never met, never talked with, and wouldn't recognize. I called and said to his secretary, 'Hi, this is so-and-so, I'm a partner in the New York office,' and he got on the phone and said, 'So-and-so, how ya doin'?' And I said the same back: 'Hi, Joe, how ya doin'!'

"We pretend that we know each other. It's required. It's not written down anywhere and no one tells you, but, from the early years at Skadden, you learn to do that." And: "On a lot of occasions, when a partner has called me, I've flipped madly through the Skadden picture book to see who's calling, and find something about him." (The book is a gray-covered, inch-thick, 5¼-by-8½-inch paperback with large black-and-white headshots of every firm lawyer presented alphabetically by geographic office.) "I've done that when I was going to a meeting with a client in Dallas and a partner from Los Angeles was going to be there, and I didn't want to have to guess who he was and introduce myself in front of the client."

On the other hand, each Skadden practice group operated separately—boutiques in an upscale department store. Distinctions among the firm's geographic offices may have been clearer than those among its practice groups (Matt Rosen: "In New York, the more you work with another office, the better you feel about the value of a One Firm culture. If you don't, you get resentful—because other offices seem to work less hard"), but some tensions between the practice groups lay very close to the surface, if they were buried at all.

The major division was between M&A lawyers and others. M&A powered Skadden's growth; no one at the firm seriously disputed that. In case others missed the fact's significance, however, M&A lawyers reminded them regularly of the tangible payoff for all partners from the success of their practice. A mid-level M&A partner summarized: "For many years, people outside M&A made a lot more money than their peers at other firms, because of M&A."

Some lawyers in other practice groups didn't like what they heard in this view. In 1985, Les Arps wrote: "While I certainly do not intend to minimize in any way the contribution that the M&A work made to the firm, I suggest that there were other areas which have and are now contributing." Barry Garfinkel, a litigator, said, "I've never considered us an M&A firm. We've always done lots of other things." Henry Baer, who was a labor partner and became of counsel, told me, only half jokingly, "M&A lawyers believe that, without them, none of us could feed and clothe our families."

The M&A and other departments sometimes clashed over their respective abilities. "Do you respect the smarts of other people, if you're outside, of the people in M&A; if you're inside, of the people outside?" was how one partner put the question. But it was usually about money: "You think you work harder than those in other areas and don't think that the difference in compensation reflects this difference in 'dedication,' as it's put," the same partner explained.

The lawyers whose compensation caused this debate to swirl especially fast were mid-level M&A partners, in their late thirties to mid-forties. They were known as the Lucky Sperm Club. In the eighties, senior partners handed them hundred-million-dollar deals that were too small for the seniors, who had billion-dollar deals going; the members of the "club" developed relations with the investment bankers who worked on the lesser deals; and when the bankers called them directly the next time around, their own practices flourished. Steve Axinn observed: "If you were lucky enough to be in M&A, then you would go onto an astounding earning curve."

In 1990, Fin Fogg, then chairman of the firm's compensation committee, said, "My perception of the most serious problem we face is that, on the one hand, you have an M&A group that has a Green Beret mentality—we're the guys who, year in and year out, jump into the bush and knock off the Vietcong, and the other troops clean up later. Over the last three years, M&A has made extraordinary money for the firm, wildly in excess of budget. The M&A group think they should get a big hunk of that. And, on the other hand, some M&A lawyers don't appreciate that there are other parts of the firm that are steady and profitable. And the rest of the firm resents the M&A group, because we have been so profitable.

"I don't think this is aimed at Aaron or Atkins or Kramer or me, but it comes up for the four guys who made partner around the same time, and the M&A guy eventually gets more and the antitrust guy thinks he's just as good and that his practice is as important, even if it's not as profitable. That's where the schism is. There are some people who sort of hope M&A is not as good in 1990 as it's been—that it goes down. That's not rational. But a lawyer from L.A. said that to me on the phone today. I think that's the most serious problem we face."

To address the problem, in the mid-eighties the firm put into effect a new system for dividing its profits among partners. Mullen described the system as "the heart of the firm's culture." Its goal was to reward conduct that, to Skadden leaders, reflected the firm's priorities.

Among large law firms until not long ago, there were two main models for compensation systems. One paid all partners of the same class so that their salaries increased together, reached a peak, and then moved down together always on a par, reflecting a lawyer's seniority. The other also paid all partners of the same class equally, but, after a long proving period (say, twelve years), paid them the same as every other partner more senior, until the seniormost (say, the sixty-five-year-olds) passed another benchmark (going into the chute, one firm calls this), when the group's compensation would begin to decline until they retired. Firms employed these systems primarily to keep money from becoming a wedge among partners—to buffer law firms from the meanness of the market, creating utopian islands in the rough waters of capitalism.

When Joe Flom became a partner at Skadden in 1954, the firm used the second, plateau, approach. Two years into his partnership, Flom began to make as much as the three founding partners. Because of the disparity between the amount of business that Flom brought into the firm and what the founders generated, however, the system wasn't satisfactory for long. Soon after Mullen became a partner in 1962, according to Flom, Mullen remarked that in some cases the partnership distribution was unfair and that a system based initially on seniority and then on what Skadden called merit would be more sensible.

Skadden began to pay partners by class for the first five years, and then to award compensation based on a partner's contribution to the firm—a formula that lawyers sometimes call "Eat What You Kill." In unusual cases, the firm would make exceptions to the class rule even in the first five years of a lawyer's partnership. The partnership classes then were small and irregularly sized, however (three new partners in '62, one in '65, three in '68, three in '70, four in '72, for example), so allowing exceptions to the class rule meant that the firm could in fact pay any partner whatever it wanted.

The factors for determining contribution were said to be a partner's abilities as a lawyer, his success in developing business from new or existing clients, how much work he billed to clients, whether he helped manage the firm, and his standing among other lawyers—in the firm's shorthand: "If that partner weren't around, how much would the firm as a whole suffer."

Initially, Flom took charge of compensation, dividing the firm's profits and proposing why each partner should get what. He devised a compensation plan for each upcoming year, based on the income that the firm projected, so that a partner could know generally how much money to expect and could plan accordingly. Mullen made adjustments, and once a year Flom and Mullen jointly circulated a list of the results.

When Mullen became chairman of the administrative committee, in 1972, he did a draft of the firm's annual allocation, Flom reviewed it, and the committee either tinkered with or approved their proposal. The firm paid partners by awarding fractions of the firm's profits, so when the firm made a new partner and none left, it was mathematically unavoidable that each existing partner's fraction would shrink, even though the dollar amount of his income went up. By the mid-seventies, as the number of partners began to multiply, the firm carried out its division of profits to the third decimal point—one one hundred thousandth of the firm's profits.

Arthur Liman, a senior partner at the Paul Weiss firm and a friend of Flom's, suggested that instead of making fine distinctions and seeming to take points from each partner annually, the firm should change its system. He recommended awarding units, as in a mutual fund, so that the firm could reinforce the psychological benefit of the pay hike that most partners enjoyed each year as a result of the firm's increasing profits, by increasing his shares as well. Skadden made the change. As before, the distribution list established a clear pecking order at Skadden, as well as who got what, and partners were keenly aware of the order of the names on it.

Moves up and down the list were accompanied by speculation and study. They caused anguish and glee. One year, Flom cut the draw of a recently arrived partner who had brought in less business than the firm expected him to. ("He was brought in to be a rainmaker, and he was a drought," another lawyer who was a partner then said.) As was his habit, Flom called the lawyer late in the evening to deliver the unwelcome news. Another year, the firm did the same to a different partner. Flom: "I remember we wanted to cut back on the percentage for one guy. We did. All the other partners of his level came in and said they'd give back a portion of their take to make up what he lost. Peter stuck to his guns and said, 'No, we're trying to give a message and it's important to do that.'"

Another year, according to Fin Fogg, "Flom decided to pop one guy above the rest of us in my class." (It was Alf Law, who then worked closely with Flom. He later described the premium as "hazard pay.") Fogg recalled that he went "screeching in to talk with Mullen," who calmed him down. It was a common view that Flom encouraged rivalries (Law: "Joe would play people off against each other"), and he sometimes used the list to aggravate them. Law: "Money was the principal tool for keeping lawyers on their toes."

Rivalries also flared up on their own. Bob Pirie, a partner from 1973 to 1982, observed: "People at Skadden like to talk about it being collegial, but it was a mean, tough place to work." In the late seventies, according to a partner then, three of the Fab Four (Peter Atkins, Roger Aaron, and Morris Kramer) pushed hard for a larger share for themselves than the system would have allocated, arguing that the heady takeover days might end soon, leaving them ineligible for the money that they thought they deserved and that was going to partners at the flexible end of the scale. (They had become partners in 1975 and were in the five-year lockstep period.)

They became known as "a pack of sharks," by "targeting" the partnership share of one partner to make more money available for themselves. They succeeded, and later went after shares tagged for other senior lawyers as well. No one was sacred. The firm eventually cut the draw of Les Arps, one of the founding partners. Arps, to me in 1983: "Younger partners thought someone as old as I am wasn't worth the money they were paying me." And: "The more aggressive a firm you spawn, the more apt you are to get kicked in the ass."

The firm's saving grace was the cascade of money it was generating from takeover business. Even partners who made less than they hoped to compared with colleagues made more than lawyers with their level of experience at most other firms in the country. Pirie said, "We found the one color wallpaper that covers all cracks. It's green."

Mullen and Flom began showing their compensation decisions to the Fab Four before releasing them to the partnership in 1980. The next year, they asked the four to help divide the money, and by 1982 the four were regularly involved, without camouflage. (Fin Fogg: "Mullen would flash a list for inputs to us four." Steve Axinn: "The oldsters didn't say, 'Fuck you.' They said, 'This is great.' Mullen managed that.") According to Fogg, however, while he and his peers had a say about compensation, Flom retained final authority until 1983. Then things began to change in earnest—in Fogg's words, it became obvious that Flom no longer had "a real good fix on what everyone was doing."

At the end of 1986, Skadden amassed the largest pool of profits to date in the firm's history. The firm had a policy that when its profits reached 140 percent of the amount that had been projected in its budget, as happened then, any further profits would be (in one partner's words) "subject to redistribution." Rather than have the money allocated to partners by units, the firm's administrative committee decided that it should be divvied up as bonuses, with M&A lawyers getting the bulk. The fund became known as the Pig Pool.

Mullen observed recently, "In retrospect, the pool should have been a good thing, but it was misperceived by a lot of partners. There is no magic solution to compensation. The best system is where no one knows what anyone else makes. I think we're too competitive for that to work at Skadden. People would want to know what everyone else makes. The concept of a performance bonus has a lot to be said for it, in theory. In practice, it didn't work for us. It is divisive enough to fix compensation once a year. You aggravate the problem by forcing people to reckon with their differences a second time in a bonus pool."

By Skadden lore, Roger Aaron and Peter Atkins drew up a long list of lawyers to get bonuses from the Pig Pool, including Flom, themselves, the rest of the Fab Four, and other senior deal lawyers, as well as younger lawyers to whom they had passed along deals. "The biggest problem was the acolyte system," explained Edmund Duffy, a corporate lawyer, "when the big M&A guys tried to take care of their followers." According to Duffy, Mullen blocked the plan and was "heroic in avoiding its dangers": of creating a class system, with M&A lawyers the Brahmins and everyone else feeling like an Untouchable.

In the end, according to a lawyer, nine deal lawyers benefited from the Pig Pool: Flom, the Fab Four, and a quartet of others. "Flom said he wanted twice as much as the next guy," the lawyer said, and he apparently got it. By one lawyer's account, Flom received $4 million, Aaron and Atkins got $2 million, and the bonuses tapered down to $350,000 for Frank Gittes, then a rising partner and later head of the M&A department. This was in addition to their regular shares. Mullen initially kept himself off the list ("I took the position that I could have more influence if I were removed from the pool"), but the firm's administrative committee voted him a $500,000 add-on.

"The way some partners tell it, the thing was fueled by absolute greed," Mullen recounted. "It was misperceived that these guys just came in and grabbed. One of the tensions within the firm as we developed a broad base of practice has been that M&A produced the best economics and lots of other practice areas that were reasonably lucrative didn't measure up. We want to be a firm and to be collegial, and yet if you don't pay some attention to the economic realities, then you run the risk of losing the most profitable partners to somewhere else."

The limits set on the number of partners in the Pig Pool did not keep it from dividing the partnership. Many lawyers opposed the idea because they were not included. A lawyer: "Everyone who worked on M&A and who was not in corporate M&A got knocked off, and was left unalterably bitter." So were many others: "ERISA, tax, litigation—they all felt like they were just employees." The lawyer, again: "The Pig Pool was the most corrosive and destructive event, and created a 'we' versus 'they' at the firm."

Michael Diamond, the head of the firm's Los Angeles office and a litigator who worked on many takeovers, said of the M&A group, "They showed an arrogance that pissed people off. They insisted that they were entitled to a major portion of the money. It was the first time they'd really been that assertive. People recognized the attitude, gave the money to them, and resented it all at the same time. Until then, we all said, 'We're all making a load of money here,' and it seemed that people didn't care that some had more points than they did. That just disappeared."

In 1987, after the flare-up over the Pig Pool, Skadden adopted its new compensation system. Mullen explained it like this: Because of the size of the firm (there were then one hundred forty partners), it was not realistic for an informal group to make compensation decisions. Atkins: "We grow, we evolve, we change." Others said that Mullen no longer wanted to catch flak from partners who thought they hadn't gotten what they deserved.

Mullen appointed (and initially chaired) an eight-member committee of lawyers from different practice groups and offices who divided the task of assessing each partner's contributions to the firm. One of the committee members compared their task to that of scholars judging the academic qualifications of a candidate for tenure at another university: They reviewed the work of lawyers outside their own practice groups and offices.

The committee was asked to look at three groups of factors. In the first were the quality of a partner's legal work (the transactions he or she had worked on and what he or she contributed), the intensity of effort (how many hours billed and under what circumstances), the profitability of the area and practice, and any contribution made to the management of the firm. In the second were a partner's efforts to promote the firm, his or her achievements in the profession and in the community, contribution to the firm as part of a team, and attention to the economic health of the firm. The third category consisted only of seniority. The range of factors reflected an aspiration to move beyond the simplistic logic of the Pig Pool, in which lawyers who generated and took charge of the most lucrative business were most richly rewarded, and, in a time of plenty, to recognize the spectrum of contributions required to sustain prosperity.

Members of the committee interviewed each partner about him- or herself, and gave each the chance to present his or her major accomplishments. Some partners submitted memos, some produced charts, and some handed in computer printouts of their billings. From senior partners, like leaders of practice groups and of geographic offices, committee members also got information about the contributions of junior partners.

For relatively new Skadden partners, the inquiry was a freestanding performance review rather than a report card with money riding on it. For the first four years of partnership, Skadden usually paid everyone in a partnership class the same amount of money, increasing their pay as a group. For partners in the following four years of seniority, the review affected what they made, but if they were considered to be performing well, their pay was likely to increase with that of classmates, until they reached a plateau called the "benchmark," after eight years. In the first years of the new system, partners whose compensation advanced faster than that of their classmates were regularly in M&A. Mullen said that the firm had to keep them happy so they wouldn't leave to become investment bankers.

Since the compensation committee was largely filled with older partners, some younger partners were loath to accept their judgments. A mid-level partner said about his junior colleagues, "They're less powerful and have less to say about how the money gets divided. So they are angry and powerless, but earning more money than they ever expected to and, as their compensation increases, increasingly co-opted. A lot of this is prompted by looking at the distinctions between people you know and figuring if you can live with that or not. What does this say about the firm culture? Rather than being something you embrace, it gets foisted on you and it weaves into your skin."

In many cases, partners reached the plateau of benchmark before they were forty. To rise above that level, a partner had to do something "extraordinary"—lead a practice group, run an office, handle an unusually complex piece of work. When Skadden adopted the new approach, it also modified the unit system into broad bands of compensation. Flom: "A guy's making a million dollars, and, under the unit system, say he would make ten thousand dollars more than another. All that does is create ill will, and it has nothing to do with economics." There were seven bands below benchmark and seven above, or fifteen in all. The benchmark itself covered a range of compensation, rather than being one number.

In 1990, approximately half the firm's partners were below the benchmark, about one-quarter were within the benchmark range, and one-quarter were above. Between 1986 and 1990, according to senior partners, the ratio between the compensation of those at the top and those at the bottom of the list ranged between ten and six to one, excepting Joe Flom from the calculation. To avoid another fight like the one over the Pig Pool, senior M&A partners were given more units to assure them the same high take as before.

The shifts and wrinkles in the compensation system sometimes confused even Skadden partners. One partner told an associate, "Most of the time, I believe that Mullen keeps a large sack of money under his desk and whenever the partners get restless, he sends Earle Yaffa around to throw handfuls of money at partners, and what is left Flom, Mullen, Atkins, and other powerful partners divide among themselves."

Beginning in the mid-seventies, when takeovers made Skadden a highly profitable firm, Joe Flom's annual compensation was taken off the list. It rose from approximately $1.1 million in 1978 (according to one report), when the average Skadden partnership share was $330,000; to $5 million in 1988 (by a variety of other reports), when the average was $1,155,000; to between $7 and $8 million, a well-informed senior partner said, during Flom's best year, 1989, when the firm partnership average was almost $1.2 million and, according to senior partners, the benchmark centered on $1 million.

Rumors about Flom's income have been passed along outside the firm. One investment banker said to me, "Felix"—meaning Felix Rohatyn, the well-known investment banker with Lazard Frères & Company and a friend of Flom's—"told me that Joe insists on making three times as much as the next-best-paid guy." (According to Mullen, there was never any such formula about Flom's compensation, although the multiple passed along the grapevine might have been an inflated version of the one Flom was said to insist on in the Pig Pool.) Through 1991, the public stance of Skadden partners was: Whatever Joe makes, he deserves.

In 1991, a senior partner said, the partners at the top of the firm compensation sweepstakes ranked as follows:

1. Joe Flom
2. Roger Aaron, Peter Atkins
4. Peter Mullen
5. Fin Fogg
6. Morris Kramer
7. Mark Kaplan
8. Michael Schell
9. Ken Bialkin, Jim Freund, Frank Rothman

The list reduced the firm's real culture to basics. Roger Aaron and Peter Atkins headed the firm's corporate practice and were among its most accomplished deal lawyers. They each made more money than Mullen, the firm's chief executive. (In 1991, a senior partner said, "Every year Roger and Peter fight with [Mullen] about compensation, and it's become an annual ritual. Mullen's been trying to knock back the cut of M&A and they're hawks on the subject.") Fin Fogg and Morris Kramer, the other two of the Fab Four, made less money than Aaron and Atkins, but more than other senior partners who held leadership positions in the firm.

Mike Schell, in his mid-forties, was the youngest partner in the top ten. He climbed there by building an independent M&A practice, rather than developing business through one of the Fab Four, as was typical of the rest of Schell's generation. (These included the Lucky Sperm Club, whose members clustered in the low twenties on the list. They were paid more than 90 percent of their colleagues.) Mark Kaplan, Ken Bialkin, Jim Freund, and Frank Rothman, sometimes called the firm's wise men, were in the top ten because (among other reasons) each had "a book of business." (Rothman was a former chairman of MGM/UA Entertainment Company and a former name partner in another firm in Los Angeles, where he is a senior Skadden litigator.) All but Mullen and Rothman were deal lawyers.

The men on the list were masters of first impressions: controlled but not quite intimidating, seemingly confident, agreeable without being deferential. Most of them had fit naturally into the Skadden culture, if they hadn't shaped it. At some point, they had had something to prove. Flom felt he had to "show the bastards," as he said. Mullen moved to Skadden after being passed over for partnership at Dewey Ballantine. Fogg was told he wasn't cut out to be a lawyer. Kramer was told that his chances for partnership elsewhere were poor. In his words, Kaplan "came to Skadden to lick his wounds."

Schell, as a Boston University Law School student, couldn't get a summer job at a Boston law firm, because of the "Harvards." He went to the first firm that offered him a summer job, which was in New York. When he moved from that firm to Skadden, his goal was simply to survive. As one of Joe's boys, the last in the line, apparently, he had done far better. Bialkin had been stripped of his authority at Willkie Farr, and had had little choice about whether to leave the firm. Freund felt he had to build a reputation for himself that was separate from Flom's and the firm's.

The list emphasized that Skadden was a market where reputations were built in different ways, like fortunes in the worlds that Skadden served. A lawyer's standing at the firm could rise—and fall. But, through 1991, compensation tended not to respond suddenly to changes in status. What a mid-level or senior partner made depended in part on the capital of reputation that he had built over time.

In practical terms, a partner's share was likely to rise with his accomplishments and level off if his performance slackened or fell. In 1990, a mid-level partner called the system "genteel." He complained that the principle of accumulated reputation favored seniority as much as merit, and protected "nonproductive" partners—who, in theory, didn't exist at Skadden, because the culture purported not to tolerate them.

The official standard was called "merit," but assessing merit was plainly a subjective enterprise. The Skadden philosophy was that partners could show merit by contributing to the firm's prosperity in many ways. It accepted no formula for reducing key factors to a common measure (business generated, business managed, and so on).

Atkins: "If people perceive, and people can perceive this, that compensation results from an exertion of power, I think that's a misperception." Yet judgments about how much a partner contributed to the firm invariably reflected his relative power—the ultimate, elusive differentiator. Power defined people, in terms of seniority, responsibility, and contribution to the firm.

Skadden anthropologists carefully observed and tracked the attributes of power. "He was the first associate to have a speakerphone, in 1969," a senior partner recalled about a colleague twenty years later, when explaining the Skadden scoring system in an Arrowwood talk. "We're practical," he said, and want to know "the relevant status symbols."

An older partner's name once came up in a conversation I had with a Skadden administrator. She said, "He must have been powerful once, because he has a corner office." The name of James Levitan, the head of the firm's tax practice, cropped up in a conversation with an associate in the tax group. He marveled: "He's third on the letterhead of the whole company!"

The preoccupation with status in such ambiguous circumstances reinforced the cues of the culture that self-promotion was a rational choice for lawyers who wanted to prosper. It colored Skadden autobiography. Current and former partners regularly volunteered to me that they had achieved some "first" at the firm: the first partner to have come through the firm's summer program (John Feerick); the first woman partner (Peggy Kerr); the first woman invited to a partners' meeting (Sheila Birnbaum, while she was being interviewed as a potential senior colleague and Kerr was still an associate).

And because rating power was as vague and subjective as judging merit, where a partner ranked on the compensation list became the official measure of his value in the Skadden market. His position was a surrogate for his power. When the compensation committee finished its deliberations each year, the firm circulated to partners a list of the new allocation of units. "We're very, very interested in compensation," a partner confided. The firm required that they return the list within a day to Mullen, but partners could consult it whenever they wished—to be reminded of how many units they had, perhaps, although they were likely to remember, and to see where others stood. They fixed on the differences.

14

Pro Bono

When the firm's quest for profits seems to obscure its other goals, the activity that Skadden points to is its support of legal work in the public interest. In Joe Flom's words: "An institution, if it's to be worthwhile, has to be more than just a moneymaking organization." To commemorate its fortieth birthday, in 1988, Skadden vowed to make "an original philanthropic gesture"—what Peter Mullen described as "a very unique contribution" to the public interest.

The idea came from Flom. He is often cited as the instigator of Skadden's program of providing free legal counsel—work done pro bono, for the good of the community. Over the years, his pet personal projects have included stumping for higher judicial salaries, working to improve New York City's public schools, and helping to invigorate the city's economy. Some of his many pro bono activities—not just honorary positions—have included service on the Mayor's Management Advisory

Task Force, and as a trustee of the New York University Medical Center, of Barnard College, of the New-York Historical Society, and, as the mayor's representative, of the Metropolitan Museum of Art. He has also given his time to the New York City Commission on the Status of Women, the Archdiocesan Task Force on Crime Prevention and Youth, the New York City Holocaust Memorial Commission, and numerous other public-spirited endeavors, municipal and national.

In 1986, Flom began his sponsorship of a class of sixth-graders at PS 96 in East Harlem as part of the "I Have a Dream" program. (In 1993, there were 156 groups sponsored through the supervisory foundation, which Flom helped to establish, and which operates in forty-eight cities.) For his part, Flom pledged to provide support for the class through junior and senior high school, and to make it possible for the students who finished high school to go to college, by assuring that each one received adequate financial aid and by providing at least a partial scholarship for any student who needed it.

The foundation asks potential sponsors like Flom to contribute at least $350,000 initially, for investment in an annuity whose income will cover long-term costs. It expects sponsors to pay an additional $45,000 to $150,000 a year, depending on the size and needs of a class, during the ten or more years leading up to graduation from college.

Of the sixty students who were active in the Flom Dream class, forty-six graduated on schedule from high school in 1993, and thirty-five went to college (58 percent of the class, as opposed to 10 percent of the high school students in the class's East Harlem district). The colleges they attended range from Bronx Community College, La Guardia Community College, and John Jay College of Criminal Justice, in the city, to Swarthmore College and Union College.

For several years, Amy Coccia worked with Flom's Dream class as his assistant. (Flom also hired Sylvia Rivera, a social worker, as a full-time coordinator for the class.) Coccia is a graduate of Swarthmore who grew up in Bethlehem, Pennsylvania, and Birmingham, Alabama. An art history major in college with no real idea what she might do afterward, she applied to work as a legal assistant at Skadden. She got "the Flom job," she said, because she "had worked for three Screamers in M&A and had proved she could work with them—had the confidence to stand up to them, not take their guff, deal with someone short-tempered, difficult."

Coccia described Flom as a father figure and a role model for his

Dreamers, who were "bright, plugged in, politically attuned." He went to holiday parties with the kids and to "recognition events" for them. He was "very good at support groups," one of them a four-hour session with almost every student confessing having contemplated, talked about, or tried to commit suicide. Flom made sure that his law firm provided part-time and summer jobs for the students who wanted them. The students also turned up on the front page of *The New York Times* with Ed Koch, during his tenure as New York City's mayor (he is a friend of Flom's), in a photograph taken when they visited him on a field trip.

At a high school graduation ceremony for Flom's Dreamers in July 1992, at Riverside Church in Manhattan, "things got a little spontaneous," Coccia said. When it was time for Flom to go onstage and award diplomas to his class, he was overwhelmed by emotion and couldn't talk. The Dream class engulfed him in a collective hug and gave him a plaque with their names on it. Flom replied, "It's you who oughta be thanked, not me."

Flom's public engagement was matched by his wife's. One of the Floms' two sons, Peter, was born prematurely and developed a serious learning disability. (He is now studying for a Ph.D. in psychology at Fordham University. The Floms' other son, Jason, is a record producer.) When Claire Flom saw how little the available New York schools seemed to offer him, she started a new one. Opened in 1965, and designed to help young children with learning disabilities to get into the mainstream of education, it is called the Gateway School of New York.

In 1979, Claire turned to a second major project. She said recently, "I thought: Things are really in awful shape out there. The one thing I thought I could help with was schools, so I figured I would give it a shot." She founded the New York Alliance for the Public Schools, whose purpose was to involve the city's universities and business and professional communities in the elementary and secondary schools, and to promote the strengths of the public schools. She ran the organization for a decade.

In 1988, Claire accompanied Joe when he debated about the legal profession at a Federal Bar Council meeting in Puerto Rico. "We started discussing that the firm should do something far more significant than they'd ever done before in the way of public service," Claire remembered. "We had time to talk about it, and had a lot of ideas. We narrowed down to one, which we thought was a real winner."

After their return to New York, Flom proposed that the firm pledge

$10 million to fund "a Nobel Prize for people who had made contributions to democratic values." A committee of partners led by Mullen was formed to work on the proposal. Some thought that the firm should get something directly for its money. Mark Kaplan said, "My attitude was that we should put up money as matching funds, so a partner might put fifty thousand dollars into a charity board and we'd match it and he'd go on the board." But Flom wanted the firm to make a pledge with no strings attached. (Kaplan: "Joe Flom likes the idea of doing good. He's the guy who forced the firm to put up ten million dollars.") The result was the Skadden Fellowships.

In the "largest commitment to legal-assistance organizations" ever made by a private law firm, according to *The New York Times*, the firm undertook to provide "storefront lawyering" to the poor, the elderly, the homeless, the disabled, and others in need. The lawyering would be done by Skadden Fellows—recent graduates of law school, sponsored by a public-interest group with whom they would work while receiving a salary from the foundation established in 1988 to oversee and fund the fellowships.

The director of the foundation is Susan Butler Plum. Keen and stylish, she had been working for two years as a consultant to foundations and was also a trustee of Joe and Claire Flom's private foundation. Before her foundation life began, she had worked as a counselor to draft evaders in the late sixties, for Planned Parenthood in the era when abortion was legalized in New York State, and for a range of nonprofit groups and foundations. When Mullen and others hired her, Plum recounted, they had "no preconceived notion" of what the fellowship should be. "They simply wanted to encourage young lawyers to do good, and work with the poorest of the poor."

The only issues that fellows would not be permitted to address in their legal-assistance placements were abortion and the environment, the latter because it was seen as heavily supported by other foundations and no longer involving storefront legal work. As to the former: Skadden lawyers had helped write friend-of-the-court briefs on both sides of major abortion cases in the U.S. Supreme Court, but abortion was too controversial a subject for the firm as an institution to take on.

The original trustees of the Skadden Foundation included three Skadden partners (Flom, Mullen, and Barry Garfinkel) and nine respected American leaders: Tom Bradley, then mayor of Los Angeles; Archibald Cox, a professor emeritus at Harvard Law School and former Solicitor

General of the United States; Marian Wright Edelman, the founder and president of the Children's Defense Fund; Ellen Futter, then president of Barnard College; Reverend Theodore Hesburgh, president emeritus of the University of Notre Dame; Edward Levi, former Attorney General of the United States; Henry Cisneros, former mayor of San Antonio, Texas; Richard Ravitch, a New York City lawyer and businessman; and Sargent Shriver, the first director of the Peace Corps and of the Office of Economic Opportunity.

The firm committed to supporting five classes of twenty-five fellows, for a total of one hundred twenty-five lawyers, and set their salaries at the rate of law clerks to federal judges, which was $32,500 in 1988. That was 30 percent higher than the average starting salary among public-interest lawyers, and not quite half the starting salary of a first-year Skadden associate. In addition, the firm decided to pick up the tab for medical insurance and other benefits ordinarily provided to lawyers by the organization where a fellow worked, and to cover interest charges on the student loans of fellows during their tenure.

The fellowships were each to last for one year. The firm pledged to renew them once for fellows in good standing with their sponsors. On the assumption that the full compensation for each fellow, including salary and benefits, was approximately $40,000 a year, and that almost all one hundred twenty-five fellows would serve for two years, the cost of the five-class program would be the $10 million that the partners had agreed to support. By *The American Lawyer*'s figures, one year's portion of that total amounted to $2 million, two-thirds of 1 percent of the firm's 1987 revenues. (The program's annual cost was equal to the compensation of one well-paid senior partner.) Peter Mullen told a reporter that $10 million overall was "a meaningful amount and didn't cause all the partners to have heart attacks."

According to the internal Skadden newsletter, regularly published since 1974, lawyers there had long been involved with pro bono activities of various kinds, but moneymaking jobs had clearly and of necessity taken precedence. Firm historians sometimes cite Les Arps's work for the Crime Commission, in the fifties, as early evidence of the firm's public engagement, forgetting, perhaps, that Arps signed on with the commission because he needed the work. Mullen, calling pro bono activities "a basic part of the firm," said "there was a period of time when we were really up to our ears in the takeover business, maybe in the seventies, where there wasn't as much emphasis put on it."

In 1979, not long after the firm was singled out by *The American Lawyer* and the *New York Post* as the richest in the United States, but not visibly active in pro bono work, Skadden responded in two ways. Internally, it circulated a memo which said, "In view of certain erroneous information which has recently appeared in various newspapers with respect to the Firm's involvement in pro-bono matters, you might be interested in the attached letter from Community Law Offices," a project of the Legal Aid Society. Flom had received the letter from the project's director, who reported that the news about the lack of pro bono work at Skadden "came as quite a surprise since your firm has been one of our biggest and consistent contributors of volunteer lawyers over the past five years"—"one of the top five contributors from about forty of our New York City firms."

For public consumption, the firm informed observers that Flom had directed the partner who coordinated Skadden's pro bono work to concentrate on increasing it. (The *New York Post*: "What's to be embarrassed about making lots of money? Obviously plenty.") Some high-profile projects were undertaken: During the next few years, the firm's notable projects included helping to write a book-length brief designed to persuade Congress to maintain funding for the Legal Services Corporation (1981) and, with the American Civil Liberties Union, successfully challenging an Arkansas state law that violated the Constitution's separation of church and state by requiring the teaching in public schools of creationism (1982).

In 1984, Skadden joined nearly fifty other New York City law firms and corporate law departments in a new program of the city bar association. It was called Volunteers of Legal Services, and its members agreed "to use their best efforts" to have lawyers in their offices donate an average of thirty hours a year to pro bono projects.

In 1985, Skadden brought John Donovan, a former partner in the law firm of Hughes, Hubbard & Reed, into its Los Angeles office. Donovan had worked regularly with Ron Tabak, another Hughes Hubbard lawyer, who was based in that firm's New York office. Tabak successfully coordinated the pro bono work at Hughes Hubbard, helping to increase the number of lawyers involved in its program, spending 40 percent of his time on pro bono work. Tabak had also handled a major appeal in a death-penalty case for the NAACP Legal Defense and Educational Fund, and had done well: the case ended up at the U.S. Supreme Court, where Tabak's client prevailed.

Donovan asked Tabak to move to Skadden, too, and Tabak agreed, with conditions: He wanted to remain in New York, to continue to spend 40 percent of his time on pro bono matters, and otherwise to work exclusively for John Donovan, no matter how much he, Tabak, had to travel. Skadden accepted the terms and in 1985 Tabak made the jump. Not long after, Mullen asked Tabak, still new to the firm, if he would head up a pro bono program at Skadden, to help bring its lawyers' average pro bono hours up to the goal of the bar program.

Tabak wears thick glasses, somber suits, and clunky wingtips. He shouts when he gets excited, and even when he is on the phone, he chops the air with a hand to punctuate his words. Among lawyers working to limit the use of the death penalty, who generally praise him for extraordinary dedication to their cause, Tabak is considered an inspired noodge as much as a capable advocate.

Tabak told Mullen he would take the coordinator's job, again with conditions: He wanted the backing of "top management" (Flom and Mullen) "in a credible way"; he wanted lawyers who spent time on pro bono work at Skadden to be "given sufficient respect" that, when a lawyer working on a case was averaging "enough hours already," the case be considered part of a normal load and not in addition to it; and he wanted Mullen to support pro bono efforts by signing memos about the program that Tabak wrote for him and by coming to pro bono lunches and similar events. Mullen agreed.

Relentlessness was Tabak's chief tactic. He solicited Skadden lawyers by sending memos describing the range of pro bono projects they could do, and asked that everyone respond to the invitation and choose one. If they didn't answer, he nagged. ("I believe that, if you commit yourself in writing," Tabak said, "that's a strong reminder.") By 1988, over two hundred lawyers in the New York office, or more than one-third of the office's total, did some kind of pro bono work. Tabak also took on the common problem of people committing to do pro bono work and then not following through. He would offer them the kind of project they said they wanted to work on, and ask if that was what they wanted. If they said they didn't have time for it, he would ask when he could call again. Lawyers refused the first time and the second, but finally came around.

By 1988, Skadden lawyers spent an average of forty-two hours a year on pro bono work, with the work defined narrowly to include legal services that are most needed by the poor. The average was fifty-four hours, if the definition was broadened to include legal services provided at no charge for a government agency, for example, or service on the board of a nonprofit organization, like a hospital.

Skadden lawyers represented criminal defendants in their appeals from convictions, hosted training seminars for lawyers working with the Gay Men's Health Crisis, and helped create the first publicly funded program of home equity loans for low- and moderate-income senior citizens in New York. They advised residents in some Harlem apartment buildings how to buy them from a financially troubled landlord, counseled political refugees on how to get asylum in the United States, and aided disabled workers in qualifying for Social Security benefits.

According to the *New York Law Journal*, Skadden's per-lawyer average of pro bono work then was creditable, although not nearly the highest of the city's large law firms. Its costs represented a lower proportion of revenues than at many other big firms, the *Journal* reported. The large number of lawyers at the firm, however, meant that its annual total of eighty thousand pro bono hours was higher than anywhere else. Figured conservatively at $125 per hour (in 1993, the firm's so-called blended billing rate, which reduced its various rates for lawyers to one number, was $205 per hour, according to a senior partner), the pro bono hours represented an annual donation of $10 million—in addition to the $2 million annual cost of the Skadden Fellowships. Tabak found Skadden's approach to pro bono work "consistent with its market orientation": The firm did not require such public service, but, to his mind, it had eliminated some of the disincentives that usually accompany nonpaying projects.

An intriguing detail of Skadden's pro bono program is that Tabak is not a partner, but a special counsel—a status more permanent than associate, but without the prestige of a partnership. Tabak explained that he had been a special counsel at Hughes Hubbard and wanted to be the same at Skadden; that it was more important for him to have Mullen's backing for the program than to be a partner; and that recognition for the Skadden pro bono program from the American Bar Association and elsewhere was more meaningful to him.

I asked him why he couldn't meet the same goals as a partner. He told me that when Mullen had inquired whether he wanted to be considered for a partnership, he answered that he wasn't seeking it, but wouldn't turn it down. As a Skadden special counsel, he went on, he made twice as much money as he had in the same role at Hughes

Hubbard—he was probably the highest-paid public-interest lawyer in America.

An alternative reading of Tabak's special counselship is that it reflects the second-class status of pro bono work at Skadden. Matthew Mallow is the head of the firm's corporate finance department. In the 1960s, when he was an associate at another firm, he helped found an organization designed to persuade large firms to let young lawyers do more pro bono work. I asked him about the standing of lawyers doing pro bono work in the Skadden culture. His answer was: "Sure, you can do the work, but at some cost to a steady rise at the firm."

In 1986, the Legal Aid Society of New York chose Joe Flom to be the recipient of the highest honor it bestows on lawyers who make contributions to the public interest, the Servant of Justice Award. (The previous year's winner had been Vernon E. Jordan, Jr., a partner in the law firm of Akin, Gump, Strauss, Hauer & Feld and the onetime head of the National Urban League.)

The dinner chairmen were friends of Flom's and sometime clients: Edward L. Hennessy, Jr., the chairman of the board of Allied/Signal; Frederick H. Joseph, the chief executive officer of Drexel Burnham Lambert; and Jerome Kolhberg, of Kohlberg, Kravis, Roberts & Company. The dinner's host, the president of the Legal Aid Society, was Maurice Nessen, a senior partner of Kramer, Levin, Naftalis, Nessen, Kamin & Frankel, and a onetime Skadden associate.

In a written introduction to the dinner's printed program, Nessen described Flom as more "a flood creator" than a rainmaker. "The success story in the world of high-powered big law firms of our generation," Nessen declared, was that of Flom and his firm. " 'Get Joe Flom' was not a message of Chicago gangsters, but a direction from the boardrooms of major corporations all over the land."

The heart of Nessen's message was this: "Some say Flom made the lawyers' roles in mergers and acquisitions respectable. There is a bit of truth in that: No senior partner anywhere in this nation, no matter how staid or ancient the law firm, frowns when he or she hears that there is a new tender offer in the shop; rather, he or she smiles. But to a much larger extent, that notion of Flom making merger and acquisition advice and action respectable is a false scent; for never should great advocacy for clients indulging in legitimate pursuits have been considered anything less than respectable. Flom has reminded us over the past decades that good lawyers should be dynamic as well as ethical and that stuffiness and snobbery stand in the way of the proper performance of the lawyer's job."

For several years, beginning with the creation of the award in 1978, Louis Auchincloss had written the biographical sketches of the lawyers who received the award. When he was asked to write the sketch of Flom, he demurred. Making a point that Nessen addressed in his writing, Auchincloss recounted to me: "I was asked, 'What's wrong with him?' I said, 'What's right about him? Why is *he* a great and noble character?' "

Nessen used the extended metaphor of a proxy fight for the poor when he spoke at the Legal Aid Society dinner. Heralding the "Year of Joe Flom," Nessen's figure of speech suggested why Auchincloss may have turned down the Society's request. Linking Skadden's pro bono support to the areas of practice that made it possible, as Nessen did, gave pause to more than Auchincloss: "What [the Flom year] means is a great proxy battle for humane and sensible treatment for the poor. It means an expansion of what we do and our resolve to do it, with greater quality. It means daring ventures and more people co-opted to do them. It means a takeover battle for the hearts and consciences of more lawyers in private practice and in the law departments and corporations found here in the city." Nessen declared, "We want the Legal Aid Society of New York to be the Skadden Arps of legal service organizations in the United States, not a tiptoeing servant for the poor."

At a 1988 news conference called to announce the Skadden Fellowships, Peter Mullen sought to break that unwelcome linkage and to draw attention to his firm's pro bono activities in their own right. "This will tend to contradict the view that the established bar has about large law firms," he predicted, "the view that we take from society and do not give back. We have been successful, and we have made money, and we have decided to put some of it back."

The firm also emphasized that the fellowship program was not intended to substitute for its "considerable pro bono efforts." As a report of the Skadden Fellowship Foundation stated: "We devised this project to complement those efforts because we believe that full-time public interest work is critically important and differs greatly from volunteer work."

Of the original twenty-five fellows, sixteen were women and nine men. Fifteen were white and ten were people of color (four African Americans, three Asian Americans, two Latinos, and one Native American). They came from sixteen law schools, and the organizations sponsoring them included well-known public-interest groups (the American Civil Liberties Union, the Legal Aid Society of New York City, the NAACP Legal Defense Fund) and others that served communities with special needs for legal assistance (the Appalachian Research and Defense Fund, California Rural Legal Assistance, and the Disability Law Center).

In terms of public attention, the program was an immediate success for Skadden. As members of the first class of fellows were arriving for work in the summer of 1989, the American Bar Association's Committee on Lawyers' Public Service Responsibility awarded Skadden its certificate of commendation. An article about the award appeared in the ABA's journal, and was accompanied by a photograph of Flom and Mullen, identified simply as trustees of the Skadden Fellowship Foundation.

In Skadden offices across the country, the fellowship program quickly became what Susan Butler Plum called "a fabulous recruiting device." In Los Angeles, she said, the fellowship alone seemed to turn around the firm's reputation, from being arrogant to being committed. The program was designed for people who were unlikely to want a career at a firm like Skadden; the work of the fellows was at the other end of the spectrum from that of Wall Street lawyers. Yet its significant cost and the fidelity to justice that it represented enhanced the firm's standing. One Skadden Fellow explained: "It has a feel-good quality, like the Peace Corps, with the promise of creaming off the best and the brightest. That's what gets the publicity."

In the spring of 1991, the law firm held a one-day meeting of the Skadden Fellows in the main conference room of the New York office. Gathered to address a range of issues, the group consisted of approximately eighty people—the first class of fellows who were completing two years of service, the second class in the middle of its term, a third about to begin, and a few others, like me. Susan Butler Plum and Michael Connery, a Skadden partner who chaired the firm's fellowship committee, acted as hosts.

The fellows were bright and intent, alternating sly good humor with self-protective irony. They weren't turned out like corporate lawyers. Andrew Ko, a member of the class of '89 and a graduate of New York University Law School, worked at the Legal Aid Society of New York City. He is a tall, fine-boned Korean American with curly black hair then shoulder-length, and he wore a charcoal-gray suit jacket, a red open-necked print shirt that wasn't tucked in, checked trousers, and funky black shoes.

Rebecca Hall, also in the class of '89, is a graduate of the University of California Law School at Berkeley and worked for the Berkeley Community Law Center. A solidly built African American with wire-rimmed glasses, she wore a black jacket over a loose-fitting gray-and-black patterned jumpsuit, and black high-topped Reeboks. Her hair was in a complex do with a fade cut on one side of her head, cornrows on the other, and a long ponytail in back.

Mike Connery, one of the firm's three labor partners, also dressed for the occasion, but Skadden-style. He wore a dark blue suit, a crisp striped shirt with French cuffs and a white collar, and a red silk tie. One fellow declared that, in the group's eyes, Connery personified Skadden: tall and commanding; white, male, sophisticated; macho, Ivy League. (On the last point, they erred, for Connery is a graduate of Georgetown University's School of Foreign Service and of the University of Connecticut Law School.)

Opening the formal session, Connery said that one of the purposes of the meeting was to discuss the question: Where do the fellowships go from here? He asked: What can I do for you? What kind of contact do you want with us? What can you do for yourselves? What can we all do collectively to address some of the problems you work on every day? With that in mind, Connery continued, the agenda for the morning would focus on two subjects of concern to the group: legal services to youth and the problem of homelessness.

The main speaker was Mark Soler, a graduate of Yale Law School, who directed the Youth Law Center in San Francisco. He spoke about the effects of the "system" on an abused youth—how the system designed to help the boy had failed him. Soler concluded: "I want to say to the people of Skadden Arps: the Skadden Fellowship program is the most exciting in the country, and there's nothing in second place. The next-best program in the country is light-years behind. I congratulate the fellows, and I especially congratulate the people from Skadden for making it all possible"—enabling lawyers who wanted to do a special kind of legal work to do it without interruption, distraction, or split loyalties.

During the course of the day, the Skadden Fellows followed Soler's lead and expressed a range of views about the "system." John Sullivan worked at Covenant House, in lower Manhattan, in a short-term crisis center for runaways and homeless kids. Twenty percent of his clients had been in and out of psychiatric care, 70 percent had been sexually abused, and 10 percent were HIV-positive. Sullivan: "The statistics are endless and oppressive."

A young mother had asked him: Will it affect my being able to get my child out of foster care if they find out I shot his father this week? A couple of thirteen-year-old boys had stolen a car in Connecticut, driven to Covenant House, and handed Sullivan the key. "Remember in professional responsibility class when they ask, 'What are you going to do if your client hands you the gun and tells you the crime he committed with it?' This happened to me," twice.

Andrew Ko, who worked with homeless families, said, "Lately, the importance of family has really come home to me. Families need a place to be. They need stability and security and, in New York, this is something they can't always get. The social welfare agency in New York, I've heard people say, is a big dumb animal. It's another agency designed to rip families apart, to create misery, and to exercise power."

To Ko, the question he and other young lawyers had to face about the "system" was: If you're so good, why aren't you on the inside? His answer was: "They're never going to let us do that and, if they do, once we're on the inside, they're going to force us out." When Ko was asked what he might do differently if he could start over as a fellow, he said, "I would be less polite. I'm basically a very timid person. For better or for worse, and I think for worse, we're in sort of a macho profession, and you have to make your adversaries respect you. What I've learned is that manners in the face of stupidity and cowardice are not a virtue."

Rebecca Hall told how she had worked as a paralegal for a social welfare agency, gone to law school, and, during the first year of her Skadden Fellowship, worked on policy research about homelessness. Her main conclusion was that being homeless was a full-time job. On average, she reported, people spent thirty-seven hours a week trying to take care of basics, like getting a shower, cleaning their clothes, and securing a place to sleep.

In her second year as a fellow, she switched to representing tenants faced with homelessness. She concluded that the best defense for tenants was to keep them from being evicted. When Berkeley tenants were represented in eviction proceedings, they won three times out of five. Otherwise, only one in twenty kept their apartments. Often they had strong defenses against eviction. Sometimes they could keep their apartment by demonstrating that it fell below standards of habitability. Others, Hall said, tried to use litigation as a threat: "I'll drop this lawsuit if you give my client two thousand dollars, six months' free rent, and possession immediately."

When Hall was asked what she would do differently, she replied,

"Get more sleep." For many fellows, who were intense, dedicated, engaging, and impressive, the overriding problem of their work was burnout. Karen Cole, a member of the class of '89 from New York University Law School, who was working with homeless people as a lawyer for the Legal Aid Society, told the incoming group, "You all have, like, these incredibly concerned faces. You all look so earnest. You become incredibly involved when you do this work, and every time you're beaten back, you have to find a way to keep going. So how? The people who have been involved a long time say: Distance yourself. For me, that's not the answer. It's the commitment that keeps me going."

Toward the end of the day, a different kind of discussion was led by Diane Chin, an Asian American from Northeastern University Law School, in Boston, assigned to the Lawyers' Committee for Urban Affairs in San Francisco, and Sheila Thomas, an African American from Georgetown University Law Center, in Washington, D.C., assigned to the NAACP Legal Defense Fund. Their focus was the range of diversity among the Skadden Fellows.

They complained that the program hadn't gone far enough to assure a representative mix. In their view, the Skadden program had altered public-interest law in the United States. They expressed "heartfelt appreciation" for the firm's support. But, they went on, "diversity" was something that few people thought seriously about in the context of public-interest law. According to fellows who had studied the issue, their roster should have included more fellows of color, from a wider range of law schools. That there weren't more such fellows suggested to them that law students of color were intimidated by the Skadden name and took themselves out of the running by not applying, or that color was a "risk factor" in the application process: To raise the chances that an applicant of color would meet the standards of the white working world, a higher percentage of them were graduates of a "heavy-duty" law school.

The consensus was that the fellows should set an example themselves to get more lawyers of color in the program. Rebecca Hall urged, "People of color need to be sent to schools. They need to say, 'Apply. I did it. I made it.'" Mike Connery responded: "I absolutely agree with that. Clearly, the best thing you can do is go out yourself. You are the best example of what this program is, and you represent it very well. Show people how the process works."

Then, instead of ending the program, the discussion was transformed into a sparring contest.

A lanky white man, Jeffrey Selbin, stood up in the back of the room. In the fellowship class of '89, from Harvard Law School, and working at the Berkeley Community Law Center in his second year as a fellow, he wore a small gold ring in his left earlobe, a blue work shirt, blue jeans, and heavy work boots.

He began: "I think that what's good for the goose is good for the gander. I think that Skadden has to change the way it does business. Until I met Martin yesterday," referring to a Korean American paralegal who assisted Susan Butler Plum, "the only people of color I met at Skadden were the people from the kitchen staff who serve us at these functions."

Mike Connery asked cautiously, "What are you saying?"

"I'm saying that you need to change your ways. I've never met a person of color who is an attorney at Skadden. How many African American partners do you have? How many women?"

Selbin seemed unaware of Skadden's founding and history as a house of tolerance and diversity, compared with many major law firms, and Connery referred to those facts only indirectly, asking, "Don't you think we're sensitive to that?"

Selbin: "It's just that the picture you present to the world doesn't reflect that. I think the fellowship program is wonderful. It's had a wonderful impact on people's lives, certainly those who are fellows. But the values represented by the program don't seem to be matched by those at the firm."

Connery: "Recognize that the firm is different from the fellowship, and that at the firm we work hard to get people of color and diversity. Remember, though, that the pool is very small and that we are competing with a lot of other institutions for our share."

Other fellows soon joined in, airing discomfort about the relationship between the firm and the fellowship and questioning Connery's implication that different standards should apply in each.

Nina Perales is a Latina in the fellowship class of '90 and a graduate of Columbia Law School. She was working at the Puerto Rican Legal Defense and Education Fund in New York. She summarized what seemed to be on the minds of others in the room. "The problem," she said, "is that part of the big bad-guy image of Skadden is leaking into the fellowship."

One fellow complained specifically (with at least one glaring inaccuracy) that the program was tainted by its tie to "a law firm that's big, white, male-dominated, aggressive, competitive—not just white but really Wasp—and that is a hired gun for big business." The reason the firm wasn't enthusiastic about improving the diversity of the fellowship program, the fellow charged, was that it already had what it wanted: wonderful publicity from a big tax write-off.

The fellow articulated a view that was not uncommon among lawyers and bankers. It was expressed to me one night at a private club on Park Avenue by an investment banker: The Skadden Fellowships and other commitments that Joe Flom and his partners made in the name of the public interest were for show. The lawyers were primarily dedicated to advancing the name of the firm, in pursuit of their own glory.

When I raised these criticisms with Flom, he waved his hand dismissively. He said, "I like what someone once said about us: 'It doesn't matter what our motives are if we do the right thing.' That's what counts."

15

The Merger Movement

Skadden's image was established during its conspicuous part in what Flom called "the most massive restructuring of American industry in history." He has regularly endorsed the merger movement that brought it about. Flom once defended the drastic consequences of takeovers, such as the firings of workers, on the grounds that the shareholders of the company involved and, more broadly, the American economy usually benefited. "This is capitalism," he said. "I thought profit was what it was supposed to be about."

In July of 1989, in a symposium published in the *Institutional Investor*, Flom said, "Merger and acquisition activity has performed a critically important function. Companies have become leaner and meaner. Even companies that have not gone through the trauma of a takeover or of having to restructure because someone is breathing down their necks are coming up with new discipline. They're working their assets as hard as they can for their shareholders. And they've eliminated a lot of sacred cows."

After the takeover wave ended in a tailspin for the American economy, Flom stuck by his basic position, but put it in more refined terms. In a 1991 article called "The Future of Takeovers—a Personal View," he wrote, "The debate continues over whether 'hostile' takeovers and related takeover activity are a major positive force for improving the efficiency of American business. The answer probably lies between the extreme positions of those who see such activity as an unmitigated evil and those who feel that companies should trade freely as commodities.

"Most of the debate, unfortunately, is based on idiosyncratic examples or data viewed and skewed to reach a preordained conclusion. Having been enmeshed in the two major takeover movements that have occurred since the Great Depression, in which I represented both targets and aggressors, I would urge that, overall, takeovers have been a positive force for enhancing competitiveness through the repositioning of assets as a result of a business combination or the causing of needed reforms in company operations through restructuring. However, as with any broad economic phenomenon, undesirable extremes have occurred."

The business of buying and selling corporations (or large pieces of them), which Skadden helped create and took part in as the dominant law firm, comprised what became known as the market for corporate control. Flom's "personal view" tracked that of the market's proponents. The market was seen as the solution to a profound problem for large corporations, the "separation of ownership and control," in the classic phrase used by Adolf Berle and Gardiner Means.

The corporation as a legal form is often judged to be a seminal development of the nineteenth century, because it enabled entrepreneurs to raise large sums of money while spreading the risk among many shareholders, to draw on a pool of managers much broader than those who could afford to own a company, and to limit the liability of the shareholders and the managers for the actions of the company.

But, to Berle and Means, writing after the Great Crash of 1929 and during the ensuing Depression, the separation also allowed managers to make decisions that didn't yield the maximum benefit for shareholders. If competition in the marketplace didn't discipline managers to seek that standard, however, a number of scholars responded two generations later, the market for corporate control would.

According to Alfred Chandler, the business historian, the "unprecedented diversification" of the 1960s led large corporations to adopt new structures of organization that seriously limited communication between top executives and the managers of operating divisions. That, in turn, reduced their collective ability successfully to guide divisions of the company that were operating in markets unrelated to the main enterprise of a corporation.

He observed: "This separation affected the competitive strength of American companies and industries far more than the separation of ownership and management ever had." Some of the activity in the market for corporate control in the 1970s grew from decisions of corporate executives to undo what they had vainly attempted to accomplish through mergers in the previous decade.

The main determinant of those decisions was the relatively poor financial performance of the divisions that had been acquired. Unable to oversee operations as they once had or to make decisions about the use of corporate resources based on firsthand knowledge about their firm's full portfolio of businesses, top executives increasingly relied on financial measures as ultimate standards. Beginning in the sixties, many executives with a background in finance rose to the top of American corporations. The logic of finance, previously used as one of several tools of management, became a shortcut to judgment about overall corporate performance—the bottom line.

In the market for corporate control, return on investment was also a key factor to executives, indirectly. The currency of exchange in the market was the price of a share of a company, which was assumed to reflect its overall performance. The primary test of performance was the return on investment, or capital, in the company. If performance was good and the price remained high, measured in terms of the company's earnings per share of common stock, the company was safe. Otherwise, the firm was vulnerable to a takeover.

According to Michael Jensen, a professor at Harvard Business School and at the University of Rochester, and the most vigorous academic proponent of the market for corporate control in the eighties, the market addressed the critical problem that resulted from the separation of ownership and control after the Second World War—what managers did with any surplus of corporate funds.

The money that remained after they made appropriate new corporate investments, called free cash flow, should have been paid out to shareholders as dividends, Jensen argued. When it wasn't, but was used for acquisitions, for example, managers were shielded from having to ask new investors for help in financing fresh ventures, which would have required that they prove their ability to deliver a competitive return on capital. The market for corporate control stripped managers of this protection. It zeroed in on the basic element of capitalism.

Through the 1970s, according to proponents, changes that the market for corporate control prompted companies to make amounted to a cure for the ills caused by blundering, mismanagement, and waste of American corporations in the previous decade. It altered the balance of power between managers and shareholders. By returning some control to the owners, it brought a kind of democracy to the governance of corporations. (The democracy was limited, however. The voters, or shareholders, were generally given no information about a bidder's plans for the corporation in which they owned shares, except for the price it would pay to accomplish a takeover.) The benefits of the shift were restricted by government enforcement of antitrust laws, which limited the size and scope of deals, and by financial regulations and conventions, which limited the amount of capital available for deals. But, to believers, the advantages were evident nonetheless.

The proof lay in the stock-market value of corporations involved in control contests. Beginning in the mid-seventies, a new kind of study found that soon after a friendly merger or a hostile takeover was announced, the price of the target company's stock went up beyond what the normal fluctuations of the market would have caused, and the price of the acquiring company's stock changed little beyond what was normal. The overall effect was that shareholders gained. Mergers, takeovers, and other deals done in the market for corporate control were judged to increase corporate value all around.

An acquiring company never paid less than what a target was selling for in the stock market before the bid was announced. It usually paid much more. The increase was called a control premium. To proponents of the control market, who believed in its rationality, there was a reason for payment of a premium. The stock market valued each share as a minority share, and shareholders in the minority had little say about a corporation's management. But a majority shareholder, especially one that bought a company outright, could transform the company and increase its worth. According to the theory behind the control market, an acquirer that paid a premium could still make a good return on its investment because of gains in efficiency. The upticks of the stock prices for target companies reflected that fact.

In the 1980s, the curtailment of antitrust enforcement and the deregulation of American finance that led to the rise of junk bonds enabled the control market to operate at a pace no one had anticipated, with almost no constraint. The laissez-faire philosophy at the heart of the argument in favor of the control market reigned in America: Society functioned as Economics One courses taught that it did; capital flowed to its maximum use, and the country benefited.

In the middle of the decade, the President's Council of Economic Advisers included an extraordinary and unqualified endorsement of the control market in its annual report. When the American Economic Association sought to present a balanced set of views about takeovers in its journal, the contributions that it received heavily favored the market for corporate control. There were few heavyweight economists making counterarguments.

Michael Jensen declared that the "gains to shareholders" from takeovers and related transactions were "huge." In the ten years from 1977 through 1986, he asserted, they totaled "$346 billion (in 1986 dollars)." By Jensen's tally, the gains realized by shareholders of the buying firms added "at least another $50 billion to the total."

By the mid-eighties, however, it was also clear that the control market was booming for reasons other than those giving coherence to the theory behind it. Rather than being used as a form of discipline against poor performance by corporate managers, it turned out, many takeovers were simply one corporation capturing another. W. T. Grimm & Company, the leading collector of data about mergers and acquisitions, reported in 1985 that "many of the merger participants in the last decade were large, well-managed concerns acquiring financially healthy and well-managed companies enjoying strong market positions. The acquired companies, in most cases, ranked first or second within their industries."

The rise in the use of junk bonds underscored that the market for corporate control had a life of its own, which the ideas of Jensen and others had not anticipated. Junk bonds made all but the very largest corporations vulnerable to takeovers. From 1977, the first year there was a substantial market for junk bonds, through 1981, the market averaged about $1.2 billion of new bonds a year. In 1982, it doubled to $2.5 billion. In 1983, it more than doubled again, to $6 billion. In 1983, bonds underwritten by Drexel Burnham Lambert were first used to finance hostile takeovers, and in 1984, T. Boone Pickens, Carl Icahn, and others who called themselves financial entrepreneurs used junk bonds in bids by relatively small companies or groups of investors for much larger companies.

Junk bonds expanded the sources of financing for the entrepreneurs, who sometimes had difficulty obtaining it from commercial banks. They multiplied the size of deals that the entrepreneurs could do, because of the amount of funds that they were able to raise directly through junk and through other means, since some banks would finance up to half the cost of a deal if the other debt that bidders took on was secondary to their own. In 1984, the amount of new junk bonds issued almost doubled again, to almost $11.5 billion.

In 1986, it peaked at $31 billion, before settling to a plateau somewhat below that level, where it stayed for several years until the junk market collapsed in 1989. The amount of junk bonds used in hostile takeovers was a fraction of the total of new bonds each year, but increasingly a larger one. The bonds enabled Michael Milken to act as a puppeteer of the control market, picking targets for entrepreneurs and assuring the completion of deals by placing junk bonds issued by the entrepreneurs' companies with other clients of Drexel Burnham Lambert.

Along with the deals of the entrepreneurs, the most dramatic use for the bonds lay in a relatively new form of financing for a corporate acquisition called the leveraged buyout, or LBO. In the 1950s and 1960s, the technique was called the bootstrap. It was generally used when the owner of a small, privately controlled company wanted to raise money, either to solve a short-term financial problem or to cash out of the business by selling to someone who couldn't raise the funds necessary for purchase any other way. In a bootstrap, the company took on as much debt as it could service with the cash it generated in the normal course of business ("leveraging"), and the buyer used the funds raised to purchase the business. The assets of the corporation usually secured the loan.

Jerome Kohlberg refined the bootstrap in the sixties as an investment banker with the firm of Bear, Stearns & Company, so that managers of companies could use the technique of leveraging to take part in buyouts of their firms. Kohlberg oversaw a number of LBOs on his own, and in 1969, two new Bear Stearns bankers, Henry Kravis and George Roberts, helped him for the first time on a deal. In the next half decade, they regularly worked together, specializing in LBOs that took private (turned into privately owned companies) former divisions of conglomerates whose stock was publicly traded. The deals were often divestitures.

The premise of KKR, as the trio was called, was that, standing alone, a new company could often be managed to yield more value than it had done as part of a conglomerate. Investors in an LBO could therefore realize large gains: The company could go public again, and issue new stock at a price that was higher than the cost of the buyout; or the company could be resold at a higher price. The business of LBOs was described as financial engineering. Its payoff (the "pot of gold") was expected to arrive in short order.

In the seventies, for example, Kolhberg and his colleagues were involved in a $38 million buyout of the Vapor Corporation, which made industrial valves and pumps and had been part of the Singer Company. The new company's shares increased in value from $2.80 to $33 apiece, or by a factor of twelve, between the buyout and the company's resale to another corporation six years later. This was a typical return on an LBO investment at the time. By some measures, annual returns averaged 40 percent in the early years of buyouts. Although some LBOs didn't work out, the deals of KKR became the most lucrative done by Bear Stearns. In 1976, the three left to found Kohlberg, Kravis, Roberts & Company, the first small investment firm to specialize in leveraged buyouts. Joe Flom sent them their first deal.

To Kohlberg and company, the risks of LBOs, represented by their defiance of longtime convention in having a company take on a maximum load of debt, required the group to look for buyout candidates that would reduce the odds of the debt sinking the company created by the buyout. Among the conditions they sought, according to the writer Max Holland, were that a company had to have little debt to begin with; it had to have a steady flow of cash from its business to service the debt taken on in the deal; it had to compete in a mature market, so that it was unlikely to need new technology and, therefore, require an infusion of capital to pay for it; it had to have fixed assets of physical plants, property, and equipment that were usable, had been fully depreciated for tax purposes, and cost more to replace than their recorded value on the company's accounting books; and it had to have proven managers who would stay on after the buyout.

To proponents of the market for corporate control, LBOs were even more effective in serving the interests of shareholders than the threat of a takeover. Where managers might get away with retaining a company's free cash flow and not distributing it in dividends in a traditionally financed company, they had a legal obligation to use that cash to service debt taken on in a buyout. If they didn't, they would lose the equity they gained in the deal.

But the KKR insistence on retaining proven managers again contradicted the premise of the market for corporate control that buyouts would improve a company's performance by replacing bad managers with good ones. Furthermore, to Kohlberg and his colleagues, the benefits of LBOs were less in discipline than in the advantages provided them by the American government. Once a buyout was accomplished, the company could raise the value of its assets on its accounting books to the level of the cost of replacing them, which was invariably higher than what the buyout had paid for them, and it could again fully depreciate them under federal tax law—using the depreciation to offset income from the business. The company could also write off the interest payments on its debt. As long as it made enough profit, the company had two large shelters against corporate taxes that it could take advantage of: Without changing anything but its accounting books and its financial structure, the company could significantly improve its "profit."

Through most of the 1970s, no one attempted a leveraged buyout of a company that cost more than $100 million. Most were much smaller. In May of 1979, with Skadden as counsel, Kohlberg and his colleagues engineered the first buyout well beyond the old limits, for $355 million, of a manufacturer of machine tools, pumps, automotive products, and construction materials called Houdaille Industries. According to the Skadden newsletter, the financing for the deal involved "a line of credit and a revolving credit agreement, senior notes, senior subordinated notes, junior subordinated notes, two classes of preferred stock," and more. The size of the buyout was reflected in its financial complexity.

However, the deal involved no junk bonds. (In 1986, junk bonds were used to refinance it.) Within a few years, many buyouts did. The bonds permitted bidders to attempt much larger deals, and their targets became whole companies rather than divisions. From 1985 to 1989, investors' purchases of publicly traded companies through leveraged buyouts made up almost one-quarter of all the deals of $100 million or more; in 1987, they represented one-third.

In 1987, Joe Flom told an interviewer for the *Institutional Investor* that he was "delighted" to have been involved in the "three major areas" of financial change during the previous generation—"the growth of nonconsensual transactions, leveraged buyouts, and high-yield bonds." Flom spoke of them as if they were neutral innovations in means that could serve a variety of ends. In his view, however, the ends they served were generally good ones.

The hostile takeovers of the 1970s were momentous because they opened up the field of mergers and acquisitions. "Once these takeovers got started," Flom said, "we were off to the races." The advent of junk bonds was important because it allowed corporations and others to undertake deals that were much larger than ever before: they "leveled the playing field" between small and large companies and subjected large ones to the discipline of the market just like others. Leveraged buyouts were, after takeovers, the next major innovation in dealmaking.

Yet, by the early eighties, hostile takeovers, junk bonds, and leveraged buyouts were not simply means that could be used to good or bad effect by American and other corporations. According to Alfred Chandler, they allowed corporations to be "bought, sold, split up, and recombined" as never before. The breadth of this activity suggested that the measure of the merger movement should not simply be its effect on shareholders, as believers in laissez-faire economics contended, but on the companies themselves and, in broader terms, on the country.

The business of buying and selling corporations sometimes served the long-term interests of companies. In the chemical industry, for example, one of the most important to the American economy (it is about twice as large as the automobile industry), some companies successfully used mergers and acquisitions to gain lines of specialty chemicals that were more demanding to make than basic chemicals and yielded higher profits. Similar advantages accrued to companies in other industries.

But the buying and selling developed its own dynamic that served the long-term interests of companies far less than it required them to focus on the short term. For a few years, it appeared that a takeover—domineering, sudden, with the likelihood of ending the life of a corporation—could be warded off if executives improved the performance of their companies, according to the financial measures that influenced decisions in the control market. When it became clear that aggressors were choosing strong targets, so that the odds that a company would be a target of a takeover in fact increased with the level of its financial performance, the takeover threat led companies to adopt defensive ploys that could be self-destructive.

They made acquisitions so that they would be less attractive as targets. They sought partners for otherwise unsought friendly mergers that would remove them from the takeover market. Their governing boards adopted procedures of governance that made it more difficult for them to be taken over. They bought off aggressors with tribute.

The takeover game, as many participants called it, came to describe an arena with its own rules. Deals were regularly done for the sake of financial gains from the transactions themselves. Deals were initiated by companies which otherwise might not have pursued them, because they wanted to maintain some control over the company's direction. Deals caused purchases by misadventure, creating chain reactions, when one company that lost out to another used the treasury of cash and credit it had amassed to buy a third company.

For a time in the 1970s and early 1980s, the first aggressor in a takeover contest was almost guaranteed to lose to another company invited into the fray by the target company as a more acceptable acquirer. (The third party was generally called a white knight, although its intentions weren't necessarily gallant.) To avoid the white-knight problem, a tactic described as a bear hug became popular, in which a potential aggressor proposed a supposedly "friendly" merger, with the threat that it might undertake a hostile bid if the target didn't cooperate. By the mid-eighties, executives sometimes kept companies from being taken over by taking them private, often through a leveraged buyout. LBOs became an alternative to hostile takeovers. At the same time, LBOs were also done on a hostile basis, and became a mechanism for takeovers.

In the eighties, an increasingly common defensive ploy by corporations that wanted to make themselves less attractive to takeover was converting equity (a form of ownership) into debt (an obligation). This was described as self-help. The idea was to eliminate a corporation's capacity to borrow as a reason for another company to take it over. In the year and a half between January of 1984 and July of 1985, for example, almost half of the 850 largest American corporations bought back their own stock, took on more debt, and engaged in other forms of financial restructuring, apparently with their vulnerability to takeover in mind.

In the logic of finance, debt was better than equity. Capital raised through taking on debt was cheaper than capital raised through issuing equity: The interest on it was deductible whereas dividends on equity were not. Servicing debt, in the language of the control market, didn't "waste cash flow." Paying dividends did, because they were twice taxed as income: once to the corporation and a second time to the shareholder. In the long term, debt might be riskier for a corporation than equity. If the economy turned down, a corporation could cut dividends to holders of equity but it could not fail to service its debt. A large amount of debt could severely limit its flexibility. During the takeover era, however, relatively few were thinking of the long term, or of a straitened economy.

According to Margaret Blair of the Brookings Institution, the "great corporate restructuring movement of the 1980s" was caused, in part, by "the combination of high real interest rates and sagging returns" that had characterized U.S. industries since the late sixties, when they began to seek growth through diversification rather than through new investments. (The real interest rate is the difference between the interest rate charged by banks and the rate of inflation.) The low returns made it more profitable "for financial entrepreneurs to dismantle whole corporations, to siphon funds away from physical production, and to redeploy them in financial investments" than to commit them to long-term investments. To Blair, "corporate restructuring and the rush to leverage can be viewed as another symptom of the widespread shift in the U.S. economy of the 1980s away from savings and toward debt-financed consumption."

But even if the merger movement was not primarily a symptom of stagnant productivity, as Blair argued, and if it lacked a clear, simple explanation, the phenomenon was not the result of irrationality. The United States has the largest pool of capital in the world and, in the heyday of the movement, the managers of the institutional funds that owned an increasingly large portion of the shares of publicly traded companies increasingly sought short-term returns on investment rather than long-term appreciation. As fiduciaries, they were obliged to maximize returns, by custom, if not law. The size of the premiums paid for target companies meant that even the best-managed companies could rarely produce equivalent results for shareholders.

If shareholders hesitated to sell in response to a tender offer, because a takeover looked like it might not go through, for example, the market for corporate control had another set of players—arbitrageurs—who eliminated that risk for shareholders by assuming it themselves. They bet on the success of takeovers by paying shareholders more than the market value of their holdings but less than the premium promised in a tender offer. Since they were most interested in buying large blocks of stock, institutional investors were their best suppliers. If the arbitrageurs were right, they profited from the difference between what they had paid and the size of the premium offered for a company, multiplied by the number of shares that they owned.

Arbitrageurs did more than assume risk. Once stock was in their hands, they had a stake in the success of a takeover. Their very presence raised the chances that a takeover would go through. They became the company's shareholders, with every incentive to help the takeover to succeed. If it didn't, the value of their shares, which fluttered up on takeover rumors, was likely to sink back down. The central role of arbitrageurs, for whom a month of holding stock was a long time, emphasized how intensely the merger movement was riveted by the short term.

During the eighties, corporations were often treated less like complex institutions that served a variety of sometimes conflicting interests (e.g., short-term profits for shareholders versus long-term investment in research and development) than as collections of assets that could be combined and recombined in various configurations, like a deck of cards that could be dealt to yield losing or winning hands.

Gregg Jarrell, the chief economist for the Securities and Exchange Commission during the Reagan administration, and two co-authors expressed this outlook when they declared that transactions in the market for corporate control reflected "economically beneficial reshufflings of productive assets." The language that Joe Flom used to defend the merger movement closely echoed that of Jarrell and his allies.

Flom and Jarrell served together on an advisory committee appointed in 1983 by the chairman of the Securities and Exchange Commission to study the takeover phenomenon. Other members of the committee included Martin Lipton, Flom's chief rival and a skeptic about the universal benefits of takeovers, and Robert Rubin, the leader of Goldman Sachs & Company, the investment bank, who was later appointed chairman of the National Economic Council in the Clinton administration.

The appointment of the panel was prompted by a messy takeover involving three major corporations (Bendix, Martin Marietta, and Allied), in which the first two wound up immobilized, as owners of a majority of each other's stock, and the third put an end to what its chairman, Edward Hennessy, called "a pretty sorry spectacle for American business," by buying all of Bendix and 39 percent of Martin Marietta.

The committee made fifty moderate recommendations for changes in the regulation of takeovers, but the equivocating tone of its 171-page report was set in the first recommendation: "The purpose of the regulatory scheme should be neither to promote nor to deter takeovers; such transactions and related activities are a valid method of capital allocation, so long as they are conducted in accordance with the laws deemed necessary to protect the interests of shareholders and the integrity and efficiency of the capital markets." (Flom and Robert Greenhill, then of Morgan Stanley, were co-chairs of the subcommittee that dealt with the issue of regulation.) The committee concluded that the Reagan administration's hands-off approach to takeovers should essentially be left alone, as it was.

The panel did so over the protests of Lipton, who felt that the group's makeup and its views reflected a pro-takeover bias, and of another panel member, former Supreme Court Justice Arthur Goldberg, who filed a short dissent which concluded: "The abuses in the tender [offer] situation are substantial, serious and continuing." The panel's report was criticized from the other flank by Jarrell and Frank Easterbrook, a conservative legal scholar, who was appointed to be a federal judge by Ronald Reagan. The Jarrell-Easterbrook statement faulted the committee's report as "a plea for more regulation." According to an account of the panel's deliberations by Steve Coll and David Vise, Jarrell believed that the representatives of Wall Street "wanted to create just enough regulatory delays during [takeover] battles to enhance the market for legal and financial advice."

During the period of the commission's hearings, in 1983, Joe and Claire Flom invited me to dinner at their town house in Manhattan. That day, Flom had taken part in a debate about takeovers sponsored by *The Atlantic Monthly*. His opponent was Robert Reich, then a teacher at Harvard's Kennedy School of Government. (Years later, Reich served as a principal economic adviser to Bill Clinton during his presidential campaign. In 1993, he became Secretary of Labor.) Reich had argued that takeovers represented the highest form of "paper entrepreneurialism"—big deals in which little new wealth was created for society, while enormous sums of money changed hands, a lot of it filling the pockets of investment bankers and lawyers like Flom. Claire Flom told me that she had found the galleys for the book in which Reich made this argument in a wastebasket next to Joe's bed. Flom confirmed that he had thrown out the book.

Flom's beef against Reich was almost philosophical. Reich and others were barely heard above the roar of enthusiasm for takeovers, but they contended there was sound, if imperfect, evidence to support their judgment that takeovers were often harmful.

Flom and others asked: By what standard? For the country? What if there had been no takeover wave? Would business as it had been going in American corporations have served the country better? For the industries involved? Would they have been as competitive without take-overs? For the shareholders of companies? How could they have fared better? The evidence of Jensen and others of a generalized benefit was clear and convincing. No data contradicted it. (One of Flom's partners put it: "If the argument is that companies that get left alone focus on long-term strategic planning and build for the future, that's a lot of horseshit.") Otherwise, each deal was sui generis, so distinct that the lot of them gave rise to no obvious patterns supporting a respectable coun-terclaim. Flom brushed off the possibility of a coherent negative appraisal.

If the stock-market evidence had been as clear as Flom and others made out, given the prevailing American ideology, it would have been difficult to refute them. But the effort to simplify the debate about takeovers to a consideration of the price of a corporate share was open to criticism on its own terms, because it regularly overlooked the actual reasons for the increases in the price of a share. The American capital markets were effective for shareholders, but increasingly at the expense of other interests.

The laissez-faire position depended on, among other things, the belief that takeover premiums accurately anticipated improvements in oper-ating performance for corporations under new ownership, which would pay for the premiums retroactively. But by the eighties a growing body of economic analysis indicated that takeover premiums were often paid for by other means, and that some of the run-up in stock prices could be attributed to the market's anticipation of the premiums, not to real increased value.

Economists called the other means "transfers of wealth." The transfers came to shareholders from employees of the target company (through layoffs and wage cuts); from pensioners (through so-called reversions, or seizures, of pension funds); from bondholders (through the decrease in the value of their bonds); from governments (through the loss of tax revenues); and from other so-called corporate stakeholders to whom executives were responsible. Some transfers could be justified in terms of the primacy of shareholder interests over those of other stakeholders (e.g., employees) and in terms of rationality (any corporation that didn't minimize taxes acted against its self-interest). But, over time, they could be justified less often in terms of efficiency, let alone fairness.

Furthermore, because of the lure of the control market—reflected in the increasingly high premiums paid for corporations in order to clinch deals and the increasingly heavy loads of debt taken on to complete them—takeovers beginning in the early eighties were notably less successful than the most impressive ones of the half decade before, in the financial terms favored by the control market. Rather than correctly anticipating improvements in operating performance, hikes in premiums made it more difficult for takeovers to succeed. The profits of bidders declined sharply in the years right after the deals.

As Edward Herman, of the Wharton School at the University of Pennsylvania, and Louis Lowenstein, of Columbia Law School, wrote: "Eventually, those who bid for companies in order to operate them showed mediocre results, even while those who played the game for speculative purposes only were able to profit handsomely." A growing body of evidence indicated that, in the long term, the value of shares of companies that did takeovers went down, as a result of the drag of the company taken over.

The story of LBOs took a similar turn. According to the economists William Long, of the U.S. Census Bureau, and David Ravenscraft, of the University of North Carolina, the early leveraged buyouts yielded "strong evidence" that such deals improved the "operating performance" of companies. In a comprehensive sample of LBOs done before 1985, they found that company income rose between 20 and 30 percent, on average, after a buyout, and that 60 percent of the companies involved in them showed improvements in performance—although improvements came less often from streamlining production than from tax savings, reductions in overhead, and cuts in capital expenditures that could be argued to yield a short-term benefit at the expense of future returns.

Companies in deals done after 1985 "failed to improve" performance, on average, according to the same study. Almost half the LBOs were done on nonmanufacturing companies, rather than the manufacturing firms that made ideal candidates for LBOs, and they proved to be marginal candidates for buyouts. Because of the competition simply to do deals (the fees that investment bankers charged for putting together buyouts rose in the late eighties from an average of 2 percent of the cost of a deal to 6 percent), bidders paid increasingly higher premiums to stockholders (in 1988, the average premium paid in an LBO was twice what it had been in 1975). They took on a lot more debt to complete buyouts, leaving them little financial flexibility to withstand a downturn in the economy. (Until the mid-eighties, even the LBOs that issued some junk bonds didn't rely heavily on them, because they depended largely on traditional means of financing, like commercial bank loans. But in the next five years more than half of the major LBOs depended on junk-bond financing, and deals that relied on junk bonds were much more likely to default.)

When a deep recession came, in 1989, the consequences were stark. Steven Kaplan, of the University of Chicago, and Jeremy Stein, of the Massachusetts Institute of Technology, found that of LBOs over $100 million in size, only two of forty-one that were done before 1985 defaulted on their debt. In contrast, of eighty-three LBOs that size done after 1985, twenty-two, or over one-quarter, defaulted.

The run of sobering news about deals done through takeovers and through leveraged buyouts from the mid-eighties until the end of the decade was magnified by the run-up in the number and size of those deals. Both factors crested at very high levels, as the wave of dealmaking peaked before crashing. Almost half of the LBOs of the takeover era were done in the three years between the start of 1986 and the end of 1988. While some contend that this increased intensity made sense, because the success stories of earlier years had finally persuaded the cautious to plunge in, it was more like a belated binge.

In 1992, *Fortune* reviewed forty-one of the LBOs that the magazine had designated one of the "Deals of the Year" between 1985 and 1990. Some were in bankruptcy and the rest were in weak condition. Even for the winners, the results were not widely impressive. The writer George Anders summarized: "In broad economic terms, the biggest surprise about buyouts was how transient they turned out to be. They instigated dangerous, thrilling journeys for companies over a span of several years. At the end of the cycle, however, many businesses found themselves surprisingly close to where they had been at the start."

According to Alfred Chandler, no American industrial corporation was helped in the long term by a deal done solely for the sake of a deal, when companies were traded in the control market. The mergers and acquisitions of the preceding generation had been concentrated, first, in so-called stable-tech industries (such as automobiles, metals, and the like, where the final products change little over time and competition occurs in the improvement of existing products and the processes for making them, as well as in marketing, distribution, and better relations with suppliers and the work force) and, second, in low-tech industries (such as beverages, food, and tobacco, where the final products change little and competition occurs in the improvement of marketing and distribution more than in production).

In the low-tech area, where competition was not intense, managers used mergers and acquisitions to carry out long-term strategies and corporations made fortunes buying and selling other companies. But takeovers and other speculative deals were concentrated in the stable-tech area, where options for new products were limited and competition was intense, making cash flow tight and research and development and long-term capital investment critical. To Chandler, "the short-term horizons of those involved in such transactions had the most devastating impact on U.S. competitive strength."

Chandler's study reached results similar to those of F. M. Scherer, of Harvard, and David Ravenscraft. To answer whether mergers and acquisitions in general yielded "economic efficiency," they undertook a comprehensive survey of six thousand corporate acquisitions in the United States that occurred between 1950 and 1977. They studied how often acquired lines of business were sold off after an acquisition, the effect on corporate profitability of the sell-offs, and the profitability of surviving lines of business.

The good news they found was that the profitability of corporations making acquisitions decreased only moderately after deals were completed. The bad news was that more than one-third of the acquisitions had resulted in sell-offs—and a division that had been acquired, as opposed to one that was created through expansion, was twice as likely to be sold off. The minority of firms that expanded through internal growth had fewer divestitures and higher profits. The only deals that succeeded consistently were mergers between firms of the same size.

In a summary of the findings that he reached with Scherer, Ravenscraft wrote: "In the merger game, the target shareholders are like the house: They always take their cut and therefore strongly support the game. The bidding firms and the capital providers are the gamblers: They must assess the odds and the amount they wish to risk. History suggests that the odds are against a bidder's success."

According to Scherer, studies of the stock prices of corporations that succeeded in making a takeover confirmed that view. While prices often went up slightly or remained approximately the same during the weeks after deals were completed, they went down significantly in the few years following. The declines illustrated the phenomenon of the winner's curse.

For some companies, as Flom contended, mergers and acquisitions were valuable transactions, in terms of financial performance, economic efficiency, and other standards. For many others, they were not. The hostile takeover that heralded the new merger era, in 1974, and the leveraged buyout that transformed the modestly used mechanism into a major innovation, in 1978, both had bleak outcomes. In 1981, when INCO reported its first operating loss in fifty years, it declared a loss of a quarter of a billion dollars on its investment in ESB and sold off the company in pieces. The LBO of Houdaille Industries floundered and went through a distress refinancing in 1986. The refinancing gave a four-to-one profit to holders of equity in the original buyout, but, because the event raised the company's debt to 152 percent of its book value, the refinancing made dismembering and selling off the company the only realistic way out of its daily financial problems. Those piecemeal sales happened in 1987. The INCO and Houdaille deals became troubling and unavoidable reminders that the merger movement did not often serve long-term economic interests.

The evidence didn't have to be negative to prove a big premise of the era wrong. In the decade that ended in 1990, according to Lipper Analytical Services, an investment in the average junk-bond fund grew by 131 percent. The same amount of money in the obvious alternatives did much better: in U.S. government bonds (191 percent); in general equities, or stocks (203 percent); and in A-rated, investment-grade corporate bonds (210 percent). Michael Milken's basic pitch was that "investors obtained better returns on low-grade issues than high-grades." In that key period, the facts refuted him.

In general, the merger movement led to a preoccupation with short-term performance that made it more difficult for publicly traded corporations to make commitments to research and development, the training of workers, and other investments that, by the late eighties, were widely seen as essential to long-term competitiveness. While general improvements in American corporations occurred during the movement and some might have been furthered by it, the movement reinforced unproductive tendencies of corporations and stymied productive ones, in years when global competition made the consequences matter deeply to the nation.

As Robert Pollin of the University of California at Riverside judged, the merger movement at best was a decade-long experiment in laissez-faire economics that failed. It left the United States less equipped to compete in global markets than it had been beforehand. At the end of the period, rather than simply continuing to stagnate, the rate of American productivity actually decreased. The American standard of living slipped notably in the world rankings.

For Skadden, the merger movement framed a large irony. Between 1985 and 1990, when the firm was doubling in size from five hundred to over one thousand lawyers, and when it seemed to stand in the forefront of the American legal profession, the movement turned into a speculative surge. As the movement grew out of control, Skadden profited handsomely. But, to a broad consensus of experts, the market for corporate control was ultimately animated by anxiety, self-preservation, and greed, not efficiency and productivity. Skadden served that market, so it fueled those instincts and, to some degree, could be expected to share them.

Skadden had no need to defend the control market, because it could invoke the traditional definition of the lawyer's role to support its representation of Wall Street: It could very plausibly disclaim accountability for the consequences of its clients' actions. About the rights and wrongs of takeovers, Flom once told the writer John Brooks, "I have many different moods depending whether I'm on offense or defense, and afterward I look out the window and laugh at myself."

But Skadden had long asserted that it provided more than legal counsel in the deals that defined it, and, consistent with that approach, Joe Flom eventually stepped forward. Sometimes, Flom sounded like a moderate for whom the outcome of the wave of takeovers, LBOs, and whatnot was a kind of justice. About LBOs, he said, "You had a lot of great transactions in the early days, but the wave fed on itself and, of course, what finally happened is that not only did it feed on itself but a lot of other people got in the act who really didn't have the discipline—they were just bidding—and so the pricing got crazy, in addition to everything else which led to the debacle."

But in response to a mood of revisionism about the merger movement and in the face of mounting evidence of the transactions' harmfulness, Flom joined the most ardent defenders of the market for corporate control. He seemed to make its vindication a resolute commitment.

Privately, Flom signaled his views in a letter of endorsement about Michael Milken to federal trial judge Kimba Wood in July of 1990, when she was considering the length of Milken's sentence for violating securities laws.

"I take the liberty of urging leniency," Flom wrote. "In my entire experience with Mr. Milken"—more than fifteen years—"he demonstrated great acumen and punctilious concern for what was ethical. He also demonstrated an unusual degree of personal commitment to the interests of his clients both during a transaction and thereafter. There did arise occasions when our firm's advice was not what he or his associates wanted to hear. However, I can think of no case where our advice as to legal requirements was not followed."

And: "I do not condone the acts to which Mr. Milken pleaded guilty. I can only assume that they were the result of his preoccupation with his clients' interests. This may have caused him to overlook some of the rules setting limits on the means by which he fostered those interests. Perhaps he was too original and too unconventional to function in the highly regulated environment of the securities business where there are an overabundance of rules."

Publicly, at Oxford University and in other distinguished forums in the early nineties, Flom lectured about his position. A striking element of his argument was the use of history. In the heat of the deal years, Flom had been a trailblazer for whom the intricacies of mergers and acquisitions were novel and, therefore, not comparable to corporate and financial inventions of the past.

Now, in the nineties, Flom suggested that recent M&A activity was merely more of what had gone on before, in the "three other great merger waves in the U.S. in this century." Dealmakers and deals, he said, were "not all that new." To prove it, he quoted from a paper in the *American Economic Review*, dated March 1931: "During 1928 and 1929 some investment houses employed men who did nothing but search out mergers. One businessman told me that he regarded it as a loss of standing if he were not approached at least once a week with a merger proposition."

Flom's argument also centered on his views about causation and capitalism. To him, there was "no adequate methodology for evaluating who is right" in the debate about the consequences of the deal decade, and there was no "meaningful consensus on which effects should be evaluated, or how such effects should be weighed," or "which type of transactions should be aggregated." The problem was too many variables: "Even when attempts to isolate and evaluate specific elements have been made, there are a multiplicity of factors raising questions as to how meaningful the conclusions are."

About capitalism, he said, "We go out the same door we came in. One can argue about the social impact of mergers, but they will thrive so long as there are economic dislocations or anomalies which they can effectively address and those anomalies will continue to be created, providing for additional activity."

Flom was a leader in the group that maintained the belief that the merger movement had helped equip the American economy for the future. But the movement's apparent consequences were not easily refuted. Instead of establishing that Skadden had filled a swashbuckling role in a campaign whose splendor was manifest in its outcome—the renewal of corporate America—the finale of the merger movement was widespread financial distress, business failure, and corporate bankruptcy.

For a decade, as its boosters claimed, the movement was widely seen as a grand end justifying intricate, protean, controversial means, which Flom and Skadden championed with impudent delight. The idea of a renegade law firm serving the nation's fortunes turned the Skadden story into a great adventure, which was hurtling, bounteous, and panoramic.

The demise of the movement tinged the story with darker shades of reality.

The Crucible

16

Skaddenfreude

The first quarter of 1990 was the best in Skadden's history. At its close, the firm named twenty-three new partners, thought to be the largest group ever elected at one time by a Wall Street firm. A downturn in mergers and acquisitions and in the business economy was then affecting most corporate law firms. Some lawyers who had doubted that Skadden's success was durable accepted the size of the group as evidence that Skadden could withstand a poor economy as well as any large firm. At Skadden's annual gathering of partners and their spouses, held in Washington, D.C., in mid-April of 1990, talk about the future was largely bullish.

Signs of Skadden's success were visible externally and internally. Along with the regularly elected group of new partners at the retreat came three laterals led by Robert Bennett. He had recently joined Skadden's Washington office with fourteen other lawyers as part of the largest group to join Skadden en masse from another firm. Bennett was then in the news as special counsel to the U.S. Senate's Select Committee on Ethics, and was running its inquiry about the group of senators known as the Keating Five. (The five senators were under investigation for their involvement with Charles Keating, the former savings and loan president who was later convicted for his part in the S&L cataclysm.) Hearings about the five senators were of intense public interest and were broadcast daily on cable television. Bennett's role in the inquiry was cited in the firm as proof that his group had one of the country's major practices in white-collar criminal law—in Bennett's view, rivaled only by that of the Washington, D.C., firm of Williams & Connolly, developed by the late Edward Bennett Williams.

Like other Skadden lawyers, Bob Bennett had left the first firm he had worked at and had moved to another Washington firm, which eventually carried his name. (An emissary of the first firm later asked him whether he would be interested in coming back.) Until Bennett was recruited by Skadden, he hadn't even known that it had a Washington office. ("That's the God's honest truth," he swore.) Skadden considered it a coup to bring him in. At a dinner during the Washington event in the spring of 1990, Bennett was seated next to Joe Flom. The arrangement pleased them both.

During the partners' business meetings, Bennett explained why it made sense for Skadden to have a large group of white-collar-criminal lawyers who would represent both companies and individual managers. In response to the perception of corporate excesses in the 1980s, he said, the federal government had stepped up its prosecution of white-collar crime to perhaps the highest level in American history. "Yes, there is a secret school where government investigators go to learn the tricks of their trade," Bennett and two co-authors wrote in a white paper presenting their views that was only partially satire. Lesson One was that corporations spent "all their time devising greedy schemes to cheat the government and the public."

Bennett commented later: "A cynic would say that the government is using the criminal law to reform how corporations do business." (He conceded that he was a cynic.) The government couldn't send a corporation to jail, but it could stop a company from doing business: "Where it really counts—in terms of dollars and acceptance by the public—the government can really hurt a company. They don't charge you with obscure crimes. It's conspiracy and fraud. It's of real interest to those who manage companies. Skadden decided criminal law was of real interest, and that they should be able to say, 'We've got the best in the business.' "

The most talked-about internal sign of Skadden's development at the 1990 meeting was the announcement of a new management structure for the firm. Eight years after naming Mullen the first full-time chief executive of a major law firm, Skadden was taking another step unprecedented for a Wall Street law firm. Skadden had tripled in size in those eight years, and partners said it had to manage itself differently: Skadden was too large to be guided only by Mullen, as executive partner, and Earle Yaffa, as managing director.

The new structure seemed to emphasize how different the firm was from most of its American counterparts. The management authority followed a corporate model, used by chairmen of boards of directors. It was called the Office of the Executive Partner. Consisting of Mullen, Yaffa, and five senior lawyers, it comprised a new council of leadership at Skadden.

The five lawyers were Roger Aaron, Peter Atkins, Mike Diamond, Bill Frank, and Benjamin Needell. Each of the first four had been at Skadden for almost a generation, or longer. Aaron, Atkins, and Frank had become partners on the same day in 1975, and were among the firm's obvious leaders. Needell had been at Skadden for nine years. As head of the real estate practice, he ran a group that Mullen described as one of the best-managed at the firm. Needell also implicitly represented partners who had arrived laterally from other firms. By including him, the firm said that partners brought in by that route had as much opportunity to guide Skadden as did partners who had come up through the ranks.

Diamond was included as the leader of the Los Angeles office, because Mullen viewed the office as the best-run outside New York, and it seemed sensible to give the two West Coast offices a clear voice on the council. Aside from Diamond, the members of the OEP (as it was called) doubled as practice coordinators (Atkins of M&A, Aaron of corporate areas besides those specializing in M&A, Frank of litigation, and Needell of the remaining practice areas), to whom leaders of individual departments reported. A chart laying out the organization gave Skadden the look of a large corporation.

In addition, the firm replaced the old administrative committee with a new policy committee. It consisted of the executive partner, the practice coordinators, the leaders of the five American offices, some partners with special functions (the head of hiring, for example), nine rotating members, and the managing director (Yaffa). On the Skadden chart, the policy committee sat above the OEP. In theory, it was the forum of final review at Skadden.

Although, with Aaron and Atkins, Fin Fogg and Morris Kramer were part of the Fab Four and were widely viewed as leaders in the firm, they were not on the OEP. Mullen explained exasperatedly: "We couldn't put on all four!" Fogg and Kramer had standing as rotating members of the policy committee; Fogg was named head of the firm's compensation committee, with Kramer and six others.

The new structure was the result of a yearlong exercise assisted by McKinsey & Company, the management consulting firm. At the 1989 partnership retreat, McKinsey consultants led Skadden lawyers in a discussion about the firm's values, about the professional development of its partners, and about other topics bearing on management. They heard about a "fault line" growing between the values of the firm's older partners (aged forty and over) and those of the younger (under forty). They heard about an incipient identity crisis among some senior lawyers: When older, homegrown partners expressed why Skadden was unique to them ("All the old-timers were saying, 'We're fantastic lawyers and we walk through walls and we get the job done,'" a partner reported), lawyers who had moved there from other law firms pointed out that their former firms had felt the same way. ("The old-timers were floored by that. Some lawyers felt that we might not be as special as we thought we were.")

The keepers of the firm's values (as the older, homegrown partners saw themselves) responded by questioning whether others, especially younger partners, were as dedicated to the ethic that had made the firm soar. ("Skadden Arps was yuppified long ago," a senior partner in New York complained. "We have a bunch of kids who don't know how to get home at night by bus and have never ridden the subway since joining us. They only know the way to Dial-a-car.") One purpose of the OEP was to encourage leading partners to reach out to one another and renew that ethic as the firm grew in size and complexity. Making the office and practice leaders "more robust as managers," in McKinsey's phrase, was one mechanism. Another was creating "a leadership body" that might "forge ways of working that could have tremendous impact further out."

The primary questions that had led Skadden to form the OEP, however, were who should succeed Mullen as executive partner, and when. In the absence of consensus about the answers, the OEP was designed to let the contenders prove themselves as managers and, in effect, to audition for the executive job. At a dinner in Washington's Union Station, the 1990 retreat's social highlight, Mike Diamond led the Not Ready for Prime Time Partners in a series of songs spoofing the firm. In one about Mullen, to the tune of a lazy ballad, "I'm Bidin' My Time," the laugh line was: "As to suc-ces-sion, I keep 'em guessin,' 'cause I'm bidin' my time."

A popular view at Skadden was that Mullen had set up the OEP as a way of defusing the impatience of those who wanted to replace him, of extending his tenure, and of delaying the selection of his successor. One theory was that, with the OEP, Mullen had divided and conquered his would-be replacements with great finesse. To McKinsey, proponents of this theory seemed to regard the sole task of management as decision making, and the aim of the executive partner, who decided many matters for the firm, as preserving his own power to do so. The team of consultants dismissed this view and its premise. To them, the challenge of management was to lead. They were unreservedly impressed by how Mullen and others at Skadden first explored, and then adopted, the new leadership structure.

"What is the mark of a successful institution?" one consultant asked. "The ability, when at the top, to look ahead, with the idea of perpetuating itself, but not necessarily with the old approaches." While McKinsey viewed Joe Flom as a man with "well-earned clout" and "his values, the stamp of the firm," his power at the firm seemed "atavistic." The central figure in the Skadden attempt at self-renewal was Mullen.

In the judgment of McKinsey's group, Mullen was "a very strong leader," with an unusual mix of humility and self-confidence, and a style that made people "feel involved and part of decisions." The OEP would be run under his guidance. A McKinsey consultant remarked that the new structure gave Mullen the chance to use his colleagues "like a stereophonic booster—he could put his message through these other speakers and blast it throughout the firm." Mullen's message was that the firm needed to change for the sake of its future.

Despite the general good feeling at the Washington retreat, the effects of the nation's economic downturn were becoming apparent in Skadden's practice. It was widely acknowledged among the partners that the biggest short-term issue facing the firm was how it would deal with the decline in M&A activity. The loudest applause for the Not Ready for Prime Time Partners came as they sang "There Is Nothing Like a Deal!" knocked off from *South Pacific*. "What ain't we got?" the punch line asked: "We ain't got deals!"

The first quarter had brought high revenues because corporate deals initiated the year before had been completed in the first part of the year. New transactions had not fully replaced them, however. In remarks to the partners, Mullen cautioned that the firm would have to watch the situation closely.

Like other Skadden partners, he treated with resigned good humor and a touch of defensiveness some rumors about the firm's decline, whose appearance seemed both to coincide with the hiring season (Mullen: "Other firms say, 'I wouldn't go to Skadden because . . .' ") and to reveal a general wish for the firm's comeuppance. Instead of general *Schadenfreude*, he suggested, competitors felt Skaddenfreude.

The firm was used to rumors that garbled its actions. When Erica Ward, a partner in the Washington, D.C., office, moved to Detroit in March of 1989, because her husband had the chance to join his family's large business, Skadden set up an office for her in her home so that she could maintain her practice. Her computer was connected to the firm's main computer in New York to allow her to use its word-processing and other systems, and, through a fancy phone system, Ward was tied to the Washington office, so people there could reach her by pushing four digits.

Word got out that she had moved to Detroit and was not joining a local firm. It blossomed into a full-fledged report that Skadden was opening a full office in that city, pregnant with the warning that Detroit law firms should consider merging in order to compete with New York's boldest. Associates at Detroit firms applied for jobs at Skadden's new Detroit office.

The Detroit rumor provided another detail for the picture of Skadden's relentless, unstoppable expansion—the Skadden juggernaut. A further detail of it, passed along among partners at a first-rank New York firm who were convinced they had to formulate a defensive strategy, had Skadden pursuing a five-year plan to reach five thousand lawyers.

The rumors in late 1989 were different. Skadden began to hear reports of its demise in October of that year. They came from many directions and, in the firm, were referred to collectively as "the rumor that wouldn't die." The whispers arose from the common conviction that the collapse of the junk-bond market in October of 1989 and the subsequent demise of Drexel Burnham Lambert, the investment-banking firm, must have severely undermined the firm's economic footing.

The rumor of Skadden's imminent disintegration gained plausibility from the specifics of its premise. Skadden had done junk-bond work and Drexel had been very important to Skadden: From 1985 through 1989, Drexel had been Skadden's highest-billing client. The rumor also gained plausibility from the explosion, in 1987, of the national law firm of Finley, Kumble, Wagner, Heine, Underberg, Manley, Myerson & Casey. Finley Kumble had formed in 1968, had grown to over seven hundred lawyers, and had billed itself in aggressive, Skadden-like terms. Its dissolution left behind a tangle of lawsuits claiming fraud and mismanagement, a load of debt and acrimony, and a lot of worried lawyers. (Joe Flom represented one of Finley Kumble's primary lenders, who sought to recover $83 million from the remains of the firm.)

Lawyers and administrators at other firms began calling Skadden to offer sympathy and to commiserate at the reported breakup. Chase Wilson, the firm's director of publications from 1984 until 1990, recalled: "The thought went, 'Sure Skadden denies it, but they're really taking it in the neck.'" Talk about a Skadden layoff of twenty-five lawyers in its Los Angeles office, which had handled business for Michael Milken's Beverly Hills outpost of Drexel Burnham Lambert, grew to a generally bruited firm-wide layoff of one hundred. Then the number murmured rose to two hundred fifty—fully one-quarter of Skadden's lawyers—with the rumored cuts allocated in detail to firm offices across the country.

In the winter of 1990, when leaders of the firm grew concerned that the rumors might balloon into a public relations problem suggesting a disaster like Finley Kumble's, an internal memo was drafted "about the Drexel/Skadden relationship that was intended to throw water on the rumors of Skadden laying people off," a firm insider reported. But Mullen decided that the reasons for not releasing the memo outweighed the ones for release. In response to my inquiry, Mullen dismissed the rumor about the L.A. and other layoffs as ill-founded and, in any case, dated.

Drexel had been Skadden's best client in the mid-eighties, but as the investment bank's financial activities decreased in the late eighties, Mullen said, so did the law firm's work for it—even though Drexel remained the firm's highest-billing client through 1989. When the holding company of Drexel declared bankruptcy in February of 1990, Skadden was "relatively undamaged," Mullen reported, because it had never done work for the holding company. By contrast, Cahill, Gordon & Reindel, the New York firm, had reportedly billed fees of $40 million to the Drexel holding company in 1989. The Cahill Gordon firm laid off eleven lawyers soon after the holding company filed for bankruptcy protection.

Drexel's investment-banking group owed Skadden 1 percent of the firm's gross billings for 1989, or approximately $5 million, but Skadden expected to be paid eventually. (It was substantially paid.) Skadden had also taken on new clients in investment banking to make up for the loss of the Drexel business. In Mullen's words, the "Drexel tragedy" was "not in terms of business." It was "a personal one," from Skadden's point of view, because the firm had close relationships with people who had worked there. They were finding new jobs at other banks and financial companies, often with help from Skadden. The firm intended to keep working with them.

About another part of the rumor, Mullen was puzzled. "The concept of shutting down Los Angeles is weird." After seven years, the office had one hundred twenty-five lawyers. (It had opened in 1983.) If it had been an independent firm, it would have been among the dozen largest and one of the most profitable in that city. Its litigation department was very busy, Mullen said. With one-quarter of the lawyers in the office in that department, it alone could make up for the loss of Drexel business in the city.

At the 1990 retreat, the performance of the Not Ready for Prime Time Partners ended with a production number, an off-key, not quite in unison, sentimental ballad, a takeoff on "Drink with Me" from *Les Misérables*. The firm's new partners, almost two dozen of them, filed in front of the stage and introduced themselves in the spotlight. They joined the ensemble in song. One verse went: "Here's to lawyers with superior skills / Here's to clients who pay all their bills / Here's to them / and here's to us."

The year before, when the annual skit had closed with the same ballad, the line had been: "Here's to clients who pay *premium* bills . . ." Due to circumstances beyond the firm's control, it had been necessary to revise the text.

17

The Morning Line

Soon after the 1990 Washington retreat, Mullen met with Robert Sheehan, a partner who chaired a firm committee charged with evaluating
candidates for partnership. They began to compile a list of lawyers who
should be considered for election the following year—to decide who
should go on "the morning line." The phrase was drawn from the horse-
racing-style pool sometimes formed by firm lawyers who assign odds to
the chances of the various partnership candidates—as Sheehan called
them, "serious candidates and cross-your-fingers candidates, who are
loved by their mentors and colleagues" (but whose odds of making
partner are long). Along with the firm's decisions about how to divide
its profits among the existing partners, Skadden considers the election
of new partners the most important choice it makes each year.

Sheehan was forty-six, and a stocky banking lawyer. He has thinning
blond hair framing a round face and crooked teeth with a gap in the

front. Sheehan talks like a tough guy, in a scratchy voice. His cool is belied by his nervous habits. One is jiggling his feet incessantly as he works at his desk. He had been a partner for a dozen years.

"I was always a fair-haired boy. I had an easy trip," Sheehan said about his election to partnership in 1978 when the firm had forty partners and one hundred fifty-three lawyers in all. "Everybody knew everybody else. They knew your strengths, they knew your weaknesses. They didn't need a committee." When the firm felt the need for a formal committee in 1985, Mullen asked Sheehan to join it. Another Skadden partner explained: "The firm's gotten so big that, essentially, departments are evaluating their own people and people aren't really seen by other departments. And some departments are harder graders than others." In 1989, the first chairman of the partnership committee stepped aside. Sheehan: "Mullen asked me to head the thing."

In 1990, the associates whom Mullen and Sheehan considered as candidates for partnership were six to ten years out of law school. All but a few had been at Skadden for five years or longer. "In five years," Bob Sheehan advised, "you develop all the sweat equity you're going to develop." Their performances as lawyers had been formally evaluated twice a year and, while the firm had not enunciated its standards of quality, reasoning that each lawyer defined them for himself, it had developed some rules of thumb about the ingredients for success.

They included analytical ability, detailed knowledge about an area of law important to firm clients, the ability to take charge of work for a client, the promise of generating new business from new or ongoing clients, and—the unteachable but essential for lawyers—good judgment. They also included the sort of commitment that was revealed in Skadden's version of hard work: stamina, tenacity, and aggressiveness.

For an hour or so, Mullen and Sheehan reviewed senior associates with high ratings who were obvious candidates for partnership and others who had been proposed by sponsors. One office leader advised: "Any partner with an associate can put him on the morning line. It has to be credible, but some people who get put up are softer candidates than others." A senior associate affirmed: "Not everyone who gets that far is cut out to be a partner." Some lacked the personal qualities: They were "selfish," or "sandbaggers." Others lacked breadth: They had "kept to a very narrow line of work." Others hadn't proven their mettle. Advice from partner to associate: "Get fanatical to become a partner." Mullen and Sheehan spent another hour "to see that no one fell through the cracks" (Sheehan's words).

In the weeks that followed, Mullen spoke with the heads of each of the firm's offices and departments to round out the list of those who should be considered, and with other associates and special counsels. (Usually, special counsels were former associates who had been passed over for partnership but had been asked to stay on because of their utility to the firm, or relatively senior lawyers who had joined the firm laterally and had not been made partners).

By the end of June, the morning line was complete, with forty-five lawyers on it. A large cluster of the candidates had just been passed over for partnership in the preceding year. Kent Coit, of the firm's Boston office, which had approximately thirty lawyers, was one. He practiced in mergers and acquisitions.

He was a trim thirty-eight-year-old of medium height, with close-cropped blond hair, a mustache, and an alert, pleasant, precise manner. When I noticed a Grateful Dead sticker in his office and mentioned it to him, Coit explained: "I wasn't a Deadhead, but I'd go out of my way several times a summer to see them, like driving from Boston to Washington."

Coit had worked in Skadden's Boston office during the summer of 1981, after finishing both his second year at Harvard Law School and his doctorate in American history at Harvard. (His dissertation, *The Diffusion of Democracy*, studied how and why the original American states changed their constitutions in the nineteenth century.)

When Coit had interviewed with Boston law firms for a summer job, he felt that Skadden had "stood out in a way that I couldn't understand." He went there thinking that the experience would turn out "pretty good or very bad," and that, if the latter, his risk was low, because it was only for the summer.

Nineteen eighty-one was the summer of the takeover fight among Conoco, Seagram, and Du Pont. A number of other lawyers in the Boston office were swallowed by the firm's work for Conoco, and when a smaller ($60 million), regional deal came into the office at the same time, a third-year associate at the firm and Coit, one year shy of his J.D., were assigned to handle it.

The two did much of the work on the deal, with a partner overseeing their efforts. Coit thrived on the project. When he was offered a permanent job to begin after he finished law school in 1982, he accepted it. "I was awfully busy from the time I came in the door," he recalled. Five years later, with slight misgivings, he decided to "take a shot at partner."

"I had my first child in 1986," Coit explained. "My wife will tell you that during our daughter's first year I wasn't there very much." He went on: "My wife has a love-hate relationship with Skadden. She loves it because I love it. And she hates it because I love it." No one had told him how he ended up on the morning line, but he wasn't surprised when he became a candidate. "I consistently did good work and people knew about it."

In a videotape about Skadden that the firm uses to recruit at law schools, Roger Aaron, the senior partner who was the head of recruiting when the tape was made in 1989, presents the firm. He informs viewers: "We promote people from within the associate ranks, and from the associate ranks to the special counsel and partner ranks, purely on the basis of merit."

According to Bob Sheehan, Coit easily met that standard. "You don't have to be narrow about him," Sheehan advised recently. "He's an excellent technical lawyer, and has the drive and personality to attract and draw in business to the firm that it otherwise wouldn't have, as well as the ability to do the institutional work which the firm draws." Another partner elaborated: "We tend to judge individual lawyers in terms of competence, but the ability to generate legal business counts as merit."

Yet while the firm promoted only lawyers who, in its judgment, met these tests, even this broad definition of merit was not the decisive criterion for promotion. Internally, the firm described the other critical factor as "need." In 1990, Skadden defined need primarily in terms of economics, measured in the contexts of geographical grouping and area of specialization. If work in a particular practice within a specific office was flourishing and showed promise of continued growth, a strong candidate for partnership in that area and office had a chance to be elected, although other factors could still affect what happened. If not chosen, he (or she) might be held over for reassessment until the following year. Working in tandem with the committee chaired by Bob Sheehan, which reviewed Skadden lawyers for quality, was another that assessed the firm's needs. It was sometimes called the "balance committee."

In 1990, the firm used "need" as much as "merit" in making its partnership decisions. An able specialist in an area that wasn't growing, or seemed unlikely to grow in the near future, was unlikely to make partner. An able specialist in a booming area whose long-term prospects were uncertain might not make it either. The definition of need was also subject to eleventh-hour revision.

According to the *New York Law Journal*, in April of 1989, when

Skadden named twenty-two new partners, seven others were initially in the group that had been told that they were "shoo-ins." Then a core of partners decided that twenty-nine new arrivals at the table was too many. In a collision of judgments about need, the firm's yearlong partnership process gave way to a last-minute assertion of power.

The head of the Skadden office in Boston is Louis Goodman. He is a thoughtful, offbeat man with a surface calm, who graduated from Harvard Law School and joined Skadden in New York City in 1970. While he liked the firm ("These were crazy, driven people, having an enormous amount of fun," he said), he left after two years in search of a saner life, to practice with a small Boston firm. A year later, he was eager to return to Skadden when it opened a Boston office to accommodate Bob Pirie. About the small firm in Boston which he joined, then spurned, Goodman said, "It wasn't Skadden Arps. It had fine lawyers, but no drive or desire to be the best, to conquer."

Goodman became a Skadden partner in 1978 and the head of the Boston office four years later. He is an M&A partner—in 1990, one of the fifty or so in the firm explicitly described as specialists in the area, aside from the many others who sometimes practiced in it. Of the new Skadden partners named in the second half of the eighties, more were specialists in mergers and acquisitions than in any other area. They were carried to partnership by the boom in deals and by special aspects of the practice.

"If the CEO of a company that is a target of a takeover hires us," Goodman explained, "he needs a partner to hold his hand." The ratio between partners and associates in mergers and acquisitions (its leverage) was lower than in most other areas at Skadden; the balance between the two groups was closer than in other departments. During the second half of the eighties, Goodman said, "we went and made as many partners as possible." On the other hand, he recalled, no one was voted in lightly. "I think M&A is very hard," he observed. "Partly, it's an ego thing, to hold ourselves and the people we work with to high standards. It's more a crucible. If you join Skadden Arps, you're more likely to be interested in M&A, so the competition is tougher."

By the first quarter of 1990, the economic downturn was more pronounced in New England than in other regions where Skadden had offices. Goodman felt no compunction about admitting that the extraordinary increases in business that made the eighties so profitable for many law firms and propelled some to grow at extraordinary rates were over for Skadden, along with many of its clients involved in dealmaking. "The overheated environment which was very good to lawyers" was gone.

To Goodman, the change demanded realism, but not alarm. Referring to the development of the firm's practice in bankruptcy, financial restructuring, and reorganization, for example, he went on: "Skadden will remain a central part of things. Skadden is like a conglomerate now, with countercyclical businesses as well as cyclical."

Describing what he did as an office leader, he admitted that, among other things, he spent "a certain amount of time on gossip." By phone with partners across the country, toward the end of his day, he discussed a range of topics: Did a recent decision by the Delaware Supreme Court on a basic question of corporate law change how some deals had to be put together? In general, how much equity in a company was a client required by banks to seek in order to obtain financing for a deal? And what about the upcoming partnership decisions?

In the 1990 partnership round, Goodman vigorously supported Kent Coit and David Brewster, another Boston associate in M&A. To colleagues who knew them best, Coit and Brewster seemed virtually identical as candidates: They were members of the same class at Harvard Law School, had started together at Skadden as summer associates, and proved themselves similarly adept in practice. Their children were the same age and they lived in the same town outside the city. They were close friends.

When the needs committee ruled that the firm's economic prospects justified only one new M&A partner in Boston, Goodman and the three other partners in the office decided to make their own decision about who it should be rather than leaving it to another group at the firm, like the M&A department, run from New York. The choice was close enough so that Goodman tipped the balance, as the office leader. According to an observer, the Boston partners picked Brewster over Coit "by focusing on minutiae."

Goodman called Coit to deliver the bad news. "David won by less than a hair," he and other partners told people in the Boston office. Coit was surprised and extremely disappointed. "It was pretty bad," Coit remembered about the call. "Lou said that it [partnership] hadn't happened [for me] and that he was trying to be hopeful about '91."

To Coit, the reason for the decision was business: "I knew tough times were ahead. I could look at the economics and see it was going to be a tough year." Since Skadden was naming such a noticeably large group of partners, however—twenty-three of them—it was hard for Coit not to take his omission personally. Feeling that a judgment had been made about him alone on the basis of merit (he told me he didn't know that it had come down to a choice between him and Brewster), Coit brooded later: "I thought it was the wrong decision."

During the next few weeks, the Boston partners tried to convince Coit to stay at Skadden rather than to leave for a job somewhere else. They had a large corner office that was not being used, so, to entice Coit, the partners did not give it to Brewster, the obvious claimant, but promised to save the office for Coit as a gesture showing how they hoped things would turn out. Coit gave some thought to taking a legal job with a corporation, and spoke with a couple of legal recruiters about his possibilities. He also reviewed his options outside the firm with colleagues in other Skadden offices. They told him they would understand if he decided to leave, but stressed that he was highly valued at Skadden.

The words of a respected, fortyish partner in New York, Alan Myers, with whom Coit had worked closely, were regularly repeated in conversations about Coit. Myers on Coit: "This is the best lawyer we've never made a partner."

To emphasize how serious Skadden was about keeping him, Goodman arranged for Coit to fly down to New York to speak with Mullen. Goodman advised: "If Peter Mullen says anything different from what I said, listen to him." Mullen's message to Coit was: If the world doesn't change drastically, you should be made a partner next time around, in 1991. Coit was working on long-running matters for clients and a new project had just come his way. (Coit: "The following morning, after I heard the news in the evening, I had to be on a telephonic board meeting.") He decided to stay at the firm and try for partnership one more time.

18

Recession

By June of 1990, most observers assumed that the downturn on Wall Street, sometimes described as Skadden's "major client," must have seriously undermined the firm. No one at Skadden denied that the firm's business was off. Steve Axinn, the head of the antitrust department, grumbled a few months later: "In the summer, it was so slow that everyone took vacation. That's the way it's supposed to be, but not here." Matt Rosen, a tax partner, explained: "The biggest problem for us when there's less activity is that this is a place where people are used to going flat out. I personally am most happy when I'm mildly overstressed. Most people like a backlog of matters. Everybody in the tax department is busy now, but we all have a little more time on our hands. The pace is slower. The sex is out of it. We all like to have to be in four places at the same time, and now we're only getting called to two."

Speculation about the effect of Drexel's demise on Skadden was mixed with big new rumors. In late summer, one jarring piece of scuttlebutt (flatly denied by Skadden management) was that firm profits had fallen so far that the partners had taken no money since July, and were seriously contemplating substantial layoffs. In October, the *New York Law Journal* turned part of the rumor into news, reporting that Skadden had frozen the salaries of associates, that it had failed to promote some associates from one level to the next, and that it had laid off sixty young lawyers. Detailed, carefully worded, and based in part on unnamed sources, the piece had an authoritative ring. Earle Yaffa was quoted as confirming the salary freeze—defined as not escalating the overall compensation of associates. Yaffa was also quoted as saying that the decision not to promote some associates was "nothing new" and that associates who were promoted had moved to the next level of pay. The only major item that Yaffa might have been disputing was the report that "some sixty" associates had been laid off. In each of the firm's two annual reviews, Yaffa said, "somewhere between eight and thirty" associates had been given notice. If it had been thirty each time, the total would have been sixty.

The piece was widely talked about among other lawyers (a partner in a firm in Baltimore, Maryland, said that a senior lawyer had brought it up at a meeting of their management committee, for example). The news it contained was reprinted by national publications: *The Wall Street Journal* carried an item about the layoffs on November 1, which Skadden associates quickly dubbed Black Thursday. After adding new lawyers at more than 20 percent a year for a decade, and making broad promises of opportunity based on merit, Skadden was reported to have made an abrupt, cold reversal.

Internally, the firm sought to counteract the story. Every Thursday, in New York and at most other Skadden offices, the firm provided lawyers with the chance to meet informally over a free lunch. Unlike the firm's weekly partnership meetings, which were centered in New York but attended (through a high-tech telephone hookup) by partners in each of the firm's other North American offices, the informal lunches were not regularly attended by senior lawyers or managers in any of the offices.

In Washington, D.C., according to an associate there, the office leader, Neal McCoy, rarely showed up. On Black Thursday, however, McCoy attended to make an announcement. Its gist, reported one lawyer, was that "the *Wall Street Journal* story was not accurate, and that Skadden wasn't laying people off." McCoy's explanation, he confirmed later, was that Skadden was simply getting more businesslike about its regular evaluations of associates. If they hadn't met the firm's standard, they were being asked to leave. Partners delivered similar messages in other Skadden offices.

Soon after, Mullen purported to respond to the *New York Law Journal* article but seemed to criticize a different piece from the one that had run: "Saying that Skadden Arps has frozen salaries is terrifically inaccurate. The salary level has gone up more or less every year, and much faster than inflation, though we have never been a leader in those raises. This year, all firms in New York did not raise first-year salaries, so we didn't raise the scale of other salaries, either. . . . We decided this wasn't a year to raise salaries. It would be stupid. The economy has made what was a seller's market, from the point of view of law students, into something that has the possibility of being a buyer's market. But we have given raises to associates. What we haven't done is raise the whole scale, to avoid the problem of having first-year associates make more than associates in subsequent years.

"The trickier thing is the concept of cutting back on staff. The bottom line is that we have not cut back on staff. . . . The trickiness is this: Firms evaluate their lawyers regularly and, if you want to avoid the stigma of having others say you are laying off lawyers, you could just raise your standards of evaluation. Rightly or wrongly, we just didn't do that. Twice a year, we do evaluations and the more important one comes in October, when we give raises. I told practice leaders to apply the same standards we have in the past. Every year, some people get a raise and a good progress report. Some are given a warning that there are things they need to improve in order to stay on track. Some have been told before and are given a more severe warning. Finally, some people are told—after two previous warnings—that this is not the place for them and to look for another job.

"The number being terminated as a result of October evaluations this year was less than for last year, which was around twenty. That is the ultimate test whether you are using evaluations to cut back on staff. Two years ago, when things were almost unmanageable in terms of people's lifestyles [because the firm had so much business and everyone was working very hard], we did the same type of evaluations. But then, when somebody was told they should leave, they were able to beat the system and find work that no one else could do. That wasn't good for us, but it happened. This year, both in April and October, we have given an absolute deadline of three months. We told people that they didn't have to work, that they should just look for a job. For some, we've extended the period of time, but cut their salaries by twenty-five percent, on the theory that they aren't really working for us anymore and, also, as a signal that we are serious.

"A reporter for the *New York Law Journal* allegedly called fifty associates here"—the article in the *Journal* mentioned no figure—"many of whom said what I've told you, but some who said something different. The conversation I imagine them having is something like, 'Yes, Skadden must be cutting back, because I've been told to leave.' Associates don't see the big picture at the firm. That has produced some troubles for us in terms of recruiting.

"The bottom line is: We are less busy than we were at the beginning of the year, but 1990 will be a pretty good year. The uncertainty is 1991. Nineteen ninety was a disaster for Wall Street, not for Skadden Arps. If Wall Street continues as is, '91 will be no better than '90 for us, but no worse. If the recession really gets bad, Skadden Arps could have a harder time. Associates are jittery about this. I tell them that we can't guarantee what will happen in the future, but I can assure them that we will be no worse off and probably better off than other firms. We are not proposing real cuts at this time.

"A law firm, ideally, is a little more collegial than another type of organization, and we want to avoid losing that."

In 1990, Skadden's policy about partnership had been in flux compared with those at some other major law firms. At one extreme, it was the practice at some to hire a small number of first-year associates each year and eventually to make a relatively high percentage of them partners. At Wachtell, Lipton, Rosen & Katz, Skadden's main rival in mergers and acquisitions work and a much smaller firm, the average accepted into the partnership from 1980 to 1985, according to the 1992 Employer Directory of Harvard Law School, was three out of initial classes that averaged seven associates. By 1991, that firm had fifty-eight partners and forty-five associates.

At the other extreme, some firms hired a large number of first-year associates and made only a small fraction of them partners. With an occasional exception, Cravath, Swaine & Moore has long pulled only a handful of partners from its incoming classes—between 1979 and 1984, it awarded one of every twelve associates its brass ring from classes that averaged forty. In 1991, it had seventy partners and two hundred sixty-three associates.

The Wachtell approach is to be highly selective in hiring associates, and, even though most do not make it, to hire with the declaration that all can become partners. The Cravath model is described as being as selective as possible, since the firm's partners will come only from its pool of associates, but it does not hold out to them the likelihood of a partnership. According to a recent survey, most large firms fall between the two extremes, with 20 to 40 percent of their first-year lawyers eventually becoming partners.

When Skadden was asked by law schools for similar statistics, so that prospective associates could compare the chances for partnership there and at other firms, it rebuffed the request, maintaining that the numbers would be "meaningless." The Skadden line was that a firm that grew quickly, as it did, was different from one whose growth was slow and steady, like Wachtell and Cravath, and that a firm that hired a large share of lawyers laterally, as Skadden had for a generation, couldn't be compared to firms that didn't.

From Skadden's point of view, in 1990 the telling statistic was the absolute number of partners it had made, rather than the fraction of starting associates who became partners. In the eighties, Peter Mullen regularly said about Skadden, "Here, you don't have to wait for someone to die to become a partner." Setting up a straw man that represented the reality at no large law firm, the phrase nonetheless conveyed what Mullen wanted it to: the promise of opportunity.

From 1980 to 1990, the Skadden partnership quadrupled in size. In the category of partnerships offered to associates, the average in each of those years was thirteen. In the five years from 1986 to 1990, the average was twenty. Those numbers seemed far more promising than the ratios asked for by law schools.

In 1975, according to the Skadden newsletter, the class of first-year associates at the firm included ten lawyers. Six eventually made partner. In 1978, the entering class numbered twenty-seven, of whom three made partner. In 1981, the class had thirty-three. Six made partner—one in 1988, three in 1989, and two in 1990.

To Skadden, however, the large number of partners that it elected in the 1980s from its associate ranks did not fully represent the opportunities at the firm. In order to keep senior associates who did not make partner but had skill and knowledge that the firm could use, in 1985 it began to confer the status of special counsel. Sheila Birnbaum, a partner, explained: "They are like middle managers in corporations, who keep their jobs and get well paid but don't get constant promotions." Between 1985 and 1990, Skadden named forty-two special counsels who had been associates (it brought in eleven lawyers from other firms as special counsels).

The firm also kept a large number of senior associates for longer than the eight- or nine-year tenure commonly allowed by other firms. A Skadden partner asked, "The whole weird thing at law firms is: Either you make partner, or what?" The firm answered by replacing the up-or-out policy, favored at most major firms from the fifties until the eighties, with a more flexible one. In the firm's view, the new rule served Skadden interests and those of lawyers who wanted to stay.

Associates experienced the Skadden system differently. About the demise of the up-or-out policy, some said that the firm was extending the time until partnership to hold on to experienced lawyers in a period of intense demand. "The firm needed warm bodies" was a common phrase. A senior associate observed: "There's a tension there, because if your work is good enough, they'll want you to stay around, even if the prospects of a partnership for you aren't certain at all. . . . It's certainly not fair, but that's the way the system works." Beginning in 1988, according to one young partner, Skadden explicitly deferred candidates because so many were up for partnership in some practice areas. As a consequence, it increased the number of years during which the partnership could make a nice, clean profit from the labors of salaried associates.

According to Brian Krisberg, an associate, the arrangement was part of the "business contract" that Skadden implicitly made with each lawyer. "If the pie goes your way—if the firm's economic needs create needs in your area—it is possible for a lawyer to remain as a ninth- or tenth-year associate," Krisberg said. "It's a very straightforward place."

The special counsel position was reportedly offered to lawyers who were as capable as partners and, in view of their legal achievements, proved the worth of the new title. But most special counsels were viewed by associates as figures marked by an asterisk—different, if not second-class, and kept on primarily because the firm needed an experienced lawyer to fill a technical role that no partner did. Matt Rosen (a partner): "A client called up and asked whether he could take a security interest in somebody's tax-refund claim. I made some phone calls and found there was a woman here"—a special counsel—"who knows everything there is to know about this."

Some associates viewed accepting a special counselship as settling for something less than the real prize. Some who were passed over for a partnership and offered a special counselship said they turned it down in favor of trying again for partnership. A lawyer: "I was offered a special counsel's spot, in 1988, I think. It was relatively new. I was told at that time that I was the only associate in my department to whom it was offered. I declined. It was my perception that it was a good job, but a dead end." Between 1987 and 1990, Skadden offered partnerships to four special counsels, out of the total of eighty-one partners chosen from the firm during those years. A special counselship was not a likely stepping stone, but it could be one.

During the early and mid-eighties, when Skadden grew rapidly and regularly felt the need for more partners who could supervise the work of less experienced lawyers (according to some associates), the firm invited a high percentage of the associates on the morning line to become partners. In the mid-eighties, Earle Yaffa, the firm's managing director, reported, the firm tried to elect no more than three-fourths of the serious candidates, to keep candidates on their toes. But throughout most of the eighties, one senior associate reflected, "once you got past the quality committee"—or its equivalent—"you pretty much had it made."

Nineteen eighty-nine was the first year that the firm's long expansion among junior and mid-level associates unequivocally caught up with the process for deciding what to do with the senior ones. It was the first year when lawyers who had made it through the merit committee were not made partners—and, according to the *National Law Journal*, when one-fourth of the lawyers approved for partnership on the basis of the firm's need as well as of the lawyers' merit still were not made partner.

"There were about seventy-five people eligible for partnership," an associate said, "and that number was cut by the departments to around forty-five for the morning line. In the high thirties made it through the quality committee, and, with twenty-two new partners, roughly two-thirds of those made partner."

The addition of another large class of eligible associates to the number of deferred, passed over, or belatedly denied candidates who chose to try again made the 1990 competition even stiffer. The number of senior associates competing for partnership was far larger than the group that could conceivably be elected. By then, some associates strongly disagreed with the firm's description of the extent of opportunity for a lawyer rising through the ranks to become a partner at Skadden. If not a Cravath-style partnership, Skadden's was far less accessible to them than what the firm's leaders, and its recruiting videotape, had portrayed.

A lawyer who was passed over: "I had never wanted to be a lawyer, but I went to law school because it seemed interesting and I became a lawyer and they paid me well, and it became harder to look around and consider other options. Then I was encouraged to stay and make partner. I was told I deserved to make partner. I could go do something after, if I wanted. When the head of my department wasn't able to make me a partner, the thing that made me feel bad was when Peter Mullen told the press: We made all of the quality people partners."

One senior associate estimated that over one hundred lawyers were candidates in 1990. (Bob Sheehan said that forty-five were placed on the morning line.) Some had arrived at Skadden in 1982, when the firm had seventy-five partners and approximately three hundred lawyers. Others had arrived in the classes of '81 and '80, when the firm was smaller. Most had come in laterally, during years of prodigious expansion. Still other associates in the eligible seventh-, eighth-, and ninth-year classes were not included among the candidates, although some had received excellent evaluations. Seth Schwartz, a well-reviewed associate who eventually became a partner, admitted: "I was told there was no way I would become a partner in 1990, because so many people were up for partner. I was told that I would be considered in '91 and that I should stick around and see what happens."

Many at Skadden agreed with the firm view that statistics about associates becoming partners were not reliable predictors, but for a different reason: To them, the key to the process was power. Skadden associates believe, one reported, that it helps to have sponsors who are "strong and not despised" and that it's crucial to have sponsors who stick up for them. ("He's on my shit list," a onetime Skadden associate said about a partner who didn't protect him. "He let another lawyer take credit for one of my ideas.") Many partners agree.

"He was a guy I made partner," bragged a former partner about one still at Skadden. "Ben wasn't allowed to make any partners" is how an associate described the firm's decision in 1989 not to make any partners in the real estate department led by Ben Needell. "If each of the Fab Four pushes someone, and there are other pressures, the numbers add up," a partner calculated during another partnership season. "My candidate wasn't on the list," complained a disgruntled senior partner, talking about a recent partnership decision.

The saga of Joseph Coco suggested how confounded the power calculus can seem to Skadden lawyers. Known as "Mr. Skadden" when he was an associate, he was a legend in the world of big-firm lawyers for having billed more than five hundred hours in one month—an average of almost seventeen hours a day—on an M&A deal. Coco: "We were in the middle of a hostile battle, and just spent all of our time in the office, doing one thing or another in preparation. It's not what people usually did then, or certainly what they do now, but we were just there."

In 1989, by some accounts, the M&A department used Coco in a gambit to get an extra partner made from among the group's candidates. The department had been allotted four slots and Coco was said to be among the winners. But to finesse the limit, the story went, the M&A department ranked Coco fifth, to force the full partnership to take all five. It didn't. The Fab Four were then expected to choose who, between Coco and another, would get the fourth slot, a partner said. They split, two to two. Unable to resolve the split, they threw the choice to a vote by the department. ("At the time," a lawyer said, "I thought it was a very serious leadership error.") The vote went against Coco. Another lawyer reported about the aftermath: Coco "was promised by *the institution*, it might have been in writing, that he would be made a partner in 1990." He was.

According to Mullen, the Coco tale was "romanticized" and "full of misinformation." As he told it, there was strong disagreement within the M&A department and among leaders in the firm outside the department about whether it should get five new partners or four, as happened. "Because the supporters of Joe were very persistent, it was a close call," Mullen said. He also disputed that "power plays" had anything to do with who became a Skadden partner.

Peter Atkins seconded Mullen's view. He stated: "It's absolutely critical to the process that we are perceived as acting in a fair manner. To be sure, there are people who have strong views about candidates. That means they are comfortable with the lawyers they are promoting. That's what we live and die for. I've been through this process a long time. I have always been comfortable that people feel they are working for the interests of the firm, and not for the individual. It has worked very well, whether it involves a friction and a rub. Unless I have completely misperceived the process, it is the antithesis of one involving back-room deals. It is remarkably open."

But by many other accounts power has long infused the process. In theory, in the mid-seventies, the firm had each of its departments choose candidates for partnership and then selected from among them in a firm-wide meeting at which partners with candidates lobbied for support among partners from other departments and traded deals. The process was said to be collegial, in the sense that confrontations, guided by a modicum of civility, can take place among people who know each other well.

In practice, partners with a large portfolio of business that kept many lawyers busy had more influence than others. As Mullen put it, "an important partner" could stand up and say, "This guy is great," and (Mullen again) "no one would dare challenge him." Not surprisingly, no partner had more influence than Flom. One partner shrugged about efforts made to "secure" a partnership for a candidate: "Anyone who had anything serious to talk about went right to Flom so his message wouldn't get filtered." Bob Sheehan assured me that "Joe could make anyone a partner he wanted, but he tended to stay out of the process." Yet, according to Sheehan, Flom could count on having the final word: "Mullen would get Flom a list and he would O.K. it with Joe."

In the early eighties, with the guidance of McKinsey & Company, the process was made more orderly—"to level the playing field" (Mullen). Skadden formed its quality and needs committees to assess the candidates and the requirements of the firm. But decisions about partnership remained contentious. Candidates were sometimes blackballed by partners—permanently or, to make a point, for a year. In 1983, when the candidacy of a protégé of Les Arps met with opposition, Arps, who was then Skadden's senior partner, threatened to take his name off the firm's letterhead if his young colleague was not elected. ("Of course, he would never have removed his name," the lawyer said recently. "Les was devoted to the firm.") The protégé got through.

By the mid-eighties, conflicts between departments arose as often as they did about particulars of individual candidates—which is why the needs committee was sometimes said to make judgments about internal "balance." For the firm as a whole, the issue that increasingly came up was need. The firm's diversification into new legal areas led to a perception that there were guidelines about the amount of new business required in a department before it would be allowed a new partner, although management claimed there were no such things.

A candidate for a partnership in the mid-eighties in a specialty department, as the smaller ones were called, confided that she understood that she would be considered when her group had one million dollars of new business. The departments were spoken of as product lines. The firm acted as if it expected each line to pay its way, although rich departments like M&A were understood to subsidize the start-up of specialty lines. In the allocation of partnerships, the strong got stronger. Others labored to maintain their standing.

Some stable departments, like antitrust, resented the booming ones, like M&A. Yet within the M&A department as well there were tensions created by its structure, for the group was divided into teams. Each was led by one of the Fab Four. A lawyer observed: "You've created a set of mini-firms, with the leaders like rabbis, who have to get their people made partners in order to keep the loyalty of the team." In general, a young partner said, "anyone who thinks that the process is as neat as feeding variables into a computer and coming up with obvious results is deluding himself. My impression is that the selection of partners is an integrity-driven process with a lot of friction."

In March of 1990, Skadden chose not to make the economic downturn a dominant factor in deciding how many partners to make. A few months later, that approach was judged imprudent for the 1991 cycle. The recession officially started in July of 1990. By then, Skadden's monthly profits were clearly off. The latest in a long run of superlative years for the firm turned into a merely fine one.

Another way to look at Skadden's 1990 was as two halves: The first comprised the end of the preceding financial year and was strong in terms of profits; the second marked the beginning of the next financial year, and was notably weaker. By the end of 1990, Skadden lawyers were speaking about competition in an era of constraints.

Even so, for Wall Street and large New York law firms, the start of 1991 was far worse than anyone had projected. For Skadden, the unrelieved severity of the downturn in mergers and acquisitions, the continuing economic recession, and an unexpected slowdown in large business ventures during January and February, resulting from the Persian Gulf War, made the first quarter dismal.

According to one well-placed partner at Skadden, it was the worst quarter for the firm in twenty-five years—a melodramatic contrast with the first quarter of the previous year, which had been the firm's best. "Partners get these quarterly statements of our earnings, and one of the young partners said to me, 'My housekeeper makes more than I made,'" he recounted in April. "There's a lot of nervousness around old Skadden Arps now."

Partners focused on two statistics in particular: the firm's cash revenues and its hourly billings. The downturn in mergers and acquisitions meant that the firm could not expect that department to generate regular premium payments, as it had increasingly through the eighties. In Skadden terms, the "quality" of the firm's billings fell drastically. They delivered a much lower profit margin. The slowdown on Wall Street meant that other departments in the firm were less busy than they had been, too, with the average annual billings of all lawyers slipping from approximately 2,000 hours to less than 1,800 hours.

A more revealing look at the firm's hourly billings came when they were subdivided. According to a well-placed partner, in 1990, 12 percent of the firm's associates billed more than 2,400 hours, 60 to 65 percent billed around 1,600 hours, and 25 percent or so billed less than 1,400. He observed: "You have a bunch of people killing themselves, and there is just a wide discrepancy in the productivity and the value to the firm of associates." The firm's reputation as a sweatshop, which it had bragged about, was no longer deserved.

The partner also noted: "There's a feeling that costs are way out of whack. We used to bring almost fifty percent to the bottom line, then it went to forty-five percent, and now it's not much more than thirty percent. There's a feeling around the partnership that we ought to do more about the firm's costs by letting people go."

In the winter of 1991, Mullen explained the situation differently. His view turned on an understanding of accounting, law-firm economics, the varying tides of the firm's practice areas, and Skadden psychology. He began: "The numbers are more complicated than they appear."

For taxes, the firm used financial reports generated on a cash basis: From one January to the next, it subtracted expenses from revenues and the remaining profits were divided among the partners. A poor quarter of revenues meant a poor quarter of income for each partner.

To Mullen, however, the cash system was not "a fully reliable measure of the firm's profitability." If Skadden worked for a client in June and sent a bill in October, it might be paid in December or in January of the following year. The firm's reported income would be skewed in one year or the other. For a stable firm, the cash method could give an accurate picture of profitability. For a growing firm, as Skadden had been for twenty years, cash accounting tended to understate profitability. A firm taking on new lawyers had to begin paying them and related expenses the day they arrived. Bills to clients for the time the lawyers worked didn't go out for months. Revenues didn't come in for another four to seven months.

For management purposes, Skadden also kept a second set of books using the accrual method. There, Skadden matched expenses more closely against work when it was actually done and chargeable to a client and the right to revenues had accrued. The management books were more instructive than the tax ones as a planning tool, for accrual income was a more reliable measure of the firm's performance. "The ups and downs in the year on a cash basis are really so much at random that you don't pay much attention to them, comparing this quarter of this year to the same last year. We don't even deal in the concept," Mullen said.

Mullen allowed that the firm's billings in M&A and in corporate finance were substantially down, but emphasized that the M&A department was still the firm's largest. He asserted that its lawyers were busy by almost any standards but Skadden's: "They are going home at seven versus eight, or six versus seven, and probably taking a real lunch, but they are leading relatively normal, busy lives." In other areas, such as banking, bankruptcy and restructuring, energy, and environmental law, business was so strong that the firm was transferring into them lawyers from less active areas or it was hiring from outside.

A major source of the Skadden jitters, then, was expectation. For a generation, the firm's size, revenues, and profits had grown rapidly to unanticipated and very high levels, by the standards of any law firm. A year when they went anywhere but up felt disconcertingly out of character, and in 1991 Skadden was on its way to a second consecutive year of declining profits. In 1990 (Mullen had projected it would end up a "pretty good year"), Skadden's revenues were $503 million, according to *The American Lawyer*, and its profits $207 million—a decline of 3 percent and 11 percent, respectively, from the previous, record-setting year.

To most Skadden partners, however, the declines felt steeper. Each year there were more of them dividing the pie: two hundred twenty-five partners in 1990 as opposed to one hundred ninety-seven partners the year before. Two hundred and seven million dollars divided among an extra twenty-eight partners brought the average share down by well over $100,000, or one-eighth—although the effect of the extra partners was muted for the most "productive" partners, since they took a higher share of the firm's income, and correspondingly amplified for the less productive partners.

The drop-off seemed to feel even more precipitous because of the change in the nature of Skadden's income—the drop in its "quality." During the boom years for deals, from the mid-eighties to the late eighties, Skadden's premium fees lifted the firm's income high over the amounts that it projected annually—"wildly over budget," Fin Fogg had said. In this respect, contrary to what Mullen maintained, the numbers were as simple as they appeared.

Skadden had "net write-ups"—premiums minus write-offs and partial write-offs of bills to clients—of over $100 million in its best year, most of it from M&A. That money went almost directly to the bottom line. Earle Yaffa said then about the firm's profits, "The key variable is revenues rather than costs." In 1990, premiums almost doubled the take of every partner. Without them, Skadden would not have been Skadden.

Officially, the firm treated premiums as a passing thing. "It was an absolute rule in the firm that no estimate of premiums could be included in the budget—not five cents," Flom said. Along with quarterly payments timed to help each member pay estimated taxes, a partner's monthly income was derived from his share of revenues as projected by the budget. The firm made extra payments when it was confident that revenues were running ahead of budget and seemed likely to continue doing so. Partners were told not to count on the extra payments—to think of their monthly draws as their salary and the other money as extraordinary bonuses.

But, as the extraordinary became the usual, bonuses also became entitlements. Many partners seemed not to distinguish between regular income and bonuses, and to count on making much more than the firm projected for them in its budget. The Skadden office directory was filled with addresses on the Upper East Side, on Central Park, and in other glamorous neighborhoods in the midtown section near the New York office, for example. Many partners listed an additional address for a weekend, summer, or winter place, and some gave three addresses.

During the boom years, the firm raised the amount of life insurance it funded for each partner to four million dollars. A senior partner said, "I sometimes think that's to take care of partners' real estate debts," so that the family left behind when a partner died would be protected from the loss of income required to service a jumbo loan.

Around the office, where the decor of the place limited how ostentatious partners could be, they sometimes displayed pictures of large, lovely sailboats they owned, and spoke about cruising together in the South Pacific. A Finnish make, called the Nautor Swan, whose starting price for a forty-six-foot sloop was three-quarters of a million dollars, seemed in vogue; among partners, it had displaced boats of the same quality built in Maine by the Hinckley Company. Other details of wealth seeped out: of the white Rolls-Royce a partner kept in France for forays in Europe; of the antique store that a partner put money in as a hobby; of the gifts that a partner gave to a friend for his wedding (a car) and to his secretary for Christmas (ditto). A Skadden partner, after the big wave of prosperity broke: "It's been a great ride for us, but people here are almost relieved not to be spending."

In the fall of 1990, when it was plain that the firm's revenues would be less flush than in earlier years, Skadden began taking steps to reduce costs and improve its balance sheet by firing members of the support staff. Mullen explained: "A recession has some very salutary effects. It gives you a motivation to look at a lot of things—maybe everything you're doing—and see how effective it is. In our firm, I think we have highly competent managers, but we have lawyers who have spent their lives in areas where cost really didn't mean a lot. In the takeover business, getting things done quickly means a lot. Some of our procedures were not terribly cost-effective under normal circumstances.

"I would say that, because the current climate has caused us to take a hard look at everything we're doing, it will cause us to be a much more efficient operation than we were. The most significant thing we've done is to reorganize some of our approaches to word processing and some other office systems. We think we can accomplish some of the same things we did, with fewer people. From office to office, we've averaged a little over ten percent in terms of cuts."

Each office leader made cuts as he saw fit. In some cases, they prompted fresh discussion about firm philosophy. Lou Goodman, the Boston leader, commented soon after: "For the first time, we're laying people off. It's people's lives at stake and it's very important to me that we not get rid of the newest people here in Boston—our moral compact is that we're a meritocracy.

"In Washington, when the office had to get rid of support staff, Neal McCoy took the twenty most junior people. I insisted that we get rid of the weakest people—and, in one case, we got rid of a senior person who happened to be the weakest in her area." McCoy: "It is correct that I would have applied a time and service principle." But, first, he offered money as an inducement for staff members to leave. It worked. "When people had to be asked to leave, it was the most junior, but it wasn't that many."

The view among some Skadden lawyers was that the obvious method for the firm to cut costs was to fire lawyers. But, as Mullen put it, the firm's position at the end of 1990 and into the start of 1991 was that it planned no "real cuts"—layoffs of lawyers for economic reasons. It announced a no-growth strategy: The firm would be the same size in October of 1991 that it had been a year before.

Skadden expected one hundred ten new lawyers to have joined it by then. It assumed that, since its recent annual attrition rate had been approximately 15 percent, about the same proportion of lawyers would leave over the coming year. A few years before, when the firm was growing quickly, it had replaced lawyers lost through attrition by hiring from other firms as well as taking on recent graduates from law schools. In the no-growth strategy, Mullen said, if Skadden stopped hiring laterals, "attrition would take care of things."

Attrition was a changeable notion. In the mid-eighties, the concept included the departures of some lawyers lured to take other jobs, such as in corporations and in investment banking, and of some who left because Skadden wasn't the firm for them or because they were moving to another, Skadden-less city. When Skadden tightened its personnel policies, in 1989 and 1990, "attrition" began to include the score or so of associates who, twice a year, were asked to leave because they weren't meeting the firm's standards.

By early 1991, the downturn in demand for the services of large law firms in New York and in other American cities where Skadden had offices altered the meaning of attrition again. Fewer Skadden lawyers were being lured to other jobs. Many who might have looked for work elsewhere were staying because they believed there weren't other jobs available.

During the first quarter, the combination of Skadden's relatively weak economic performance and its low rate of attrition made speculation about whether, or when, the firm would fire associates for economic reasons a regular topic of conversation there. The official word remained that the firm would not take that step. It would follow its no-growth plan. It would rely on attrition to thin out the ranks. Skadden would only fire associates who had had fair warning. It expected to get rid of twenty lawyers, or fewer, each evaluation period.

Around the time that Mullen pronounced this policy, however, some other Skadden lawyers gave a different impression of the firm's treatment of associates. By 1991, they said, the firm was using quality reviews to accomplish ends heavily influenced by economic circumstances.

A senior partner recounted in the spring: "Peter tells you we haven't really let anyone go except through attrition. I think it's gotten a lot stricter and that we're doing more than that. There is such nervousness about the L-word: layoffs. It makes no sense to me. Maybe we believe our own notices that Skadden is the best-managed law firm in the world and never made a mistake. I think our clients would understand that we run a business just like them, and that our costs are out of whack and that we have to do something about that."

A senior associate confided: "One thing they won't talk about generally with associates is that they've gotten a lot tougher in the review process. It is not officially acknowledged so far." Speaking about the 1991 spring evaluations, the lawyer went on, "I heard that in the latest review, fifty-three people were being asked to leave. They were so-called quality cuts, but there is no question that today's standard is very different from that used three years ago. A year ago, the firm went to a new system of review. The departments were asked to rate people one to five: one was a star; two was someone working at class level; three was a good, solid person; four was someone with a perceived problem who was told to shape up; and five was someone who was seen as having no opportunity at Skadden. To get to five, you had to be a four first. The fifty-three people were all said to be fours and fives. In corporate finance, I know, some of the people being given deadlines had been rated the equivalent of a two throughout their careers. That fifty-three is also deceptively low. It doesn't include people in individual departments—ten or so in real estate, I heard—who were told to leave but were given more time—longer than the standard three months."

The associate concluded: "Some of the people say, 'I could have gone to be an investment banker and made a lot more money, knowing that I could be turned out tomorrow. I chose to be a lawyer because I thought it provided some security.' They feel cheated by the change. Headhunters are not interested in people from Skadden, I'm told, because they've heard that everyone is being cut for quality reasons. But that's not really true. The perception among lawyers used to be that Skadden was a sweatshop, but the press was really high on Skadden. It is a great place, but a little more honesty might be appropriate. The belt tightening is consistent with a businesslike approach, but there are human costs that the firm is not dealing with well."

19

Making Partner

Under normal circumstances, Bob Sheehan would have called a meeting of the quality committee to talk about how candidates on the morning line had fared in the firm's evaluation of associates in October of 1990. Then he would have talked with Mullen about the firm's likely needs for new partners in different practice areas and offices.

Since Sheehan became chairman of the quality committee, however, he had tried to coordinate it with the needs committee: "Wherever the line is drawn, some are going to be way above it, some way below it, and some very close. It is counterproductive to make a decision about someone on as subjective a basis as quality that need not be made. Otherwise, the quality review causes heartache." For the partnership decisions of 1991, the question of needs arose sooner and loomed larger than it ever had at Skadden.

To deal with this new circumstance, the OEP designated itself the needs committee. In private debate, it demonstrated the depth of its concern. In August, the OEP considered postponing all decisions about new partners from the spring of 1991 until the following fall. Mullen raised the idea. By then, he said, the economy might pick up, giving the firm a better idea of its long-term needs, and freeing it to make more partners than it was likely to do in more uncertain times. Sheehan said, "There was quite a series of discussions. People had different impressions about whether we should wait until the fall of '91 to make partners, as opposed to March, and people had different opinions about whether that would lead to more new partners or less."

Sheehan's view was that a postponement, and with it an adoption of a new schedule for partnership, would mean that Skadden was taking more than two years to consider the next two partnership classes rather than the eighteen months then expected. A change of that type would further unnerve the firm's mid-level and senior associates.

The OEP took the point, and didn't alter the schedule. Because of rampant uncertainty about how many partners to make, however, the firm continued to do little about selection. The fall passed with only slight adjustments to the morning line, made after evaluations in October pushed some candidates out of the running.

By late January of 1991, forty-two of the original forty-five candidates remained on the list and Sheehan's committee had yet to make its quality review. "They waited for the numbers to shake out," an observer said about the firm's uncertain economic shape. In February, the OEP gave Bob Sheehan "a fairly good fix" on the departments that would not be allowed new partners. Of twenty or so, depending on how some specialists were grouped, they included all but seven: the antitrust; banking and institutional investing; bankruptcy, restructuring, and reorganization; environmental; litigation; mergers and acquisitions; and products liability groups.

The OEP also advised Sheehan of the likely allocation of new partners to the various firm offices. The quality committee began its work and, by the middle of the month, eighteen candidates fell off the line. A month later, two more candidates fell off. The list was down to twenty-two—in Sheehan's words, mostly "because of needs." Of the twenty others, "half were clear or probable passes, and a very small percentage were in the category of those not likely to pass the quality test."

Sheehan explained: "Going from the forty-two down to the twenty-two, there was a lot of back-and-forth. Certain judgments were made in departments and offices, after Peter Mullen called their heads, that it made sense to trim their list from six to two, because they would have no more than two. Realism sets in—there's a trimming down that is based, in effect, on judgments at the grass roots about needs and quality. This is Mullen doing diplomacy.

"I don't attempt to review anybody on a needs basis, but quality and needs can interplay. If a partner calls me about a candidate and I know there is a needs issue in his department, I might shade my remarks toward the needs issue—if a department can't realistically hope to have more than one candidate and it's not likely to be this one. Why have friction and a rub when you don't need it?"

In the cut to twenty-two, Sheehan said, most of the close cases disappeared in the firm's large departments: "We were left with the cream of the cream." Of the remaining candidates, fifteen were judged "clear quality passes." Seven were in the gray area. In Sheehan's opinion, the quality committee had fewer difficult choices to make than in the previous two years, when the final groups of contenders had been twice as large. The difficult choices this year were posed in the departments where a candidate's chances could be eliminated or fortified.

To a partner sponsoring an associate or a special counsel for partnership, the campaign started soon after the previous year's announcement, when he put the candidate on the morning line. Following the 1990 round, Lou Goodman was known to feel a special obligation to support Kent Coit. "Lou's Telstar for the year was making Kent a partner," one observer remarked. Because of delays in the winnowing of candidates, however, Goodman waited to engage in serious efforts to lobby his colleagues until the winter of 1991.

By February, the M&A department had cut its list from ten candidates to five. Of the five candidates for whom support was strongest, two were lawyers in the Chicago office. Partners from that office made the case that the lawyers were able and that, because it was so busy, the office "had the numbers" to justify making them partners. The argument didn't convince other M&A partners, who thought that it avoided the merits of the choice. ("I wouldn't have made the case that way," said a senior partner from another office.)

A third M&A candidate was Herbert Henryson, a uniformly respected New York associate who was being considered ahead of his class. Skadden had given him the salary of a second-year associate when he arrived at the firm because he was a real rocket scientist: He had a Ph.D. in nuclear engineering as well as a law degree. But he had practiced law for only six and a half years. In previous years, he might have been recommended for partnership by the department. In 1991, due to economic conditions, he wasn't.

The other candidates were Kent Coit, from Boston, and a senior associate in the Washington, D.C., office, Brian Hoffmann, who was thirty-two and had graduated from law school at Georgetown University in 1982, the same year that Coit finished Harvard. The M&A department saw a clear line between Coit and Hoffmann, on the one hand, and the others on the short list. In a tight year, the department concluded, it was more likely to get two new partners if it backed two candidates— Coit and Hoffmann—instead of five.

Like Coit, Hoffmann was considered "a terrific lawyer," and had lost to another (Washington-based) candidate the year before. Hoffmann had been backed by the corporate lawyers in Washington ("He was our candidate," a partner there said) and had broad support among corporate lawyers in the firm. A Skadden associate said that Hoffmann "poured himself into the firm, billed high hours, and gave up his marriage for Skadden." But, as in 1989, in 1990 the M&A department had been given one less slot (four) than it had candidates it considered ready for partnership.

At a preliminary meeting of the department in 1990, one partner reported, Peter Atkins made it clear that he considered David Fox, a candidate from New York who had worked for him, the strongest of the bunch. The Boston slot had been given to David Brewster, and the other New York slot to Joseph Coco. Mike Schell (according to one partner and confirmed by other lawyers) told those at the meeting that the candidates he was highest on were Hoffmann and another Washington lawyer, Mark Smith.

It was Schell's position that the department shouldn't be limited to four new partners, but if it was, the lawyer whom the firm could least afford to lose was Smith. Schell's word mattered. A younger lawyer said about him, "If I had a bet-the-earth case, and I could be sure Schell's personal interests were the same as mine, he's the guy I'd want in charge." The main knock on Schell was that he was a free agent, not aligned with one of the Fab Four or any other lawyer, besides Flom. "He is playing it for himself," another lawyer said.

Smith's problem was that he was a transplant. He had gone to Skadden's New York office from Cravath in 1986 and in 1988 had moved to Washington, D.C., largely out of a desire to leave Manhattan. A lawyer said, "He was not a homegrown boy in D.C., and probably did more stuff in New York." It made sense that Hoffmann had the backing of the Washington partners, because he had become their protégé. In a straw vote on Hoffmann and Smith, an M&A partner recalled, "it was so close that nobody bothered to refine it, to find out whether one guy was ahead by a vote or two."

After a long discussion and some more balloting, Smith was the M&A department's choice for the partnership—in a Skadden custom, by acclamation. But the department's official unanimity was tainted by talk of a deal. It went like this: Peter Atkins's candidate was said to have been in jeopardy, in part because Schell was expected to vote against him. Atkins was said to have told Schell that if he voted for Atkins's candidate, he could "make" whom he wanted to in Washington.

Atkins was said to have worked this deal in the meeting of the M&A department without making it explicit to everyone there what he was doing. By firm rumor, when one partner figured out what was happening, he said, "What the fuck is going on here? Did we vote on this?"

Atkins: "There were only two people who could have been party to that conversation, and it didn't happen. Anyone who says it did is engaging in speculation and I don't know what." And: "I'm going to say this in as affirmative terms as I can: I do talk with my partners. I don't think any of us have ever conceived that we have the authority to present a deal about a new partner."

"I've heard the deal story," Schell said. "There are people I know, who clearly should know better, who think that I made some sort of a deal with Atkins. There is no truth to that." Hoffmann was not Schell's candidate for the Washington slot, as he had said, but he favored Hoffmann over other lawyers who were chosen.

What gave the deal story credibility was an attempt at a similar-sounding deal that lawyers involved concede had been made. The night before the partnership election, Hoffmann was summoned to New York on a pretext. In reality, there was talk of "making him" in London. If so, it would have been nice for him to be in New York to get the news. It would not have been the first time that a Skadden associate was made a partner if he was willing to move. The idea was that the London office needed "an M&A type," a partner said, and that either "one of the guys up that year might be able to fill the position" or "by moving someone else to London, the firm could open up a slot in the U.S." Neither idea worked out, however, and Hoffmann was left in the cold.

According to an observer, after the 1990 partners were announced,

Schell and Hoffmann went out for drinks, to hash over what had happened. In the view of a Hoffmann sympathizer, the partner pledged to fight for the associate's selection the following year. "Schell said he would move heaven and earth" to get Hoffmann elected, an observer said. "He said he would come out with his shield or on it."

Schell recounted: "He was angry. We talked it over. Was he going to stick it out for another year? Was he going to look for alternatives? I could certainly understand how he would feel that that represented some kind of a commitment on my part to support him, and, in a sense, it was—in the sense that I was very sympathetic to him, particularly because he was so angry, and I wanted to try to get him through that.

"I did not say to him that it was in the bag for next year, or anything like that. Or even 'You're my boy.' What I did tell him is that he might want to go make sure he was rock solid with his sponsor, Roger Aaron. I thought there was no way he was ever going to be a partner unless he was Roger's number one choice."

Hoffmann also had an audience with Mullen. According to one insider, Mullen told him that there was no one among the firm's corporate lawyers who was viewed more highly, and perhaps only one lawyer at his level—Kent Coit.

"It was merit plus the sense of moral obligation plus politics around the edges that led us to pick Kent and Brian," a partner said about the 1991 M&A finalists.

After the M&A department met, the OEP—again, in private debate—considered a radical option that would have preempted M&A's choice. Mike Diamond, a member of the OEP, told me, "There were people who seriously proposed that we make no new partners." Another member of the OEP said, "This took a lot of attention, and was an issue that had never come up. We were dealing with a new environment and different facts and hadn't ever had to deal with this before."

Another senior partner, who was not a member of the OEP, recalled soon after: "I think the OEP initially decided not to make any partners this spring. And they went to the policy committee, and the other members of the committee, almost unanimously, thought that they had to make partners now." On the firm grapevine, talk of the OEP's deliberations was downplayed as rumor and then disclaimed. But associates formed the impression that it was likely the M&A department would get only one new partner, not two.

The OEP confirmed the impression. It informed the M&A department that, by usual measures, it did not need any new partners. But the OEP redefined need in terms of the firm as an institution rather than solely on the basis of its economics. It allotted the department one partner. A senior partner explained how the message was understood: "You have the dominant franchise, and you want to keep that up. You don't want to shut the door to people and, by naming a partner, you say to candidates, 'If you're really good, you'll get through.' "

The judgment turned the department's support for Coit and Hoffmann into a contest between them. Lou Goodman quietly reengaged his campaign. In phone conversations with partners, he repeated the description of Coit made the previous year: "This is the best lawyer we've never made a partner."

Goodman told war stories about Coit's accomplishments, and asked people who didn't know Coit to talk with those they respected who did. Two of Coit's references were Bob Sheehan and Mike Schell.

Sheehan had worked with Coit on a bid for the takeover of a Boston bank. A lawyer explained: "All deals, loosely speaking, are messes for a time. They are amorphous and have to be made to work." Coit had helped give order to a very messy one. Schell and Coit worked as a team on a joint venture between Daimler-Benz and United Technologies, two of the world's largest multinational industrial companies. A lawyer: "The companies started as relative strangers, announcing a joint venture before it had much shape and when there was absolutely no meeting of the minds. The Germans asked why they needed lawyers involved. Kent is a very smart guy, and he was able to find a structure that everyone supported."

Schell was one of the few partners who had worked extensively with both Coit and Hoffmann. For weeks, Goodman tried to persuade Schell to say whom he supported and, if Coit, to advocate his candidacy. Schell and Coit had gotten to know each other well during flights between New York and Europe on the joint venture ("He's one of my best friends at the firm," Coit said about Schell), but the partner told Goodman that the choice between Coit and Hoffmann was a hard one for him. He kept his own counsel.

Neal McCoy advocated Hoffmann's case. He was less assiduous than Goodman (an observer said, "Neal is a less political animal than Lou. He's so much a good team player that, whenever he is political, it's tempered by respect for the needs of the institution"), but he had a good story to tell.

Hoffmann had been the main corporate lawyer on a large case for Skadden, which had heated up in 1990. The firm had counseled the Southland Corporation in the first attempt by an operating company at a large prepackaged bankruptcy, in which the financially troubled company sought to strike a deal with its creditors before they all went to court. The maneuver had succeeded: The company went into bankruptcy in November, moved out in early February, and was on its way by early March, as the 1991 partnership decisions approached.

A partner said, "We had two people who were unusually and equally well qualified, who had done projects in circumstances and with supervising partners that qualified them way beyond the standard that would have been required in the years before. That is the baseline."

For a time, apparently, Hoffmann looked like the winner. An observer said, "My understanding is that, a week or so before the M&A department met to vote, the Fab Four got together to decide how it should come out," and came down in favor of Hoffmann. (Atkins: "I don't think I knew either of the individuals involved. I wouldn't be surprised that we would discuss the process." Fogg: "I don't remember being part of that cabal." Kramer: "I have no recollection of that. I won't swear on my mother's grave that it didn't happen. I did back Hoffmann. I had worked with him.") Hoffmann had gone to Roger Aaron to ask if he was his number one choice, and Aaron had told Hoffmann and others that he was.

Peter Atkins told Mike Schell that the OEP was not certain whether the M&A department should be given a partnership slot and that the decision could depend on whom it chose. Schell said to Atkins, and to a couple of others, that he strongly believed the department's choice should not be predetermined, and, with the balloting of the previous two years as a precedent, that it ought to be done by a vote.

To some lawyers, it appeared that Schell was breaking his commitment to Hoffmann, for the sake of a principle and something else. One said, "The only way what he did makes sense is that he disliked what the big guys had done, and decided that their choice would not stand, that the decision should be made out in the open in a democratic process. The only thing that keeps coming up is that Mike wanted to show that he was a big swinging dick."

To others, it appeared that Schell was caught in the same box he had found himself in the year before: believing that both candidates should become partners, and forced by a limitation imposed on the M&A de-

THE CRUCIBLE | 271

partment to choose. He told Neal McCoy that he was going to vote for Coit and hoped that it would not affect their personal relationship. He told Lou Goodman that he would speak for Coit and vote for him, but that he would not campaign for him in advance of the M&A meeting. Coit: "He's a very independent guy."

Virtually all of the partners in the M&A department—almost fifty lawyers—took part in its decision. Morris Kramer recounted: "Before we voted, I said that I felt there was good reason to consider not making an M&A partner, and that that logic applied to some other departments as well. I said that the numbers this year should be as small as possible, and that every new partner should have to stand up to the highest standards in terms of quality and needs. We have been part of the leadership of the firm from the beginning. We have the responsibility to bend over backwards to be leaders. This time, I thought, that meant not making an M&A partner, unless the numbers really justified it."

Kramer's argument did not carry the day, and the department moved to choose between Coit and Hoffmann. Roger Aaron spoke for Hoffmann. Although Peter Atkins did not, as some partners remembered the meeting, it was understood that he also preferred Hoffmann. Schell spoke for Coit, as did Goodman and others. Intermittently, the M&A department tried to sort out its position in a series of votes. They were inconclusive, with some going for Coit by a few votes, and some for Hoffmann by the same margin. Finally, a secret ballot was held, and Coit won. According to a senior partner, the votes were almost evenly divided—it was virtually a tie. The department made the selection unanimous by a voice vote. The choice was said to be by acclamation.

Afterward, a senior partner commented: "I think that everyone feels that Mike Schell has his own agenda. He led a revolt of the M&A partners in this year's go-round. The powers that be wanted Brian Hoffmann in Washington. Mike Schell led a very deliberate and well-executed plan which resulted in Kent Coit getting it. I have no idea why."

Schell viewed his participation differently. He said, "Basically, all I did was make a speech and cast a vote. In terms of Aaron, Atkins, and Kramer, I have no desire to be in an arm-wrestling match with them." And: "I think the process by which we did that was a salutary one, in that there was almost universal participation. There was a high level of interest. There were a minimal number of procedural rules. Almost fifty people made a collective decision and were convinced of its legitimacy. Even if some weren't happy with the result."

Morris Kramer judged: "Aaron and Atkins didn't realize they were in a political contest. It wasn't a rejection of leadership. They were away, and they didn't realize it was going to be a horse race." He added about Coit and Hoffmann: "In the eighties, both those guys would have been partners in a second."

Lou Goodman was congratulated for the victory of his candidate, but to Hoffmann's sponsor, Neal McCoy, he said that he felt bad about the outcome. He explained: "I was pro-Kent, I wasn't anti-Brian." Later, McCoy said the same: "I think the world of Kent, but I wish Brian had won." Hoffmann stayed at Skadden until 1992, when he left to become a partner in a Denver law firm.

When the OEP made its final recommendations about partnerships to the policy committee, Coit was on the list. A senior partner recounted: "Then Morris, more or less as an effort to put Mike Schell back in his place, tried to get the policy committee to say no M&A partners this year."

Kramer: "The policy committee had the final vote and I thought it was still appropriate—despite or because of our vote—to raise the view that M&A and other departments might not warrant new partners. . . . My bottom line was that we could not justify the need for a new M&A partner, even though we had some of the best people up in a long time. If we were going to say need was important and mean it, that was the way to go. Otherwise, that wasn't the right thing to say."

The policy committee didn't accept Kramer's argument, and it elected Coit a partner.

Another dispute drew last-minute attention. The OEP recommended seven new partners. Sally Henry, of the bankruptcy, restructuring, and reorganization department, who was Fin Fogg's candidate, because he had been put in charge of that group of lawyers, was not on the OEP list. Henry had also been supported by Joseph Halliday, the leader of the banking department, who said she was well qualified and that the firm needed another bankruptcy partner. Skadden was then representing "a major lending institution," in Halliday's words, and Henry was "acutely involved." Invoking Halliday's judgment and his own, Fogg asked the OEP to reconsider.

The OEP stuck by its decision that the firm's overall finances didn't justify making a bankruptcy partner that year. But Roger Aaron called Fogg before the policy committee met, and asked, "Are you going to raise this there?" Fogg replied, "You bet your ass." Bill Frank reported, "We knew Fin was going to make that particular case and we said, 'Sure, make the pitch.' "

Over the following weekend, Fogg lobbied the policy committee by phone. (Another lawyer said that Halliday did, too, but recently Halliday said he hadn't known that Henry's partnership wasn't already secure.) On Monday morning, Fogg presented his case in person. Aaron switched his vote, Frank changed his, and eventually each member of the committee voted to include Henry. Frank: "It happens many times that people will make a very persuasive case for somebody who was on the short list but not at the head of it. Fin said that it would be good for his group institutionally if we made a bankruptcy partner and we agreed."

A month or so later, I had breakfast with Henry. A short, plump woman, she wore no makeup and little jewelry. She was forty-two, and had an easy laugh and an unpretentious way of talking. She told me about teaching social studies in middle schools for nine years before she went to law school. Despite her sociability, however, Henry seemed unusually cautious about how she answered my questions. I asked her why. "Lawyers know the importance of even one word in conveying impressions and information," she explained, "and want to choose their words as carefully as possible."

I asked her if she knew whether a rabbi (a sponsor) had played a part in her selection as a partner. She answered, "The term 'rabbi' is not one I have heard. My relationship with people in the department is a professional relationship that is based on trust and confidence—that I have the ability to do the work and have the ethical standards you want in a partner, that I am willing to walk through walls to meet the clients' needs. I have spent a great deal of time working to be the best lawyer I can be. I haven't spent a lot of time thinking about who makes the decision about new partners, and I really don't know the basis on which the decision about me was made."

Bob Sheehan said, "The final steps, then, are that the OEP makes needs judgments, and the policy committee makes the final decision. As a political matter, one would have that happen, to be more democratic, either in appearance or in reality." At the end of March, without a vote, the full Skadden partnership approved the elections of the committee. Of the scores on the original list of candidates and from the forty-five on the morning line, Skadden formally made eight new partners—to bring the total number of partners in the firm to two hundred thirty-one.

Joshua Schwartz, an associate who arrived at Skadden in 1987, remarked about the selections: "The rules of the game have changed a lot since I've been here. Skadden's gone from making twenty-odd partners a year to making eight. I don't think that should surprise anyone. Business isn't what it was. Along with that comes a recognition that quality is no longer determinative. It's got to be quality and marketing. People making partner are seen as important to the development of an area. If you go down the list, that's so, though I don't know any of the partners personally.

"A few years ago, the firm had the luxury of rewarding people who had been around in the really big growth years because they had worked hard and given their all. I don't know if firms have that luxury anymore. If the pie's not getting bigger, it doesn't make sense to keep slicing it in smaller pieces."

Stuart Finkelstein, an associate who went to the firm in 1985 and, in his words, became "a tax dude," said then, "Some people were like, 'Oh, my God!' Most people with a practical attitude figured it was six to ten"—that six to ten lawyers would be made partner. "It's a timing thing."

The Future

20

Global

Shortly after the new Skadden partners were named, they joined their predecessors at the annual retreat to talk about the state of the firm. Each year the retreat had been an upbeat affair, its tone set by the firm's big plans for the future and amplified by the hum of success. The firm had usually made a point of welcoming partners' spouses at the event and thanking them for their forbearance. In 1991, the event was for partners only.

"It's no secret that business is off and no secret that we met in Rye, New York, and not Boca Raton," a partner advised. "Nobody's going to say it's a terrific time for us. It was the only hard retreat we've ever had. All the others have been celebrations, of the best year ever for Skadden and any other law firm in the world."

The gathering lasted approximately twenty-four hours, beginning with drinks and dinner on a Friday evening, and running through two meetings for the full partnership the following day. Meeting time was devoted to presentations about the firm's economic condition and about its international practice, which was a primary focus of the firm's anxiety.

Isaac Shapiro oversaw the practice. In 1986, after twenty-nine years, he had left the one-hundred-twenty-year-old firm of Milbank, Tweed, Hadley & McCloy to join the upstart firm. A controlled, soft-spoken man, he was known less for his legal expertise, which was substantial, than for his cosmopolitan background. Although he had long been a Milbank lawyer, his was a Skadden story, with elements of hardship and daring and dramatically seized second chances.

His mother's parents were Orthodox Jews who fled from a pogrom in Russia across six time zones to Harbin, China, where his grandfather found work on the Trans-Siberian Railway. His father's parents were White Russians who, escaping the Bolsheviks, ended up in Japan.

Lydia, his mother, was a pianist and Constantine, his father, a cellist. In 1923, in Berlin, where they both had landed (she was eighteen, and he, twenty-seven), they were introduced and married soon after. The rise of Hitler forced them to move on, to Paris and then to Palestine, where he became the principal cellist for the Tel Aviv Symphony. She gave birth to twin boys.

Two years later, when she was pregnant with a third son, the Shapiros journeyed to live with Lydia's father, who was still in China. But one year later, the family continued on to Japan, where Constantine and Lydia found work teaching at the Tokyo Musical College.

In 1931, Isaac was born in Tokyo. By 1932, Lydia and Constantine's marriage was fracturing; Lydia took the boys west to Harbin, but four years later brought them back to Japan. The reunion—Isaac was five —gave Isaac his first memory of his father.

For the next ten years, the Shapiros lived in Yokohama, where they had a house with neither plumbing nor telephone. Largely because they were sponsored by a prestigious Japanese family whom Constantine had known through his music, the Shapiros escaped the ostracism to which Japanese would regularly subject Westerners.

Constantine enrolled his sons in a private British school in Yokohama. They spoke English at school, Russian at home, and Japanese everywhere else. Isaac took French lessons from a tutor, and also learned some German. At the end of 1943, when the war was going badly for the Japanese, the government ejected foreigners from Yokohama. The Shapiros moved to Tokyo. By then, Lydia and Constantine had a fifth son, born in 1939. The twins were at school in the Gora Mountains. Isaac and another brother (they were thirteen and sixteen) went to a special public school in Tokyo, for foreigners and native Japanese returning from overseas.

In August of 1944, as the war depleted Japan's resources, the Shapiros were often short of food. The size of the family (seven, plus a governess) aggravated the hardship, so Constantine sent the two oldest boys across Manchuria to Lydia's father in China. In 1945, American B-29 raids were igniting fires throughout Tokyo, and in March the Shapiros sent Isaac and their two other sons (with the governess) to the mountains. In June, Lydia and Constantine joined them there, where the family survived on potatoes and other staples bought from local farmers.

After the war ended in August, Isaac, then fourteen, one day told his parents he was going out to buy some food. Instead, he hopped a train to Yokohama to watch the American troops arrive. Isaac struck up conversations with U.S. troops, and before long was taken on as a helpful mascot by the commanding officer of the new American naval air base in Yokohama.

When a new chief, Colonel John Calvin Munn, took command of the air base, he took command of Isaac, too, and made the teenager his driver and interpreter. From that summer through the following spring, Isaac lived on the base, either with Munn or in junior officers' quarters.

Munn was reassigned to Pearl Harbor in 1946, and asked the Shapiros if he could take Isaac with him, to help the boy get an American education. Constantine admired the ideals of Woodrow Wilson and Franklin Roosevelt (the Internationalists, he called them), and he and Lydia agreed to the proposal. The Shapiros were technically stateless, so the American consulate invented a document for Isaac to use as his passport.

In June of 1946, at age fifteen, Isaac crossed the Pacific by military plane and arrived in Honolulu. A generation after the family had departed from Russia, the Shapiros had fanned out in their own diaspora: Isaac's parents and two of his brothers were in Japan; another brother was in China and the fourth was in the Soviet Union; and his father's brother was in South Africa. Isaac was the first Shapiro to emigrate to the United States.

Isaac became an American citizen and graduated from high school in Honolulu. He was nicknamed Ike, after Dwight D. Eisenhower. When Munn was transferred to Washington, D.C., Shapiro went East to college, at Columbia University. Delayed by a stint in the Army during the Korean War (he reached sergeant, working as a Japanese translator for an intelligence unit), in the mid-1950s he graduated from Columbia's college and then from its law school.

Shapiro married a classmate from law school and won a Fulbright scholarship to France. He hoped to do international legal work, and he believed that a tour in Europe would give him a lift as a lawyer. When the scholarship ended, in 1957, he joined Milbank Tweed in New York.

Shapiro made a place for himself there by defending the Swiss watch industry in a large antitrust suit brought by the United States government. The case helped him become a partner in litigation in 1966. Over time, he came to dislike the friction of the work and, in 1973, at age forty-two, he made an unusual jump to the firm's corporate side.

According to Ellen Joan Pollock in *Turks and Brahmins: Upheaval at Milbank, Tweed*, Shapiro endured relatively lean years when he shifted practice areas. But his career was recast by the Chase Manhattan Bank, Milbank's main client. With 20 percent of its business in Asia, the bank asked Milbank to open an office in Hong Kong and it agreed. In 1976, Shapiro and a colleague made a fact-finding trip to Tokyo. Persuaded that their firm should open a shop in Japan, too, to service the Chase and other accounts, they convinced the Milbank partnership to make the move.

For a generation, the Japanese bar had kept foreigners from establishing law practices in the country. (A grandfather clause had protected foreigners already there.) Australian lawyers tried to breach the barrier in the sixties and were rebuffed. An American firm made an attempt in the seventies, but had to settle for an affiliation with a Japanese firm. In 1977, when a Japanese firm reciprocated Milbank's interest in opening a Tokyo office cooperatively, Shapiro smoothed the path by finding a professor at Tokyo University who would write an article arguing it was legal for the Americans to come into Japan.

Shapiro was the obvious candidate to lead Milbank's venture. He spoke Japanese fluently. He knew people in the country intimately. One of his brothers lived there. He had been the president of the influential Japan Society in the United States. Not surprisingly, Shapiro got the assignment. He arrived in Tokyo through the front door, unnoticed by the official bar.

Shapiro soon caused a commotion. Japanese headlines compared his arrival to that of the reviled Commodore Matthew Perry and his Black Ships, in 1854. Threatened with a criminal suit for his boldness in beginning a practice, Shapiro hired Tasko Matsuo, a well-known Japanese lawyer, as his counsel. Matsuo treated him like a star. Correctly predicting that the criminal matter would melt away, he took Shapiro to meet some of the justices of Japan's Supreme Court. Other obstacles also shrank. With Shapiro at the helm, Milbank began doing business in Tokyo for the Chase Manhattan Bank and for Japanese clients.

In 1979, Shapiro returned to New York. His homecoming coincided with a period of international expansion, when many American law firms began to open offices abroad. Skadden was not among them. Bob Pirie, the senior partner in Skadden's Boston office, made twenty-six round-trip flights between the United States and London on client matters in 1980 and 1981. The travel might have been expected to make him an advocate of opening a Skadden office in London, but it didn't. As long as the Concorde could get him to Europe in three hours, he saw no reason for Skadden to bear the cost of running a London branch. His view prevailed at the firm.

In 1985, Peter Mullen and other senior partners were moved to think differently about the question. When they attended a London meeting of the American Bar Association, they were courted by British firms. To British and European lawyers, Skadden's rapid growth, its apparent wealth, and its hegemony in the American M&A business gave it a powerful allure. But the firm continued to rely on the Concorde as the firm's link to London, and took no steps toward opening a real branch in the City.

The firm was more interested in Tokyo. It took three times as long to fly there from the East Coast of the United States as it did to get to Europe. The firm's business in Japan was increasing and Skadden decided to explore opening an office there. In 1982, it had made a false start down that path, when it came close to taking in a new partner who was an expert on East Asian law. The Skadden partnership had voted, two to one, to approve the hire and, with it, the opening of a Tokyo office. But, with so many opposed, Mullen and others judged that the move lacked a real consensus. The lawyer joined another firm.

In 1983, the firm sent a team of partners to Japan to present a seminar on mergers and acquisitions at the Comparative Law Center in Kyoto. In 1984 and 1985, Skadden lawyers made similar presentations in Australia, New Zealand, and Beijing, as well as in Japan. By the end of 1985, the firm had determined it would open a Tokyo office as soon as it found the right lawyer to lead it.

Ike Shapiro, at Milbank, was on Skadden's short list. Bob Pirie (he knew Shapiro from a business deal) and Elizabeth McCormack (a distinguished mutual friend of Shapiro's, Pirie's, and Joe Flom's) had hatched a scheme to introduce Shapiro to Skadden. Although Pirie had left the Skadden partnership in 1982 to become an investment banker, he dealt with Skadden regularly and knew about the firm's Tokyo plans. He asked McCormack whether she thought Shapiro might be interested. She responded that he should be, because Skadden would give him a larger stage.

Pirie: "I called Joe Flom and said, 'I've got just the guy for you.' Joe had never heard of him. He went to talk with Mullen, and called me right back. He said, 'I've just talked with Mullen and he says you're out of your fucking mind. He'll never leave where he is.' I said, 'That's not the question. The question is: Do you want him? and What's the best way to go after him?' "

A former nun and a past president of Manhattanville College, McCormack is a senior adviser to the Rockefeller family and the chairman of the board of the John D. and Catherine T. MacArthur Foundation, one of the largest and most respected private foundations in the United States. Not a person who shies from change, she sought and obtained a papal dispensation allowing her to give up her religious vows so that she could marry a man who was Jewish and divorced.

McCormack knew Shapiro through her Rockefeller family work: The Chase Manhattan Bank, Milbank's longtime client, is controlled by the Rockefeller family. According to Ellen Joan Pollock, McCormack told Pirie that Shapiro was not happy at Milbank. McCormack told me that she believed that Shapiro was not challenged enough at the firm. To her, it seemed old and conservative. A remaking of Milbank, whose aspirations were obvious by 1990, had only just started.

After her conversation with Pirie, McCormack mentioned to Shapiro that he might hear from Skadden—that the firm wanted to get advice from him about opening a practice in Japan. Indignantly, he asked why he should advise a competitor. She explained that Skadden was interested in him. His response was adamant: "After all these years, I do not intend to make a change." She replied calmly, "I would ask you to go with an open mind." By encouraging Shapiro to move to the younger, bigger, and, in her view, more exciting firm, McCormack gave an imposing benediction to Skadden.

The firm then had five hundred fifty lawyers. Shapiro had heard only about its M&A practice, nothing more, when he got the call from a

Skadden partner he had known in law school. As a discussion between Shapiro and Skadden took shape, Peter Mullen and Earle Yaffa conceded to Shapiro that Skadden had been built on American deals, but described its ambition to have a broad-based international practice. A Tokyo office would be a crucial first step toward that goal, and Skadden offered Shapiro a partnership.

In April of 1986, leaving partners of twenty years on terms that ranged from friendly and gracious to cool and bitter (Milbank withheld money that Shapiro believed he was owed, and he sued to get it), Shapiro took an unprecedented step for a senior partner in good standing at an old-line New York firm: He accepted Skadden's offer.

By Ellen Joan Pollock's account, Skadden provided him a way out of a worrisome situation, for he had been less successful in attracting international business than his eminence as an East Asian hand suggested he would be, and had expressed concern about his security at Milbank. At the time of the move, Shapiro admitted his concern about the vitality of Milbank. In his first year and a half at Skadden, he brought in $4 million of business.

But Shapiro's magnetism for new business was less important to Skadden than his experience with and insight into an uncomfortable polarity, between the global spread of business and the local character of much legal practice. For an American law firm intent on becoming international, the contrast between the forces of capitalism and the strictures of tribalism presented a delicate challenge. Skadden needed Shapiro for his skills as an anthropologist as well as for his knowledge of international practice.

Shapiro expected to concentrate on Japan. But not long after he switched firms, Mullen suggested that Shapiro compose a memo outlining the steps Skadden should take to " 'internationalize' its scope of practice." Shapiro undertook the assignment. Called "A Global Strategy for Skadden Arps," his memo's premise was that Skadden lagged significantly behind other major American firms in attracting overseas clients and international business.

The net surplus for services in the American balance of trade had climbed from $2.3 billion in 1970 to $18.9 billion in 1986 (the balance on manufactured goods had fallen from a surplus of $2.6 billion to a deficit of $145.1 billion in the same period). While legal services represented a small fraction of total services (less than 1 percent), Skadden had barely a sliver of this growing business. The main reasons for the firm's deficiency, Shapiro contended, were its lack of overseas offices and its failure to market itself as aggressively overseas as it had in the United States.

Shapiro theorized that the domination of the market for legal services in the 1990s by "a few mega-firms," which was sometimes predicted domestically, would occur in the international arena as well. The successful mega-firms would be "truly global in the ability to provide multi-national services to multi-national clients," he argued.

The most obvious step in the firm's global strategy would be the establishment of Skadden offices in the world's "major international financial centers." The firm was already in two, New York and Los Angeles. The next candidates were London (the second-ranked financial center, following New York) and Tokyo (ranked third).

Soon after Shapiro's arrival, Skadden had begun informal operations in Tokyo, having recruited a well-qualified lawyer, Anthony Zaloom (fluent in Japanese and Chinese as well as in English), to run the branch. Skadden was subletting space from the Kawasaki Steamship Line until Zaloom could register as a foreign law solicitor under a new Japanese law scheduled to take effect in April of 1987.

Shapiro presented a London office as an equal necessity, referring to the British capital as part of the financial world's "golden triangle." By 1986, approximately forty American law firms had London offices, as did many major American investment and commercial banks. To Shapiro, Skadden could rely on three particular strengths to make up lost ground as a late entry in a crowded market: its expertise in corporate law, in corporate finance, and in banking; its geographic diversity; and its administrative and legislative "clout."

He recommended that Skadden do abroad what it had in the United States, by developing a "brand name" that would give the firm an advantage in the international market for legal services as it had at home. The firm should lead "with its M&A and commodities expertise" and then sell "corporate finance and banking expertise." The idea was for Skadden to reposition itself as a truly international firm, with Europeans and Asians on a London staff connected directly to Tokyo, where most U.S. firms with London offices didn't have an office. Shapiro recommended opening a Hong Kong office sometime in the future, as a fifth important site in the financial world network.

As for marketing the firm's services in other "important capitals of the world," Shapiro observed that a "relatively low-cost method" would be "to form close correspondent relationships with major law firms in those cities"—the kind of fraternal links that leading firms in New York, Boston, and Washington, D.C., for example, had made with London firms during the middle decades of this century. Skadden already had such an arrangement with a firm in Australia. Shapiro mentioned as other possible locations China, Korea, and Taiwan (in Asia) and Belgium, France, Germany, the Netherlands, Sweden, and Switzerland (in Europe).

Shapiro's memo was circulated in 1986, an intensely busy year of deals for Skadden. No one paid much attention to it. But the Tokyo office advanced to official status, as planned, and within a year it appeared to have been opened just in time: The firm took part in what it considered its fair share of mergers there in 1987 and 1988 (it had a role in four of every ten involving Japanese and American companies in those two years).

In 1987, at the firm's annual partners' retreat in Boca Raton, Shapiro made his "golden triangle" argument again: Of all the American firms that had recently gone to Tokyo, he told his new partners, Skadden was the only one without a London office. It, too, needed an office in the City. While some partners greeted the pitch caustically, calling it the promise of the "magic" triangle, the firm accepted Shapiro's reasoning. Skadden had gone to Tokyo because the move seemed to make good economic sense on its own terms. The firm decided to establish itself in London because, whether that office met the same test, firm leaders thought it was time for Skadden to be there, too. In January of 1988, six months after Skadden opened its doors in Tokyo, it began a London operation.

In 1989, a memo signed by Peter Mullen outlined the reasons for Skadden to take further steps in its global strategy and to start up offices in Beijing, Hong Kong, and Sydney. Since Shapiro had first proposed an "international game plan" for the firm in 1986, its international practice had billed over $18 million, the Tokyo office had been "extremely busy," and London was "off to a good start." The firm also represented "a larger number of Chinese enterprises than any other law firm in the United States."

Mullen's case for opening the offices rested on three broad premises. First, the future of "business and law practice" was "global." Opportunities outside the United States were growing faster than those inside. Second, with "frequent visits," the firm had already begun to develop business in the proposed office sites, working from its New York office. It needed to maintain its success by "establishing a presence in the two regions" (mainland Asia and Australia). Third, Skadden's "size, client base, reputation and ability to support development efforts" put it in "an excellent position to carry out these expansions successfully."

Mullen concluded: "This expansion makes sense if we are going to be a major international player, which I strongly believe we should and must be." No one of the proposed offices could fill the roles of the other two, because of the distances involved. (A flight from Sydney to Hong Kong took nine hours, and to Tokyo, ten and a half hours. Flights from Tokyo to Beijing or to Hong Kong took five hours, and from Hong Kong to Beijing, four hours.)

"We have already thrown our hat in the ring of global law firms of the future," Mullen reminded his partners. "I think these next steps are very important to sustain our efforts in that direction." In October of 1989, Skadden established offices in Hong Kong and Sydney. Not long after, the firm decided to open in Brussels (1990), Paris ('90), and Frankfurt ('91), and to operate informally in Budapest ('91) and Prague ('91). The political events at Tiananmen Square led Skadden to postpone the opening of a Beijing office until 1992.

The firm took Shapiro's view: It was late in making its international move and needed to recover lost time. Between 1987 and 1989, the annual number of international matters for the firm (projects either taking place abroad or involving a foreign client) had risen from 137 to 469. Between 1986 and 1990, the number of foreign offices of the ten major investment banks—among Skadden's highest-billing clients—rose from 127 to 169.

Among the world's twenty largest industrial companies, which Skadden worked for or sought to work for, eleven were foreign. Among the twenty largest banks, on Skadden's roster or in its sights, only one was American. Thirteen, including the first eight, were Japanese. Skadden already had a number of major foreign clients. In order of 1989 billings, for example, they included Daimler-Benz (Germany), Hitachi (Japan), Fiat (Italy), Matsushita Electric Industrial Company (Japan), and Nissan Motor (Japan).

The economic promise of expanding internationally, however, was probably even stronger than these numbers suggested. The most obvious advantage for American (as well as English) lawyers lay in words. They were masters of the language of international business: The legal documents used in most deals, even those that don't involve an American or English corporation, are usually written in English.

A second advantage lay in experience. American (and, increasingly, English) lawyers were more involved in business and commerce than their counterparts anywhere else in the world. They had invented many of the methods relied on in international deals—sometimes called Anglo-Saxon legal, or corporate, technology. As Skadden discovered when it surveyed the world, the transformation that it and other American firms had undergone since 1970 was modest compared with the changes that lawyers in many other places had endured. They were grappling with historical restrictions on their roles while struggling to modernize.

In the 1970s and 1980s, for example, the French legal profession reinvented itself as it had not done for hundreds of years. Until 1971, the profession was fractured in many parts, with various legal functions carried out by different groups of professionals (*avocats, notaires*, etc.). The *avocats*, who were the most prestigious because they represented clients in court, were required by law to operate largely as they had since the sixteenth century, out of the apartments where they lived.

They were defined by prohibitions—against establishing separate offices, because that would be a form of solicitation for clients; against affiliating with legal counselors to businesses, called *conseils juridiques*; and against associating with more than five other advocates—that was thought to compromise their independence. (Until 1956, *avocats* had not been allowed to form partnerships at all.) In France, the largest and most respected law offices handling business matters were those of two American firms, Coudert Frères and Cleary Gottlieb, which had practiced in Paris since 1879 and 1949, respectively. The French lawyers offering similar services generally operated in firms of ten or fewer.

In 1971, the French government passed a law that created a profession of *conseils juridiques*. The law maintained the prohibition against affiliations between them and *avocats*, and included limits on foreign lawyers' access to legal practice of all kinds in France. Only lawyers from countries in the European Community could qualify as *avocats*, and to set up a French office a foreign firm had to create a French firm whose partners registered as *conseils juridiques*.

During the following decade and a half, the number and size of French corporate law firms in Paris, where most of the country's major business is done, grew steadily, as did the size, although not the number, of American and other foreign firms in the city. The young French drawn to the law had considered it more prestigious to become advocates instead of legal counselors, but the rise of business practice strengthened the pull of corporate firms. Increasingly, graduates of France's *grandes écoles*, in literature, politics, and business, who had long been destined for positions in government or at a university, went on to study law and join *cabinets d'affaires*, or law firms.

Still, offices of American and other foreign law firms in Paris attracted new business that French lawyers believed was rightfully theirs. This new legal work stemmed from the increase in corporate deals involving France and other countries, the privatization of formerly state-owned enterprises, the growth in business regulation by the European Community in anticipation of European unification in 1992, the expansion of financial activity sown by deregulation of the French market, and the ground swell of all kinds of international financial activity.

Daniel Soulez Larivière practices in the old French style with two other *avocats*, working from his apartment off the avenue de la Grande Armée, near the Arc de Triomphe in Paris. In 1987, the anachronistic profile of the French legal profession moved Soulez Larivière to run for a position as a member of the Paris bar counsel on a platform of change. Once elected, at the request of the bar's president he wrote a report on the state of the profession that accused French lawyers of the sin of pride (*"un excès de suffisance"*) and proposed a major reorganization. Soulez Larivière: "The report had a lot of success. The press realized that this was a new story to tell. It ended with a cover story of *L'Express*, called 'Avocat: Profession de l'Avenir' "—the profession of the future.

Soulez Larivière had reported that in the mid-eighties there were only eleven hundred French legal counselors registered in Paris—one hundred fewer than the number of foreign lawyers registered in the city. The entire Paris corps of *avocats*, nine thousand strong, billed a fraction of the revenues of the foreign lawyers. Besides losing business to foreign lawyers, the French had allowed the Big Eight international accounting firms to gain a large share of the legal market in Paris. To Soulez Larivière, the one paradoxical advantage of the French legal system at this point was its archaic nature. It was so irrational and outmoded that only a complete reconstruction would solve its problems.

Most of his recommendations became law in 1990. The key change was the unification of France's courtroom and office lawyers into one profession, called *avocats*. While lawyers like Soulez Larivière could continue to practice as their predecessors had for many generations, others were liberated to band together and compete with foreign lawyers in Paris for a share of the increasing amount of sophisticated legal business in the country. American law firms showed the way. At a ceremony awarding the rank of commander in the French Legion of Honor to the longtime head of the Paris office of Coudert Frères, Charles Torem, France's President, François Mitterrand, thanked him for helping to make Paris a center of legal practice in Europe.

The chief theoretician behind the movement for French law firms to challenge the American was a French partner in Cleary Gottlieb, Laurent Cohen-Tanugi. His book *Le Droit sans l'Etat* (*The Law without the State*) included a preface by Stanley Hoffmann, a professor of international relations at Harvard University, which began: *"Voici le plus tocquevillien des ouvrages sur les Etats-Unis écrits depuis Tocqueville—et, pour cette raison même, le meilleur."* Here is the most Tocquevillian of the works written about the United States since Tocqueville—and, for this very reason, the best.

Born in 1957, Cohen-Tanugi is an alumnus of the Ecole Normale Supérieure, from which he took a degree that entitles him to teach literature, and of Harvard Law School, where he received a master's degree. He worked for Cleary Gottlieb in New York and in 1983 moved to the firm's Paris office. There he became a partner in the firm. He explained: "I started writing fairly soon after coming back. The question I wanted to answer for my readers was: Why are law and lawyers so important in the United States and so unimportant in France?"

He argued that, in contrast to the United States, where the role of lawyers was assured by the complex legal machinery of a constitutional government and by the distribution of rights and responsibilities throughout the society, the position of lawyers was limited in France because of the centralization of power in the state. It was run like a giant monopoly by a network of civil servants who had little need for legal counsel. To the French, the American legal system was a "pathology." Cohen-Tanugi presented its benefits: "My point was: If you really want to reduce the role of the state, then you have to increase the role of law and lawyers."

Le Droit sans l'Etat was published to wide notice in 1985, and Cohen-Tanugi became a regular on French television, an intellectual celebrity. His punditry focused on the relationship between law and politics in France, but the role of lawyers in business and finance was increasing dramatically, and many prominent French lawyers were moving from American firms to the growing number of expansionist Parisian firms. Cohen-Tanugi articulated for French lawyers a grand purpose they hadn't felt in generations.

Some critics of large American firms (*"Les Law Firms Américaines,"* they were called at a Paris conference about them organized by a French institute in June of 1991) contended that the American model posed a threat to the collegiality of the French bar. To Cohen-Tanugi, the question was "a completely lost cause." There was "really no alternative, to practice effectively," he said.

By 1991, the largest French law firm, Gide Loyrette Nouel, which was founded in 1920, and in 1962 had five lawyers, had grown to one hundred and sixty lawyers, who practiced in Paris, Brussels, Warsaw, Riyadh, Tokyo, and New York. (A respected member of the French bar concluded that the Gide firm was in fact responsible for the Soulez Larivière report on the legal profession: It had "whispered instructions" in Soulez Larivière's ear.) The style and intensity of practice in Paris resembled that of New York in the sixties more than that in the nineties, some lawyers observed, but, to Cohen-Tanugi, the differences were minor, between "the margin and the core." The larger point was that French firms had adopted the American-style integration of key specialties (corporate law, litigation, tax, and the like) into multipurpose law firms.

"The French have a curious relationship with money," explained Xavier de Roux, a senior partner of the Gide firm, contrasting the new firms and their predecessors: "For the traditional bar, business was equated with money and, for a long time, *avocats* didn't court it. Fees were a voluntary thing, in a way—a sign of *bienvenue* from a client. Until 1971, if a client didn't pay a lawyer, the practice was not to sue a client." Dominique Borde, a onetime partner in Cleary Gottlieb and now the senior partner of Moquet, Borde & Associés, one of several highly thought-of French firms considered offspring of Cleary Gottlieb, completed the point. He said, "We're a Catholic country and, to many Catholics, the pursuit of profit is evil. We're also France and what was commercial was not intellectual. That has totally changed."

To French lawyers who felt they had to catch up with lawyers from more established bars, the cost of not succeeding was that French lawyers would be permanently relegated to second-class status as bag carriers for the cosmopolitan foreign counselors who had mastered the glamorous business practice. To the extent that there was debate about the clash between values of professionalism and those of the market, retreating to embrace the former was seen as a step toward isolation and self-destruction—a way of ceding the latter to realists. Among the few concerns presented by the French bar under the heading of professionalism were rules governing practice for new and foreign lawyers, which, for foreigners especially, amounted to large barriers to entry into the market.

The French Assembly crafted one exception to the barriers, expressly for some American lawyers. They were from Skadden. In the original draft of the law fusing various pieces of the French legal profession, a draft supported by longtime American lawyers in Paris, all foreign lawyers practicing in offices that were established as of January 1990 were automatically allowed to become *avocats* if they met certain other minimal requirements. Skadden's office in Paris hadn't opened until June of 1990, so the rule made it significantly more difficult for the firm's lawyers to build a practice in France.

Working in Washington, D.C., through the United States government, Skadden pushed the French Assembly to consider extending the automatic approval for foreign lawyers to those who had arrived by the end of 1990, rather than the beginning. The proposed rule to that effect passed in the lower house of the French legislature. The Senate turned it down—in Skadden's view, because jealous American law firms "tried to sabotage Skadden's efforts," according to a Skadden lawyer involved in the process. "Through a French lawyer we asked to help us in Paris, we learned that the U.S. firms would have been just as happy to see us frozen out."

One December evening in the French Senate, Skadden's case received an injection of support when the Minister of Justice took the floor and called the amendment fair and reasonable. After a night of trade-offs, the two houses of the legislature agreed to the change. Just before Christmas, the French President signed it into law. Ike Shapiro recounted: "The amendment didn't have our name on it, but no one was naive enough not to think that this rollback was designed to benefit us."

The amendment saved Skadden from a predicament. In June, Skadden had once again seized the attention of its American and other competitors by announcing a new "working arrangement" with a small and highly prestigious Parisian firm, founded in 1964 as Badinter, Bredin & Associés. Its original partners were Robert Badinter and Jean-Denis Bredin. The third-ranking partner was Jean-François Prat, who had a practice that particularly interested Skadden.

By the mid-eighties, Bredin's novels and other books, including a bestselling history of the Dreyfus affair, had made him France's best-known lawyer. Robert Badinter was also prominent, for in 1981 he had left the firm to serve as France's Minister of Justice and had provoked a national controversy by opposing the death penalty. Prat, in turn, was distinguished by his handling of some of the most publicized mergers and acquisitions in France.

An unmistakable mark of the French firm's prestige was the understatement in its presentation to the world. Its receptionist answered the phone, *"Cabinet d'avocats,"* not naming its principals. Underscoring that those needing the services of the firm would know where to find it, its lovely old offices above a courtyard off the rue du Faubourg St.-Honoré, on Paris's Right Bank, bore no nameplate. The Skadden-Bredin understanding also swept in a small, new Parisian firm called Schepard Baxter, composed of two American lawyers from the firm of Coudert Frères and a French *avocat.*

Some in the Parisian legal community had a cynical view of the three-way alliance: The Bredin firm had been "essentially disbanding," in the words of a senior Paris lawyer whose firm had recently hired two *avocats* from there, and the choice Prat himself faced was "to become a solo practitioner or to put some strength around him."

When Bredin Prat, Schepard Baxter, and Skadden announced their respective deals together in 1990, Richard Schepard arranged for a French magazine, *Le Nouvel Economiste,* to run an article about the affiliation that emphasized its bright side. The article described the deal as a *"mariage du gotha"* (between two princely families, roughly speaking) and, as translated, began: "The most famous lawyer on Wall Street, Joseph Flom"—*"M. J. Flom"*—"has just chosen an ally in France, one of France's best, the law firm of Bredin-Prat."

Jean-François Prat was born in the South of France in 1941. He studied political science and law at the University of Aix-en-Provence, took a diploma at King's College in London, and joined what is now the second-largest firm in France, Jeantet & Associés, in 1965, when it had three partners and three associates. After three years, he moved to Badinter Bredin, where he became a partner in 1969.

Prat, on the most intriguing element about his alliance with Skadden: "Morris Kramer called to say that he would like to meet me with some of his partners. So I had a dinner with them. They asked, 'What would you think about doing something together?' In my mind, I thought: It's a good idea, but you are so huge—one thousand lawyers—and we are so small." And "I said to them, 'I know your idea is to eat me. I do not want to be eaten by anybody. If you want my friendship and association, that might be fine. If it is your intention to eat me, then I do not want any part of it.' "

Schepard had been talking with Prat about joining forces for several months when Prat got the call from Skadden. Schepard: "We came to see Prat one Saturday morning and he said, 'Have you ever heard of Skadden?' " The three parties struck a deal that appeared no firmer up close than it did from afar. The Bredin Prat/Schepard Baxter firm would retain Skadden if it required counsel in locations of the American firm and would be billed for the services. If Skadden needed local counsel in Paris, it would hire the French firm and be billed for the services.

The strength of the affiliation was its aura of exclusivity and power. Skadden acquired the social and literary cachet of the small, mysterious Paris firm. Bredin Prat, incorporating Schepard Baxter, acquired the backing of a giant. "They are not the most traditional American lawyers, certainly not," observed Xavier de Roux about Skadden. "They are terribly business-minded."

In the summer of 1990, members of the new alliance drove off in a caravan to celebrate not far from Paris, at a castle owned by Moët et Chandon, the great champagne maker—and a mutual client of Prat and Skadden. The vehicle leading the caravan was a vintage white Rolls-Royce, provided for the occasion by Ike Shapiro, who several months later seemed to make good the firm's risk of setting up in Paris by orchestrating the passage of the Skadden amendment in the French Assembly. Despite the amendment, however, the Paris bar rejected the firm's application to operate as French *avocats*. With distinguished local counsel, Skadden took the bar to court and won the right to practice as it wanted.

The outcome of the story highlighted Shapiro's uncommon contribution to his firm as an anthropologist: In the match between Skadden and Bredin Prat that Shapiro completed, both sides felt they were marrying up; in securing the Skadden amendment and the victory in court, Shapiro assured that the dowry in the marriage had value.

But Shapiro's abilities as a cultural interpreter and guide were not foolproof. That had been proven by some slapstick dealings he had with the East-West Business Circle Foundation in Moscow. The foundation was run by Vladimir Kvint, a Soviet economist who was chairman of the Moscow Business Club, vice-chairman of the Economic Institute of the Academy of Sciences of the U.S.S.R., and, as the leading Soviet expert on economic free trade zones, a deputy to one of the architects of *perestroika*.

At a New York conference for Skadden clients interested in doing business in Russia under the new regime (it was presided over in Russian by Kvint, with his wife solemnly translating his remarks into English), Shapiro described Kvint as having more business cards than anyone he knew. Shapiro praised him as a hustler.

Not long after, a cooperative arrangement between Skadden and the foundation was announced. Then, without warning, Kvint disappeared in Vienna. A few weeks later, he resurfaced in Israel, claiming (as Shapiro recounted) that he had gone underground because he was being harassed by the Russian government. A Skadden partner helped Kvint get asylum in the United States, where he found a job teaching international business at Fordham University and became a contributor to *Forbes* and an adviser to Andersen Consulting. The law firm quickly ended its relationship with Kvint and the foundation.

Shapiro: "I had egg on my face. Kvint took us for a ride."

To close the Kvint chapter, at the 1990 annual partners' meeting, Shapiro proclaimed Kvint a leader of an imaginary new foreign office, in Antarctica.

By the time of the partners' retreat in 1991, the foreign operations of Skadden had not been expected to turn a profit and they hadn't. But changes in the firm's financial picture made the costs of the operation more painful to bear than the firm had foreseen. No one argued that Skadden should shut down abroad. ("I think there would be only a handful of people who would be in favor of shelving the whole international thing completely," a senior partner reported.) In the new context of economic constraint, however, many partners gave the program close scrutiny for the first time.

At the 1991 meeting, Shapiro, Mullen, and Yaffa addressed the complaints of partners that the firm had only a sketchy understanding of the international program's costs and benefits. Mullen stressed the program's mission, recycling material from previous presentations to remind partners that they themselves had approved the plan. Yaffa summarized its expenses and revenues for 1990 and its budget for 1991. His prediction was that the performance of the young program (Skadden's initial foreign office had been open only four years) would improve significantly. In 1990, only the London office had made money; in 1991, Brussels and Hong Kong were also expected to be in the black. (They were.)

Shapiro described plans to cut international costs, as the program did its part in the new Skadden drive for efficiency. A Skadden partner based overseas was being heavily criticized by some of his partners for having over $200,000 of unreimbursed travel expenses the previous year, as he jetted around Southeast Asia trying to develop business. His globe-trotting helped earn the whole international program a rap as "a rogue operation," and Shapiro was held partially responsible. Shapiro's goal was to cut $2 million in costs from the program, through a reduction in travel expenses, cost-of-living adjustments, and other items, which represented perhaps 20 percent of the firm's shortfall from the international program.

Morris Kramer, who had helped establish the London office and visited there regularly, argued for the continuing need for the globalization of the firm's practice. Still, one senior partner explained his skepticism about the program like this: "I think most people buy Morris's overall shtick—that corporations are multinational, that our U.S. corporate clients have significant opportunities overseas, that our competition has set up offices there, and that we have to do the same thing to meet the competition. And that there is going to be an increasing amount of cross-border work, in M&A and related areas, and that we ought to be in position to get our fair share of it. But the question is: What does that mean, office by office, in terms of costs and income? What the fuck does it mean?"

In economic terms, the case for the international program in 1991 turned out to depend on the amount of work generated for Skadden in the United States as a result of its foreign offices. Skadden called this "but-for business"—the firm would not have attracted it but for one of its foreign offices. At some firms with international practices, identifying and quantifying the amount of that business was considered so difficult that it wasn't done. At Cleary Gottlieb, but-for business was called "throwaway work."

This partner summed up: "The economic argument for the international expansion goes like this: After all the costs of our expansion, which, so far, counting expenses and the shares of partners in those offices minus the revenues they've earned, are about seven to ten million dollars, the program makes sense because they claim that more than that amount has been earned in the United States offices on deals that we would not have had *but for* those overseas offices.

"Say the number is fourteen million dollars, which they say it is, giving us a margin of between four and seven million dollars. Why not skinny back? Can you skinny back your foreign operations, and save a lot of money, and still generate that fourteen million dollars? Do you need the Paris office? The Paris and the Frankfurt office?

"Another thing: We hear that the partners overseas all have special deals, that they get houses and cars. I've heard that one of our guys in Australia, who isn't even a partner, has a huge house that the firm is leasing for him at eight thousand dollars a month. And that our senior partner in London has a house and a car with a driver. I don't know if those rumors are true. But there are bruised feelings about all this."

He continued: "The argument is that there is something called Anglo-Saxon corporate technology that is now being adopted on the Continent, right, and that lawyers there are walking around saying that and envying us. But you've got to know the law of the country where you're doing business to be able to practice it, you've got to know the culture of the country, and you've got to know the language. You can't just waltz into Germany and France or wherever and say, 'There is something called Anglo-Saxon corporate technology, and you're an asshole if you don't hire us.' "

21

Spooked

The international program offered a lightning rod for anxiety, but the more profound worry was about the firm's economic slippage. At the 1991 retreat, Mullen saw Skadden as "spooked." Skadden began a period of "extreme self-scrutiny," Mike Schell called it, which took place "in almost encounter-group sessions" for the next year.

Partners criticized the leadership of the firm: "Leadership takes credit for the good times. It should take responsibility for the bad."

They ridiculed the firm's management structure: "I think we ought to ditch the OEP and send those five lawyers back to doing what they do best, which is getting business and doing it. They're super at that. I sort of cringe when the OEP meets. It's a prescription for doing nothing. Six people"—including Mullen—"sit around and debate who should be fired."

They lamented some of the firm's past choices: "Would I have voted for all this expansion? No. I would have preferred to stay small, like Wachtell Lipton, making more money in the good years and having a bigger cushion to rest on in the bad."

They suggested that Skadden was vulnerable because it had yet to grow beyond its dependence on Flom: "I think it's fair to say that Joe Flom has produced most of the business that the firm has. There's no doubt that people who do the work for the firm bring clients back. But it's Joe who built the firm. It's Joe who made it rain."

While Mullen was occasionally irritable about partners' complaints— "a herd of cats," he called them—his main response to the outpouring of frustration was to try to get partners talking with each other. He had them begin at the retreat and continue for months afterward in lunches held for small groups of partners. The lunches were billed as opportunities to quiz Mullen about the state of the firm and to express urgent concerns.

Mullen's fans said he was at his best in this period, minimizing disagreements among partners and finding common ground, steering the firm through turbulent times while maintaining the calm of his crew. To critics, he was hard to read or mealymouthed ("Have you ever talked with Mullen?" a lawyer asked me. "Could *you* tell what he said?"). The downturn in 1991 supplied one plausible motive for him to have chosen to act as noncommittal as the critics charged. The firm that was known for its mastery of the market could not control it. The big adjustments that the market seemed to require of Skadden were painful to concede.

A fortyish partner, soon after the partnership retreat: "Next week, it will be no secret that, for the first time in the history of the firm, people in the hardest-hit areas [at the firm] are being laid off for economic reasons, mostly in New York. That's a horrible thing to have to do. Some people said we should start doing it sooner. We're doing something that is pretty extreme. A couple of years ago, we kept people around who weren't up to quality standards because we needed the bodies. Last year, people said we were laying people off and we weren't. Compassion hung on for a while. Now, the official posture is that we are doing some things that are pretty serious but that this is not a crisis."

Mullen: "I'm looking for excuses not to excess lawyers"—a euphemism for firing them. "The main reasons are institutional and humanitarian and a sense of fairness overriding pure economics. Somewhere along the line every partner has a point to which he's willing to tighten his belt, and for everyone there is a balancing of the values of this firm—of collegiality and professionalism—against the pull of economics."

Addressing the matter of layoffs, indirectly: "Last year, we made a judgment that we shouldn't have to excess people, but for [because of] attrition. This year, we started to do some aiming out of people who were not inadequate performers. There were a couple of areas where we haven't been able to solve the overcapacity problem. We gave some people the option of changing areas, and some are taking it, some are not." Of those who didn't take the option, he estimated, only "a handful" would end up being fired for economic reasons.

He said, "I'm doubtful we will go any farther."

Fin Fogg recommended that Skadden go farther. After the partners' retreat, he proposed that the firm institute a system of compensation for associates based on a new definition of "merit," which would reduce their salaries and use a portion of the savings to make up a bonus pool for distribution among "productive," or busy, associates at the end of the year. The policy committee dismissed the idea. A senior partner commented: "Why not do this? I think Peter and the OEP feel that maybe business will pick up and that we'll just revenue our way out of this. Hope springs eternal."

The immediate source of hope was the firm's April 1991 billings, the best they had been since April the year before. The numbers for May and June fell down some, but the whole second quarter was far better than the first and made up a large part of the shortfall in the firm's budget left over from the winter. At the end of July, one month into the third quarter, the firm projected that its second half would be better than the first and more or less on budget. The budget had been set lower than the one for the year before, however. Reaching it meant that the firm would not "revenue" its way to new prosperity. The year was going to be the kind the firm had "expected and not much better," Mullen predicted.

He and the other members of the OEP decided to take fresh action. The group directed partners to weed out associates, office by office and department by department, using "staffing capacity" as the key criterion for firings. The standard was almost purely Darwinian: In most cases, it meant that busy lawyers would be protected, and less busy ones vulnerable.

In the 1980s, the annual billings of Skadden associates averaged roughly 2,000 hours. For 1991, confronted by the downturn in business,

Skadden had budgeted 1,800 hours per associate. Using that figure as a guide, the firm calculated whether associates were performing above, at, or below expectations, and it compiled a list of associates whose average monthly billings were less than the targeted annual number would require.

They ranged from junior to senior lawyers, and came from almost every office and department. After some "superstars" were excised from the list (the list was meant to reflect quality as well as economics), the firm came up with an official dismissal list of forty-five lawyers whose layoffs were approved by the OEP and office and department leaders. Twenty-four were lawyers who, in better times, would have been welcome to stay despite their low billability that year, and they were told as much. The others were fired outright. For public purposes, the groups were treated similarly, Mullen said, to avoid imposing a stigma of failure on lawyers in the second category.

In a choreographed series of meetings during the last week of September, the firm notified the associates being laid off of their fate, and explained the move to those remaining. One motive for the layoffs had been to improve staff morale by some clear line-drawing. Some lawyers whom the firm said it favored, but who weren't as busy as the firm or they wanted them to be, had expressed uneasiness about their future at Skadden. ("People were looking over their shoulders," Mullen said.) The meetings were intended as pep talks about the future of the firm, its economic position, and the long-term prospects for legal services.

A lawyer who attended one meeting explained: "My understanding is that the script for the talk was to say that the firm is very strong, that there is plenty of work to keep people busy, that the firm has no debt, and that the legal business is still a very good one." Ben Needell, the member of the OEP and the head of the real estate department, informed his lawyers that the firm wanted associates to bill an average of two hundred hours per month. In previous months, the average had been close to one hundred fifty. He and others also told associates that if they hadn't been asked to leave by then, their positions at Skadden were secure. Neal McCoy, recapping his talk to associates in Washington, D.C.: "The message was that we had done what we had to do, we were through doing it, and I didn't expect we would have to do it again."

The news received sober and attentive coverage in the national press. ("Skadden, Arps, Slate, Meagher & Flom, the law firm that most reflected the soaring fortunes of lawyers in the 1980s, laid off about 45 lawyers this week," began a story in *The Wall Street Journal*.) The dismissals were treated as a sign that the eighties were over for Wall Street law firms and for many across the country. Almost half the large firms in the country had fewer lawyers in 1991 than they did the year before.

Peter Mullen professed to be surprised by the attention. Speaking of the recession, the drop in M&A, and a depression in the real estate market, Mullen observed gravely that the firm was dealing with the "worst combination of circumstances I've known in the last couple of decades" and was simply "facing reality rather than deterioration."

In doing so, he acknowledged, the firm had shifted policies: "At the beginning of the year, I said that ours was a no-growth scenario—that with normal attrition and departures following quality reviews, we'd be around the same size this fall that we were last. That's changed somewhat. We'll be about fifty lawyers smaller, once all of our new people arrive." The firm was "responding prudently" to "important changes in the economic and business environment," he commented to *The Wall Street Journal*.

"We don't expect this to happen again," he declared. "It's a one-time thing."

A senior associate complained afterward: "The thing that has bothered me is the failure of the firm to acknowledge publicly that they've let a lot of people go already: fifty to seventy-five, and maybe one hundred. Far more than a 'handful' of people have been let go for reasons other than quality. In each class, there are a few people who are above reproach—the superstars. Otherwise, there are a lot of lawyers, especially mid-level associates, who, if the firm were busier, would have gotten work and been judged solid performers, even if they probably would not make partner. And those lawyers, whom the firm has asked to leave, it is calling quality layoffs."

Skadden wasn't the only major law firm to lay off lawyers, and the ambiguity of its approach wasn't unique. In the spring of 1991, Skadden associates literally faxed around the world copies of an article from a legal journal that anatomized the downsizing of a law firm, so buddies on different continents could confirm the relevance of what they thought they were seeing. But the combination of the large number of layoffs at Skadden and of the suggestion in many cases that lawyers had been fired because they had failed to meet a standard of quality rather than for economic reasons made it particularly hard for lawyers in that group to find other work.

In response to the general problem, in September of 1991 the Association of the Bar of the City of New York issued guidelines about layoffs that articulated why the ambiguous approach that Skadden and others had taken appeared to be unjust. The guidelines directed that "a law firm should not state or imply that a termination caused essentially by economic considerations was based on performance evaluations." The guidelines went on: "To represent the decision as having been based on the attorney's professional performance is unfair to the attorney and can unduly diminish the attorney's prospects for finding new employment."

By the Skadden associate's account, all the steps taken at the firm to trim the ranks of associates in 1991 were of a piece. Only a handful of lawyers had been explicitly laid off by the firm for economic reasons before September 1991 (some, after they chose not to move from one department to another). But far more had actually been asked to leave in that period, by departments making "voluntary" cuts, as distinct from those made in the name of the firm. Although the firm usually offered associates three months of severance pay and asked them to be gone within that time, departments (with the firm's approval) sometimes offered six, as an incentive for associates to leave before the firm asked them to. The advantage to departments was an improvement in the balance between their revenues and costs and in their contribution to the firm's profits.

By the associate's tabulation, between the fall of 1990 and the spring of 1991, the number of Skadden associates who were asked to leave because of economic conditions, even if their departures came as a result of so-called quality layoffs, was double the number cited by Skadden: one hundred as opposed to fifty. Because many laid off by the firm or by departments had been unable to find new jobs and remained in a kind of purgatory at Skadden, however, they hadn't been included in the official number of associates departing to make room for new ones.

Some associates who hadn't found new jobs obtained extensions of their salaries and benefits from the firm; some continued to show up after their salaries and benefits had run out. If all had been included in the layoff figure, and that number was compounded by the forty-five others unambiguously fired in September, it would not have been accurate to say that the firm's no-growth strategy had been "changed somewhat": the total number of departing associates would have been almost half again as large as the number of incoming Skadden lawyers.

Later, when I asked Mullen to comment on the associate's impression, he confirmed it, with an explanation: "To the extent that quality was used as a standard for sorting people out beyond [the publicized forty-five], it was not done at the direction of the firm. It was at the instigation of practice leaders. They were not told to, but I can see why they felt committed to doing it." When I asked for data to corroborate what Mullen had told me, he responded that the numbers were too complicated to prove that there had, or hadn't, been "a purge."

By late in the fall of 1991, however, the firm was noticeably smaller than it had been the year before. Rather than a 1,133-lawyer firm (the largest number it admitted to reaching), Skadden now described itself as a 975-lawyer firm. A senior partner reported: "Among the large majority of associates, I think, based on individual conversations, there is a high level of anxiety about when the ax is going to fall again. We've said that we have no present intention of laying off any more associates, but you can't assure people entirely, after you've done it once. There's definitely a layer of anxiety among the associates."

And by focusing on associates, discussion about Skadden's personnel decisions bypassed other telling elements. According to an associate, throughout the spring and summer of 1991, the firm had also encouraged half a dozen special counsels to leave. Some partners had received a similar message (Mullen confirmed this, too) and others chose to walk away for a variety of reasons. "Once the dam broke, we noticed we had lots of partners, maybe more than we needed," a senior partner said. "Why not encourage people to go?"

Beginning in the spring of 1991, a run of partners announced their departures from the firm. In the following seasons, the number of departing partners (they included Peggy Kerr, the onetime trailblazer) reached eighteen, with partners leaving for large law firms and small—destinations that, a year earlier, had been unknown to any former Skadden partner.

Skadden's distress was aggravated by a cover story in the September issue of *The American Lawyer*, called "Skaddenomics." Based on a report by Florida's attorney general, the article presented a trove of titillating detail about a $6 million bill from Skadden to the South Florida Water Management District, in a large case about pollution of the Everglades. (The firm later settled for a payment of $4.9 million.) The essence of the report was that, instead of covering the costs of doing business through some factor for expenses built into the firm's regular charges for service, Skadden had billed separately for, and marked up, almost everything it could.

Coffee and Danish for four people from the firm's cafeteria was billed at $33.60—$23.80 for the food, plus a 40 percent surcharge for overhead. The fee for one of the firm's messengers to deliver a package ten blocks was $22, or four times as much as it would cost to use a messenger from an independent service. Time that secretaries spent on the case was billed at $45 an hour. Time spent by messengers to tend printers was billed at 45 cents a minute, or $27 an hour. Faxes were billed by the cost of the phone call, plus a surcharge of $2.50 a minute.

The law firm billed for meals and parking when its staff worked on weekends and after hours. It billed for the laundry tabs of lawyers when they stayed in hotels while working on the case. It billed for the fees of two lawyers who had to pay for a license to appear before the federal appeals court that handles Florida cases.

The article noted that other large law firms followed similar practices and sometimes charged even more for the same services. It included Skadden's justification of this method of billing: If the firm hadn't passed on the specific costs of support services in this way, it would have had to raise its professional fees generally and would have taxed some clients for services that didn't benefit them. But the piece identified Skadden as employing a particularly aggressive approach to billing ("abusive," some lawyers called it), a deep embarrassment at a time when Wall Street was growing intolerant of the style, and the levies.

In March of 1991, for example, Morgan Stanley's legal department had issued a policy statement about the billing practices that it expected of law firms retained by it. It warned against billing for word processing and secretarial overtime, excessive billing for photocopying, charging for overhead on phone calls and fax transmissions, charging for personal as well as business expenses while traveling on bank matters, and other questionable habits for which Skadden was criticized in *The American Lawyer*. "Skaddenomics" stained Skadden when it was vulnerable.

Steve Brill, the editor in chief of *The American Lawyer*, said that Skadden wasted no time in griping. "Mullen called up and said he felt particularly betrayed, because we had used Skadden as a focus. They hated the article. They said it had cost them a lot of money. Even a docile general counsel had to say to them, 'You didn't charge me for this stuff, I hope.' Then Skadden had to eat the cost. That piece cost them a lot of profit centers"—although to Skadden, it was simply covering its costs.

Mullen, on why he was unhappy about the piece: "There are three things that annoyed me about the article. The first is that it suggested we were doing something different from other firms, or something new. We've been doing this for forty years, and all the major firms in New York do it.

"Second, it made it look as if we didn't care, that we pass on costs willy-nilly. That isn't true. In the eighties, during a no-holds-barred deal, maybe, we might have. Not today. In the last year or two, we've really clamped down on the cost of add-ons. We have had to justify our cost accounting to major insurance companies paying the bills of clients. Last year, we negotiated three cost reductions in express mail charges.

"The other implication is that this is a matter of ethics. It isn't. I would characterize *The American Lawyer*'s as a mean-spirited article that was just stupid."

The "Skaddenomics" article asked rhetorically, "Is this the best that the world's supposedly best-run law firm can do in the way of cost-effective client care?" But at Skadden, a more important concern resided in the question's premise: Given the decline in its prosperity and its leadership's seeming drift, could Skadden call itself the world's best-run firm? There was broad consensus that the current management system wasn't working as effectively as it should.

Stuart Shapiro, who had been a member of the firm since 1976, raised the topic at a weekly lunch of the Skadden partners. (Shapiro was the son of Irving Shapiro, the former chairman of Du Pont who had joined Skadden when he retired from the chemical company.) Since the partners owned the firm, he observed, it was odd that they didn't have a direct say in who ran it and how.

According to some lawyers who were at the lunch, Shapiro's remarks got under Mullen's skin. Mullen parried by answering that the full partnership wasn't in a position to decide the leadership question wisely—it didn't have all the facts at its command.

If Mullen's goal was to isolate Shapiro's sentiment before it proved contagious, he didn't succeed. ("He sometimes blunders in his sincerity," one lawyer commented about Mullen, "because he doesn't understand how others hear what he has to say.") As the firm continued to seek new economic bearings, the partners' extended conversation about the fate of Skadden took the form of talk about revamping the firm's governance.

Sheila Birnbaum was in the midst of it. She had come to the firm in 1979 in a special arrangement while she taught at New York University Law School, and had joined the firm as a full-time partner in 1984. In seven years, she had built the products liability group into one of the fastest-growing and most successful at the firm. Massive legal cases in which classes of plaintiffs sued for injuries caused by asbestos, DES, and other infamous products had become as important to some corporations as takeovers had to others.

Like Joe Flom talking about takeovers and Bob Bennett about white-collar-criminal defense, Birnbaum located her advocacy on the moral high ground. "I like representing the underdog," she told me. Plaintiffs "overreached for damages" and juries indulged them by voting much bigger awards against large corporations than against small ones for the same kinds of injuries. The law was hampering the creation of new products, she asserted, and was further dulling the edge of American companies against Japanese, Korean, and other competitors. Stephen Gillers, one of Birnbaum's former colleagues at New York University Law School, pointed out that Birnbaum's corporate clients tended to be rich and powerful. He commented: "Lawyers posture all the time."

Birnbaum felt that she was a natural participant in the discussion about governance at Skadden: "My role in the firm increased as the level and intensity of my business increased." To others, she had been "very unhappy" with the limits of her role and sought more respect by plunging deep into the debate over management. Steve Axinn: "Sheila was quite outspoken. She was a symbol of what had gone on here. In a difficult environment, she had brought in more and more business in her area. In her own opinion, she wasn't being treated well," in terms of money and authority.

A new, ad hoc group called the "structure committee" got going at the end of 1991, with Birnbaum as its chair. After canvassing some lawyers in the firm, the committee came up with a management structure that it found "representative." The basic format called for a chief executive, like Mullen, who would be chosen by and report to a policy committee of up to twenty-one members. The committee members would represent the firm's major constituencies: its big practice areas, whose leaders tended to be in New York; partners from outside the New York office; the best-paid partners; relatively new partners; and some others. The existing Skadden policy committee approved the new structure in principle, and asked Birnbaum's group to present it in meetings around the firm—"to get input and suggestions," she said.

One of the meetings was at a luncheon in New York, in March of 1992. It was jammed. The structure committee's proposal had been unveiled in a memo that, in Mullen's word, was "argumentative." It was marked by "footnotes, bullets, and turgid prose," according to one lawyer. The memo attracted partners to the show-and-tell session, because, as the lawyer described it, it was "a highly convoluted proposal which essentially didn't change the management structure in a serious way and left the leadership with no accountability." It was like the current structure, only bigger.

Another partner was critical for a different reason: "I believe that Sheila and others tried to ram this down the firm's throat in an impolitic way, mainly because they had so many other things to do. Sheila, for instance, didn't have the patience for building consensus. It takes time, and she didn't give it." The wisdom of this view was apparent at the New York meeting.

Proponents of firm democracy (who generally opposed the Birnbaum proposal) expressed a simple theory. If the Skadden partners ran themselves as a democracy and didn't like the direction in which their leaders took them, they could change leaders. If not, what motivated the partners was not a stake in the firm's performance but fear—of retribution through compensation, "being penalized if you don't perform by someone else's standards," a lawyer said. "In that case," he continued, "the only time change occurs is when there's a catastrophe."

Many partners at the luncheon were skeptical about the proposal of the structure committee. Not all skeptics were proponents of firm democracy. But the democrats—or dissidents, as they later called themselves (they dreamed of "a Prague spring," one confessed)—posed the questions that got remembered. The dissidents included Stuart Shapiro and Douglas Kraus, a litigator in his early forties, who in 1990 had "started screaming that costs were out of control," one lawyer put it.

Kraus's dissent was rooted in a history of commitment to Skadden. In the 1970s, he was the first and only associate in the Get-to-know-Joe program and, twenty years later, his frustration was born of a rationalist's certainty that Skadden could be run better than it was. Kraus had been put in charge of a committee that recommended almost $7 million of cuts in firm costs in 1991 through a variety of measures: for example, by limiting overtime for secretaries, by reducing the rentals of sky boxes at sports arenas around the country, by ending the program of subsidizing legal assistants at law school, and by eliminating free box lunches for lawyers who wanted to eat at their desks. Although Shapiro and Kraus did not speak until after others at the luncheon meeting about the

Birnbaum committee's recommendations, they were quickly identified as the primary adversaries of the status quo.

Why shouldn't partners vote for the CEO of the firm? they asked. What evidence had persuaded Birnbaum and others that it would be unwise? What was wrong with having the people who owned the firm have a say in who managed it? ("I'm sure that was the gist of some of the questions," Birnbaum advised.) As the proponents of democracy saw it, the problem with the Birnbaum proposal was the same as with the current management: By having a policy committee that picked a nominating committee that picked the policy committee, the system was elitist and incestuous.

Birnbaum conceded nothing about her committee's proposal. She dismissed as "an absurdity" the notion that the firm should be run by any means democratically—that was "a prescription for chaos." (A partner: "She rejected that out of hand. She said that her committee thought it was preposterous. She stated that the vast majority of the partners—all right-thinking people—thought it was just silly.") Birnbaum: "The view that a lot of us had was: If the selection of leadership turns into a popularity contest, you could have very skewed representation."

To some of the proponents of democracy, her unwillingness to respond directly to their questions provided a form of pleasure. They enjoyed grilling her. A lawyer in their camp reflected: "It's been my experience that people who exercise power without accountability tend to develop thin skins, and that makes them vulnerable to good questions." When Birnbaum appeared to get in trouble, a lawyer reported, Roger Aaron stood up in her defense. "Basically," the lawyer reported, Aaron said, " 'Shut up.' Anyone who disagreed [with the Birnbaum proposal], he said, was undermining the management of the firm."

Stuart Shapiro objected, "We have to talk about this," and Mullen replied, "You know what? You're outrageous!" Shapiro told Mullen, "You're right!" When the meeting threatened to become a shouting match, Jim Freund assumed a statesman's role. A lawyer: "He said something like 'In all the years I've been at this firm, I can't remember an issue that got resolved if the firm didn't have a consensus. If Stu and Doug feel this strongly, it's not right to push this thing through. I'm seriously troubled by this process, when a significant number of partners feel that they have something to say and haven't been heard.' "

Another lawyer: "Jim Freund stood up and said that the exploration of a new form of governance had gotten 'very disruptive.' To him, the

Birnbaum committee's recommendations weren't 'ripe for a decision.' "
(Freund confirmed this later.)

The March meeting seemed to be a catalyst for the Prague spring.
The gathering had been held in New York, but was broadcast throughout
the North American offices of the firm. A lawyer: "Instead of hearing
the leaders of the firm [Mullen, Aaron, Birnbaum] sound reasonable,
they heard them shout others down and get defensive." Birnbaum: "Once
there was a vocal group that felt strongly about the original report, we
went back to the drawing board. The whole point was to have an open
process, and to reach as much consensus as possible."

Doug Kraus wrote a proposal described by one lawyer as being for
"a democratically elected board of governors"—"a small, effective leadership that was legitimate." He proposed a group of about a dozen. The
plan was modified by a number of partners and drew a nucleus of
supporters, including Stuart Shapiro, Fin Fogg, and Edmund Duffy, a
corporate lawyer. According to Sheila Birnbaum, her committee took
account of the concept: "Afterward, there were discussions between all
kinds of people, with all kinds of views, in an effort to build consensus."

To others, the overt tensions of the March meeting got internalized
in firm politics. A lawyer: "Initially, Sheila Birnbaum told the proponents
of democracy to come talk with her about all this. Maybe the partners
would have a firm vote on her plan versus some other structure. She
retreated from that very quickly and made her second major mistake.
She said hers was the legitimate committee, that its recommendations
had been unanimously backed, and that the dissidents had no right to
study the issue."

Ed Duffy: "I remember attending a policy committee meeting at which
Doug Kraus and I stated our reasons that there ought to be some kind
of election. Several members of the committee were of the view that
there was no broad consensus supporting our proposal. It was the pet
bugaboo of a small number of disgruntled dudes, and it wasn't worth
delaying getting on with the new structure just for us. The Birnbaum
proposal was a carefully thought-through, well-constructed plan. Some
others said, 'The partnership meeting is close [meaning it would take
place soon]. Let's see what the partnership as a whole has to say.' "

The annual retreat was scheduled for April. In the weeks leading up
to it, Mullen, Birnbaum, Aaron, and others controlling the agenda agreed
to hold a debate and a referendum at the retreat about the question of
democracy in firm governance. Fogg, Duffy, and others not on the

structure committee asked to see the question that would be presented to the partnership. Birnbaum said she would get the language to them. It didn't arrive. They asked again and it came around two days before the retreat.

The preamble to the question was this: "The Structure Committee has recommended a governance structure which includes a ratification vote by the full partnership for selection of a new Executive Partner but does not include a multiple candidate election process for members of the Policy Committee or other positions. The Structure Committee believes instead that a broad-based representative committee structure is the best way to insure participation by the largest number of partners. Some partners, however, believe that an electoral process is necessary for purposes of accountability and to give legitimacy to the governing body of the firm."

The democracy camp found the referendum question loaded against their position. They said they wouldn't participate unless it got changed, and offered some suggestions.

Eventually, the partners agreed to vote on this statement:

The Firm's governance structure:

☐ should
☐ should not

include some additional form of electional process to that recommended by the Structure Committee.

_____

UNITS

_____

NAME
(OPTIONAL)

Mullen: "One guy says, 'This doesn't make sense. It's not English.' Another says, 'As I read it, it doesn't say what it should.' That's what happens when a lot of lawyers get together. Sometimes there is a substantive disagreement. I don't want to suggest this was just nitpicking, but still . . ."

At the retreat, the panel of lawyers arguing that the Skadden partners should back some form of democracy at the firm were Fogg, Duffy, and Kraus. Duffy italicized their position by comparing the Skadden management to that of the former Central Committee of the Soviet Communist Party: "It was a self-perpetuating governing body that was isolated from most of its constituency and absorbed in its own view of reality." Kraus anchored the team. Word for word, he read a long statement that he had prepared so he would not stray from his argument.

Voting for leadership, Kraus proposed, was a way for all Skadden partners to feel that the system was "responsive to them" as the firm grew "larger and more diverse." As Kraus put it, other successful firms (like Davis Polk and Shearman & Sterling) selected leaders by voting and Skadden was more like them than firms reported to have had trouble with democracy. As to the apparently large concern that a "high-unit partner" who was not elected "might threaten to leave if he was not given a significant role in management," Kraus outlined two solutions. The "quarrelsome partner could be given an appointed role," or could be "well compensated in accordance with his or her value" to Skadden, so he or she would want to stay. If neither solution worked, Kraus declared, "my own view is that we should probably accept his resignation, because giving in to that kind of anti-collegial behavior only encourages more such threats, and will ultimately do much more damage to the Firm than the loss of a few selfish people, even if they do control some business."

Kraus ended with what he called "just one last thought." He stated: "We've been incredibly fortunate at this Firm. The world has beaten a path to our door, and we've worked hard and made the most of it. But now the world is changing, and we're going to have to make some hard choices to keep what we've achieved, and to build on it. Each one of us deserves to participate in those choices. We've worked hard to earn that right, and we're all smart enough to choose wisely. That's what voting is all about. I urge you not to give up the right to participate in those choices."

Representatives of the opposing camps had agreed that the ballots would be counted two ways: per capita (one partner, one vote); and by units (with each vote weighted by a partner's share in the firm's profits). Because the statement on which the partners were voting was not detailed or specific, the proponents of democracy expected they would get support from at least 25 percent of the Skadden partners. They weren't confident they would get much more.

Mullen reported: "Many of the older partners were against democracy. Many of the younger ones were for it"—although some of the firm's leading older partners (Ken Bialkin, Mark Kaplan, Ike Shapiro) were actually for it. If partners voted their hopes, more than one-quarter of the group might back democracy, its proponents guessed. If they voted their fears, only the small core of supporters would vote "should."

Per capita, the vote yielded a victory for the proponents of democracy, they claimed. (Mullen: "I can't remember the outcome. Per capita, it may have won by a small majority.") By units, the vote tipped against democracy. (One lawyer: "Per points, there were about five thousand units separating the sides, out of one hundred twenty thousand or so units, I think. That was a difference of about four percent.")

The unexpected and relatively large vote for democracy reinforced the judgment of the structure committee that electoral leadership at the firm would be uncontrollable and, from their point of view, doomed to failure. Management's plan went unrevised. Sheila Birnbaum: "I had and continue to have a strong view: You could not have direct voting by the partnership for the CEO and the policy committee, because you could end up with a very unrepresentative leadership.

"Half the partners in the firm have been so for under five years' duration. [Giving a direct role in choosing the firm's leader to so many young partners] would be a disaster for this law firm, based on its history. You don't run law firms through popularity contests. In other places where that has happened, it has led to a great deal of dissension, electioneering, and tension. The vast majority of my partners agree that that would be very distracting for us. I don't think young people understand all the issues, when they haven't had a management role."

The new structure of governance at Skadden was this: The executive partner was charged with focusing on "key issues facing [the] firm" and "developing consensus" about them, as well as with serving as the firm's "principal voice" and chairing its compensation and policy committees. He was given a "five-year renewable term" that could be reviewed "sooner under extraordinary circumstances." Two practice coordinators were authorized to help run the firm, overseeing the corporate and litigation practices, respectively. They were given three-year terms, and would serve at the executive partner's discretion. Responsibility for composing the budget of the firm and for assessing its financial performance went to a new financial oversight and audit committee (FOAC), consisting of three members, with a chairperson to be picked by the policy committee and to serve as a member of it—along with the executive partner and the practice coordinators.

The policy committee was assigned seventeen members, including the four who would receive automatic, ex officio appointments. The thirteen at-large members were to be "a cross section of the firm," as long as they included "at least one senior-level member from each of the Chicago, Los Angeles, and Washington offices." The thirteen would be chosen by an appointments committee of eight: four of the appointments committee would be picked by the policy committee itself, to assure that the appointments group had a broad representation of partners, "in terms of geography, seniority, and practice area"; and four would be elected, with votes tabulated per capita. (That was the new structure's democratic element.) No member of the appointments committee could be on the policy committee.

The structure was approved by approximately 85 percent of the partnership, with most of the other 15 percent made up of partners who were spread around the world doing business and who didn't vote. Mullen was retained as executive partner; Roger Aaron and Mike Diamond, who had been members of the OEP, were named practice coordinators; and Fin Fogg was appointed chairman of FOAC. Though FOAC was the logical extension of the cost-cutting committee that Kraus had chaired, he was not given a seat on the new committee.

In the history of Skadden, some partners believed, the democracy debate was trivial. A senior partner who practiced outside New York dismissed it as "a New York thing." To Joe Flom, it was silly. "Idle hands do the devil's work," he observed. Mullen summarized the meaning of the debate like this: "We found that the sentiment for democracy was stronger than the anti-democracy people had thought, but that it was not universally supported."

But the meaning of the debate was complicated, as Mullen himself suggested when he tried to write off the episode. Declining to get into details of some events leading up to approval of the new structure, after I mentioned how passionately some partners spoke about the topic, he said, "I think someone has led you on a wild-goose chase with this one. The whole process was a drop in the bucket. Yes, feelings and opinions ran high. There was a certain amount of acrimony." But all in all, it didn't amount to much, he said. It was a family quarrel that blew over and left no scars.

Another partner, when I passed on Mullen's comments, only reemphasized the significance of the event: "If Mullen and everybody thought the governance thing was a non-event, I don't know why they got so upset about it." Mullen got so exercised, the lawyer said, that he had hung up the phone on a partner who disagreed with him.

Sheila Birnbaum also suggested the importance of the debate in the vehemence of the words she chose to describe what the victors had successfully avoided: "The democracy that finally got the firm's consensus is as far from what the proponents wanted as night from day."

And a dissident felt as strongly: "You have this simple, human story: People in power want to defend the system that worked for them."

Almost a year after the debate was officially ended with a vote, feelings about both the substance and the process remained almost fiercely high. "This guy has to jump in and dump shit on me whenever I open my mouth," one partner who had been involved in the debate said about another. Telephone conversations seemed the most comfortable way for some Skadden lawyers to talk with me about the debate. Speaking with me as a faceless voice from the privacy of an office seemed easier than having a conversation in person. "I've got you on the speaker box, but my door is shut and I'm alone" is how one lawyer began a long talk.

One anecdote, told by a lawyer who was intensely interested in the democracy debate, suggested how personal the infighting had gotten and why it felt so loaded. The lawyer: "There was a meeting of the policy committee about a final detail of the new structure, and Doug Kraus, who was expected to attend, didn't come. People said, 'Call Kraus.' Mullen said, 'I wouldn't do that.' People said, 'Why not?' Mullen brushed it off, so Stu Shapiro said, 'I'll tell you.'"

At the retreat, one of the arguments against democracy had been that it could be corrupted, say, by partners selling their votes. ("'If you vote for me, and I go on the compensation committee, you'll get more money,'" is how a partner put a hypothetical.) In defense of democracy, one of its proponents recalled, Kraus had said that any system could be corrupted, including the firm's current one. Kraus's exact words had been: "Ultimately, however, all partners should recognize that no system of governance can be made immune from 'corruption.' If people want to corrupt the system by making 'deals' or by other means, they can do it equally well under any structure. In fact, many say that it is going on right now under the current system."

On the firm gossip mill, Mike Diamond was said to have been stung by Kraus's remark. By calling management corrupt, Diamond was said to feel, Kraus had lodged a personal accusation against everyone involved.

One lawyer said, "Earle Yaffa was certain that Kraus had people in mind, and that view was reinforced when Mike Diamond said to someone, who reported it to Earle, that he [Diamond] felt like he should resign the partnership." It didn't happen, but Yaffa told Kraus that the near-miss was his fault. He had nearly caused the resignation of a major senior partner. (By Yaffa's account, he simply told Kraus that he had to choose his words more carefully, because of the "sensitivities of people like Mike Diamond.") By one account, Kraus immediately called Diamond in Los Angeles to say that he hadn't meant to accuse anyone, and Diamond said he knew that. But the damage had been done.

Kraus said he had understood the anger that Yaffa and other leaders felt toward him. ("Without intending to be nettlesome, I was raising issues of significance to the firm, which a lot of people told me they supported but didn't want to speak to.") But after the confrontation, he decided to disengage from the struggle for democracy. ("It was unpleasant to be at odds with my partners.") Kraus resigned from all the committees he was serving on, except the one that reviews the quality of candidates for partnership, and he effectively stopped going to partnership meetings.

To a Kraus supporter, the encounter between Yaffa and Kraus couldn't be dismissed as a product of the usual heat generated when Skadden partners were working something out. Or of an unfortunate misunderstanding, as Kraus wished. Or of a forgotten family quarrel, as Mullen preferred. To this lawyer, it hadn't been by chance and Mullen was partially behind it: "Mullen and Yaffa's were bullyboy tactics. Kraus is a nice man and less sophisticated than you might expect, given his intelligence and accomplishments as a lawyer. What Mullen and Yaffa did showed a lack of measure."

Mike Diamond told a different version of the story. In his view, Kraus had said something that definitely could be interpreted as an accusation that the current system of management and leadership was corrupt. He found that offensive. "I thought it was a loose use of a volatile word," Diamond said. "I went right up to Mullen and said, 'That must really make you angry.' He [Mullen] said he was used to it. He got that all the time. But that statement didn't lead to my considering leaving the firm. . . . I think Stu Shapiro told me this story"—Shapiro, in part out of his own frustration, resigned the Skadden partnership at the end of 1992—"and I called Doug. I said, 'Doug, if you're being told this' "—

about Diamond quitting—" 'this is bullshit. If anybody is telling you this, forget it.' "

But to Diamond, while the democracy debate hadn't changed the law firm much, it did carry a serious warning. The debate's fervor came from personal mistrust between the structure committee and partners not on it, and, in a larger sense, from a "distrust of leadership." Different explanations for the acrid feelings were possible, ranging from all managements' being distrusted, to the failure of the current management to get across "its devotion, the wisdom of its decisions, how it operates," to ones he wouldn't detail. "I'm sure Peter is aware that people distrust him," Diamond said. "He may subscribe to the view that it's built into the position."

At the same time he affirmed, "There is a lot of sentiment to get the process started." Or, as another partner put it, the democracy debate could serve as "a symbol about the whole question of succession."

For many years, by and large, Mullen had been praised for his leadership of the firm. Since the firm's fortieth anniversary (in 1988), however, the question of succession had been on partners' minds. It had grown from an agenda item for the future (in 1989), to a cause of uncertainty that was sufficiently under control so that it could be made fun of at the partners' retreat (in 1990), to something far more pressing (from 1991 on). It had become a subject of discussion behind closed doors, a topic of regular speculation, and a source of disquiet for a growing number of partners.

Critics of Mullen sounded several themes: That he had allowed a powerful group of deal lawyers the run of the firm and, in doing so, had permitted a system that created divisions, wounds, and enmities. That he and others had not understood the shift in the firm's practice areas and had kept on too many lawyers in mergers and acquisitions, for example, and not redeployed them soon enough into new areas. That he had not successfully controlled the firm's costs, as reflected in Skadden's diminished margin of profits. That his form of patient consensus building was no longer what the firm needed. Or that he no longer had the patience to build consensus.

A provision for a succession committee appeared in the firm's new governing structure. The committee was charged with recommending a partner (or partners) to serve as the next executive partner. The succession committee would have five members ("reasonably representative of the firm"), with Mullen not a member but to be "consulted extensively." No member of the committee could be executive partner; the committee's recommendation of its selection was to be made to the policy committee within three months. If that committee approved, the partnership would vote on the name, or names, by secret ballot. ("If one-third of the total units or one-third of the partners disapprove the selection, the Policy Committee and the Succession Committee will reconvene and consider and select another candidate.") The policy committee, with Mullen, "should determine his tenure and the timing of the initiation of the succession process."

In January of 1993, I asked Mullen when the succession process would be initiated. Mullen: "My view is that, doing what I do, you have to be involved full-time or not at all. I'm not sure how I'm viewed today. Last year, I had lost a lot of credibility with the firm. I wasn't the moving force in the restructuring. I stayed out of it. No one last year wanted to have a referendum about whether I should be executive partner. That would have been a real wrench.

"I really do serve at the pleasure of the policy committee and they can decide they want a change of leadership. I am very flexible. I have a heavy stake in the firm and I'm not about to retire this year, of my own volition. If nature takes its course—if I stay healthy—I still feel it is very challenging to get this firm set for the nineties. We've come a good way and have more to go."

Soon after, a senior partner who is an admirer of Mullen's mused: "I think Peter is waiting for some consensus to develop around a candidate, or candidates, to succeed him. Over the years, in my opinion, he has shown great sensitivity to the political pulse of the firm as a whole. He has shown a talent for being able to avoid treading on toes unnecessarily, emphasizing what holds people together and not what divides them. The person, or group, who succeeds him is going to have to be something that, to some extent, is seen as backed by a consensus. That means what people say to each other over lunch and behind closed doors. I don't think we have that consensus. I suspect that's what Mullen—and Flom—are waiting for."

Another senior partner said, "I think there are a lot of partners who feel Peter is out of touch. The partners are hungering for a strong leadership, and not the kind of benign refereeing that worked many years ago." In response to my asking about Mullen's assertion that he served "at the pleasure of the policy committee," this partner barked: "Peter doesn't serve at anybody's pleasure." He predicted: "If Mullen doesn't quit, he may receive a visit, suggesting that it's time for him to go."

22

Succession

One pervading question behind much of the self-scrutiny at Skadden
was: Is this law firm still unique? In 1992, it was not hard to array the
facts in a pattern that made Skadden look undeniably mortal, falling
slowly and painfully down from Olympian heights. Two months before
the end of the year, Joe Flom admitted, his firm was running at least
25 percent behind its projected budget, and partners were wringing their
hands. The firm's profit margin had withered to less than 20 percent,
from the roughly 50 percent that many remembered from the eighties.
The firm's contingency plans included further layoffs of associates. When
December turned out to be a phenomenal month, with clients paying
bills at a torrential pace (approximately $75 million splashed in—twice
as much as the average monthly income for the year), the firm's annual
revenues went somewhat over budget. Still, they were significantly below
what Skadden had once enjoyed. For the first time since *The American*

Lawyer began ranking law firms financially, Skadden's '92 revenues placed it second rather than first. It grossed $440 million to Baker & McKenzie's $503.5 million, although, because Baker is a much bigger firm, it had lower profits per lawyer.

The big change in Skadden's finances had, again, to do with the disappearance of takeovers. Premium billings had virtually evaporated and, with them, vanished the camouflage for the firm's high costs. The effects were all too evident in the levels of compensation that the firm was delivering to its partners. At its peak, the firm's benchmark (roughly equivalent to average profits per partner, a senior partner said) surpassed one million dollars. For 1993, the benchmark was set at $475,000.

By most measures, the partners of Skadden were prospering handsomely. But the ghost of the eighties shadowed the firm. Some partners and associates were frustrated, they said, because, unlike more senior lawyers, they would not have the chance to get rich practicing law. One lawyer theorized that Skadden's conservative financial practices (funding its own growth, not borrowing money, saving for a rainy day), which cushioned it during the recession, had actually put the firm in jeopardy.

"A partner of fifteen years or so has a significant, seven-figure amount in his capital account," the lawyer explained. "The account pays no interest and earns nothing." If a partner chose to leave, the firm was obligated to pay the lawyer half of his capital account after one year, and the rest after one more. It was possible for a partner in his forties to withdraw $3 to $4 million from the firm's capital account in the space of two years: "For a partner who no longer feels excited about the practice, or feels he is bringing in more than he's getting out, or is worried about the future of the firm, there is an economic incentive to leave." If twenty partners followed suit—less than 10 percent of the partnership—they would seriously deplete the Skadden treasury.

According to one observer, the splintering of Skadden was a scenario spotlighted by a list put together by a middle-aged head of a practice group and circulated among partners toward the end of 1992. The list named those partners whose compensation was above benchmark, but whose 1992 billable hours were projected to be less than 1,250. Although some on the list were apparently on track to bill fewer than 1,000 hours, the memo was considered noteworthy more for the names it included than the precise level of billable hours that was its standard: The list contained some of the best-paid senior partners in the firm.

At the end of 1992, the firm projected that by the following April its New York office (with four hundred seventy-six lawyers) and Chicago office (with ninety-four lawyers) would be at 90 percent of their peak number of lawyers. Washington (with one hundred forty lawyers) would be at 80 percent. Los Angeles (with ninety lawyers) would be at 73 percent. Boston (with twenty lawyers) would be at 60 percent. The whole firm would contract to nine hundred fifty lawyers. The number working on corporate finance and mergers and acquisitions would fall to one hundred fifty-seven, little more than half as many as at the crest of the deal wave, and less than one-sixth of the lawyers in the firm.

In the same cluster of facts that made some partners pessimistic, however, was a pattern of welcome adjustment. The facts might have been unpleasant to face, but it was good news to some at the firm that a new reality was being acknowledged. In 1992, for example, Ike Shapiro recounted, "we took the painful hit of trying to get our write-offs up to date." Partners who had not been able to collect fees from a client for all the time that they and other lawyers had spent were told to forget about it. The firm's "early bad numbers" that year (Shapiro's words) were due in part to the decision to wipe the slate clean, so Skadden would start 1993 without carrying on its books revenues that it wasn't likely to collect. This was a part of life in the new world.

To a variety of partners, one of the firm's primary accomplishments in 1992 had been the work of FOAC, headed by Fin Fogg. By squeezing an additional $12 million of costs out of the firm's budget for 1993, when revenues were projected to be the same as for 1992, the committee had increased the projected bottom line per partner by an average of over $50,000. A survey of law-firm management done by Price Waterhouse had taught Skadden that "the number of days we had invested in clients was significantly more than other firms" (Fogg). The firm sought "to realize its investment faster" by collecting active bills sooner.

The compensation structure for partners was also changed dramatically in 1992. According to one partner, the best-compensated partners were reduced from the number of units they had reached in 1991 to the units they held in 1989. Fogg, on compensation: "What happened generally beginning in '92 was compression. The spread between the top and the bottom, excluding Flom, fell from about six to one to about five to one: The top came down. In '92, before we did anything else, the people at the top—above a certain level—were reduced by a significant percentage, like twenty percent."

Mullen confirmed that, for the first time at Skadden, some senior partners had lost as much as 20 percent of their units in the firm during this reconfiguration. Members of the Lucky Sperm Club plunged to less lofty positions on the roster than they had occupied in years. The 1992 list signaled that the glory days for the M&A group were over. The rest of the firm no longer owed it anything but payment for what it contributed to Skadden in a current year. The flip side of M&A's decline was the growth of other practice areas and the firm's new stars—Bob Bennett, the head of Skadden's white-collar practice; Sheila Birnbaum, the head of the products liability group; Joe Halliday, in charge of the banking practice—moved up the list.

On the 1993 compensation list, the compression continued, to four to one, and the new stars moved into the firm's top ten. Most symbolically, for the first time since the firm had been stamped by him in the late fifties, Joe Flom didn't lead the pack. ("From 1992 to 1993, Flom gave up forty percent of his compensation," one lawyer reported.)

Roger Aaron and Peter Atkins were now slotted above Flom. They were credited with more business than anyone else in the firm—although one partner, who praised Atkins and Aaron for keeping clients "happy and in the fold," questioned whether they were truly responsible for much of the business attributed to them and argued that "a lot" of their clients were "institutional" and would have stayed with the firm even if the lawyers had moved on. And, in their elevated places at the top of the list, Aaron and Atkins had also lost units; the 1993 budget scheduled them to make less than they had the previous year. "Over time," philosophized Mike Schell, whose own compensation was also reduced in the 1993 budget, "you can't have compensation be at war with the underlying political ebbs and swells of the firm, without doing serious harm to the institution itself."

In addition to compensation decisions, the strongest signal of the firm's sense of caution or confidence came in the annual selection of partners. In April of 1992, the firm had named only seven partners. Of those, only one was chosen from the class of partners being considered for the first time. In effect, the firm had postponed until then the partnerships of lawyers who had previously qualified. In 1993, in a reflection of some increased optimism, the firm named twelve partners, including several who were up for the first time. The group of new partners included three of particular note for their locations: one because he was a lawyer in Houston, where Skadden was about to open an office, and two because they practiced overseas.

The Houston story showed the free-form side of Skadden, and the labyrinthine process by which the firm made Lyndon Taylor the new partner there irritated some partners. In the winter, the energy department removed Taylor from the morning line in favor of two other energy associates: Although he was highly regarded, the others were viewed as more well-rounded and riper for partnership. He wasn't in the final set of candidates for 1993.

Just before the quality committee offered final recommendations at the end of March, however, Taylor was put back on the line. Lynn Coleman, a leader of the energy practice, had persuaded Mullen and others that the firm should open an office in Houston, where Taylor was operating as an associate out of space provided by a client. The firm considered moving different partners to the city. It decided instead to propose making Taylor a partner for a variety of reasons, including that he was a member of the Texas bar and, as an alum of Oklahoma State University and of the University of Oklahoma College of Law, seemed a natural pick for the oil patch.

Bob Sheehan, the chairman of the quality committee: "This coincided more or less with the tail end of our selection process, but not quite." A week or so before new partners were to be announced, the quality committee was asked to review Taylor. They balked at the deadline but launched into the task. Taking a couple of weeks, Sheehan verified that Taylor was as good as the energy group claimed. Banking lawyers with whom Taylor had worked told Sheehan that, with flying colors, he passed their test of quality, too. On April 7, the Skadden partnership approved Taylor's selection retroactive to April 1, when the firm had made eleven other new partners.

On the Skadden grapevine, explanations for the last-minute push were that the energy department had worried the partnership into it, arguing that the firm would be in violation of a Houston bar rule if it didn't have a resident partner in Houston who was qualified to practice in Texas, once the firm changed the status of its city work space to a full-fledged office. (Sheehan: "That's unfair and inaccurate.") They complained that, when the firm sent Taylor and another lawyer to Houston on a temporary assignment, in the fall of 1992, it was sucking the partnership into a bigger, unannounced commitment. (Mullen: "That wasn't the case. We were simply accommodating a client so we could get more business from them.") Some Skadden partners said they felt they'd been had.

Mullen portrayed the Houston story as old-fashioned opportunism—

of Skadden taking advantage of a business break that developed faster than expected. The unusual feature of the scramble, he said, was that the firm had reversed the standard process, appraising Skadden's need before confirming Taylor's merit.

Overseas, Christopher Baker, in Paris, and Jonathan Pedersen, in Hong Kong, represented two strands that Skadden now considered integral to its culture. Pedersen was a homegrown boy, having started at Skadden as a legal assistant and, in the estimation of his mentors, having succeeded admirably throughout his career as an associate. Baker, a lateral from Coudert Frères in Paris, brought a pedigree of legal aristocracy: his grandfather was a founder of Baker & McKenzie, the largest American firm and the farthest-flung internationally; his father, its fifth partner, had founded its Paris office; and Christopher was talented in his own right.

The larger significance of the election of two new international partners was that it reflected a new position of strength for the firm's young international operations. Through 1992, Skadden's international offices had not been profitable. In 1993, for the first time, the firm predicted black ink from the operations. The income that the firm expected those offices to accrue was for the first time greater than all the costs of all the international offices, including the shares of partners.

When the firm included in its calculation estimates of revenues from "but-for" business (work it believed it would not have gotten if it hadn't been operating in a foreign location), the international picture was even more promising. When the firm factored in all of the international work it was doing in the United States, even if the work had originated there and might have come in if the firm didn't operate abroad, the picture improved yet again. At the beginning of 1993, fully half the revenues in the Chicago office came from international work (broadly defined), the firm was surprised to learn. For all of Skadden, the ratio of international to all revenues was between one-quarter and one-third, depending on how some work was allocated.

Skadden's international offices were beginning to make their mark on the identity of the firm. The sixty-five lawyers who were assigned abroad constituted less than 7 percent of the lawyers in the firm, but the very existence of the overseas offices and their surge of growth (from no lawyers in 1986 to twenty in 1990 to forty in 1992 and so on) changed the look and feel of Skadden operations both internally and externally. For one thing, the firm was putting in place a global communications system—SKADNET—an electronic highway linking all offices. Ike Shapiro explained confidently: "Skadden today thinks of itself as an international firm based primarily in the United States."

As Shapiro had proposed in 1986, the core offices abroad were London, Tokyo, and Hong Kong, the foreign capitals of finance. The offices in Brussels and Paris, as capitals of decision, also represented long-term commitments: There were partners in each of those places, as well as in Frankfurt. The other offices (Prague, Budapest, Sydney, Beijing, and Moscow) were question marks; no partners yet practiced there. Their longevity depended on their performance. Toronto was in a class by itself, a foreign office managed by a partner in New York. In May of 1993, the *International Financial Law Review* recognized Skadden's accomplishments in Europe by publishing an article ("Who's the king of the castle?") that compared the "unprecedented expansion programme" there of the *"parvenu"* with the well-established "softly-softly approach" of Cleary Gottlieb.

When I visited the offices in London, Brussels, and Paris, conversations I had with Skadden lawyers in the firm reminded me of some I had had on the first visits I made to Skadden's New York office, in 1983, when the firm had no foreign outposts and was just opening in Los Angeles. They spoke matter-of-factly about the heady sensation of being catapulted by Skadden into lawyering ventures they had not imagined possible.

Sharon Semenza, in her mid-thirties, grew up in Scranton, Pennsylvania, and went to Bucknell College and the University of Pennsylvania Law School. She worked for Community Legal Services in Philadelphia, for a commercial law firm in Pittsburgh, and then was hired by Skadden in New York. She became an expert in letters of credit issued by Japanese banks, some of which were the firm's clients. Passed over for partnership, she was made a special counsel and was asked to go to London. There, she became the main Skadden lawyer in an African deal, representing a company chartered on the isle of Jersey, off the English coast, which was set up to manage iron-ore mining in Liberia, as a joint venture between Liberia and Guinea.

Scott Simpson, also in his mid-thirties, was born in Los Angeles and grew up on Long Island. After he graduated from high school, he left for California and then Hawaii, to surf. At seventeen, he was living on Oahu, near Pipeline Beach. His housemates were all in their late twenties and living on food stamps—that convinced him to go to college. He started at American University in Washington, D.C.; transferred to George Washington University, where he studied Sino-Soviet affairs; and worked as an intern for a congressman. He did a year at New York University's business school, got a J.D. from Fordham Law School, and finished up his M.B.A. as a Skadden associate.

In the eighties, Simpson was a deal lawyer. When he moved to the London office as a young partner in 1990, he expected to do international mergers and acquisitions, but there were none for him to do. Instead, an investment banker he had been encouraged to look up involved him in a negotiation on behalf of a state-owned company that makes cars in the Czech Republic, first with General Motors, and when GM pulled out, with Volkswagen. The deal was closed in the hills of Bratislava, in a castle overlooking the Danube, the first in a series of projects for Simpson in Eastern Europe.

Barry Hawk, in his fifties, was a former professor at Fordham Law School and an expert on European competition (or antitrust) law, who had moved from the law school to Skadden when it opened its Brussels office. One morning when we spoke, Hawk was contemplating this itinerary for the following day: a flight from Brussels to Paris in the morning for a meeting with the general counsel of a large international airline; a flight back to Brussels for a run of meetings in the Skadden office; a return flight to Paris to sit on a jury of academics empaneled to hear the defense of a French doctoral thesis.

Hawk, on his background: "Working-class father—Depression—tries a couple of businesses—doesn't work out—Second World War—back from the war—tries another business—fails again—bounces around—ends up in steel mill—Reading, Pennsylvania—he is the best-dressed steelworker—reminds me more of a dance-hall entertainer—I don't see him working in a mill—retires from steel mill. Me—Catholic schools—Fordham University in New York—junior year abroad. The two most important things about who I became were my parents, whom I loved, and Paris. I went to Paris and never recovered."

In the 1970s, Hawk found his specialty. He inaugurated an annual conference on the European Economic Community. ("Why the EEC? Paris, I think. It was more fun to go to Paris for conferences than to St. Louis, I figured—though I've never been to St. Louis.") Because of the conference, a member of the European Commission who dealt with questions of competition invited Hawk to join his directorate for a year. Hawk became a regular consultant to the commission, started an academic center on European Community law at Fordham, and became one of the world's mavens on the subject: "A nice thing in all this: one year, the ABA antitrust section presented a seminar on EEC issues— one day in Brussels and one in Luxembourg. The night before the Luxembourg program, the president of the European Court had a private dinner for judges and advocates in my honor. . . . A friend of mine says, 'This would be like Rehnquist having a dinner in honor of some European guy who was teaching American constitutional law in Europe.' "

When I was in London, Sharon Semenza was sent to Skadden's Sydney office to help out for a while. An associate I met in Brussels was transferred to work in London. A partner I spent some time with in New York traveled out to Jakarta for four days because a colleague in the Skadden Hong Kong office needed assistance on a Southeast Asian matter. The firm was extending its reach, sometimes in patterns that seemed rash and inefficient, but the effect of the movement was stirring.

In Skadden's new world, where the protocol of business was dictated by time, London sometimes seemed at the center of things, halfway between the West Coast of the United States and the Far East when time was the measure. I thought occasionally about a breakfast I had with a New York associate who recounted how, when she had worked for Skadden in Tokyo, fourteen time zones ahead of New York, she had often spent the first few hours of the day in her apartment, talking by phone with lawyers in New York, while listening to music and sipping coffee, as the light streamed in through a floor-to-ceiling window that overlooked an ancient Tokyo tree.

In Paris, a Skadden associate told me that he hoped the firm would eventually provide free legal services to Americans who needed it in the city. Otherwise, the model of professional responsibility that both challenged and dogged Skadden in the United States was never mentioned when I spoke with American and other lawyers in Europe.

The talk was of Skadden, and other American firms, bidding for work as part of and against consortiums of law firms, investment banks, and accounting firms. Of Skadden doing R&D on behalf of some clients and making special fee arrangements that included some payment for the firm's time and a share of the returns, if the financial and other instruments that Skadden played a part in inventing were successful in the market. Of Skadden now doing some work as a loss leader, to get a toehold in a promising market.

The notion of legal service abroad was almost completely uncoupled from the duty to the public regularly seen as a professional responsibility in America, and tales about the business paralleled those about the lore of the proxy world in the 1950s, with lawyering on the run and a free-for-all in fresh territory. Skadden was taking its sense of American exceptionalism (the yearning for the frontier, yet respect for the airs and accomplishments of civilization) to surprisingly virgin terrain. The old country was the new frontier. The rest of the globe defined the full scope of opportunity.

Skadden literally took on the world, representing a group that called itself the U.S. Steel Coalition in an action to prevent major foreign steel exporters from dumping steel in the United States. There was Skadden advising about the privatization of Hungary's national airline, serving as international counsel to the tax administration of the Republic of Kazakhstan when it negotiated a tax treaty with the United States, and counseling Venezuela about the sale of a large piece of its national telephone company to GTE Corporation. There was Skadden retained by the Fujisankei Group when it sold its share of the Virgin Music business to Thorn EMI, by the People's Construction Bank of China to advise on a dozen financings worth $1.2 billion, and by commodities, futures, and other exchanges in Amsterdam, Paris, Barcelona, Singapore, Kuala Lumpur, Sydney, and New Zealand. Capitalism was breaking out where it hadn't functioned for generations, and where it had, it was in the midst of transformation. In all cases, Skadden was eager to assist.

For 1992, Skadden led the list of the "Top 15 Worldwide Legal Advisors" in mergers and acquisitions, according to *IDD Information Services*. It also led the *National Law Journal* lists of "Who Represents Corporate America" and "Who Represents Financial America," in which law firms were ranked by how frequently they were used by major companies and financial houses. Skadden was counsel in the largest sale of an American insurance company and in the first of certain kinds of financings, involving geothermal electric projects and the issuance of securities with standing trees as collateral.

The firm represented the National Football League in the lawsuit brought by players to challenge part of the league's draft system, and the Dow Corning Corporation fighting lawsuits dealing with silicone gel breast implants. It was retained by Clark Clifford and Robert Altman to defend them against prosecution for their part in the Bank of Credit and Commerce International scandal, and by Caspar Weinberger to defend him against charges related to the Iran-Contra affair and to counsel him in obtaining a presidential pardon.

Skadden helped Yoko Ono Lennon settle a suit brought by the Elephant's Memory Band, which backed up John and Yoko in two charity concerts at Madison Square Garden in 1972, and claimed that its rights of privacy and publicity were violated by the release of videotapes of the concerts. It counseled the Marvel Entertainment Group in settling a suit brought by the Hell's Angels, complaining that a Marvel comic book that retold the legend of Dr. Faust and was called "Hell's Angel" had misappropriated the name of the motorcycle club. In pro bono news, the firm was given the Liberty Award by the Lambda Legal Defense & Education Fund, a national organization dedicated to the protection of the rights of gays and lesbians. Honoring the Skadden Fellowship program and Skadden's legal work in support of equal rights, the award went to a law firm for the first time.

In the spring of 1993, as economic activity in the United States seemed to pick up and as Skadden's international program found momentum, the firm's lawyers were as busy as they had been in several years. I thought of a young lawyer I had once noticed dictating into a palm-size tape recorder as he strode up Third Avenue in Manhattan. It had been around nine o'clock on a rousing morning and, as the lawyer headed into Skadden's building and hopped an elevator to the floor of the firm where I happened to be going, he radiated a gleaming clarity of purpose.

Without fanfare, in March, Peter Mullen appointed a new ad hoc committee, again chaired by Sheila Birnbaum, to consider the questions of his tenure and succession. By the time of the annual partners' retreat in April, it was an open secret that, in consultation with the committee, Mullen had begun the process of choosing his successor.

The goals that Birnbaum (not Mullen) articulated at the retreat were that a new executive partner would be selected by the turn of the year, that there would be a period of overlap between the outgoing and incoming leaders for a few months in early 1994, and that a passing of the baton would happen by the firm's forty-sixth anniversary, on April 1. Birnbaum's report was greeted by silence from the partnership: no burst of applause for Mullen, in appreciation of his service; no emotional speeches by him or anyone else. "There was no anything, one way or the other," a senior partner reported. "We just went on to the next order of business."

In small groups, partners began trading odds about the candidates for running the firm—making a new morning line. Roger Aaron was the favorite, though he was considered to have high negatives and his name stirred grumbling about removing such a productive partner from practice. Mike Diamond, like Aaron a colleague with Mullen in the triumvirate running the firm, was a solid bet: to do the job, he would have to move back to New York from Los Angeles. Bill Frank, the head of the New York office and a steadying force; Fin Fogg, from his perch as head of FOAC; Bob Sheehan, of the quality committee—these five were the handful with the best odds, partners guessed, although others filled out the list. There was also talk about a new model of leadership, with the equivalent of a chairman of the board filling that role while continuing to practice law and of a chief operating officer managing Skadden day to day.

Since succession had been an issue of increasingly edged concern for years, triggering the selection process was uncontroversial. The timing was something else. In January, Mullen had told me that he harbored no plans to step down. Among partners I spoke with during the winter, no one predicted that Mullen would be out of power within a year. What happened to change Mullen's mind and the expectations of the partnership was not easy to sort out.

According to one partner, the Birnbaum committee's original mission had been murky, involving the task of judging the performance of Mullen, Aaron, and Diamond in their management roles, as a basis for setting their compensation. Through its conversations with Mullen and other partners, the committee evolved into an agency of change, with a message for Mullen. To another partner, the message must have been reinforced by a series of visits that Mullen received from various senior partners. "People sense that the firm's introspective period can be brought to a close if we just face up to succession," a partner observed, "and Peter may sense that, too."

"Was he pushed?" a senior partner asked. "Who the hell knows? It's Skadden Arps. It could have been done with bare knuckles and it could have been done gracefully."

Mullen: "I was getting a certain amount of heat from my wife, and I had a growing feeling that I did not want to be as fully occupied as I had been and that I didn't want to continue working twelve- to fourteen-hour days, as this job requires. There were reports that some of my contemporaries at other firms were cutting back at sixty-five. I said, 'I really don't want to do this very much longer, and *you* decide whether to push me to the limits of my work here for another two years, or how long you'd like me to stay.'"

The decision of the Birnbaum committee, backed by the policy committee and accepted by the partnership as a whole, was that it was time for Skadden to enter the future. The era of Joe Flom, seventy years old in December of 1993, and of Peter Mullen, sixty-five in April, was ending like the run of two professional athletes whose careers defined a generation in a sport, with a final season that would allow tributes in arenas around the country. At the 1993 retreat, Flom didn't speak to the question of succession either. His remarks about the state of the firm ("short and sweet," he said later) began simply: "What a difference a year makes!"

To perpetuate itself, Skadden felt that it had no choice but to adjust, trimming the take of lawyers whose work was less fruitful, favoring partners whose practice was succeeding now, bringing in new lawyers to build for the future, "excessing" those no longer as productive, and selecting a new leader. The firm's moves were dictated by business—just business. Skadden was striving to prove itself once again.

Not long before I finished my reporting about Skadden, I stopped to see Flom in his office in New York. I wanted to hear something oracular from him about Skadden, and he wanted to talk common sense. It was important not to miss the obvious about his firm, he instructed. "We're very strong. We're permanent. We're an institution. The firm has proven its value. Like anything else, nothing here happens without some adjustment, and adjustment involves pain. Four years ago, in the heyday of M&A, you didn't worry so much about controlling costs. You had to get rid of excess personnel when the downturn came, and that was painful.

"Now, we have lots of business. We're out hiring new lawyers. We're thinking of opening a new domestic office," he continued, referring to the Houston office that hadn't yet been announced. "Five years ago, we had one foreign office and now we have twelve."

How to measure the firm's strength?

"Take the partners' accumulated capital, the value of all our work in progress, and our outstanding bills to clients, on the asset side. On the liability side, we don't owe much, if anything. We've still never borrowed a nickel from a bank. So take the assets minus the liabilities to get a balance sheet, and that is a very big number—I think you're going to see a number well over $500 million."

I asked Flom what he would tell a young partner who felt that, with all the riches of the firm as an institution, he had missed the firm's golden years. The most senior partner replied, "I would tell him *he's* gotta make the future. I'm not gonna."

Flom's office is on the thirty-fifth floor of 919 Third Avenue. When we had finished talking, I went from there by an interior stairway to my favorite place in the New York office, one floor below. It is a small waiting area outside the firm library, guarded by the gilded cast of an eagle. Like other places in the firm that day, it struck me as supremely quiet. Occasionally, I heard an echo from a speakerphone or a riffle of laughter from behind a closed door. Otherwise, Skadden was at work. Like any other place where brainwork is done (a library, a school, a scientific lab), it was defined primarily by the absence of noise.

On one wall of the waiting area hangs a display of photographic portraits called the Rogues' Gallery. Ten men are pictured: six of them dead (Skadden, Arps, Slate, Lyon, Meagher, and Ensher) and four living (Bill Timbers, the senior federal appeals judge; Bob Sweet, also a senior judge, on the federal trial bench in Manhattan; Bob Pirie, who left Skadden to go to Rothschild & Co.; and John Feerick, who became dean of Fordham Law School in 1982, and in 1992 was elected president of the New York City bar).

Across from the gallery is a conference room. At the head of a long table inside it hangs an oil painting of Flom. In the portrait, Flom is sitting on a chair in a sunlit wood-paneled study that opens onto a garden. (The painting was done at his home in Westchester County in 1990.) He wears a white shirt with French cuffs and blue suit pants. His tie is loosened. In his right hand is a pen, resting on a pad balanced on his right leg, which is crossed over his left.

The Flom in the portrait appears slightly on edge and a little hunched at the shoulders—himself, yet not. It is the picture of an agile leader in a moment of repose: seasoned, almost gentle, roughly handsome, distinguished. This is the way the lawyers who make Skadden's future will see Flom when he's gone.

A Background Note

I became interested in writing about Skadden in 1983, after learning about Joe Flom and his role in the history of American corporate take-overs. In 1988, I presented a proposal for this book to Flom, as the firm's senior partner, and to Peter Mullen, then the executive partner. Mullen presented the query to the firm's administrative committee, which approved the firm's cooperation with me. They did not commission or pay for my work. I approached the firm as an independent writer, and did my reporting and writing as such.

Mullen explained that he supported the project on the theory that I could be thoughtful about the firm and study it with some perspective, as he and his colleagues could not. I'm sure that the soaring economic fortunes of the firm when I made my proposal in 1988 reinforced the confidence of partners in the Skadden story. Flom reported to me when I began that same year, "I told the guys, 'Warts and all'!"

What the firm's cooperation was going to mean was left open. Its approach to my work was sometimes genuinely cooperative. In the round of conversations I had had at the firm about takeovers, in 1983, and in the periodic stints of intensive reporting I did there between 1988 and 1993, many Skadden lawyers, other professionals at the firm, and members of the firm's staff spent hours talking with me. I'm indebted to each of them. These interviews allowed me to venture inside an important private institution in a way usually unavailable to outsiders.

At other times, the firm was only guardedly cooperative. The directions that Flom articulated, "Warts and all," were not widely followed. To the contrary, many at Skadden were unwilling to discuss or even acknowledge the existence of any warts.

Sometimes the firm cooperated not at all. I requested information about the firm's finances and other subjects that I considered essential to a profile of the place, but that it considered private and would not disclose to me on the record. (I pieced together the financial data reported in this book from material provided by individual lawyers at the firm and other sources.) I requested permission to attend a partners' meeting, to sit in on negotiations by Skadden lawyers, and to observe other events, and in each of these cases, I was turned down. Some Skadden clients met my attempts to interview them about the firm with the tremor of the intimidated, or with a superficiality that suggested they themselves had decided that they should reveal nothing.

Skadden's most direct effort to control the contents of this book was embodied in an agreement drafted by a lawyer at the firm, and amended and signed by me and by Peter Mullen, as the firm's executive partner, in January of 1990. It addressed the question of confidential client and "insider" information that I might learn through Skadden in the course of my reporting. Skadden required me to sign the agreement before it would let me continue to interview extensively at the firm. In it, I acknowledged that my work "generally" wouldn't "require the use of any privileged confidential information relating to clients" of Skadden, and I agreed to cooperate with the firm's efforts "to take reasonable precautions to prevent the receipt by me of such client information."

To avoid any confusion about the sponsorship of my work while I spent time at Skadden, at my request the firm established a billing account for me, which allowed me to keep track of and reimburse the firm for meals I shared with its lawyers in their offices, for photocopying, and for other expenses.

For this book, I drew on materials from general and scholarly books, academic journals, general and trade periodicals, general and trade newspapers, Skadden records, and a range of unpublished papers. Writing any book, even one based exclusively on documents, involves an accumulation of judgments: about what seems true and what seems false, what should be included and what should be left out, what details to give the reader about conflicting accounts.

In addition, much of this book is based in significant part on over three hundred interviews, more than half with people at Skadden. This aspect of my reporting in particular required me to make many judgments. I have looked for independent corroboration and consistency in oral accounts where possible, and I have assessed the credibility and plausibility of what I was told. I have tried to present opposing views where I have been aware of them.

When I was satisfied that the shape and contents of this book made sense in light of my reporting, I went back to Skadden lawyers and presented what I considered the most critical elements of my narrative, to give them the chance to respond. I also tried to speak again with those on whom I had relied in telling key parts of the story, to give them the chance to amend or expand their versions where appropriate.

The narrative I've presented here conveys many of the stories, impressions, and insights I gained in the course of years of reporting about Skadden. They make a portrait that is faithful to the firm as I came to know it, and that I believe holds more general insights about the business of large American law firms and their transformation since the Second World War.

Acknowledgments

A grant from the John Simon Guggenheim Memorial Foundation, in 1989–90, enabled me to engage fully in research for this book. I'm grateful to the Foundation and to Joel Conarroe, its president. The Foundation's aid made a significant difference in the scope of work that I could undertake.

For supporting my application to the Foundation, I want to thank David Ignatius, who is a novelist and an assistant managing editor of *The Washington Post*; J. Anthony Lukas, whose book *Common Ground*, about the effort to integrate Boston's schools through the busing of students, is a landmark in the field of nonfiction; and another accomplished supporter who prefers to remain anonymous. In addition, the late Paul Freund, for generations a leading student of the U.S. Constitution and of the Supreme Court at Harvard Law School, supported my quest for funding.

With the hospitality of Robert Nelson and Rayman Solomon, I was the guest of the American Bar Foundation at a conference about the relationship between ethics and economics in the legal profession, in 1988, which marked the reconstitution of the profession as a subject of scholarship. With guidance from Anne Grant, Seymour Hersh, and Morton Mintz, I received a grant from the Fund for Investigative Journalism, in Washington, D.C., in 1992. In 1993, I received a Pope Journalism Award. It paid for costs related to the book's completion. David Yount, of the National Press Foundation, in Washington, D.C., kindly played a part in my receiving the award, and Catherine Pope administered it with dedication. I'm grateful for all this support.

To do some of my research, I spent three extended periods living in New York City, besides making many other trips to the city. (My home is in Washington, D.C.) During one stint, Margaret Conklin and David Sabel lent me their apartment, and by the time I visited Skadden's offices in Brussels, Margaret and David had moved there (with a new baby daughter) and put me up again. Others who gave me shelter or valued company while I was on the road include Candy Lee and Joe Ward and Diane McWhorter and Richard Rosen (in New York City), John and Cleo Carney and Ellen Semonoff and Daniel, Joshua, and Jonathan Meltzer (in Boston), and Ruth, Richard, Roo, and Bo Rogers (in London). My thanks to all.

A book like this requires collaboration between a writer and his subject, however cautious on both sides. The Skadden administrative committee gave me access to much of its excellent New York library and, as I describe in my "Background Note," let me interview many people at the firm during the course of hundreds of hours. These interviews were indispensable to the book. I couldn't have obtained the committee's permission for them without the backing of Joe Flom and Peter Mullen. No one was more generous with time or more fascinating to me than Flom, and no one was more available or diligent in explaining the firm's view of itself than Mullen.

In addition, James Freund, the firm's unofficial historian; Barry Garfinkel, its unofficial curator; and Isaac Shapiro, the head of the firm's international practice, responded at length to my many inquiries. At the firm's New York library, Carrie Hirtz and Cornelia Locher regularly answered my questions and supplied me with helpful material. Chase Wilson, when she was the firm's director of publications, and Sally Feldman, her successor, fielded my requests for help and responded cooperatively and quickly, as did Anthony Arbisi, the firm's director of administration, and his assistant, Ellyn Jarmel.

Others not connected with the firm generously shared their insights with me as well. Some who deserve special mention are Alfred Chandler, the distinguished historian of American business and emeritus professor at the Harvard Business School; Yves Dézalay, of the Centre National de la Recherche Scientifique, in Paris; Stephen Gillers of New York University Law School; Donald Gogel, a principal with Clayton, Dubilier & Rice, Inc.; Robert Gordon of Stanford Law School; David Luban of the University of Maryland; Robert Nelson of the American Bar Foundation and Northwestern University; Stephen Waldman, a partner in Covington & Burling, in Washington, D.C.; and David Wilkins, a professor and director of the program on the legal profession at Harvard Law School.

I owe a debt to others whose writings I have relied on: Gerald Dunne of St. Louis University; Robert Ferguson of Columbia University; Marc Galanter and Thomas Palay of the University of Wisconsin Law School; Ronald Gilson of Stanford Law School; the writer Max Holland; Geoffrey Hazard of Yale Law School; Louis Lowenstein of Columbia Law School; the writer Martin Mayer; Robert Pollin of the University of California, Riverside; the sociologist Michael Powell; Deborah Rhode of Stanford Law School; Theodore Schneyer of the University of Arizona Law School; Rayman Solomon of Northwestern University Law School; and Charles Wolfram of Cornell Law School.

In addition, Ruth Arps; Charlene Cuniff of the Baker Library at the Harvard Business School; Eve Harlan Dillingham and, with her approval, Dean Turner, of the law firm of Dewey Ballantine; Paul Friedman, a Washington, D.C., lawyer; Sharon Kissel, the librarian at the Washington, D.C., firm of Shea & Gardner; Mary Ellen Slate; and Tinsley Yarbrough of East Carolina University helped me obtain material important to the book.

Other libraries whose resources I was glad to have available to me include the Boston Globe Library, the Georgetown University Library, the Langdell Library of the Harvard Law School, the Library of the Association of the Bar of New York City, the Library of Congress, and the Library of the Washington College of Law, at the American University. The library of the law firm of Cleary, Gottlieb, Steen & Hamilton provided me with a copy of Leo Gottlieb's memoirs and with two other biographies. The Oral History Project of Columbia University furnished me with a copy of an interview with Henry Friendly.

The work of Jill Abramson, Stephen Adler, Steven Brill, James Stewart, and other former and current reporters for *The American Lawyer* and its sister publications; of reporters for *The National Law Journal* and its sister publication, *The New York Law Journal*; and of other legal reporters, in particular David Margolick of *The New York Times*, provided me with material that sometimes became integral to my narrative and with a record on which I sometimes built my own reporting.

Jonathan Galassi, the editor in chief of Farrar, Straus & Giroux, edited this book. He provided penetrating counsel, in one astute observation after another. His intellectual power was equaled by his reassuring patience. It was a privilege to have his guidance and support, and the benefit of his great gifts. They reflect the love and feel for books that pervade the publishing house he helps lead.

Others at the house helped me as well: Helene Atwan, the firm's sophisticated and gracious associate publisher and director of publicity, and her fine associate, Elisabeth Calamari; Elisheva Urbas, the managing editor, who was wise about every stage of publication and a pleasure to work with; and Phyllida Burlingame and Paul Elie, able assistants of Jonathan Galassi. The house's copyediting, design, marketing, and sales departments also gave me a lift at key junctures. When I undertook this project, it was under the aegis of Linda Healey. Her belief in the idea helped launch my work.

John Sellers, who helps run the fact-checking department of *U.S. News & World Report* as deputy chief of news desk research, assisted me by checking facts presented in the book. His work was organized and precise. It was carried out with the grace of a diplomat and the endurance of a medical intern, and it tightened my work appreciably. Errors that remain are mine alone.

Seth Rubin took photographs for this book, using materials at Skadden or lent by the firm. I thank him for his skillful work.

James Fallows guided me through some thickets of journalistic ethics, with clarity and good sense. Daniel Meltzer and Jeffrey Rayport read a draft of this book. While they don't necessarily agree with my conclusions, they gave me valuable critiques. Rafe Sagalyn, my agent, was a fine counselor and ally. And to Robert Gottlieb, my deep thanks. I would not have undertaken this project without his strong encouragement or finished it without his intrepid support.

I want to express my gratitude to three others whose constancy and friendship were instrumental to the completion of this book: David Ignatius (mentioned above), Robert Shapiro, and William Yeomans.

Jamie Gorelick and Richard Waldhorn were mainstays as counselors and friends, as were Paul and Anne Goldenheim, Wendy Gray and Stephen Pearlstein, Vicki Jackson and Robert Taylor, and Ellen Semonoff and Daniel Meltzer. My sisters, Margi and Joanna Caplan, were there for me, as always, with their families.

My daughter, Molly, sprouted from a baby to a five-year-old girl while I worked on the book. When I wasn't on the road, it was my great joy to watch her life unfold from the special vantage point of a home office. When my sense of purpose dwindled, she sparked it again.

To my wife, Susan, my immeasurable thanks once more: for backbone; for clear measured judgments about intricate issues; for close thoughtful editing of material I found difficult to elucidate; for patience rooted in faith; and for love.